INDIAN CAPTIVITIES

OR

LIFE IN THE WIGWAM

AMS PRESS

NEW YORK

TORTURING A CAPTIVE

DERBY. Del.

N. ORR. Sc. N.Y.

INDIAN CAPTIVITIES

OR

LIFE IN THE WIGWAM;

BEING

TRUE NARRATIVES OF CAPTIVES WHO HAVE BEEN CARRIED AWA
BY THE INDIANS, FROM THE FRONTIER SETTLEMENTS
OF THE UNITED STATES, FROM THE
EARLIEST PERIOD TO THE
PRESENT TIME.

BY

SAMUEL G. DRAKE,

AUTHOR OF THE "BOOK OF INDIANS."

AUBURN:
DERBY AND MILLER.

1851.

Library of Congress Cataloging in Publication Data

Drake, Samuel Gardner, 1798-1875.
    Indian captivities; or, Life in the wigwam,
being true narratives of captives who have been
carried away by the Indians . . .

    Reprint of the 1851 ed. published by Derby and
Miller, Auburn.
    Originally published under title: Tragedies of
the wilderness.
    1. Indians of North America—Captivities.
I. Title. II. Title: Life in the wigwam.
E85.D75   1975   973'.04'97   74-7961
ISBN 0-404-11849-6

Reprinted from the edition of 1851, Auburn
First AMS edition published in 1975
Manufactured in the United States of America

AMS PRESS INC.
NEW YORK, N.Y. 10003

READER—

This volume consists of entire Narratives; that is to say, I have given the originals without the slightest abridgment; nor have I taken any liberties with the language of any of them, which would in the remotest degree change the sense of a single passage, and the instances are few in which I have ventured to correct peculiarities of expression; yet I designed that, with regard to grammatical accuracy, there should be as few faults as the nature of such a performance would allow. All expressions of an antiquated date are not attempted to be changed. Some redundancies have been dropped, which could only have been retained at the expense of perspicuity.

I am not unaware that there may be persons who will doubt of the propriety of laying before all classes of the community a work which records so much that is shocking to humanity; but the fashion of studying the book of Nature has now long obtained, and pervades all classes. I have done no more than to exhibit a page of it in this collection. To observe man in his uncivilized or natural state offers an approach to a knowledge of his natural history, without which it is hardly obtained.

We find volumes upon volumes on the manners and customs of the Indians, many of the writers of which would have us believe they have exhausted the subject, and consequently we need inquire no further; but whoever has travelled among distant tribes, or read the accounts of intelligent travellers, do not require to be told that the most endless variety exists, and that the manners and customs of uncultivated nations are no more stationary, nor so much so, as are those of a civilized people. The current of time changes all things. But we have elsewhere observed* that similar necessities, although in different nations, have produced similar customs; such as will stand through ages with very little, if any, variation. Neither is it strange that similar articulations should be found in languages having no other affinity, because imitations of natural sounds must everywhere be the same. Hence it follows that customs are as various as the face of nature itself.

A lecturer on the manners and customs of certain tribes of Indians may assure us that no others observe certain barbarous rites, and that, as they by some sudden mortality have become extinct, the knowledge of those rites is known to none others save himself, and that therefore he is the

* Book of the Indians, Book i., p. 10.

only person living who can inform us of them. But he may be assured that captives and other travellers have witnessed customs and ceremonies, which, together with their performers, have passed away also. And there is another view of the matter. Many a custom, as it existed fifty or a hundred years ago, has become quite a different affair now. From these reflections it is easy to see what an endless task it would be to describe *all* of the manners and customs of a single tribe of Indians, to say nothing of the thousands which have been and still exist.

These observations have been thrown out for the consideration of such as may be looking for some great work upon Indian manners and customs, to comprehend all they have been taught to expect, from those who have, perhaps, thought no deeper upon the subject than themselves. When the reader shall have perused the following narratives, I doubt not he will be convinced of the truth of what has here been delivered.

This is truly an age of essay writing, and we have them in abundance upon every thing and nothing, instead of facts which should be remembered. If a new work upon travels or history appears, we shall doubtless be delighted with descriptions of elegant scenery and splendid sketches about general matters, but arise from its perusal about as ignorant of the events of the history we desire as before. Compositions of this description form no part of these pages.

I have on other occasions stood out boldly in favor of the oppressed Indian, and I know that a book of INDIAN CAPTIVITIES is calculated to exhibit their character in no very favorable light; but the reader should remember that, in the following narratives, it is not I who speak; yet I believe that, with very small allowances, these narratives are entirely true. The errors, if any, will be found only errors of judgment, which affect not their veracity.

A people whose whole lives are spent in war, and who live by a continual slaughter of all kinds of animals, must necessarily cultivate ferocity. From the nature of their circumstances they are obliged always to be in expectation of invasion; living in small communities, dispersed in small parties of five or ten upon hunting expeditions, they are easily surprised by an enemy of equal or even a lesser force. Indians, consequently, are always speaking of strange *Indians* whom they know not, nor do they know whether such are to appear from one direction or another. When New England was first settled, the Indians about Massachusetts Bay were in a miserable fright from fear of the Tarratines; skulking from copse to copse by day, and sleeping in loathsome fens by night, to avoid them. And all the New England Indians were in constant expectation of the Mohawks; and scarce a tribe existed in any part of the country who did not constantly expect to be attacked by some other. And such was the policy of those people that no calculation could be made upon their operations or pretensions, inasmuch as the honor of an action depended on the manner in which it was executed. No credit was obtained by open combat, but he that could ensnare and smite an unsuspecting enemy was highly to be commended.

It must have very often happened that the people surprised knew nothing of any reason why they were so dealt with, and the injury for which they suffered may have been committed by their ancestors long before they had existence; and the only sure means a tribe had to avert retaliation was extermination! Hence the perpetual warfare of these people.

As there are a few other collections of Indian Narratives of a similar character to this, it may be necessary to advertise the reader that such are *similar* in title only; for in those collections the compilers speak *for* their captives, whereas, in *this*, they speak for themselves. Those collectors have not only taken upon themselves to *speak for* their captives or heroes, but have so abridged the majority of their narratives that the perusal of them only gives dissatisfaction even to the general reader. Mr. McClung's "Sketches of Western Adventure" is a work of thrilling interest, but its value is entirely lost in particular instances from the above considerations. Dr. Metcalf was earlier, and set out right, but looked back with his hand to the plough. I know of no others worthy of notice.

As several prominent narratives may be looked for in this collection without success, such as those of Hannah Duston, Rev. John Williams, &c., it will be proper to apprize the reader that those, and many others, are contained in the Book of the Indians.

I did not design to notice the works of others, in Indian history, in this introduction; but accidentally falling upon some acts of pre-eminent injustice to my former labors, committed by several compilers, whose works, from their peculiar point of emanation, or ostentatious external attractions, are calculated to fix in the minds of their readers wrong impressions in respect to the sources whence they have drawn their information, I could not, in justice to myself, let them pass without a notice. For an author to spend many of his best years in the most laborious investigations to bring out a train of facts upon an important inquiry, which, in all probability, no other would ever have taken the pains to have done, from the peculiar nature and difficulty of the undertaking, or situation of the materials out of which he had brought them, and then to see them, no sooner than produced, transferred to the pages of others without even a demand for them upon their author, is matter of which I complain, and, to say the least, is too barefaced a piracy even for this age of freebooting in matters of literature. Had the author of the Book of the Indians been dead, leaving but a single copy of his work behind, and that an unpublished manuscript, some of the compilers, to whom I allude, could scarcely have been freer in their use of it without the hope of detection. No charge is

1*

here intended against such as have copied whole pages into their own works, where they have even acknowledged their source of information; but I would point the eyes of all such as may read this to their own pages, which have been transferred from that work, or so concocted out of it as to induce the belief that it was the fruits of their own labor. Such compilers, doubtless, presume only their own works will be read on the subject of the Indians; or that the obscure and humble author of the Book of the Indians had no means of exposing their piracies. And even now, "after all said and done," perhaps Queen Victoria will never read this preface, or compare the pages of the GREAT FOLIO "Biography and History of the Indians" with those of the Book of the Indians; yet there may be those on this side of the Atlantic who may be benefited by this, though indirect, information. Besides, I am too late now to send a book to her majesty, with the slightest prospect of her ever reading it, for the very reason that she has already several books by American authors on hand! And if she has read even one, is it to be presumed she would ever read another? Moreover, what would she care whether Col. Stone gave me credit for a fact, or Mr. Thacher, or Henry Trumbull?

CONTENTS.

The following Table contains the names of the captives, the time of
their being taken, and the duration of their captivity, where the dates
could be ascertained.

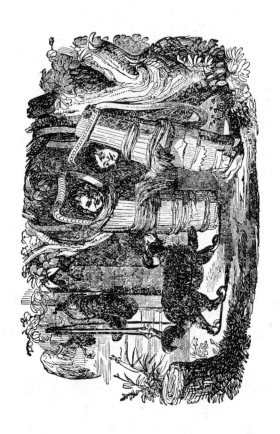

INDIAN CAPTIVITIES

NARRATIVE

OF THE CAPTIVITY OF JOHN ORTIZ, A SPANIARD, WHO WAS
ELEVEN YEARS A PRISONER AMONG THE INDIANS OF
FLORIDA.

In the year 1528 Pamphilo de Narvaez, with a commission,
constituting him governor of Florida, or "all the lands lying
from the river of Palms to the cape of Florida," sailed for that
country with 400 foot and 20 horse, in five ships. With this
expedition went a Spaniard, named John Ortiz, a native of
Seville, whose connections were among the nobility of Castile.
Although we have no account of what part Ortiz acted in
Narvaez's expedition, or how he escaped its disastrous issue,
yet it may not be deemed out of place to notice briefly here
that issue.

This Narvaez had acquired some notoriety by the manner in
which he had executed a commission against Cortez. He had
been ordered by the governor of Cuba to seize the destroyer
of Mexico, but was himself overthrown and deserted by his
men. On falling into the hands of Cortez, his arrogance did
not forsake him, and he addressed him thus : " Esteem it good
fortune that you have taken me prisoner." " Nay," replied
Cortez, " it is the least of the things I have done in Mexico."
To return to the expedition of which we have promised to
speak.

Narvaez landed in Florida not very far from, or perhaps at
the bay of Apalachee, in the month of April, and marched
into the country with his men. They knew no other direction
but that pointed out by the Indians, whom they compelled to
act as guides. Their first disappointment was on their arrival

at the village of Apalachee, where, instead of a splendid town,
filled with immense treasure, as they had anticipated, they
found only about 40 Indian wigwams. When they visited
one Indian town its inhabitants would get rid of them by telling them of another, where their wants would be gratified.
Such was the manner in which Narvaez and his companions
rambled over 800 miles of country, in about six months' time, at
a vast expense of men and necessaries which they carried with
them; for the Indians annoyed them at every pass, not only
cutting off many of the men, but seizing on their baggage upon every occasion which offered. Being now arrived upon the
coast, in a wretched condition, they constructed some miserable
barks corresponding with their means, in which none but men
in such extremities would embark. In these they coasted toward
New Spain. When they came near the mouths of the Mis-
sissippi they were cast away in a storm, and all but 15 of their
number perished. Out of these 15, 4 only lived to reach
Mexico, and these after 8 years wholly spent in wanderings
from place to place, enduring incredible hardships and miseries.

The next year after the end of Narvaez's expedition, the
intelligence of his disaster having reached his wife, whom he
left in Cuba, she fitted out a small company, consisting of 20
or 30 men, who sailed in a brigantine to search after him,
hoping some fortuitous circumstance might have prolonged his
existence upon the coast, and that he might be found. Of this
number was John Ortiz, the subject of this narrative.

On their arrival there, they sought an opportunity to have
an interview with the first Indians they should meet. Opportunity immediately offered, and as soon as Indians were discovered, the Spaniards advanced towards them in their boats,
while the Indians came down to the shore. These wily people practised a stratagem upon this occasion, which to this day
seems a mysterious one, and we have no means of explain-
ing it.

Three or four Indians came near the shore, and setting a
stick in the ground, placed in a cleft in its top a letter, and
withdrawing a little distance, made signs to the Spaniards to
come and take it. All the company, except John Ortiz and one
more, refused to go out for the letter, rightly judging it to be
used only to ensnare them; but Ortiz, presuming it was from
Narvaez, and containing some account of himself, would not
be persuaded from venturing on shore to bring it, although all
the rest but the one who accompanied him strenuously argued
against it.

Now there was an Indian village very near this place, and

no sooner had Ortiz and his companion advanced to the place where the letter was displayed, than a multitude came running from it, and surrounding them, seized eagerly upon them. The number of the Indians was so great, that the Spaniards in the vessels did not dare to attempt to rescue them, and saw them carried forcibly away. In this first onset the man who accompanied Ortiz was killed, he having made resistance when he was seized.

Not far from the place where they were made prisoners, was another Indian town, or village, consisting of about 8 or 10 houses or wigwams. These houses were made of wood, and covered with palm-leaves. At one end of this village there was a building, which the captive called a temple, but of what dimensions it was he makes no mention. Over the door of entrance into this temple there was placed the figure of a bird, carved out in wood, and it was especially surprising that this bird had gilded eyes. No attempt is made by Ortiz even to conjecture how or by whom the art of gilding was practised, in this wild and distant region, nor does he mention meeting with any other specimen of that art during his captivity. At the opposite extremity of this village stood the house of the chief, or cazique, as he was often called, upon an eminence, raised, as it was supposed, for a fortification. These things remained the same ten years afterwards, and are mentioned by the historian of Fernando De Soto's Invasion of Florida. The name of the chief of this village was Ucita, before whom was presented the captive, Ortiz, who was condemned to suffer immediate death.

The manner of his death was by torture, which was to be effected in this wise. The executioners set four stakes in the ground, and to these they fastened four poles; the captive was then taken, and with his arms and legs extended, was by them bound to these poles, at such a distance from the ground, that a fire, made directly under him, would be a long time in consuming him. Never did a poor victim look with greater certainty to death for relief, than did John Ortiz at this time. The fire had already begun to rage, when a most remarkable circumstance happened to save his life—a daughter of the stern Ucita arose and plead for him. Among other things she said these to her father: " My kind father, why kill this poor stranger ? he can do you nor any of us any injury, seeing he is but one and alone. It is better that you should keep him confined ; for even in that condition he may sometime be of great service to you." The chief was silent for a short time, but finally ordered him to be released from his place of torture. They had no sooner taken the thongs from his wrists and

2

ankles, than they proceeded to wash and dress his wounds, and to do things to make him comfortable.

As soon as his wounds were healed, Ortiz was stationed at the entrance of the temple, before mentioned, to guard it against such as were not allowed to enter there ; but especially to guard its being profaned by wild beasts ; for as it was a place of sacrifices, wolves were its constant visitors. He had not long been in this office, when an event occurred, which threw him into great consternation. Human victims were brought in as sacrifices and deposited here ; and not long after Ortiz had been placed as sentinel, the body of a young Indian was brought and laid upon a kind of sarcophagus, which, from the multitudes that had from time to time been offered there, was surrounded with blood and bones ! a most rueful sight, as ever any eye beheld !—here an arm fresh torn from its place, reeking with blood, another exhibiting but bone and sinews from the mangling jaws of wild beasts ! Such was the place he was ordered to guard, through day and night— doomed to sit himself down among this horrible assemblage of the dead. When left alone he reflected that his escape from fire was not so fortunate for him as he had hoped ; for now, his naturally superstitious mind was haunted by the presence of innumerable ghosts, who stalked in every place, and which he had from his youth been taught to believe were capable of doing him all manner of injuries, even to the depriving of life.

There was no reflection in those remote ages of the real situation of all the living, in respect to the great valley of death in which all beings are born and nursed, and which no length of years is sufficient to carry them through. Let us for a moment cast our eyes around us. Where are we ? Not in the same temple with Ortiz, but in one equally vast. We can see nothing but death in every place. The very ground we walk upon is composed of the decayed limbs of our own species, with those of a hundred others. A succession of animals have been rising and falling for many thousand years in all parts of the world. They have died all around us—in our very places. We do not distinctly behold the hands, the feet, or the bones of them, because they have crumbled to dust beneath our feet. And cannot the ghosts of these as well arise as of those slain yesterday ? The affirmative cannot be denied.

As we have said, Ortiz found himself snatched from one dreadful death, only, as he imagined, to be thrust into the jaws of another, yet more terrible. Experience, however, soon proved to him, that the dead, at least those with whom he was forced to dwell, either could or would not send forth their spirits in any other shape than such phantoms as his own mind created, in dreams and reveries. We can accustom ourselves to almost anything, and it was not long before our captive contemplated the dead bodies with which he was surrounded, with about the same indifference as he did the walls of the temple that encompassed them.

How long after Ortiz had been placed to guard the temple of sacrifices the following fearful midnight adventure happened, we have no means of stating with certainty, nor is it very material; it is, however, according to his own account, as follows: A young Indian had been killed and his body placed in this temple. Late one night, Ortiz found it closely invested by wolves, which, in spite of all his efforts, entered the place, and carried away the body of the Indian. The fright and the darkness were so heavy upon Ortiz that he knew not that the body was missing until morning. It appears, however, that he recovered himself, seized a heavy cudgel, which he had prepared at hand, and commenced a general attack upon the beasts in the temple, and not only drove them out, but pursued them a good way from the place. In the pursuit he came up with one which he gave a mortal blow, although he did not know it at the time. Having returned from this hazardous adventure to the temple, he impatiently awaited the return of daylight. When the day dawned, great was his distress at the discovery of the loss of the body of the dead Indian, which was especially aggravated, because it was the son of a great chief.

When the news of this affair came to the ears of Ucita, he at once resolved to have Ortiz put to death; but before executing his purpose he sent out several Indians to pursue after the wolves, to recover, if possible, the sacrifice. Contrary to all expectation, the body was found, and not far from it the body of a huge wolf also. When Ucita learned these facts, he countermanded the order for his execution.

Three long years was Ortiz doomed to watch this wretched temple of the dead. At the end of this time he was relieved only by the overthrow of the power of Ucita. This was effected by a war between the two rival chiefs, Ucita and Mocoso.

The country over which Mocoso reigned was only two days' journey from that of Ucita, and separated from it by a large river or estuary. Mocoso came upon the village of Ucita in the night with an army, and attacked his castle, and took it, and also the rest of his town. Ucita and his people fled from it with all speed, and the warriors of Mocoso burnt it to the ground. Ucita had another village upon the coast, not far from the former, to which he and his people fled, and were not pursued by their enemies. Soon after he had established himself in his new residence, he resolved upon making a sacrifice of Ortiz. Here again he was wonderfully preserved, by the same kind friend that had delivered him at the beginning of his captivity. The daughter of the chief, knowing her intreaties would avail nothing with her father, determined to aid him to make an escape; accordingly, she had prepared the way for his reception with her father's enemy, Mocoso. She found means to pilot him secretly out of her father's village, and accompanied him a league or so on his way, and then left him with directions how to proceed to the residence of Mocoso. Having travelled all night as fast as he could, Ortiz found himself next morning upon the borders of the river which bounded the territories of the two rival chiefs. He was now thrown into great trouble, for he could not proceed farther without discovery, two of Mocoso's men being then fishing in the river; and, although he came as a friend, yet he had no way to make that known to them, not understanding their language, nor having means wherewith to discover his character by a sign. At length he observed their arms, which they had left at considerable distance from the place where they then were. Therefore, as his only chance of succeeding in his enterprise, he crept slyly up and seized their arms to prevent their injuring him. When they saw this they fled with all speed towards their town. Ortiz followed them for some distance, trying by language as well as by signs to make them understand that he only wished protection with them, but all in vain, and he gave up the pursuit and waited quietly the result. It was not long before a large party came running armed towards him, and when they approached, he was obliged to cover himself behind trees to avoid their arrows. Nevertheless his chance of being killed seemed certain, and that very speedily; but it providentially happened, that there was an Indian among them who now surrounded him, who understood the language in which he spoke, and thus he was again rescued from another perilous situation.

Having now surrendered himself into the hands of the Indians, four of their number were dispatched to carry the tidings to Mocoso, and to learn his pleasure in regard to the disposition to be made of him; but instead of sending any word of direction, Mocoso went himself out to meet Ortiz. When he came to him, he expressed great joy at seeing him, and made every profession that he would treat him well. Ortiz, however, had seen enough of Indians to warn him against a too implicit confidence in his pretensions; and what added in no small degree to his doubts about his future destiny, was this very extraordinary circumstance. Immediately after the preliminary congratulations were over, the chief made him take an oath, " after the manner of Christians," that he would not run away from him to seek out another master ; to which he very readily assented. At the same time Mocoso, on his part, promised Ortiz that he would not only treat him with due kindness, but, that if ever an opportunity offered by which he could return to his own people, he would do all in his power to assist him in it ; and, to keep his word inviolate, he swore to what he had promised, " after the manner of the Indians." Nevertheless, our captive looked upon all this in no other light than as a piece of cunning, resorted to by the chief, to make him only a contented slave ; but we shall see by the sequel, that this Indian chief dealt not in European guile, and that he was actuated only by benevolence of heart.

Three years more soon passed over the head of Ortiz, and he experienced nothing but kindness and liberty. He spent his time in wandering over the delightful savannahs of Florida, and through the mazes of the palmetto, and beneath the refreshing shades of the wide-spreading magnolia—pursuing the deer in the twilight of morning, and the scaly fry in the silver lakes in the cool of the evening. In all this time we hear of nothing remarkable that happened to Ortiz, or to the chief or his people. When war or famine does not disturb the quiet of Indians they enjoy themselves to the full extent of their natures—perfectly at leisure, and ready to devote days together to the entertainment of themselves, and any travellers or friends that may sojourn with them.

About the close of the first three years of Ortiz's sojourning with the tribe of Indians under Mocoso, there came startling intelligence into their village, and alarm and anxiety sat impatiently upon the brow of all the inhabitants. This was occasioned by the arrival of a runner, who gave information that as some of Mocoso's men were in their canoes a great way out at sea fishing, they had discovered ships of the white men approaching their coast. Mocoso, after communing with himself a short time, went to Ortiz with the information, which, when he had imparted it to him, caused peculiar sensations in his breast, and a brief struggle with conflicting feelings ; for one cannot forget his country and kindred, nor can he forget his savior and protector. In short, Mocoso urged him to go to the coast and see if he could make a discovery of the ships. This proceeding on the part of the chief silenced the fears of Ortiz, and he set out upon the discovery ; but when he had spent several days of watchfulness and eager expectation, without seeing or gaining any other intelligence of ships, he was ready to accuse the chief of practising deception upon him, to try his fidelity; he was soon satisfied, however, that his suspicions were without foundation, although no other information was ever gained of ships at that time.

At length, when six years more had elapsed, news of a less doubtful character was brought to the village of Mocoso. It was, that some white people had actually landed upon their coast, and had possessed themselves of the village of Ucista, and driven out him and his men. Mocoso immediately imparted this information to Ortiz, who, presuming it was an idle tale, as upon the former occasion, affected to care nothing for it, and told his chief that no wordly thing would induce him to leave his present master; but Mocoso persisted, and among arguments advanced this, that he had done his duty, and that if Ortiz would not go out and seek his white brethren, and they should leave the country, and him behind, he could not blame him, and withal seriously confirming the news. In the end he concluded to go out once more, and after thanking his chief for his great kindness, set off, with twelve of his best men whom Mocoso had appointed for his guides, to find the white people.

When they had proceeded a considerable part of the way, they came into a plain, and suddenly in sight of a party of 120 men, who proved to be some of those of whom they had heard. When they discovered Ortiz and his men, they pressed towards them in warlike array, and although they made every signal of friendship in their power, yet these white men rushed upon them, barbarously wounding two of them, and the others saved themselves only by flight. Ortiz himself came near being killed. A horseman rushed upon him, knocked him down, and was prevented from dealing a deadly blow only by a timely ejaculation in Spanish which he made. It was in these words: " I am a Christian—do not kill me, nor these poor men who have given me my life."

It was not until this moment that the soldiers discovered their mistake, of friends for enemies, for Ortiz was, in all appearance, an Indian; and now, with the aid of Ortiz, his attending Indians were collected, and they were all carried to the camp of the white men, each riding behind a soldier upon his horse.

Ortiz now found himself among an army of Spaniards, commanded by one Fernando De Soto, who had come into that country with a great armament of 600 men in 7 ships, in search of riches; an expedition undertaken with great ostentation, raised by the expectation of what it was to afford, but it ended, as all such undertakings should, in disgrace and mortification.

Soto considered the acquisition of Ortiz of very great importance, for although he could not direct him to any mountains of gold or silver, yet he was acquainted with the language of the Indians, and he kept him with him during his memorable expedition, to act in the capacity of interpreter.

It was in the spring of 1543, that the ferocious and savage Soto fell a prey to his misguided ambition. Ortiz had died a few months before, and with him fell the already disappointed hopes of his leader. They had taken up winter quarters at a place called Autiamque, upon the Washita, or perhaps Red River, and it was here that difficulties began to thicken upon them. When in the spring they would march from thence, Soto was grieved, because he had lost so good an interpreter, and readily felt that difficulties were clustering around in a much more formidable array. Hitherto, when they were at a loss for a knowledge of the country, all they had to do was to lie in wait and seize upon some Indian, and Ortiz always could understand enough of the language to relieve them from all perplexity about their course; but now they had no other interpreter but a young Indian of Cutifachiqui, who understood a little Spanish; "yet it required sometimes a whole day for him to explain what Ortiz would have done in four words." At other times he was so entirely misunderstood, that after they had followed his direction through a tedious march of a whole day, they would find themselves obliged to return again to the same place."

Such was the value of Ortiz in the expedition of Soto, as that miserable man conceived; but had not Soto fallen in with him, how different would have been the fate of a multitude of men, Spaniards and Indians. Upon the whole, it is hard to say which was the predominant trait in the character of Soto and his followers, avarice or cruelty.

At one time, because their guides had led them out of the way, Moscoso, the successor of Soto, caused them to be hanged upon a tree and there left. Another, in the early part of the expedition, was saved from the fangs of dogs, at the interference of Ortiz, because he was the only Indian through whom Ortiz could get information. It is as difficult to decide which was the more superstitious, the Indians or the self-styled "Christian Spaniards;" for when Soto died a chief came and offered two young Indians to be killed, that they might accompany and serve the white man to the world of spirits. An Indian guide being violently seized with some malady, fell senseless to the ground. To raise him, and drive away the devil which they supposed was in him, they read a passage over his body from the Bible, and he immediately recovered.

Thus we have given all the particulars we can derive from authentic sources of the captivity and death of John Ortiz. Of Soto's expedition, about which many writers of talents and respectability have employed their pens, it was not our intention particularly to speak, but can refer those, whose curiosity would lead them to pursue it, to a new edition of my CHRONICLES OF THE INDIANS, shortly to be published ; but for a rapid and splendid glance over that ground, I will refer the reader to the first volume of Mr. Bancroft's History of the United States. And yet if he would go into minute details, there is the work of Mr. John T. Irving, which will leave little else to be looked for.

NARRATIVE

OF THE CAPTIVITY OF MRS. MARY ROWLANDSON, WIFE OF THE REV. JOSEPH ROWLANDSON, WHO WAS TAKEN PRIS-ONER WHEN LANCASTER WAS DESTROYED, IN THE YEAR 1676; WRITTEN BY HERSELF.

I print this edition of Mrs. Rowlandson's Narrative from the *second Lancaster edition*, with a selection of the notes to that edition, by JOSEPH WILLARD, Esq., which was printed in 1828. Mr. Willard calls his the sixth edition. My own notes are, as in other parts of the work, signed Ed.

ON the 10th of February, 1676, came the Indians with great numbers* upon Lancaster : their first coming was about sunrising. Hearing the noise of some guns, we looked out ; several houses were burning, and the smoke ascending to heaven. There were five persons taken in one house ; the father and mother, and a sucking child they knocked on the head, the other two they took and carried away alive. There were two others, who, being out of their garrison upon occasion, were set upon, one was knocked on the head, the other escaped. Another there was, who, running along, was shot and wounded, and fell down ; he begged of them his life, promising them money, as they told me, but they would not hearken to him, but knocked him on the head, stripped him naked, and split open his bowels. Another, seeing many of the Indians

---

* Fifteen hundred was the number, according to the best authorities. They were the Wamponoags, led by King Philip, accompanied by the Narrhagansetts, his allies, and also by the Nipmucks and Nashaways, whom his artful eloquence had persuaded to join with him.

about his barn, ventured and went out, but was quickly shot down.   There were three others belonging to the same garrison who were killed; the Indians getting up upon the roof of the barn, had advantage to shoot down upon them over their fortification.   Thus these murderous wretches went on burning and destroying all before them.*

At length they came and beset our house, and quickly it was the dolefulest day that ever mine eyes saw.   The house stood upon the edge of a hill; † some of the Indians got behind the hill, others into the barn, and others behind any thing that would shelter them; from all which places they shot against the house, so that the bullets seemed to fly like hail, and quickly they wounded one man among us, then another, and then a third.   About two hours, according to my observation in that amazing time, they had been about the house before they prevailed to fire it, which they did with flax and hemp which they brought out of the barn, and there being no defence about the house, only two flankers at two opposite corners, and one of them not finished; they fired it once, and one ventured out and quenched it, but they quickly fired it again, and that took. Now is the dreadful hour come that I have often heard of in time of the war, as it was the case of others, but now mine eyes see it.   Some in our house were fighting for their lives, others wallowing in blood, the house on fire over our heads, and the bloody heathen ready to knock us on the head if we stirred out.   Now might we hear mothers and children crying out for themselves and one another, " *Lord, what shall we do !* " Then I took my children, and one of my sisters [Mrs. Drew] hers to go forth and leave the house, but as soon as we came to the door and appeared, the Indians shot so thick that the bullets rattled against the house as if one had taken a handful of stones and threw them, so that we were forced to give back.

* Mr. Willard, in his History of Lancaster, says he cannot ascertain that attacks were made in more than two places previous to that upon Mr. Rowlandson's house; the first of which was Wheeler's garrison, at Wataquodoc hill, now south-west part of Bolton.   Here they killed Jonas Fairbanks and Joshua his son, fifteen years of age, and Richard Wheeler. Wheeler had been in town about fifteen years.   The second was Prescott's garrison, near Poignand and Plant's cotton factory.   Ephraim Sawyer was killed here; and Henry Farrar and a Mr. Ball and his wife in other places.

† Mr. Rowlandson's house was on the brow of a small hill, on land now owned by Nathaniel Chandler, Esq., about a third of a mile south-west of the meeting-house, on the road leading from the centre of the town to the village called New-Boston, about two rods from the road, which at that time ran near the house.

We had six stout dogs belonging to our garrison,* but none of them would stir, though at another time if an Indian had come to the door, they were ready to fly upon him and tear him down. The Lord hereby would make us the more to acknowledge his hand, and to see that our help is always in him. But out we must go, the fire increasing, and coming along behind us roaring, and the Indians gaping before us with their guns, spears, and hatchets to devour us. No sooner were we out of the house, but my brother-in-law † (being before wounded in defending the house, in or near the throat) fell down dead, whereat the Indians scornfully shouted and hollowed, and were presently upon him, stripping off his clothes. The bullets flying thick, one went through my side, and the same, as would seem, through the bowels and hand of my poor child in my arms. One of my elder sister's children, named William, had then his leg broke, which the Indians perceiving, they knocked him on the head. Thus were we butchered by those merciless heathens, standing amazed, with the blood running down to our heels. My eldest sister ‡ being yet in the house, and seeing those woful sights, the infidels halling mothers one way and children another, and some wallowing in their blood; and her eldest son telling her that her son William was dead, and myself was wounded, she said, " *Lord, let me die with them :*" which was no sooner said but she was struck with a bullet, and fell down dead over the threshold. I hope she is reaping the fruit of her good labors, being faithful to the service of God in her place. In her younger years she lay under much trouble upon spiritual accounts, till it pleased God to make that precious scripture take hold of her heart, 2 Cor. 12: 9,—" *And he said unto me, My grace is sufficient for thee.*" More than twenty years after, I have heard her tell how sweet and comfortable that place was to her. But to return : The Indians laid hold of us, pulling me one way and the children another, and said, " *Come, go along with us.*" I told them they would kill me ; they answered, *If I were willing to go along with them they would not hurt me.*

Oh ! the doleful sight that now was to behold at this house ! Come, behold the works of the Lord, what desolations he has made in the earth. Of thirty-seven § persons who were in this

* Mr. Rowlandson's house was filled with soldiers and inhabitants, to the number of forty-two.

† Thomas Rowlandson, brother to the clergyman.

‡ Mrs. Kerley, wife of Capt. Henry Kerley, to whom she was married in 1654.

§ We have stated in a previous note that there were forty-two persons one house, none escaped either present death, or a bitter captivity, save only one,* who might say as in Job 1 : 15,—"*And I only am escaped alone to tell the news.*" There were twelve killed, some shot, some stabbed with their spears, some knocked down with their hatchets. When we are in prosperity, Oh the little that we think of such dreadful sights, to see our dear friends and relations lie bleeding out their hearts-blood upon the ground. There was one who was chopt in the head with a hatchet, and stript naked, and yet was crawling up and down. It was a solemn sight to see so many Christians lying in their blood, some here and some there, like a company of sheep torn by wolves ; all of them stript naked by a company of hell-hounds, roaring, singing, ranting, and insulting, as if they would have torn our very hearts out; yet the Lord, by his almighty power, preserved a number of us from death, for there were twenty-four of us taken alive and carried captive.

I had often before this said, that if the Indians should come, I should choose rather to be killed by them than taken alive, but when it came to the trial, my mind changed; their glittering weapons so daunted my spirit, that I chose rather to go along with those (as I may say) ravenous bears, than that moment to end my days. And that I may the better declare what happened to me during that grievous captivity, I shall particularly speak of the several Removes we had up and down the wilderness.

THE FIRST REMOVE.—Now away we must go with those barbarous creatures, with our bodies wounded and bleeding, and our hearts no less than our bodies. About a mile we went that night, up upon a hill,† within sight of the town, where we intended to lodge. There was hard by a vacant house, deserted by the English before, for fear of the Indians ; I asked them whether I might not lodge in the house that night; to which they answered, "What, will you love Englishmen still ?" This was the dolefulest night that ever my eyes saw. Oh the roaring, and singing, and dancing, and yelling of those black creatures in the night, which made the place a lively resem-

---

in the house, in which number are included five soldiers not reckoned by Mrs. Rowlandson.

* Ephraim Roper, whose wife was killed in attempting to escape.

† *George Hill*, which has been so called for more than one hundred and fifty years. It is said to have taken its name from an Indian whom the English called George, and who had a wigwam upon it. The name includes the whole range of the fertile and delightful ridge on the west side of the town, nearly two miles in extent. From the southern part, which is almost a distinct hill, is a fine view of the town and surrounding country.

blance of hell. And miserable was the waste that was there made of horses, cattle, sheep, swine, calves, lambs, roasting pigs, and fowls, (which they had plundered in the town,) some roasting, some lying and burning, and some boiling, to feed our merciless enemies; who were joyful enough, though we were disconsolate. To add to the dolefulness of the former day, and the dismalness of the present night, my thoughts ran upon my losses and sad, bereaved condition. All was gone, my husband gone,* (at least separated from me, he being in the Bay; and to add to my grief, the Indians told me they would kill him as he came homeward,) my children gone, my relations and friends gone,† our house and home, and all our comforts within door and without, all was gone, (except my life,) and I knew not but the next moment that might go too.

There remained nothing to me but one poor, wounded babe, and it seemed at present worse than death, that it was in such a pitiful condition, bespeaking compassion, and I had no refreshing for it, nor suitable things to revive it. Little do many think what is the savageness and brutishness of this barbarous enemy, those even that seem to profess more than others among them, when the English have fallen into their hands.

Those seven that were killed at Lancaster the summer before upon a Sabbath day, and the one that was afterward killed upon a week-day, were slain and mangled in a barbarous manner, by One-eyed John and Marlborough's praying Indians, which Capt. Mosely brought to Boston, as the Indians told me.

THE SECOND REMOVE.—But now (the next morning) I must turn my back upon the town, and travel with them into the vast and desolate wilderness, I know not whither. It is not my tongue or pen can express the sorrows of my heart, and bitterness of my spirit, that I had at this departure; but God was with me in a wonderful manner, carrying me along and bearing up my spirit, that it did not quite fail. One of the Indians carried my poor wounded babe upon a horse : it went moaning all along, " *I shall die, I shall die.*" I went on foot after it with sorrow that cannot be expressed. At length I took it off the horse, and carried it in my arms, till my strength failed and I fell down with it. Then they set me upon a horse with my wounded child in my lap, and there being no furniture on the horse's back, as we were going down a steep hill, we both fell

---

* Mr. Rowlandson, with Capt. Kerley and Mr. Drew, were at this time in Boston, soliciting the governor and council for more soldiers, for the protection of the place.

† No less than seventeen of Mr. Rowlandson's family were put to death or taken prisoners.

over the horse's head, at which they like inhuman creatures laughed, and rejoiced to see it, though I thought we should there have ended our days, overcome with so many difficulties. But the Lord renewed my strength still, and carried me along, that I might see more of his power, yea, so much that I could never have thought of, had I not experienced it.

After this it quickly began to snow, and when night came on they stopt. And now down I must sit in the snow, by a little fire, and a few boughs behind me, with my sick child in my lap, and calling much for water, being now, through the wound, fallen into a violent fever; my own wound also growing so stiff, that I could scarce sit down or rise up, yet so it must be, that I must sit all this cold, winter night upon the cold snowy ground, with my sick child in my arms, looking that every hour would be the last of its life, and having no Christian friend near me, either to comfort or help me. Oh, I may see the wonderful power of God, that my spirit did not utterly sink under my affliction; still the Lord upheld me with his gracious and merciful spirit, and we were both alive to see the light of the next morning.

THE THIRD REMOVE.—The morning being come, they prepared to go on their way; one of the Indians got upon a horse, and they sat me up behind him, with my poor sick babe in my lap. A very wearisome and tedious day I had of it; what with my own wound, and my child being so exceeding sick, and in a lamentable condition with her wound, it may easily be judged what a poor, feeble condition we were in, there being not the least crumb of refreshing that came within either of our mouths from Wednesday night to Saturday night, except only a little cold water. This day in the afternoon, about an hour by sun, we came to the place where they intended, viz. an Indian town called Wenimesset, [New Braintree] northward of Quabaug, [Brookfield.] When we were come, Oh the number of Pagans, now merciless enemies, that there came about me, that I may say as David, Psal. 27 : 13, " *I had fainted unless I had believed*," &c. The next day was the Sabbath. I then remembered how careless I had been of God's holy time ; how many Sabbaths I had lost and misspent, and how evilly I had walked in God's sight ; which lay so close upon my spirit, that it was easy for me to see how righteous it was with God to cut off the thread of my life, and cast me out of his presence for ever. Yet the Lord still showed mercy to me, and helped me ; and as he wounded me with one hand, so he healed me with the other. This day there came to me one Robert Pepper, a man belonging to Roxbury, who was taken at Capt. Beers' fight, and had been now a considerable time with the Indians, and up with them almost as far as Albany, to see King Philip, as he told me, and was now very lately come into these parts. Hearing, I say, that I was in this Indian town, he obtained leave to come and see me. He told me he himself was wounded in the leg at Capt. Beers' fight, and was not able some time to go, but as they carried him, and that he took oak leaves and laid to his wound, and by the blessing of God he was able to travel again. Then took I oak leaves and laid to my side, and with the blessing of God it cured me also; yet before the cure was wrought, I may say as it is in Psal. 38: 5, 6, "*My wounds stink and are corrupt. I am troubled; I am bowed down greatly; I go mourning all the day long.*" I sat much alone with my poor wounded child in my lap, which moaned night and day, having nothing to revive the body or cheer the spirits of her; but instead of that, one Indian would come and tell me one hour, "Your master will knock your child on the head," and then a second, and then a third, "Your master will quickly knock your child on the head."

This was the comfort I had from them; miserable comforters were they all. Thus nine days I sat upon my knees, with my babe in my lap, till my flesh was raw again. My child being even ready to depart this sorrowful world, they bid me carry it out to another wigwam, I suppose because they would not be troubled with such spectacles; whither I went with a very heavy heart, and down I sat with the picture of death in my lap. About two hours in the night, my sweet babe like a lamb departed this life, on Feb. 18, 1676, it being about six years and five months old.* It was nine days from the first wounding in this miserable condition, without any refreshing of one nature or another except a little cold water. I cannot but take notice how at another time I could not bear to be in a room where a dead person was, but now the case is changed; I must and could lie down with my dead babe all the night after. I have thought since of the wonderful goodness of God to me in preserving me so in the use of my reason and senses, in that distressed time, that I did not use wicked and violent means to end my own miserable life. In the morning when they understood that my child was dead, they sent me home to my master's wigwam. By my master in this writing must be understood Quannopin, who was a sagamore, and married King Philip's wife's sister; not that he first took me, but I was sold to him by a Narraganset Indian, who took me when I first came out of the garrison. I went to take up my dead child

* This child's name was Sarah; born Sept. 15, 1669.

in my arms to carry it with me, but they bid me let it alone. There was no resisting, but go I must, and leave it. When I had been awhile at my master's wigwam, I took the first opportunity I could get to go look after my dead child. When I came I asked them what they had done with it. They told me it was on the hill.* Then they went and showed me where it was, where I saw the ground was newly digged, and where they told me they had buried it. There I left that child in the wilderness, and must commit it and myself also in this wilderness condition to Him who is above all. God having taken away this dear child, I went to see my daughter Mary, who was at the same Indian town, at a wigwam not very far off, though we had little liberty or opportunity to see one another; she was about ten years old, and taken from the door at first by a praying Indian, and afterwards sold for a gun. When I came in sight she would fall a weeping, at which they were provoked, and would not let me come near her, but bid me be gone; which was a heart-cutting word to me. I had one child dead, another in the wilderness, I knew not where, the third they would not let me come near to; "*Me* (as he said) *have ye bereaved of my children; Joseph is not, and Simeon is not, and ye will take Benjamin also; all these things are against me.*" I could not sit still in this condition, but kept walking from one place to another; and as I was going along, my heart was even overwhelmed with the thoughts of my condition, and that I should have children, and a nation that I knew not ruled over them. Whereupon I earnestly entreated the Lord that he would consider my low estate, and show me a token for good, and if it were his blessed will, some sign and hope of some relief. And indeed quickly the Lord answered in some measure my poor prayer; for as I was going up and down mourning and lamenting my condition, my son [Joseph] came to me and asked me how I did. • I had not seen him before since the destruction of the town; and I knew not where he was, till I was informed by himself that he was among a smaller parcel of Indians, whose place was about six miles off. With tears in his eyes he asked me whether his sister Sarah was dead, and told me he had seen his sister Mary, and prayed me that I would not be troubled in reference to himself. The occasion of his coming to see me at this time was this: there was, as I said, about six miles from us, a small plantation of Indians, where it seems he had been during his captivity; and at this time there were some forces of the In-

---

* This hill, in the town of New Braintree, is now known as the burial place of Mrs. Rowlandson's child.

dians gathered out of our company, and some also from them, amongst whom was my son's master, to go to assault and burn Medfield.   In this time of his master's absence his dame brought him to see me.   I took this to be some gracious answer to my earnest and unfeigned desire.   The next day the Indians returned from Medfield;* all the company, for those that belonged to the other smaller company came through the town that we now were at; but before they came to us, Oh the outrageous roaring and whooping that there was! they began their din about a mile before they came to us.   By their noise and whooping they signified how many they had destroyed; which was at that time twenty-three.   Those that were with us at home were gathered together as soon as they heard the whooping, and every time that the other went over their number, these at home gave a shout, that the very earth rang again. And thus they continued till those that had been upon the expedition were come up to the sagamore's wigwam; and then Oh the hideous insulting and triumphing that there was over some Englishmen's scalps that they had taken, as their manner is, and brought with them.   I cannot but take notice of the wonderful mercy of God to me in those afflictions, in sending me a Bible.   One of the Indians that came from Medfield fight, and had brought some plunder, came to me, and asked me if I would have a Bible; he had got one in his basket.   I was glad of it, and asked him if he thought the Indians would let me read.   He answered yes.   So I took the Bible, and in that melancholy time it came into my mind to read first the twenty-eighth chapter of Deuteronomy, which I did, and when I had read it my dark heart wrought on this manner: that there was no mercy for me, that the blessings were gone, and the curses came in their room, and that I had lost my opportunity.   But the Lord helped me still to go on reading, till I came to chap. 30, the seven first verses; where I found there was mercy promised again, if we would return to him by repentance; and though we were scattered from one end of the earth to the other, yet the Lord would gather us together, and turn all those curses upon our enemies.   I do not desire to live to forget this scripture, and what comfort it was to me.

Now the Indians began to talk of removing from this place, some one way and some another.   There were now besides myself nine English captives in this place, all of them children except one woman.   I got an opportunity to go and take my leave of them, they being to go one way and I another.   I asked them whether they were earnest with God for deliver-

* Medfield was attacked Feb. 21, (O. S.)

ance. They told me they did as they were able, and it was
some comfort to me that the Lord stirred up children to look to
him. The woman, viz. goodwife Joslin,* told me she should
never see me again, and that she could find in her heart to run
away by any means, for we were near thirty miles from any
English town,† and she very big with child, having but one week
to reckon, and another child in her arms two years old ; and
bad rivers there were to go over, and we were feeble with our
poor and coarse entertainment. I had my Bible with me. I
pulled it out, and asked her whether she would read. We
opened the Bible, and lighted on Psalm 27, in which Psalm
we especially took notice of that verse, " *Wait on the Lord, be
of good courage, and he shall strengthen thine heart ; wait I
say on the Lord.*"

The Fourth Remove.—And now must I part with the little
company I had. Here I parted with my daughter Mary,‡
whom I never saw again till I saw her in Dorchester, returned
from captivity, and from four little cousins and neighbors, some
of which I never saw afterward ; the Lord only knows the end
of them. Among them also was that poor woman before mentioned, who came to a sad end, as some of the company told
me in my travel. She having much grief upon her spirits
about her miserable condition, being so near her time, she
would be often asking the Indians to let her go home. They
not being willing to that, and yet vexed with her importunity,
gathered a great company together about her, and stript her
naked and set her in the midst of them ; and when they had
sung and danced about her in their hellish manner as long as
they pleased, they knocked her on the head, and the child in
her arms with her. When they had done that, they made a
fire and put them both into it, and told the other children that
were with them, that if they attempted to go home they would
serve them in like manner. The children said she did not
shed one tear, but prayed all the while. But to turn to my
own journey. We travelled about a half a day or a little more,
and came to a desolate place in the wilderness, where there
were no wigwams or inhabitants before. We came about the
middle of the afternoon to this place, cold, wet, and snowy, and
hungry, and weary, and no refreshing for man, but the cold
ground to sit on, and our poor Indian cheer.

* Abraham Joslin's wife.

† This was true at that time, as Brookfield, (Quaboag,) within a few
miles of Wenimesset, was destroyed by the Indians in August, 1675.
The nearest towns were those on Connecticut river.

‡ Born August 12, 1665.

Heart-aching thoughts here I had about my poor children, who were scattered up and down among the wild beasts of the forest. My head was light and dizzy, either through hunger or bad lodging, or trouble, or all together, my knees feeble, my body raw by sitting double night and day, that I cannot express to man the affliction that lay upon my spirit, but the Lord helped me at that time to express it to himself. I opened my Bible to read, and the Lord brought that precious scripture to me, Jer. 31 : 16,—" *Thus saith the Lord, refrain thy voice from weeping, and thine eyes from tears, for thy work shall be rewarded, and they shall come again from the land of the enemy.*" This was a sweet cordial to me when I was ready to faint. Many and many a time have I sat down and wept sweetly over this scripture. At this place we continued about four days.

THE FIFTH REMOVE.—The occasion, as I thought, of their removing at this time, was the English army's being near and following them; for they went as if they had gone for their lives for some considerable way; and then they made a stop, and chose out some of their stoutest men, and sent them back to hold the English army in play whilst the rest escaped; and then, like Jehu, they marched on furiously, with their old and young: some carried their old, decrepit mothers, some carried one, and some another. Four of them carried a great Indian upon a bier; but going through a thick wood with him, they were hindered, and could make no haste; whereupon they took him upon their backs, and carried him one at a time, till we came to Bacquag* river. Upon Friday, a little after noon, we came to this river. When all the company was come up and were gathered together, I thought to count the number of them, but they were so many, and being somewhat in motion, it was beyond my skill. In this travel, because of my wound, I was somewhat favored in my load. I carried only my knitting-work, and two quarts of parched meal. Being very faint, I asked my mistress to give me one spoonful of the meal, but she would not give me a taste. They quickly fell to cutting dry trees, to make rafts to carry them over the river, and soon my turn came to go over. By the advantage of some brush which they had laid upon the raft to sit on, I did not wet my foot, while many of themselves at the other end were mid-leg deep, which cannot but be acknowledged as a favor of God to my weakened body, it being a very cold time. I was not before acquainted with such kind of doings or dangers. " *When*

---

* Or Payquage, now Miller's river. It empties into the Connecticut, between Northfield and Montague.

*thou passeth through the waters I will be with thee, and through
the rivers they shall not overflow thee."*—Isa. 43 : 2.   A certain
number of us got over the river that night, but it was the night
after the Sabbath before all the company was got over.   On
the Saturday they boiled an old horse's leg which they had
got, and so we drank of the broth, as soon as they thought it
was ready, and when it was almost all gone they filled it up
again.

The first week of my being among them, I hardly eat any
thing ; the second week I found my stomach grow very faint
for want of something, and yet it was very hard to get down
their filthy trash ; but the third week, though I could think how
formerly my stomach would turn against this or that, and I
could starve and die before I could eat such things, yet they
were pleasant and savory to my taste.   I was at this time knit-
ting a pair of white cotton stockings for my mistress, and I had
not yet wrought upon the Sabbath day.   When the Sabbath
came, they bid me go to work.   I told them it was Sabbath
day, and desired them to let me rest, and told them I would do
as much more work to-morrow ; to which they answered me
they would break my face.   And here I cannot but take notice
of the strange providence of God in preserving the heathen.
They were many hundreds, old and young, some sick, and
some lame ; many had papooses at their backs ; the greatest
number at this time with us were squaws ; and yet they travelled with all they had, bag and baggage, and they got over
this river aforesaid ; and on Monday they sat their wigwams
on fire, and away they went.   On that very day came the
English army after them to this river, and saw the smoke of
their wigwams, and yet this river put a stop to them.   God did
not give them courage or activity to go over after us.   We
were not ready for so great a mercy as victory and deliverance ;
if we had been, God would have found out a way for the
English to have passed this river, as well as for the Indians,
with their squaws and children, and all their luggage.   *" O
that my people had hearkened unto me, and Israel had walked
in my ways ; I should soon have subdued their enemies, and
turned my hand against their adversaries."*—Psal. 81 : 13, 14.

THE SIXTH REMOVE.—On Monday, as I said, they set their
wigwams on fire, and went away.   It was a cold morning, and
before us there was a great brook with ice on it.   Some waded
through it up to the knees and higher, but others went till they
came to a beaver dam, and I amongst them, where, through
the good providence of God, I did not wet my foot.   I went
along that day mourning and lamenting, leaving farther my
own country, and travelling farther into the vast and howling

wilderness, and I understood something of Lot's wife's temptation when she looked back. We came that day to a great swamp, by the side of which we took up our lodging that night. When we came to the brow of the hill that looked toward the swamp, I thought we had been come to a great Indian town, though there were none but our own company; the Indians were as thick as the trees; it seemed as if there had been a thousand hatchets going at once. If one looked before one there was nothing but Indians, and behind one nothing but Indians; and so on either hand; and I myself in the midst, and no Christian soul near me, and yet how hath the Lord preserved me in safety! Oh the experience that I have had of the goodness of God to me and mine!

THE SEVENTH REMOVE.—After a restless and hungry night there, we had a wearisome time of it the next day. The swamp by which we lay was as it were a deep dungeon, and an exceeding high and steep hill before it. Before I got to the top of the hill, I thought my heart and legs and all would have broken and failed me. What through faintness and soreness of body, it was a grievous day of travel to me. As we went along, I saw a place where English cattle had been. That was a comfort to me, such as it was. Quickly after that we came to an English path, which so took me that I thought I could there have freely lain down and died. That day, a little after noon, we came to Squaheag,* where the Indians quickly spread themselves over the deserted English fields, gleaning what they could find. Some picked up ears of wheat that were crickled down, some found ears of Indian corn, some found groundnuts, and others sheaves of wheat that were frozen together in the shock, and went to threshing of them out. Myself got two ears of Indian corn, and whilst I did but turn my back, one of them was stole from me, which much troubled me. There came an Indian to them at that time, with a basket of horse-liver. I asked him to give me a piece. "What," says he, "can you eat horse-liver?" I told him I would try, if he would give me a piece, which he did; and I laid it on the coals to roast; but before it was half ready, they got half of it away from me; so that I was forced to take the rest and eat it as it was, with the blood about my mouth, and yet a savory bit it was to me; for to the hungry soul every bitter thing was sweet. A solemn sight methought it was, to see whole fields of wheat and Indian corn forsaken and spoiled, and the remainder of them to be food for our merciless enemies. That night we had a mess of wheat for our supper.

* Or Squakeag, now Northfield.

THE EIGHTH REMOVE.—On the morrow morning we must go over Connecticut river, to meet with King Philip. Two canoes full they had carried over; the next turn myself was to go; but as my foot was upon the canoe to step in, there was a sudden outcry among them, and I must step back; and instead of going over the river, I must go four or five miles up the river farther northward. Some of the Indians ran one way, and some another. The cause of this rout was, as I thought, their espying some English scouts, who were thereabouts. In this travel up the river, about noon the company made a stop, and sat down, some to eat and others to rest them. As I sat amongst them, musing on things past, my son Joseph unexpectedly came to me. We asked of each other's welfare, bemoaning our doleful condition, and the change that had come upon us. We had husband and father, and children and sisters, and friends and relations, and house and home, and many comforts of this life; but now we might say as Job, "*Naked came I out of my mother's womb, and naked shall I return. The Lord gave, and the Lord hath taken away; blessed be the name of the Lord.*" I asked him whether he would read. He told me he earnestly desired it. I gave him my Bible, and he lighted upon that comfortable scripture, Psalm 118: 17, 18,— "*I shall not die, but live, and declare the works of the Lord. The Lord hath chastened me sore, yet he hath not given me over to death.*" "Look here, mother," says he, "did you read this?" And here I may take occasion to mention one principal ground of my setting forth these lines, even as the Psalmist says, to declare the works of the Lord, and his wonderful power in carrying us along, preserving us in the wilderness while under the enemy's hand, and returning of us in safety again; and his goodness in bringing to my hand so many comfortable and suitable scriptures in my distress.

But to return. We travelled on till night, and in the morning we must go over the river to Philip's crew. When I was in the canoe, I could not but be amazed at the numerous crew of Pagans that were on the bank on the other side. When I came ashore, they gathered all about me, I sitting alone in the midst. I observed they asked one another questions, and laughed, and rejoiced over their gains and victories. Then my heart began to fail, and I fell a weeping; which was the first time, to my remembrance, that I wept before them. Although I had met with so much affliction, and my heart was many times ready to break, yet could I not shed one tear in their sight, but rather had been all this while in a maze, and like one astonished; but now I may say as Psal. 137: 1,— "*By the rivers of Babylon, there we sat down, yea, we wept, when we remembered Zion.*" There one of them asked me why I wept. I could hardly tell what to say; yet I answered, they would kill me. "No," said he, "none will hurt you." Then came one of them, and gave me two spoonfuls of meal, to comfort me, and another gave me half a pint of peas, which was worth more than many bushels at another time. Then I went to see King Philip. He bade me come in and sit down, and asked me whether I would smoke it—a usual compliment now-a-days among the saints and sinners; but this noway suited me; for though I had formerly used tobacco, yet I had left it ever since I was first taken. It seems to be a bait the devil lays to make men lose their precious time. I remember with shame how formerly, when I had taken two or three pipes, I was presently ready for another, such a bewitching thing it is; but I thank God, he has now given me power over it. Surely there are many who may be better employed than to sit sucking a stinking tobacco-pipe.

Now the Indians gathered their forces to go against North-ampton. Over night one went about yelling and hooting to give notice of the design. Whereupon they went to boiling of ground-nuts and parching corn, as many as had it, for their provision; and in the morning away they went. During my abode in this place, Philip spake to me to make a shirt for his boy, which I did; for which he gave me a shilling. I offered the money to my mistress, but she bid me keep it, and with it I bought a piece of horse-flesh. Afterward he asked me to make a cap for his boy, for which he invited me to dinner. I went, and he gave me a pancake about as big as two fingers; it was made of parched wheat, beaten and fried in bear's grease, but I thought I never tasted pleasanter meat in my life. There was a squaw who spake to me to make a shirt for her Sannup; for which she gave me a piece of beef. Another asked me to knit a pair of stockings, for which she gave me a quart of peas. I boiled my peas and beef together, and invited my master and mistress to dinner; but the proud gossip, because I served them both in one dish, would eat nothing, except one bit that he gave her upon the point of his knife. Hearing that my son was come to this place, I went to see him, and found him lying flat on the ground. I asked him how he could sleep so. He answered me that he was not asleep, but at prayer, and that he lay so that they might not observe what he was doing. I pray God he may remember these things now he is returned in safety. At this place, the sun now getting higher, what with the beams and heat of the sun and smoke of the wigwams, I thought I should have been blinded. I could scarce discern one wigwam from another. There was one Mary Thurston, of Medfield, who, seeing how it was with me, lent me a hat to wear; but as soon as I was gone, the squaw that owned that Mary Thurston came running after me, and got it away again. Here was a squaw who gave me a spoonful of meal; I put it in my pocket to keep it safe, yet notwithstanding somebody stole it, but put five Indian corns in the room of it; which corns were the greatest provision I had in my travel for one day.

The Indians returning from Northampton * brought with them some horses, and sheep, and other things which they had taken. I desired them that they would carry me to Albany upon one of those horses, and sell me for powder; for so they had sometimes discoursed. I was utterly helpless of getting home on foot, the way that I came. I could hardly bear to think of the many weary steps I had taken to this place.

THE NINTH REMOVE.—But instead of either going to Albany or homeward, we must go five miles up the river, and then go over it. Here we abode a while. Here lived a sorry Indian, who spake to me to make him a shirt; when I had done it he would pay me nothing for it. But he living by the river-side, where I often went to fetch water, I would often be putting him in mind, and calling for my pay; at last he told me, if I would make another shirt for a papoose not yet born, he would give me a knife, which he did when I had done it. I carried the knife in, and my master asked me to give it him, and I was not a little glad that I had anything that they would accept of and be pleased with. When we were at this place, my master's maid came home: she had been gone three weeks into the Narragansett country to fetch corn, where they had stored up some in the ground. She brought home about a peck and a half of corn. This was about the time that their great captain, *Naananto,*† was killed in the Narragansett country.

My son being now about a mile from me, I asked liberty to go and see him. They bid me go, and away I went; but quickly lost myself, travelling over hills and through swamps, and could not find the way to him. And I cannot but admire at the wonderful power and goodness of God to me, in that though I was gone from home and met with all sorts of Indians, and those I had no knowledge of, and there being no Christian soul near me, yet not one of them offered the least imaginable miscarriage to me. I turned homeward again, and met with my master, and he showed me the way to my son. When I came to him, I found him not well; and withal he had a boil on his side which much

---

* Northampton was attacked March 14, 1676.

† Nanuntennoo. He was taken April 6th, 1676. **See Book of the Indians, Book iii. 49, 50.—Ed.**

troubled him. We bemoaned one another a while, as the Lord helped us, and then I returned again. When I was returned, I found myself as unsatisfied as I was before. I went up and down mourning and lamenting, and my spirit was ready to sink with the thoughts of my poor children. My son was ill, and I could not but think of his mournful looks, having no Christian friend near him, to do any office of love to him, either for soul or body. And my poor girl, I knew not where she was, nor whether she was sick or well, alive or dead. I repaired under these thoughts to my Bible, (my great comforter in that time,) and that scripture came to my hand, "*Cast thy burden upon the Lord, and he shall sustain thee.*"—Psal. 55: 22.

But I was fain to go look after something to satisfy my hunger; and going among the wigwams, I went into one, and there found a squaw who showed herself very kind to me, and gave me a piece of bear. I put it into my pocket and came home; but could not find an opportunity to broil it, for fear they should get it from me. And there it lay all the day and night in my stinking pocket. In the morning, I went again to the same squaw, who had a kettle of ground-nuts boiling. I asked her to let me boil my piece of bear in the kettle, which she did, and gave me some ground-nuts to eat with it; and I cannot but think how pleasant it was to me. I have sometimes seen bear baked handsomely amongst the English, and some liked it, but the thoughts that it was bear made me tremble. But now, that was savory to me that one would think was enough to turn the stomach of a brute creature.

One bitter cold day, I could find no room to sit down before the fire. I went out, and could not tell what to do, but I went into another wigwam, where they were also sitting round the fire; but the squaw laid a skin for me, and bid me sit down, and gave me some ground-nuts, and bid me come again, and told me they would buy me if they were able. And yet these were strangers to me that I never knew before.

THE TENTH REMOVE.—That day a small part of the company removed about three quarters of a mile, intending farther the next day. When they came to the place they intended to lodge, and had pitched their wigwams, being hungry, I went again back to the place we were before at, to get something to eat; being encouraged by the squaw's kindness, who bid me come again. When I was there, there came an Indian to look after me; who, when he had found me, kicked me all along. I went home and found venison roasting that night, but they would not give me one bit of it. Sometimes I met with favor, and sometimes with nothing but frowns.

THE ELEVENTH REMOVE.—The next day in the morning,

they took their travel, intending a day's journey up the river; I took my load at my back, and quickly we came to wade over a river, and passed over tiresome and wearisome hills. One hill was so steep, that I was fain to creep up upon my knees, and to hold by the twigs and bushes to keep myself from falling backward. My head also was so light that I usually reeled as I went. But I hope all those wearisome steps that I have taken are but a forwarding of me to the heavenly rest. *"I know, O Lord, that thy judgments are right, and that thou in faithfulness hath afflicted me."*—Psalm 119 : 75.

THE TWELFTH REMOVE.—It was upon a Sabbath-day morning that they prepared for their travel. This morning I asked my master whether he would sell me to my husband; he answered, *nux ;* which did much rejoice my spirits. My mistress, before we went, was gone to the burial of a papoos, and returning, she found me sitting and reading in my Bible. She snatched it hastily out of my hand and threw it out of doors. I ran out and caught it up, and put it in my pocket, and never let her see it afterwards. Then they packed up their things to be gone, and gave me my load; I complained it was too heavy, whereupon she gave me a slap on the face and bid me be gone. I lifted up my heart to God, hoping that redemption was not far off; and the rather because their insolence grew worse and worse.

But thoughts of my going homeward, for so we bent our course, much cheered my spirit, and made my burden seem light, and almost nothing at all. But, to my amazement and great perplexity, the scale was soon turned; for when we had got a little way, on a sudden my mistress gave out she would go no further, but turn back again, and said I must go back again with her; and she called her sannup, and would have had him go back also, but he would not, but said he would go on, and come to us again in three days. My spirit was upon this, I confess, very impatient, and almost outrageous. I thought I could as well have died as went back. I cannot declare the trouble that I was in about it; back again I must go. As soon as I had an opportunity, I took my Bible to read, and that quieting scripture came to my hand, Psalm 46 : 10,—*"Be still, and know that I am God;"* which stilled my spirit for the present; but a sore time of trial I concluded I had to go through; my master being gone, who seemed to me the best friend I had of an Indian, both in cold and hunger, and quickly so it proved. Down I sat, with my heart as full as it could hold, and yet so hungry that I could not sit neither. But going out to see what I could find, and walking among the trees, I found six acorns and two chesnuts, which were some refreshment to me. To-

4

wards night I gathered me some sticks for my own comfort,
that I might not lie cold ; but when we came to lie down, they
bid me go out and lie somewhere else, for they had company,
they said come in more than their own. I told them I could
not tell where to go ; they bid me go look ; I told them if I
went to another wigwam they would be angry and send me
home again. Then one of the company drew his sword and
told me he would run me through if I did not go presently.
Then was I fain to stoop to this rude fellow, and go out in the
night I knew not whither. Mine eyes hath seen that fellow
afterwards walking up and down in Boston, under the appearance of a friendly Indian, and several others of the like cut. I
went to one wigwam, and they told me they had no room.
Then I went to another, and they said the same. At last, an
old Indian bid me come to him, and his squaw gave me some
ground-nuts ; she gave me also something to lay under my
head, and a good fire we had ; through the good providence
of God, I had a comfortable lodging that night. In the morning, another Indian bid me come at night and he would give
me six ground-nuts, which I did. We were at this place and
time about two miles from Connecticut river. We went in the
morning, to gather ground-nuts, to the river, and went back
again at night. I went with a great load at my back, for they
when they went, though but a little way, would carry all their
trumpery with them. I told them the skin was off my back,
but I had no other comforting answer from them than this, that
it would be no matter if my head was off too.

THE THIRTEENTH REMOVE.—Instead of going towards the
bay, which was what I desired, I must go with them five or
six miles down the river, into a mighty thicket of brush ; where
we abode almost a fortnight. Here one asked me to make a
shirt for her papoos, for which she gave me a mess of broth,
which was thickened with meal made of the bark of a tree ;
and to make it better she had put into it about a handful of
peas, and a few roasted ground-nuts. I had not seen my son
a pretty while, and here was an Indian of whom I made enqui-
ry after him, and asked him when he saw him. He answered
me, that such a time his master roasted him, and that himself
did eat a piece of him as big as his two fingers, and that he
was very good meat. But the Lord upheld my spirit under
this discouragement ; and I considered their horrible addicted-
ness to lying, and that there is not one of them that makes the
least conscience of speaking the truth.

In this place, one cold night, as I lay by the fire, I removed
a stick which kept the heat from me ; a squaw moved it down
again, at which I looked up, and she threw an handful of ashes

in my eyes; I thought I should have been quite blinded and
never have seen more; but, lying down, the water ran out of
my eyes, and carried the dirt with it, that by the morning I
recovered my sight again. Yet upon this, and the like occasions, I hope it is not too much to say with Job, " *Have pity
upon me, have pity upon me, O ye my friends, for the hand of
the LORD has touched me.*" And here, I cannot but remember how many times, sitting in their wigwams, and musing on
things past, I should suddenly leap up and run out, as if I had
been at home, forgetting where I was, and what my condition
was; but when I was without, and saw nothing but wilderness
and woods, and a company of barbarous heathen, my mind
quickly returned to me, which made me think of that spoken
concerning Samson, who said, " *I will go out and shake myself
as at other times, but he wist not that the Lord was departed
from him.*"

About this time I began to think that all my hopes of resto-
ration would come to nothing. I thought of the English army,
and hoped for their coming, and being retaken by them, but
that failed. I hoped to be carried to Albany, as the Indians
had discoursed, but that failed also. I thought of being sold
to my husband, as my master spake; but instead of that, my
master himself was gone, and I left behind, so that my spirit
was now quite ready to sink. I asked them to let me go out
and pick up some sticks, that I might get alone, and pour out
my heart unto the Lord. Then also I took my Bible to read,
but I found no comfort here neither; yet, I can say in all my
sorrows and afflictions, God did not leave me to have any impatient work toward himself, as if his ways were unrighteous;
but I knew that he laid upon me less than I deserved. Afterward, before this doleful time ended with me, I was turning
the leaves of my Bible, and the Lord brought to me some
scripture which did a little revive me; as that, Isa. 55 : 8,—
"*For my thoughts are not your thoughts, neither are my ways
your ways, saith the Lord.*" And also that, Psalm 37 : 5,—
"*Commit thy ways unto the Lord, trust also in him, and he
shall bring it to pass.*"

About this time, they came yelping from Hadley,* having
there killed three Englishmen, and brought one captive with
them, viz. Thomas Reed. They all gathered about the poor
man, asking him many questions. I desired also to go and
see him; and when I came, he was crying bitterly, supposing

* In the beginning of April, a number of the inhabitants of Hadley,
having ventured out some distance from the guard, for the purpose of til
lage, were attacked by the Indians, and three of them killed.

they would quickly kill him. Whereupon I asked one of them whether they intended to kill him ; he answered me they would not. He being a little cheered with that, I asked him about the welfare of my husband ; he told me he saw him such a time in the Bay, and he was well, but very melancholy. By which I certainly understood, though I suspected it before, that whatsoever the Indians told me respecting him was vanity and lies. Some of them told me he was dead, and they had killed him ; some said he was married again, and that the governor wished him to marry, and told him that he should have his choice ; and that all persuaded him that I was dead. So like were these barbarous creatures to him who was a liar from the beginning.

As I was sitting once in the wigwam here, Philip's maid came with the child in her arms, and asked me to give her a piece of my apron to make a flap for it. I told her I would not ; then my mistress bid me give it, but I still said no ; the maid told me if I would not give her a piece, she would tear a piece off it. I told her I would tear her coat then : with that my mistress rises up, and takes up a stick big enough to have killed me, and struck at me with it, but I stept out, and she struck the stick into the mat of the wigwam. But while she was pulling it out, I ran to the maid, and gave her all my apron ; and so that storm went over.

Hearing that my son was come to this place, I went to see him, and told him his father was well, but very melancholy. He told me he was as much grieved for his father as for him-self. I wondered at his speech, for I thought I had enough upon my spirit, in reference to myself, to make me mindless of my husband and every one else, they being safe among their friends. He told me also, that a while before, his master, to-gether with other Indians, were going to the French for powder ; but by the way the Mohawks met with them, and killed four of their company, which made the rest turn back again ; for which I desire that myself and he may ever bless the Lord ; for it might have been worse with him had he been sold to the French, than it proved to be in his remaining with the Indians.

I went to see an English youth in this place, one John Gil-bert, of Springfield. I found him laying without doors upon the ground. I asked him how he did ; he told me he was very sick of a flux with eating so much blood. They had turned him out of the wigwam, and with him an Indian papoos, almost dead, (whose parents had been killed,) in a bitter cold day, without fire or clothes ; the young man himself had nothing on but his shirt and waistcoat. This sight was enough to melt a heart of flint. There they lay quivering in the cold, the youth round like a dog, the papoos stretched out, with his eyes, nose, and mouth full of dirt, and yet alive, and groaning. I advised John to go and get to some fire ; he told me he could not stand, but I persuaded him still, lest he should lie there and die. And with much ado I got him to a fire, and went myself home. As soon as I was got home, his master's daughter came after me, to know what I had done with the Englishman ; I told her I had got him to a fire in such a place. Now had I need to pray Paul's prayer, 2 Thess. 3: 2,—"*that we may be delivered from unreasonable and wicked men.*" For her satisfaction I went along with her, and brought her to him ; but before I got home again, it was noised about that I was running away, and getting the English youth along with me ; that as soon as I came in, they began to rant and domineer, asking me where I had been, and what I had been doing, and saying they would knock me on the head. I told them I had been seeing the English youth, and that I would not run away. They told me I lied, and getting up a hatchet, they came to me and said they would knock me down if I stirred out again ; and so confined me to the wigwam. Now may I say with David, 2 Sam. 24: 14,—"*I am in a great strait.*" If I keep in, I must die with hunger ; and if I go out, I must be knocked on the head. This distressed condition held that day, and half the next ; and then the Lord remembered me, whose mercies are great. Then came an Indian to me with a pair of stockings which were too big for him, and he would have me ravel them out, and knit them fit for him. I showed myself willing, and bid him ask my mistress if I might go along with him a little way. She said yes, I might ; but I was not a little refreshed with that news, that I had my liberty again. Then I went along with him, and he gave me some roasted groundnuts, which did again revive my feeble stomach.

Being got out of her sight, I had time and liberty again to look into my Bible, which was my guide by day, and my pillow by night. Now that comfortable scripture presented itself to me, Isa. 45: 7,—"*For a small moment have I forsaken thee, but with great mercies will I gather thee.*" Thus the Lord carried me along from one time to another, and made good to me this precious promise and many others. Then my son came to see me, and I asked his master to let him stay a while with me, that I might comb his head and look over him, for he was almost overcome with lice. He told me when I had done that he was very hungry, but I had nothing to relieve him, but bid him go into the wigwams as he went along, and see if he could get any thing among them ; which he did, and, it seems, tarried a little too long, for his master was angry with him, and

4*

beat him, and then sold him. Then he came running to tell me he had a new master, and that he had given him some ground-nuts already. Then I went along with him to his new master, who told me he loved him, and he should not want. So his master carried him away; and I never saw him afterward, till I saw him at Piscataqua, in Portsmouth.

⁹ That night they bid me go out of the wigwam again; my mistress's papoos was sick, and it died that night; and there was one benefit in it, that there was more room. I went to a wigwam and they bid me come in, and gave me a skin to lie upon, and a mess of venison and ground-nuts, which was a choice dish among them. On the morrow they buried the papoos; and afterward, both morning and evening, there came a company to mourn and howl with her; though I confess I could not much condole with them. Many sorrowful days I had in this place; often getting alone, "*like a crane or a swallow, so did I chatter; I did mourn as a dove; mine eyes fail with looking upward. O Lord, I am oppressed, undertake for me.*"—Isa. 38 : 14. I could tell the Lord as Hezekiah, ver. 3, "*Remember now, O Lord, I beseech thee, how I have walked before thee in truth.*" Now had I time to examine all my ways. My conscience did not accuse me of unrighteousness towards one or another; yet I saw how in my walk with God I had been a careless creature. As David said, "*against thee only have I sinned.*" And I might say with the poor publican, "*God be merciful unto me a sinner.*" Upon the Sabbath days I could look upon the sun, and think how people were going to the house of God to have their souls refreshed, and then home and their bodies also; but I was destitute of both, and might say as the poor prodigal, "*He would fain have filled his belly with the husks that the swine did eat, and no man gave unto him.*" Luke 15 : 16. For I must say with him, "*Father, I have sinned against heaven and in thy sight.*"—Ver. 21. I remember how on the night before and after the Sabbath, when my family was about me, and relations and neighbors with us, we could pray, and sing, and refresh our bodies with the good creatures of God, and then have a comfortable bed to lie down on; but instead of all this, I had only a little swill for the body, and then, like a swine, must lie down on the ground. I cannot express to man the sorrow that lay upon my spirit, the Lord knows it. Yet that comfortable scripture would often come to my mind,—"*For a small moment have I forsaken thee, but with great mercies will I gather thee.*"

THE FOURTEENTH REMOVE.—Now must we pack up and be gone from this thicket, bending our course towards the Bay towns; I having nothing to eat by the way this day but a few

crums of cake that an Indian gave my girl the same day we
were taken. She gave it me, and I put it in my pocket.
There it lay, till it was so mouldy, for want of good baking,
that one could not tell what it was made of; it fell all into
crums, and grew so dry and hard that it was like little flints;
and this refreshed me many times when I was ready to faint.
It was in my thoughts when I put it to my mouth, that if ever
I returned I would tell the world what a blessing the Lord
gave to such mean food. As we went along, they killed a
deer, with a young one in her. They gave me a piece of the
fawn, and it was so young and tender that one might eat the
bones as well as the flesh, and yet I thought it very good.
When night came on we sat down. It rained, but they quickly
got up a bark wigwam, where I lay dry that night. I looked
out in the morning, and many of them had lain in the rain all
night, I knew by their reeking. Thus the Lord dealt merci-
fully with me many times, and I fared better than many of
them. In the morning they took the blood of the deer, and
put it into the paunch, and so boiled it. I could eat nothing
of that, though they eat it sweetly. And yet they were so
nice in other things, that when I had fetched water, and had
put the dish I dipped the water with into the kettle of water
which I brought, they would say they would knock me down,
for they said it was a sluttish trick.

THE FIFTEENTH REMOVE.—We went on our travel. I having got a handful of ground-nuts for my support that day,
they gave me my load, and I went on cheerfully, with the
thoughts of going homeward, having my burthen more upon
my back than my spirit. We came to Baquaug river again
that day, near which we abode a few days. Sometimes one
of them would give me a pipe, another a little tobacco, another
a little salt, which I would change for victuals. I cannot but
think what a wolfish appetite persons have in a starving condition; for many times, when they gave me that which was
hot, I was so greedy, that I should burn my mouth, that it
would trouble me many hours after, and yet I should quickly
do the like again. And after I was thoroughly hungry, I was
never again satisfied; for though it sometimes fell out that I
had got enough, and did eat till I could eat no more, yet I was
as unsatisfied as I was when I began. And now could I see
that scripture verified, there being many scriptures that we do
not take notice of or understand till we are afflicted, Mic. 6 : 14,
—"*Thou shalt eat and not be satisfied.*" Now might I see more
than ever before the miseries that sin hath brought upon us.
Many times I should be ready to run out against the heathen,
but that scripture would quiet me again, Amos 3 : 6,—"*Shall*

there be evil in the city, and the Lord hath not done it?" The Lord help me to make a right improvement of his word, that I might learn that great lesson, Mic. 6 : 8, 9,—*" He hath showed thee, O man, what is good; and what doth the Lord require of thee, but to do justly and love mercy, and walk humbly with thy God? Hear ye the rod, and who hath appointed it."*

The Sixteenth Remove.—We began this remove with wading over Baquaug river. The water was up to our knees, and the stream very swift, and so cold that I thought it would have cut me in sunder. I was so weak and feeble that I reeled as I went along, and thought there I must end my days at last, after my bearing and getting through so many difficulties. The Indians stood laughing to see me staggering along, but in my distress the Lord gave me experience of the truth and goodness of that promise, Isa. 43: 2,—*"When thou passeth through the water I will be with thee, and through the rivers, they shall not overflow thee."* Then I sat down to put on my stockings and shoes, with the tears running down my eyes, and many sorrowful thoughts in my heart. But I got up to go along with them. Quickly there came up to us an Indian who informed them that I must go to Wachuset* to my master, for there was a letter come from the council to the sagamores about redeeming the captives, and that there would be another in fourteen days, and that I must be there ready. My heart was so heavy before that I could scarce speak or go in the path, and yet now so light that I could run. My strength seemed to come again, and to recruit my feeble knees and aching heart; yet it pleased them to go but one mile that night, and there we staid two days. In that time came a company of Indians to us, near thirty, all on horseback. My heart skipped within me, thinking they had been Englishmen, at the first sight of them; for they were dressed in English apparel, with hats, white neckcloths, and sashes about their waists, and ribbons upon their shoulders. But when they came near there was a vast difference between the lovely faces of Christians and the foul looks of those heathen, which much damped my spirits again.

The Seventeenth Remove.—A comfortable remove it was to me, because of my hopes. They gave me my pack and along we went cheerfully. But quickly my will proved more

---

* Princeton. The mountain in this town still retains the name of Wachuset, notwithstanding a recent attempt to change it to Mount Adams. [I venerate the name of Adams, but I must protest against the heathen-like practice of destroying the old names of places. The interior of New York deserves to be chastised by an earthquake for such libellous conduct.—Ed.]

than my strength; having little or no refreshment, my strength failed, and my spirits were almost quite gone. Now may I say as David, Psal. 109: 22, 23, 24,—"*I am poor and needy, and my heart is wounded within me. I am gone like a shadow when it declineth. I am tossed up and down like the locust. My knees are weak through fasting, and my flesh faileth of fatness.*" At night we came to an Indian town, and the Indians sat down by a wigwam discoursing, but I was almost spent and could scarce speak. I laid down my load and went into the wigwam, and there sat an Indian boiling of horse-feet, they being wont to eat the flesh first, and when the feet were old and dried, and they had nothing else, they would cut off the feet and use them. I asked him to give me a little of his broth, or water they were boiling it in. He took a dish and gave me one spoonful of samp, and bid me take as much of the broth as I would. Then I put some of the hot water to the samp, and drank it up, and my spirits came again. He gave me also a piece of the ruffe, or ridding of the small guts, and I broiled it on the coals; and now I may say with Jonathan, "*See, I pray you, how mine eyes are enlightened because I tasted a little of this honey.*"—1 Sam. 14: 20. Now is my spirit revived again. Though means be never so inconsiderable, yet if the Lord bestow his blessing upon them, they shall refresh both soul and body.

THE EIGHTEENTH REMOVE.—We took up our packs, and along we went; but a wearisome day I had of it. As we went along, I saw an Englishman stripped naked and lying dead upon the ground, but knew not who he was. Then we came to another Indian town, where we staid all night. In this town there were four English children captives, and one of them my own sister's. I went to see how she did, and she was well, considering her captive condition. I would have tarried that night with her, but they that owned her would not suffer it. Then I went to another wigwam, where they were boiling corn and beans, which was a lovely sight to see, but I could not get a taste thereof. Then I went into another wigwam, where there were two of the English children. The squaw was boiling horses' feet. She cut me off a little piece, and gave one of the English children a piece also. Being very hungry, I had quickly eat up mine; but the child could not bite it, it was so tough and sinewy, and lay sucking, gnawing, and slabbering of it in the mouth and hand; then I took it of the child, and eat it myself, and savory it was to my taste: that I may say as Job, chap. 6: 7,—"*The things that my soul refuseth to touch are as my sorrowful meat.*" Thus the Lord made that pleasant and refreshing which another time would have been an abomination. Then I went home to my mistress' wigwam, and they told me I disgraced my master with begging, and if I did so any more they would knock me on the head. I told them they had as good do that as starve me to death.

THE NINETEENTH REMOVE.—They said when we went out that we must travel to Wachuset this day. But a bitter weary day I had of it, travelling now three days together, without resting any day between. At last, after many weary steps, I saw Wachuset hills, but many miles off. Then we came to a great swamp, through which we travelled up to our knees in mud and water, which was heavy going to one tired before. Being almost spent, I thought I should have sunk down at last, and never got out; but I may say as in Psalm 94: 18,—
"*When my foot slipped, thy mercy, O Lord, held me up.*"
Going along, having indeed my life, but little spirit, Philip, who was in the company, came up, and took me by the hand, and said, "Two weeks more and you shall be mistress again." I asked him if he spoke true. He said, "Yes, and quickly you shall come to your master again;" who had been gone from us three weeks. After many weary steps, we came to Wachuset, where he was, and glad was I to see him. He asked me when I washed me. I told him not this month. Then he fetched me some water himself, and bid me wash, and gave me a glass to see how I looked, and bid his squaw give me something to eat. So she gave me a mess of beans and meat, and a little ground-nut cake. I was wonderfully revived with this favor showed me. Psalm 106: 46,—"*He made them also to be pitied of all those that carried them away captive.*"

My master had three squaws, living sometimes with one and sometimes with another: Onux, this old squaw at whose wigwam I was, and with whom my master had been these three weeks. Another was Wettimore,* with whom I had lived and served all this while. A severe and proud dame she was, bestowing every day in dressing herself near as much time as any of the gentry of the land; powdering her hair and painting her face, going with her necklaces, with jewels in her ears, and bracelets upon her hands. When she had dressed herself, her work was to make girdles of wampum and beads. The third squaw was a younger one, by whom he had two papooses. By that time I was refreshed by the old squaw, Wettimore's maid came to call me home, at which I fell a

---

* She had been the wife of Alexander, Philip's elder brother. See *Book of the Indians*

weeping. Then the old squaw told me, to encourage me, that when I wanted victuals I should come to her, and that I should lie in her wigwam. Then I went with the maid, and quickly I came back and lodged there. The squaw laid a mat under me, and a good rug over me; the first time that I had any such kindness showed me. I understood that Wettimore thought, that if she should let me go and serve with the old squaw, she should be in danger to lose not only my service, but the redemption-pay also. And I was not a little glad to hear this; being by it raised in my hopes that in God's due time there would be an end of this sorrowful hour. Then came an Indian and asked me to knit him three pair of stockings, for which I had a hat and a silk handkerchief. Then another asked me to make her a shift, for which she gave me an apron.

Then came Tom and Peter with the second letter from the council, about the captives. Though they were Indians, I gat them by the hand, and burst out into tears; my heart was so full that I could not speak to them; but recovering myself, I asked them how my husband did, and all my friends and acquaintance. They said they were well, but very melancholy. They brought me two biscuits and a pound of tobacco. The tobacco I soon gave away. When it was all gone one asked me to give him a pipe of tobacco. I told him it was all gone. Then he began to rant and threaten. I told him when my husband came I would give him some. "Hang him, rogue," says he; "I will knock out his brains if he comes here." And then again at the same breath they would say that if there should come an hundred without guns they would do them no hurt; so unstable and like madmen they were. So that fearing the worst, I durst not send to my husband, though there were some thoughts of his coming to redeem and fetch me, not knowing what might follow; for there was little more trust to them than to the master they served. When the letter was come, the sagamores met to consult about the captives, and called me to them, to inquire how much my husband would give to redeem me. When I came I sat down among them, as I was wont to do, as their manner is. Then they bid me stand up, and said they were the general court. They bid me speak what I thought he would give. Now knowing that all that we had was destroyed by the Indians, I was in a great strait. I thought if I should speak of but a little, it would be slighted and hinder the matter; if of a great sum, I knew not where it would be procured; yet at a venture I said twenty pounds, yet desired them to take less; but they would not hear of that, but sent the message to Boston, that for twenty pounds I should be redeemed. It was a praying Indian that wrote their letters for them.* There was another praying Indian who told me that he had a brother that would not eat horse, his conscience was so tender and scrupulous, though as large as hell for the destruction of poor Christians. Then he said he read that scripture to him, 2 Kings 6 : 25,—" *There was a famine in Samaria, and behold they besieged it, until an ass's head was sold for fourscore pieces of silver, and the fourth part of a kab of dove's dung for five pieces of silver.*" He expounded this place to his brother, and showed him that it was lawful to eat that in a famine which it is not at another time. "And now," says he, "he will eat horse with any Indian of them all." There was another praying Indian,† who, when he had done all the mischief that he could, betrayed his own father into the English's hands, thereby to purchase his own life. Another praying Indian was at Sudbury fight, though, as he deserved, he was afterwards hanged for it. There was another praying Indian so wicked and cruel as to wear a string about his neck strung with Christian fingers. Another praying Indian, when they went to Sudbury fight, went with them, and his squaw also with him, with her papoos at her back.‡ Before they went to that fight, they got a company together to powow. The manner was as followeth.

There was one that kneeled upon a deer-skin, with the company around him in a ring, who kneeled, striking upon the ground with their hands and with sticks, and muttering or humming with their mouths. Besides him who kneeled in the ring there also stood one with a gun in his hand. Then he on the deer-skin made a speech, and all manifested assent to it; and so they did many times together. Then they bid him with a gun go out of the ring, which he did; but when he was out, they called him in again; but he seemed to make a stand. Then they called the more earnestly, till he turned again. Then they all sang. Then they gave him two guns, in each hand one. And so he on the deer-skin began again; and at the end of every sentence in his speaking they all assented, and humming or muttering with their mouths, and striking upon the ground with their hands. Then they bid him with the two guns go out of the ring again; which he did

---

* They may be seen in the *Book of the Indians.*

† Peter Jethro.—*Ib* .

‡ These remarks of Mrs. Rowlandson are no doubt just. The praying Indians, after all, take them as a class, made but sorry Christians. More comfortable dwellings, a few blankets every year, some small privileges, and a little increase, for the time, of personal consideration, were motives sufficiently strong to induce savages to change their religious faith, which at best hung but very loosely about them.

a little way. Then they called him again, but he made a stand, so they called him with greater earnestness; but he stood reeling and wavering, as if he knew not whether he should stand or fall, or which way to go. Then they called him with exceeding great vehemency, all of them, one and another. After a little while he turned in, staggering as he went, with his arms stretched out, in each hand a gun. As soon as he came in, they all sang and rejoiced exceedingly a while, and then he upon the deer-skin made another speech, unto which they all assented in a rejoicing manner; and so they ended their business, and forthwith went to Sudbury fight.*

To my thinking, they went without any scruple but that they should prosper and gain the victory. And they went out not so rejoicing, but they came home with as great a victory; for they said they killed two captains and almost an hundred men. One Englishman they brought alive with them, and he said it was too true, for they had made sad work at Sudbury; as indeed it proved. Yet they came home without that rejoicing and triumphing over their victory which they were wont to show at other times; but rather like dogs, as they say, which have lost their ears. Yet I could not perceive that it was for their own loss of men; they said they lost not above five or six; and I missed none, except in one wigwam. When they went they acted as if the devil had told them that they should gain the victory, and now they acted as if the devil had told them they should have a fall. Whether it were so or no, I cannot tell, but so it proved; for they quickly began to fall, and so held on that summer, till they came to utter ruin. They came home on a Sabbath day, and the pawaw that kneeled upon the deer-skin came home, I may say without any abuse, as black as the devil. When my master came home he came to me and bid me make a shirt for his papoos, of a Holland laced pillowbeer.

About that time there came an Indian to me, and bid me come to his wigwam at night, and he would give me some pork and ground-nuts, which I did; and as I was eating, another Indian said to me, "He seems to be your good friend, but he killed two Englishmen at Sudbury, and there lie the clothes behind you." I looked behind me, and there I saw bloody clothes, with bullet-holes in them; yet the Lord suffered not this wretch to do me any hurt, yea, instead of that, he many times refreshed me: five or six times did he and his squaw refresh my feeble carcass. If I went to their wigwam at any time, they would always give me something, and yet they were

* Sudbury was attacked 21st April.

5

strangers that I never saw before. Another squaw gave me a piece of fresh pork, and a little salt with it, and lent me her frying pan to fry it; and I cannot but remember what a sweet, pleasant and delightful relish that bit had to me, to this day. So little do we prize common mercies, when we have them to the full.

THE TWENTIETH REMOVE.—It was their usual manner to remove when they had done any mischief, lest they should be found out; and so they did at this time. We went about three or four miles, and there they built a great wigwam, big enough to hold an hundred Indians, which they did in preparation to a great day of dancing. They would now say among themselves that the governor* would be so angry for his loss at Sudbury that he would send no more about the captives, which made me grieve and tremble. My sister† being not far from this place, and hearing that I was here, desired her master to let her come and see me, and he was willing to it, and would come with her; but she, being ready first, told him she would go before, and was come within a mile or two of the place. Then he overtook her, and began to rant as if he had been mad, and made her go back again in the rain; so that I never saw her till I saw her in Charlestown. But the Lord requited many of their ill doings, for this Indian, her master, was hanged afterwards at Boston.‡ They began now to come from all quarters, against their merry dancing day. Amongst some of them came one goodwife Kettle. I told her my heart was so heavy that it was ready to break. "So is mine too," said she, "but yet I hope we shall hear some good news shortly." I could hear how earnestly my sister desired to see me, and I earnestly desired to see her; yet neither of us could get an opportunity. My daughter was now but a mile off, and I had not seen her for nine or ten weeks, as I had not seen my sister since our first taking. I desired them to let me go and see them, yea I entreated, begged and persuaded them to let me see my daughter; and yet so hard-hearted were they that they would not suffer it. They made use of their tyrannical power whilst they had it, but through the Lord's wonderful mercy their time was now but short.

On a Sabbath day, the sun being about an hour high in the afternoon, came Mr. John Hoar, (the council permitting him, and his own forward spirit inclining him,) together with the two forementioned Indians, Tom and Peter, with the third letter from the council. When they came near, I was abroad.

* Leverett.   † Mrs. Drew.
‡ Mrs. Drew's master was probably Monoco. Several chiefs were hanged at the same time, viz. 26th Sept. 1676.

They presently called me in, and bid me sit down and not stir. Then they catched up their guns and away they ran, as if an enemy had been at hand, and the guns went off apace. I manifested some great trouble, and asked them what was the matter. I told them I thought they had killed the English-man, (for they had in the mean time told me that an English-man was come;) they said no; they shot over his horse, and under, and before his horse, and they pushed him this way and that way, at their pleasure, showing him what they could do. Then they let him come to their wigwams. I begged of them to let me see the Englishman, but they would not; but there was I fain to sit their pleasure. When they had talked their fill with him, they suffered me to go to him. We asked each other of our welfare, and how my husband did, and all my friends. He told me they were all well, and would be glad to see me. Among other things which my husband sent me, there came a pound of tobacco, which I sold for nine shillings in money; for many of them for want of tobacco smoked hemlock and ground-ivy. It was a great mistake in any who thought I sent for tobacco, for through the favor of God that desire was overcome.

I now asked them whether I should go home with Mr. Hoar. They answered no, one and another of them, and it being late, we lay down with that answer. In the morning Mr. Hoar invited the sagamores to dinner; but when we went to get it ready, we found they had stolen the greatest part of the provisions Mr. Hoar had brought. And we may see the wonderful power of God, in that one passage, in that when there was such a number of them together, and so greedy of a little good food, and no English there but Mr. Hoar and myself, that there they did not knock us on the head and take what we had; there being not only some provision, but also trading cloth, a part of the twenty pounds agreed upon. But instead of doing us any mischief, they seemed to be ashamed of the fact, and said it was the *matchit** Indians that did it. Oh that we could believe that there was nothing too hard for God. God showed his power over the heathen in this, as he did over the hungry lions when Daniel was cast into the den.

Mr. Hoar called them betime to dinner, but they ate but little, they being so busy in dressing themselves and getting ready for their dance; which was carried on by eight of them, four men and four squaws, my master and mistress being two. He was dres-sed in his Holland shirt, with great stockings, his garters hung round with shillings, and had girdles of wampom upon his

* Wicked.

head and shoulders. She had a kersey coat, covered with girdles of wampom from the loins upward. Her arms from her elbows to her hands were covered with bracelets ; there were handfuls of necklaces about her neck, and several sorts of jewels in her ears. She had fine red stockings, and white shoes, her hair powdered, and her face painted red, that was always before black. And all the dancers were after the same manner. There were two others singing and knocking on a kettle for their music. They kept hopping up and down one after another, with a kettle of water in the midst, standing warm upon some embers, to drink of when they were dry. They held on till almost night, throwing out their wampom to the standers-by. At night I asked them again if I should go home. They all as one said no, except my husband would come for me. When we were lain down, my master went out of the wigwam, and by and by sent in an Indian called *James the printer*, who told Mr. Hoar that my master would let me go home to-morrow if he would let him have one pint of liquor. Then Mr. Hoar called his own Indians, Tom and Peter, and bid them all go and see if he would promise it before them three, and if he would he should have it ; which he did and had it. Philip, smelling the business, called me to him, and asked me what I would give him to tell me some good news, and to speak a good word for me, that I might go home to-morrow. I told him I could not tell what to give him, I would any thing I had, and asked him what he would have. He said two coats, and twenty shillings in money, half a bushel of seed corn, and some tobacco. I thanked him for his love, but I knew that good news as well as that crafty fox.

My master, after he had his drink, quickly came ranting into the wigwam again, and called for Mr. Hoar, drinking to him and saying he was a good man, and then again he would say, " hang him, a rogue." Being almost drunk, he would drink to him, and yet presently say he should be hanged. Then he called for me. I trembled to hear him, and yet I was fain to go to him ; and he drank to me, showing no incivility. He was the first Indian I saw drunk, all the time I was among them. At last his squaw ran out, and he after her round the wigwam, with his money jingling at his knees, but she escaped him ; but having and old squaw, he ran to her, and so through the Lord's mercy we were no more troubled with him that night. Yet I had not a comfortable night's rest ; for I think I can say I did not sleep for three nights together. The night before the letter came from the council, I could not rest, I was so full of fears and troubles ; yea, at this time I could not rest night nor day. The next night I was overjoyed, Mr

Hoar being come, and that with such good tidings. The third night I was even swallowed up with the thoughts of going home again, and that I must leave my children behind me in the wilderness; so that sleep was now almost departed from mine eyes.

On Tuesday morning they called their *General Court,* as they styled it, to consult and determine whether I should go home or no. And they all seemingly consented that I should go, except Philip, who would not come among them.

But before I go any farther, I would take leave to mention a few remarkable passages of Providence, which I took special notice of in my afflicted time.

1. Of the fair opportunity lost in the long march, a little after the fort fight, when our English army was so numerous, and in pursuit of the enemy, and so near as to overtake several and destroy them; and the enemy in such distress for food that our men might track them by their rooting the ground for ground-nuts, whilst they were flying for their lives: I say, that then our army should want provisions, and be obliged to leave their pursuit, and turn homeward, and the very next week the enemy came upon our town, like bears bereft of their whelps, or so many ravenous wolves, rending us and our lambs to death. But what shall I say? God seemed to leave his people to themselves, and ordered all things for his own holy ends. " *Shall there be evil in the city and the Lord hath not done it? They are not grieved for the affliction of Joseph, therefore they shall go captive with the first that go captive. It is the Lord's doing, and it should be marvellous in our eyes.*"

2. I cannot but remember how the Indians derided the slowness and the dulness of the English army in its setting out; for after the desolations at Lancaster and Medfield, as I went along with them, they asked me when I thought the English army would come after them. I told them I could not tell. " It may be they will come in May," said they. Thus they did scoff at us, as if the English would be a quarter of a year getting ready.

3. Which also I have hinted before, when the English army with new supplies were sent forth to pursue after the enemy, and they, understanding it, fled before them till they came to Baquaug river, where they forthwith went over safely; that the river should be impassable to the English. I cannot but admire to see the wonderful providence of God in preserving the heathen for further affliction to our poor country. They could go in great numbers over, but the English must stop. God had an overruling hand in all those things.

4. It was thought, if their corn were cut down, they would starve and die with hunger ; and all that could be found was destroyed, and they driven from that little they had in store into the woods, in the midst of winter ; and yet how to admiration did the Lord preserve them for his holy ends, and the destruction of many still among the English ! Strangely did the Lord provide for them, that I did not see, all the time I was among them, one man, woman, or child die with hunger. Though many times they would eat that that a hog would hardly touch, yet by that God strengthened them to be a scourge to his people.

Their chief and commonest food was ground-nuts ; they eat also nuts and acorns, artichokes, lilly roots, ground beans, and several other weeds and roots that I know not. They would pick up old bones, and cut them in pieces at the joints, and if they were full of worms and maggots they would scald them over the fire, to make the vermin come out, and then boil them, and drink up the liquor, and then beat the great ends of them in a mortar, and so eat them. They would eat horses' guts and ears, and all sorts of wild birds which they could catch ; also bear, venison, beavers, tortoise, frogs, squirrels, dogs, skunks, rattle-snakes, yea the very bark of trees ; besides all sorts of creatures, and provisions which they plundered from the English. I can but stand in admiration to see the wonderful power of God, in providing for such a vast number of our enemies in the wilderness, where there was nothing to be seen but from hand to mouth. Many times in the morning the generality of them would eat up all they had, and yet have some farther supply against they wanted. • But now our perverse and evil carriages in the sight of the Lord have so offended him, that instead of turning his hand against them, the Lord feeds and nourishes them up to be a scourge to the whole land.

5. Another thing that I would observe is, the strange providence of God in turning things about when the Indians were at the highest and the English at the lowest. I was with the enemy eleven weeks and five days,[*] and not one week passed without their fury and some desolation by fire or sword upon one place or other. They mourned for their own losses, yet triumphed and rejoiced in their inhuman and devilish cruelty to the English. They would boast much of their victories, saying that in two hours' time they had destroyed such a captain and his company, in such a place ; and boast how many towns they had destroyed, and then scoff and say they had done

* Viz. from Feb. 10 to May 2d or 3d

them a good turn to send them to heaven so soon. Again they
would say this summer they would knock all the rogues on
the head, or drive them into the sea, or make them fly the
country; thinking surely, Agag-like, "*The bitterness of death
is passed.*" Now the heathen begin to think all is their own:
and the poor Christians' hopes fail, (as to man,) and now their
eyes are more to God, and their hearts sigh heaven-ward, and
they say in good earnest, "*Help, Lord, or we perish.*" When
the Lord had brought his people to this, that they saw no help
in any thing but himself, then he takes the quarrel into his
own hand; and though they made a pit as deep as hell for
the Christians that summer, yet the Lord hurled themselves
into it. And the Lord had not so many ways before to preserve them, but now he hath as many to destroy them.

But to return again to my going home; where we may see
a remarkable change of providence. At first they were all
against it, except my husband would come for me; but afterward they assented to it, and seeming to rejoice in it; some
asking me to send them some bread, others some tobacco, others shaking me by the hand, offering me a hood and scarf to
ride in: not one moving hand or tongue against it. Thus
hath the Lord answered my poor desires, and the many earnest requests of others put up unto God for me. In my travels
an Indian came to me, and told me if I were willing he and his
squaw would run away, and go home along with me. I told
them no, I was not willing to run away, but desired to wait
God's time, that I might go home quietly and without fear.
And now God hath granted me my desire. O the wonderful
power of God that I have seen, and the experiences that I
have had! I have been in the midst of those roaring lions
and savage bears, that feared neither God, nor man, nor the
devil, by night and day, alone and in company, sleeping all
sorts together, and yet not one of them ever offered the least
abuse of unchastity to me in word or action; though some
are ready to say I speak it for my own credit; but I speak it
in the presence of God, and to his glory. God's power is as
great now as it was to save Daniel in the lions' den, or the
three children in the fiery furnace. Especially that I should
come away in the midst of so many hundreds of enemies, and
not a dog move his tongue.

So I took my leave of them, and in coming along my heart
melted into tears more than all the while I was with them,
and I was almost swallowed up with the thoughts that ever I
should go home again. About the sun's going down, Mr.
Hoar, myself, and the two Indians, came to Lancaster; and a
solemn sight it was to me. There had I lived many comfort-

able years among my relations and neighbors, and now not one Christian to be seen, or one house left standing. We went on to a farm-house that was yet standing, where we lay all night ; and a comfortable lodging we had, though nothing but straw to lie on. The Lord preserved us in safety that night, raised us up again in the morning, and carried us along, that before noon we came to Concord. Now was I full of joy, and yet not without sorrow : joy to see such a lovely sight, so many Christians together, and some of them my neighbors. There I met with my brother and brother-in-law,* who asked me if I knew where his wife was. Poor heart ! he had helped to bury her, and knew it not. She, being shot down by the house, was partly burnt ; so that those who were at Boston at the desolation of the town came back afterward and buried the dead, but did not know her. Yet I was not without sorrow, to think how many were looking and longing, and my own children among the rest, to enjoy that deliverance that I had now received ; and I did not know whether ever I should see them again.

Being recruited with food and raiment, we went to Boston that day, where I met with my dear husband ; but the thoughts of our dear children, one being dead, and the other we could not tell where, abated our comfort in each other. I was not before so much hemmed in by the merciless and cruel heathen, but now as much with pitiful, tender-hearted, and compassionate Christians. In that poor and beggarly condition, I was received in, I was kindly entertained in several houses. So much love I received from several, (many of whom I knew not,) that I am not capable to declare it. But the Lord knows them all by name ; the Lord reward them sevenfold into their bosoms of his spirituals for their temporals. The twenty pounds, the price of my redemption, was raised by some Boston gentlewomen, and Mr. Usher, [Hezekiah ?] whose bounty and charity I would not forget to make mention of. Then Mr. Thomas Shepard, of Charlestown, received us into his house, where we continued eleven weeks ; and a father and mother they were unto us. And many more tender-hearted friends we met with in that place. We were now in the midst of love, yet not without much and frequent heaviness of heart for our poor children and other relations who were still in affliction.

The week following, after my coming in, the governor and council sent to the Indians again, and that not without success ; for they brought in my sister and goodwife Kettle. Their not

* Capt. Kerley.

knowing where our children were was a sore trial to us still ; and yet we were not without secret hopes of seeing them again. That which was dead lay heavier upon my spirits than those which were alive among the heathen ; thinking how it suffered with its wounds, and I was not able to relieve it, and how it was buried by the heathen in the wilderness from among all Christians. We were hurried up and down in our thoughts ; sometimes we should hear a report that they were gone this way and sometimes that, and that they were come in in this place or that ; we kept inquiring and listening to hear concerning them, but no certain news as yet. About this time the council had ordered a day of public thanksgiving, though I had still cause of mourning ; and being unsettled in our minds, we thought we would ride eastward, to see if we could hear any thing concerning our children. As we were riding along between Ipswich and Rowley, we met with William Hubbard, who told us our son Joseph and my sister's son were come into Major Waldren's. I asked him how he knew it. He said the major himself told him so. So along we went till we came to Newbury ; and their minister being absent, they desired my husband to preach the thanksgiving for them ; but he was not willing to stay there that night, but he would go over to Salisbury, to hear farther, and come again in the morning, which he did, and preached there that day. At night, when he had done, one came and told him that his daughter was come into Providence. Here was mercy on both hands. Now we were between them, the one on the east, and the other on the west. Our son being nearest, we went to him first, to Portsmouth, where we met with him, and with the major also ; who told us he had done what he could, but could not redeem him under seven pounds, which the good people thereabouts were pleased to pay. The Lord reward the major, and all the rest, though unknown to me, for their labor of love. My sister's son was redeemed for four pounds, which the council gave order for the payment of. Having now received one of our children, we hastened toward the other. Going back through Newbury, my husband preached there on the Sabbath day, for which they rewarded him manifold.

On Monday we came to Charlestown, where we heard that the governor of Rhode Island had sent over for our daughter, to take care of her, being now within his jurisdiction ; which should not pass without our acknowledgments. But she being nearer Rehoboth than Rhode Island, Mr. Newman went over and took care of her, and brought her to his own house. And the goodness of God was admirable to us in our low estate, in that he raised up compassionate friends on every

side, when we had nothing to recompense any for their love.
The Indians were now gone that way, that it was apprehended dangerous to go to her ; but the carts which carried provision to the English army, being guarded, brought her with
them to Dorchester, where we received her safe. Blessed be
the Lord for it. Her coming in was after this manner : she
was travelling one day with the Indians, with her basket at
her back ; the company of Indians were got before her, and
gone out of sight, all except one squaw. She followed the
squaw till night, and then both of them lay down, having
nothing over them but the heavens, nor under them but the
earth. Thus she travelled three days together, having nothing to eat or drink but water and green hirtleberries. At last
they came into Providence, where she was kindly entertained
by several of that town. The Indians often said that I should
never have her under twenty pounds, but now the Lord hath
brought her in upon free cost, and given her to me the second
time. The Lord make us a blessing indeed to each other.
Thus hath the Lord brought me and mine out of the horrible
pit, and hath set us in the midst of tender-hearted and compassionate Christians. 'T is the desire of my soul that we
may walk worthy of the mercies received and which we are
receiving.

Our family being now gathered together, the South church
in Boston hired a house for us. Then we removed from Mr.
Shepard's (those cordial friends) and went to Boston, where
we continued about three quarters of a year.* Still the Lord
went along with us, and provided graciously for us.   I
thought it somewhat strange to set up housekeeping with bare
walls, but, as Solomon says, *money answers all things;* and
this we had through the benevolence of Christian friends, some
in this town, and some in that, and others, and some from
England, that in a little time we might look and see the house
furnished with love. The Lord hath been exceeding good to
us in our low estate, in that when we had neither house nor
home, nor other necessaries, the Lord so moved the hearts of
these and those towards us, that we wanted neither food nor
raiment for ourselves or ours. Prov. 18 : 24, " *There is a
friend that sticketh closer than a brother.*" And how many
such friends have we found, and now living among us ! And
truly have we found him to be such a friend unto us in whose
house we lived, viz. Mr. James Whitcomb, a friend near hand
and far off.

I can remember the time when I used to sleep quietly, with-

* Till May, 1677.

out working in my thoughts, whole nights together; but now it is otherwise with me. When all are fast about me, and no eye open, but His who ever awaketh, my thoughts are upon things past, upon the awful dispensations of the Lord towards us, upon his wonderful power and might in carrying of us through so many difficulties, in returning us in safety, and suffering none to hurt us. I remember in the night season how the other day I was in the midst of thousands of enemies, and nothing but death before me. It was then hard work to persuade myself that ever I should be satisfied with bread again. But now we are fed with the finest of the wheat, and, as I may say, with *honey out of the rock.* Instead of the *husks* we have the *fat calf.* The thoughts of these things in the particulars of them, and of the love and goodness of God towards us, make it true of me, what David said of himself, Psal. 6: 6, —" *I water my couch with my tears.*" O the wonderful power of God that mine eyes have seen, affording matter enough for my thoughts to run in, that when others are sleeping mine eyes are weeping.

I have seen the extreme vanity of this world. One hour I have been in health, and wealth, wanting nothing, but the next hour in sickness, and wounds, and death, having nothing but sorrow and affliction. Before I knew what affliction meant I was ready sometimes to wish for it. When I lived in prosperity, having the comforts of this world about me, my relations by me, and my heart cheerful, and taking little care for any thing, and yet seeing many, whom I preferred before myself, under many trials and afflictions, in sickness, weakness, poverty, losses, crosses, and cares of the world, I should be sometimes jealous lest I should have my portion in this life. But now I see the Lord had his time to scourge and chasten me. The portion of some is to have their affliction by drops, but the *wine of astonishment,* like a *sweeping rain that leaveth no food,* did the Lord prepare to be my portion. Affliction I wanted, and affliction I had, full measure, pressed down and running over. Yet I see when God calls persons to never so many difficulties, yet he is able to carry them through, and make them say they have been gainers thereby; and I hope I can say, in some measure, as David, *it is good for me that I have been afflicted.* The Lord hath showed me the vanity of these outward things, that they are the *vanities of vanities and vexation of spirit;* that they are but a shadow, a blast, a bubble, and things of no continuance. If trouble from smaller matter begin to rise in me, I have something at hand to check myself with, and say, "Why am I troubled?" It was but the other day that if I had the world I would have given it for my freedom, or to have been a servant to a Christian. I have learned to look beyond present and smaller troubles, and to be quieted under them, as Moses said, Exod. 14 : 13,—" *Stand still and see the salvation of the Lord.*"

NARRATIVE

OF THE CAPTIVITY OF QUINTIN STOCKWELL, WHO WAS TA-KEN AT DEERFIELD, IN MASSACHUSETTS, BY A PARTY OF INLAND INDIANS, IN THE YEAR 1677; COMMUNICATED IN HIS OWN WORDS, AND ORIGINALLY PUBLISHED BY THE EMINENT DR. INCREASE MATHER, IN THE YEAR 1684.

A particular account of the irruption in which Stockwell and others fell into the hands of the Indians will be found in the Book of the Indians, Book iii, p. 97 and 98. Out of *twenty-four* at that time killed and taken, we learn the names only of these ; Quintin Stockwell, John Root, Sergeant Plimpton, Benjamin Stebbins, his wife, Benjamin Waite, and Samuel Russell. Plimpton was burnt in their cruel manner, Root was killed, and Stebbins escaped. Of the others I have learned nothing.

In the year 1677, September the 19th, between sunset and dark, the Indians came upon us. I and another man, being together, we ran away at the outcry the Indians made, shouting and shooting at some others of the English that were hard by. We took a swamp that was at hand for our refuge ; the enemy espying us so near them, run after us, and shot many guns at us ; three guns were discharged upon me, the enemy being within three rods of me, besides many others before that. Being in this swamp, which was miry, I slumped in and fell down, whereupon one of the enemy stepped to me, with his hatchet lifted up to knock me on the head, supposing that I had been wounded and so unfit for any other travel. I, as it happened, had a pistol by me, which, though uncharged, I presented to the Indian, who presently stepped back, and told me if I would yield I should have no hurt; he said, which was not true, that they had destroyed all Hatfield, and that the woods were full of Indians, whereupon I yielded myself, and falling into their hands, was by three of them led away unto the place whence first I began to make my flight. Here two other Indians came running to us, and the one lifting up the butt end of his gun, to knock me on the head, the other with his hand put by the blow, and said I was his friend. I was now by my own house, which the Indians burnt the last year, and I was about to build up again; and there I had some hopes to escape from them. There was a horse just by, which they bid me take. I did so, but made no attempt to escape thereby, because the enemy was near, and the beast was slow and dull. Then was I in hopes they would send me to take my own horses, which they did; but they were so frightened that I could not come near to them, and so fell still into the enemy's hands. They now took and bound me and led me away, and soon was I brought into the company of other captives, who were that day brought away from Hatfield, who were about a mile off; and here methought was matter of joy and sorrow both: joy to see company, and sorrow for our condition. Then were we pinioned and led away in the night over the mountains, in dark and hideous ways, about four miles further, before we took up our place for rest, which was in a dismal place of wood, on the east side of that mountain. We were kept bound all that night. The Indians kept waking, and we had little mind to sleep in this night's travel. The Indians dispersed, and as they went made strange noises, as of wolves and owls, and other wild beasts, to the end that they might not lose one another, and if followed they might not be discovered by the English.

About the break of day we marched again, and got over that great river at Pecomptuck [Deerfield] river mouth, and there rested about two hours. Here the Indians marked out upon trees the number of their captives and slain, as their manner is. Now was I again in great danger, a quarrel having arose about me, whose captive I was; for three took me. I thought I must be killed to end the controversy, so when they put it to me, whose I was, I said three Indians took me; so they agreed to have all a share in me. I had now three masters, and he was my chief master who laid hands on me first; and thus was I fallen into the hands of the worst of all the company, as ASHPELON, the Indian captain, told me; which captain was all along very kind to me, and a great comfort to the English. In this place they gave us some victuals, which they had brought from the English. This morning also they sent ten men forth to the town [of Deerfield] to bring away what they could find. Some provision, some corn out of the meadow, they brought to us on horses, which they had there taken.

From hence we went up about the falls, where we crossed that river again; and whilst I was going, I fell right down lame of my old wounds, which I had in the war, and whilst I was thinking I should therefore be killed by the Indians, and what death I should die, my pain was suddenly gone, and I was much encouraged again. We had about eleven horses in that
6

company, which the Indians used to convey burthens, and to
carry women. It was afternoon when we now crossed that
river. We travelled up it till night, and then took up our
lodging in a dismal place, and were staked down, and spread
out on our backs; and so we lay all night, yea, so we lay
many nights. They told me their law was that we should lie
so nine nights, and by that time it was thought we should be
out of our knowledge. The manner of staking down was
thus: our arms and legs, stretched out, were staked fast down,
and a cord about our necks, so that we could stir noways.
The first night of staking down, being much tired, I slept as
comfortable as ever. The next day we went up the river, and
crossed it, and at night lay in Squakheag [Northfield] meadows.
Our provision was soon spent, and while we lay in those meadows the Indians went a hunting, and the English army came
out after us. Then the Indians moved again, dividing themselves and the captives into many companies, that the English
might not follow their tracks. At night, having crossed the
river, we met again at the place appointed. The next day we
crossed it again on Squakheag side, and there we took up our
quarters for a long time. I suppose this might be about thirty
miles above Squakheag; and here were the Indians quite out
of all fear of the English, but in great fear of the Mohawks.
Here they built a long wigwam, and had a great dance, as they
call it, and concluded to burn three of us, and had got bark to
do it with, and, as I understood afterwards, I was one that was
to be burnt, sergeant Plimpton another, and Benjamin Waite's
wife the third. Though I knew not which was to be burnt,
yet I perceived some were designed thereunto; so much I understood of their language. That night I could not sleep for
fear of next day's work; the Indians, being weary with the
dance, lay down to sleep, and slept soundly. The English
were all loose; then I went out and brought in wood, and
mended the fire, and made a noise on purpose, but none awaked. I thought if any of the English would awake, we might
kill them all sleeping. I removed out of the way all the guns
and hatchets, but my heart failing me, I put all things where
they were again. The next day, when we were to be burnt,
our master and some others spoke for us, and the evil was prevented in this place. Hereabouts we lay three weeks together.
Here I had a shirt brought to me to make, and one Indian said
it should be made this way, a second another way, a third his
way. I told them I would make it that way my chief master
said; whereupon one Indian struck me on the face with his
fist. I suddenly rose up in anger, ready to strike again; upon
this happened a great hubbub, and the Indians and English

came about me. I was fain to humble myself to my master, so that matter was put up. Before I came to this place, my three masters were gone a hunting; I was left with another Indian, all the company being upon a march; I was left with this Indian, who fell sick, so that I was fain to carry his gun and hatchet, and had opportunity, and had thought to have dispatched him and run away; but did not, for that the English captives had promised the contrary to one another; because, if one should run away, that would provoke the Indians, and endanger the rest that could not run away.

Whilst we were here, Benjamin Stebbins, going with some Indians to Wachuset Hills, made his escape from them, and when the news of his escape came we were all presently called in and bound; one of the Indians, a captain among them, and always our great friend, met me coming in, and told me Stebbins was run away; and the Indians spake of burning us; some, of only burning and biting off our fingers, by and by. He said there would be a court, and all would speak their minds, but he would speak last, and would say, that the Indian who let Stebbins run away was only in fault, and so no hurt should be done us, and added, "fear not;" so it proved accordingly. Whilst we lingered hereabout, provision grew scarce; one bear's foot must serve five of us a whole day. We began to eat horse-flesh, and eat up seven in all; three were left alive, and not killed. After we had been here, some of the Indians had been down, and fallen upon Hadley, and were taken by the English, agreed with and let go again. They were to meet the English upon such a plain, there to make further terms. ASHPALON was much for it, but Wachuset sachems, when they came, were much against it, and were for this: that we should meet the English, indeed, but there fall upon them and fight them, and take them. Then ASHPELON spake to us English, not to speak a word more to further that matter, for mischief would come of it. When those Indians came from Wachuset there came with them squaws and children, about four-score, who reported that the English had taken UNCAS, and all his men, and sent them beyond seas. They were much enraged at this, and asked us if it were true; we said no. Then was ASHPALON angry, and said he would no more believe English-men. They examined us every one apart, and then they dealt worse with us for a season than before. Still provision was scarce. We came at length to a place called Squaw-Maug river; there we hoped for salmon; but we came too late. This place I account to be above two hundred miles above Deerfield. We now parted into two companies; some went one way, and some went another way; and we went over a mighty mountain, it taking us eight days to go over it, and travelled very hard too, having every day either snow or rain. We noted that on this mountain all the water run northward. Here also we wanted provision; but at length we met again on the other side of the mountain, viz. on the north side, at a river that runs into the lake; and we were then half a day's journey off the lake.

We staid here a great while, to make canoes to go over the lake. Here I was frozen, and again we were like to starve. All the Indians went a hunting, but could get nothing: divers days they powwowed, and yet got nothing; then they desired the English to pray, and confessed they could do nothing; they would have us pray, and see what the Englishman's God could do. I prayed, so did sergeant Plimpton, in another place. The Indians reverently attended, morning and night. Next day they got bears; then they would needs have us desire a blessing, and return thanks at meals; after a while they grew weary of it, and the sachem did forbid us. When I was frozen, they were very cruel towards me, because I could not do as at other times. When we came to the lake we were again sadly put to it for provision. We were fain to eat touchwood fried in bear's grease. At last we found a company of raccoons, and then we made a feast; and the manner was that we must eat all. I perceived there would be too much for one time, so one Indian who sat next to me bid me slip away some to him under his coat, and he would hide it for me till another time. This Indian, as soon as he had got my meat, stood up and made a speech to the rest, and discovered me; so that the Indians were very angry and cut me another piece, and gave me raccoon grease to drink, which made me sick and vomit. I told them I had enough; so ever after that they would give me none, but still tell me I had raccoon enough. So I suffered much, and being frozen, was full of pain, and could sleep but a little, yet must do my work. When they went upon the lake, and as they came to it, they lit of a moose and killed it, and staid there till they had eaten it all up.

After entering upon the lake, there arose a great storm, and we thought we should all be cast away, but at last we got to an island, and there they went to powwowing. The powwow said that Benjamin Waite and another man was coming, and that storm was raised to cast them away. This afterward appeared to be true, though then I believed them not. Upon this island we lay still several days, and then set out again, but a storm took us, so that we lay to and fro, upon certain islands, about three weeks. We had no provision but raccoons, so that the Indians themselves thought they should be starved. They gave me nothing, so that I was sundry days without any provision. We went on upon the lake, upon that isle, about a day's journey. We had a little sled upon which we drew our load. Before noon, I tired, and just then the Indians met with some Frenchmen; then one of the Indians that took me came to me and called me all manner of bad names, and threw me down upon my back. I told him I could not do any more; then he said he must kill me. I thought he was about to do it, for he pulled out his knife and cut out my pockets, and wrapped them about my face, helped me up, and took my sled and went away, giving me a bit of biscuit, as big as a walnut, which he had of the Frenchman, and told me he would give me a pipe of tobacco. When my sled was gone, I could run after him, but at last I could not run, but went a foot-pace. The Indians were soon out of sight. I followed as well as I could, and had many falls upon the ice.

At last, I was so spent, I had not strength enough to rise again, but I crept to a tree that lay along, and got upon it, and there I lay. It was now night, and very sharp weather: I counted no other but that I must die here. Whilst I was thinking of death, an Indian hallooed, and I answered him; he came to me, and called me bad names, and told me if I could not go he must knock me on the head. I told him he must then do so; he saw how I had wallowed in the snow, but could not rise; then he took his coat and wrapt me in it, and went back and sent two Indians with a sled. One said he must knock me on the head, the other said no, they would carry me away and burn me. Then they bid me stir my instep, to see if that were frozen; I did so. When they saw that, they said that was WURREGEN.* There was a chirurgeon among the French, they said, that could cure me; then they took me upon a sled, and carried me to the fire, and made much of me; pulled off my wet and wrapped me in dry clothes, and made me a good bed. They had killed an otter, and gave me some of the broth made of it, and a bit of the flesh. Here I slept till towards day, and then was able to get up and put on my clothes. One of the Indians awaked, and seeing me walk, shouted, as rejoicing at it. As soon as it was light, I and Samuel Russell went before on the ice, upon a river. They said I must go where I could on foot, else I should freeze. Samuel Russell slipt into the river with one foot; the Indians called him back, and dried his stockings, and then sent us away, and an Indian with us to pilot us. We went four or five miles before they overtook us. I was then pretty well spent. Samuel Russell was, he said, faint, and wondered how I

* See Book of the Indians, B. ii. 85.

6*

could live, for he had, he said, ten meals to my one. Then I was laid on the sled, and they ran away with me on the ice; the rest and Samuel Russell came softly after. Samuel Russell I never saw more, nor know I what became of him. They got but half way, and we got through to Shamblee about midnight. Six miles off Shamblee, (a French town,) the river was open, and when I came to travel in that part of the ice, I soon tired; and two Indians ran away to town, and one only was left; he would carry me a few rods, and then I would go as many, and then a trade we drove, and so were long in going the six miles. This Indian was now kind, and told me that if he did not carry me I would die, and so I should have done, sure enough; and he said I must tell the English how he helped me. When we came to the first house, there was no inhabitant. The Indian was also spent, and both were discouraged; he said we must now die together. At last he left me alone, and got to another house, and thence came some French and Indians, and brought me in. The French were kind, and put my hands and feet in cold water, and gave me a dram of brandy, and a little hasty pudding and milk; when I tasted victuals I was hungry, and could not have forborne it, but I could not get it. Now and then they would give me a little, as they thought best for me. I laid by the fire with the Indian that night, but could not sleep for pain. Next morning the Indians and French fell out about me, because the French, as the Indians said, loved the English better than the Indians. The French presently turned the Indians out of doors, and kept me.

They were very kind and careful, and gave me a little something now and then. While I was here all the men in that town came to see me. At this house I was three or four days, and then invited to another, and after that to another. In this place I was about thirteen days, and received much civility from a young man, a bachelor, who invited me to his house, with whom I was for the most part of the time. He was so kind as to lodge me in the bed with himself, gave me a shirt, and would have bought me, but could not, as the Indians asked one hundred pounds for me. We were then to go to a place called Sorel, and that young man would go with me, because the Indians should not hurt me. This man carried me on the ice one day's journey, for I could not now go at all, and there was so much water on the ice we could go no further. So the Frenchman left me, and provision for me. Here we staid two nights, and then travelled again, for now the ice was strong, and in two days more we came to Sorel. When we got to **the first house, it was late in the** night; and here again the people were kind. Next day, being in much pain, I asked the Indians to carry me to the chirurgeons, as they had promised, at which they were wroth, and one of them took up his gun to knock me, but the Frenchman would not suffer it, but set upon him and kicked him out of doors. Then we went away from thence, to a place two or three miles off, where the Indians had wigwams. When I came to these wigwams some of the Indians knew me, and seemed to pity me.

While I was here, which was three or four days, the French came to see me; and it being Christmas time, they brought cakes and other provisions with them and gave to me, so that I had no want. The Indians tried to cure me, but could not. Then I asked for the chirurgeon, at which one of the Indians in anger struck me on the face with his fist. A Frenchman being by, spoke to him, but I knew not what he said, and then went his way. By and by came the captain of the place into the wigwam, with about twelve armed men, and asked where the Indian was that struck the Englishman. They took him and told him he should go to the bilboes, and then be hanged. The Indians were much terrified at this, as appeared by their countenances and trembling. I would have gone too, but the Frenchman bid me not fear; that the Indians durst not hurt me. When that Indian was gone, I had two masters still. I asked them to carry me to that captain, that I might speak for the Indian. They answered, " You are a fool. Do you think the French are like the English, to say one thing and do another? They are men of their words." I prevailed with them, however, to help me thither, and I spoke to the captain by an interpreter, and told him I desired him to set the Indian free, and told him what he had done for me. He told me he was a rogue, and should be hanged. Then I spoke more privately, alleging this reason, that because all the English captives were not come in, if he were hanged, it might fare the worse with them. The captain said " that was to be considered." Then he set him at liberty upon this condition, that he should never strike me more, and every day bring me to his house to eat victuals. I perceived that the common people did not like what the Indians had done and did to the English. When the Indian was set free, he came to me, and took me about the middle, and said I was his brother; that I had saved his life once, and he had saved mine thrice. Then he called for brandy and made me drink, and had me away to the wigwams again. When I came there, the Indians came to me one by one, to shake hands with me, saying WURREGEN NETOP,* and

* Friend, it is well.—Ed.

were very kind, thinking no other but that I had saved th Indian's life.

The next day he carried me to that captain's house, and set me down.* They gave me my victuals and wine, and being left there a while by the Indians, I showed the captain my fingers, which when he and his wife saw they ran away from the sight, and bid me lap it up again, and sent for the chirurgeon; who, when he came, said he could cure me, and took it in hand, and dressed it. The Indians towards night came for me; I told them I could not go with them. They were displeased, called me rogue, and went away. That night I was full of pain; the French feared that I would die; five men did watch with me, and strove to keep me cheerly, for I was sometimes ready to faint. Oftentimes they gave me a little brandy. The next day the chirurgeon came again, and dressed me; and so he did all the while I was among the French. I came in at Christmas, and went thence May 2d.

Being thus in the captain's house, I was kept there till Benjamin Waite came; and now my Indian master, being in want of money, pawned me to the captain for fourteen beavers' skins, or the worth of them, at such a day; if he did not pay he must lose his pawn, or else sell me for twenty-one beavers, but he could not get beaver, and so I was sold. By being thus sold, adds Dr. Mather, he was in God's good time set at liberty, and returned to his friends in New England again.

NARRATIVE

OF THE CAPTIVITY AND SUFFERINGS OF MISS SARAH GER-
ISH, WHO WAS TAKEN AT THE SACKING OF DOVER, IN
THE YEAR 1689, BY THE INDIANS; AS COMMUNICATED TO
THE REVEREND DR. COTTON MATHER, BY THE REVEREND
JOHN PIKE, MINISTER OF DOVER.

SARAH GERISH, daughter of Capt. John Gerish, of Quo-checho or Cocheco, was a very beautiful and ingenious damsel, about seven years of age, and happened to be lodging at the garrison of Major Waldron, her affectionate grandfather, when the Indians brought that horrible destruction upon it, on the

---

* His feet were so badly frozen that he had not walked for a considerable time.—Ed

night of the 27th of June, 1689. She was always very fearful of the Indians ; but fear may we think now surprised her, when they fiercely bid her go into a certain chamber and call the people out ! She obeyed, but finding only a little child in bed in the room, she got into the bed with it, and hid herself in the clothes as well as she could. The fell savages quickly pulled her out, and made her dress for a march, but led her away with no more than one stocking upon her, on a terrible march through the thick woods, and a thousand other miseries, till they came to the Norway Planes.* From thence they made her go to the end of Winnipisiogee lake, thence eastward, through horrid swamps, where sometimes they were obliged to scramble over huge trees fallen by storm or age, for a vast way together, and sometimes they must climb up long, steep, tiresome, and almost inaccessible mountains.

Her first master was an Indian named Sebundowit, a dull sort of fellow, and not such a devil as many of them were, but he sold her to a fellow who was a more harsh and mad sort of a dragon. He carried her away to Canada.

A long and sad journey now ensued, through the midst of a hideous desert, in the depth of a dreadful winter ; and who can enumerate the frights she endured before the end of her journey ? Once her master commanded her to loosen some of her upper garments, and stand against a tree while he charged his gun ; whereat the poor child shrieked out, " He is going to kill me !" God knows what he was going to do ; but the villian having charged his gun, he called her from the tree and forbore doing her any damage. Upon another time her master ordered her to run along the shore with some Indian girls, while he paddled up the river in his canoe. As the girls were passing a precipice, a tawny wench violently pushed her head-long into the river, but so it fell out that in this very place of her fall the bushes from the shore hung over the water, so that she was enabled to get hold of them, and thus saved herself. The Indians asked her how she became so wet, but she did not dare to tell them, from fear of the resentment of her that had so nearly deprived her of life already. And here it may be remarked, that it is almost universally true, that young Indians, both male and female, are as much to be dreaded by captives as those of maturer years, and in many cases much more so ; for, unlike cultivated people, they have no restraints upon their mischievous and savage propensities, which they indulge in cruelties surpassing any examples here related. They often vie with each other in attempting excessive acts of torture.

* These planes are in the present town of Rochester, N. H.—Editor.

Once, being spent with travelling all day, and lying down wet and exhausted at night, she fell into so profound a sleep that in the morning she waked not. Her barbarous captors decamped from the place of their night's rest, leaving this little captive girl asleep and covered with a snow that in the night had fallen; but, at length awaking, what agonies may you imagine she was in, on finding herself left a prey for bears and wolves, and without any sustenance, in a howling wilderness, many scores of leagues from any plantation! In this dismal situation, however, she had fortitude sufficient to attempt to follow them. And here again, the snow which had been her covering upon the cold ground, to her great discomfort, was now her only hope, for she could just discern by it the trace of the Indians! How long it was before she overtook them is not told us, but she joined them and continued her captivity.

Now the young Indians began to terrify her by constantly reminding her that she was shortly to be roasted to death. One evening much fuel was prepared between two logs, which they told her was for her torture. A mighty fire being made, her master called her to him, and told her that she should presently be burnt alive. At first she stood amazed; then burst into tears; and then she hung about her tiger of a master, begging of him, with an inexpressible anguish, to save her from the fire. Hereupon the monster so far relented as to tell her "that if she would be a good girl she should not be burnt."

At last they arrived at Canada, and she was carried into the Lord Intendant's house, where many persons of quality took much notice of her. It was a week after this that she remained in the Indian's hands before the price of her ransom could be agreed upon. But then the lady intendant sent her to the nunnery, where she was comfortably provided for; and it was the design, as was said, for to have brought her up in the Romish religion, and then to have married her unto the son of the Lord Intendant.

She was kindly used there until Sir William Phips, lying before Quebec, did, upon exchange of prisoners, obtain her liberty. After sixteen months' captivity she was restored unto her friends, who had the consolation of having this their desirable daughter again with them, returned as it were from the dead. But this dear child was not to cheer her parents' path for a long period; for on arriving at her sixteenth year, July, 1697, death carried her off by a malignant fever

NARRATIVE

OF THE REMARKABLE ESCAPE OF WIDOW ELIZABETH HEARD,
ALSO TAKEN AT THE DESTRUCTION OF MAJOR WALDRON'S
GARRISON IN DOVER, AS COMMUNICATED TO DOCTOR COT-
TON MATHER, BY THE REV. JOHN PIKE, MINISTER OF THE
PLACE.

Mrs. Elizabeth Heard was a widow of good estate, a mother
of many children, and a daughter of Mr. Hull, a reverend
minister formerly living at Pascataqua, but at this time lived
at Quochecho, the Indian name of Dover. Happening to be
at Portsmouth on the day before Quochecho was cut off, she
returned thither in the night with one daughter and three sons,
all masters of families. When they came near Quochecho
they were astonished with a prodigious noise of Indians, howling, shooting, shouting, and roaring, according to their manner
in making an assault.

Their distress for their families carried them still further
up the river, till they secretly and silently passed by some
numbers of the raging savages. They landed about an hundred rods from Major Waldron's garrison, and running up
the hill, they saw many lights in the windows of the garrison,
which they concluded the English within had set up for the
direction of those who might seek a refuge there. Coming
to the gate, they desired entrance, which not being readily
granted, they called earnestly, bounced, knocked, and cried
out to those within of their unkindness, that they would not
open the gate to them in this extremity.

No answer being yet made, they began to doubt whether all
was well. One of the young men then climbing up the wall,
saw a horrible tawny in the entry, with a gun in his hand. A
grievous consternation seized now upon them, and Mrs. Heard,
sitting down without the gate, through despair and faintness,
was unable to stir any further; but had strength only to
charge her children to shift for themselves, which she did in
broken accents; adding also that she must unavoidably there
end her days.

Her children, finding it impossible to carry her with them,
with heavy hearts forsook her. Immediately after, however,
she beginning to recover from her fright, was able to fly, and
hide herself in a bunch of barberry bushes, in the garden; and

then hastening from thence, because the daylight advanced, she sheltered herself, though seen by two of the Indians, in a thicket of other bushes, about thirty rods from the house. She had not been long here before an Indian came towards her, with a pistol in his hand. The fellow came up to her and stared her in the face, but said nothing to her, nor she to him. He went a little way back, and came again, and stared upon her as before, but said nothing; whereupon she asked him what he would have. He still said nothing, but went away to the house, whooping, and returned unto her no more.

Being thus unaccountably preserved, she made several essays to pass the river, but found herself unable to do it, and finding all places on that side of the river filled with blood and fire, and hideous outcries, she thereupon returned to her old bush, and there poured out her ardent prayers to God for help in this distress.

She continued in this bush until the garrison was burnt, and the enemy had gone, and then she stole along by the river side, until she came to a boom, on which she passed over. Many sad effects of cruelty she saw left by the Indians in her way. She soon after safely arrived at Captain Gerish's garrison, where she found a refuge from the storm. Here she also had the satisfaction to understand that her own garrison, though one of the first that was assaulted, had been bravely defended, and successfully maintained against the adversary.

This gentlewoman's garrison was on the most extreme frontier of the province, and more obnoxious than any other, and therefore more incapable of being relieved. Nevertheless, by her presence and courage, it held out all the war, even for ten years together; and the persons in it have enjoyed very eminent preservations. It would have been deserted, if she had accepted offers that were made her by her friends, to abandon it, and retire to Portsmouth among them, which would have been a damage to the town and land; but by her encouragement this post was thus kept up, and she is yet [1702] living in much esteem among her neighbors.

NOTE 1.—MRS. HEARD was the widow of a Mr. John Heard. She had five sons, Benjamin, John, Joseph, Samuel and Tristram, and an equal number of daughters. The last-named son was waylaid and killed by the Indians in the year 1723.—MS. CHRONICLES OF THE INDIANS.

NOTE 2.—It will doubtless seem surprising to the reader that Mrs. Heard should be suffered to escape captivity, when she was discovered by a grim warrior, who, without doubt, was seeking for some white inhabitant, on whom to wreak his vengeance. The facts seem to be these: Thirteen years before, namely, in 1676, when the four hundred Indians were surprised in Dover, (in a manner not at all doubtful as it respects

the character of their captors,) this same Mrs. Heard secreted a young
Indian in her house, by which means he escaped that calamitous day.
The reader of Indian history will not, now, I presume, harbor surprise
at the conduct of the warrior. For the particulars of the event con-
nected with this narrative, see THE BOOK OF THE INDIANS, Book iii.
Chap. viii.—Ed.

MEMOIRS

OF ODD ADVENTURES, STRANGE DELIVERANCES, ETC., IN THE
CAPTIVITY OF JOHN GYLES, ESQ., COMMANDER OF THE
GARRISON ON ST. GEORGE RIVER, IN THE DISTRICT OF
MAINE. WRITTEN BY HIMSELF. ORIGINALLY PUBLISHED
AT BOSTON, 1736.

INTRODUCTION.—These private memoirs were collected from
my minutes, at the earnest request of my second consort, for
the use of our family, that we might have a memento ever
ready at hand, to excite in ourselves gratitude and thankfulness
to God; and in our offspring a due sense of their dependence
on the Sovereign of the universe, from the precariousness and
vicissitudes of all sublunary enjoyments. In this state, and for
this end, they have laid by me for some years. They at length
falling into the hands of some, for whose judgment I had a
value, I was pressed for a copy for the public. Others, desiring of me to extract particulars from them, which the multi-
plicity and urgency of my affairs would not admit, I have now
determined to suffer their publication. I have not made scarce
any addition to this manual, except in the chapter of *creatures*,
which I was urged to make much larger. I might have greatly enlarged it, but I feared it would grow beyond its proportion.
I have been likewise advised to give a particular account of
my father, which I am not very fond of, having no dependence
on the virtues or honors of my ancestors to recommend me to
the favor of God or men; nevertheless, because some think it
is a respect due to the memory of my parents, whose name I
was obliged to mention in the following story, and a satisfaction
which their posterity might justly expect from me, I shall give
some account of him, though as brief as possible.

The flourishing state of New England, before the unhappy
eastern wars, drew my father hither, whose first settlement was
on Kennebeck river, at a place called Merrymeeting Bay, where
he dwelt for some years; until, on the death of my grand pa-

rents, he, with his family, returned to England, to settle his affairs. This done, he came over with the design to have returned to his farm; but on his arrival at Boston, the eastern Indians had begun their hostilities. He therefore begun a settlement on Long Island. The air of that place not so well agreeing with his constitution, and the Indians having become peaceable, he again proposed to resettle his lands in Merrymeeting Bay; but finding that place deserted, and that plantations were going on at Pemmaquid, he purchased several tracts of land of the inhabitants there. Upon his highness the duke of York resuming a claim to those parts, my father took out patents under that claim; and when Pemmaquid was set off by the name of the county of Cornwall, in the province of New York, he was commissioned chief justice of the same by Gov. Duncan [Dongan.]* He was a strict sabbatarian, and met with considerable difficulty in the discharge of his office, from the immoralities of a people who had long lived lawless. He laid out no inconsiderable income, which he had annually from England, on the place, and at last lost his life there, as will hereafter be related.

I am not insensible of the truth of an assertion of Sir Roger L'Estrange, that "Books and dishes have this common fate: no one of either ever pleased all tastes." And I am fully of his opinion in this: "It is as little to be wished for as expected; for a universal applause is, at least, two thirds of a scandal." To conclude with Sir Roger, "Though I made this composition principally for my family, yet, if any man has a mind to take part with me, he has free leave, and is welcome;" but let him carry this consideration along with him, "that he is a very unmannerly guest who forces himself upon another man's table, and then quarrels with his dinner."

CHAPTER I.—*Containing the occurrences of the first year.* On the second day of August, 1689, in the morning, my honored father, THOMAS GYLES, Esq., went with some laborers, my two elder brothers and myself, to one of his farms, which laid upon the river about three miles above fort Charles,† adjoining Pemmaquid falls, there to gather in his English harvest, and we labored securely till noon. After we had dined, our people

---

* He had been appointed governor of New York 30 Sept. 1682.—Ed.

† Fort Charles stood on the spot where fort Frederick was, not long since, founded by Colonel Dunbar. The township adjoining thereto was called Jamestown, in honor to the duke of York. In this town, within a quarter of a mile of the fort, was my father's dwelling-house, from which he went out that unhappy morning.

went to their labor, some in one field to their English hay, the others to another field of English corn. My father, the youngest of my two brothers, and myself, tarried near the farm-house in which we had dined till about one of the clock; at which time we heard the report of several great guns at the fort. Upon which my father said he hoped it was a signal of good news, and that the great council had sent back the soldiers, to cover the inhabitants; (for on report of the revolution they had deserted.) But to our great surprise, about thirty or forty Indians,* at that moment, discharged a volley of shot at us, from behind a rising ground, near our barn. The yelling of the Indians,† the whistling of their shot, and the voice of my father, whom I heard cry out, "What now! what now!" so terrified me, (though he seemed to be handling a gun,) that I endeavored to make my escape. My brother ran one way and I another, and looking over my shoulder, I saw a stout fellow, painted, pursuing me with a gun, and a cutlass glittering in his hand, which I expected every moment in my brains. I soon fell down, and the Indian seized me by the left hand. He offered me no abuse, but tied my arms, then lifted me up, and pointed to the place where the people were at work about the hay, and led me that way. As we went, we crossed where my father was, who looked very pale and bloody, and walked very slowly. When we came to the place, I saw two men shot down on the flats, and one or two more knocked on their heads with hatchets, crying out, "O Lord," &c. There the Indians brought two captives, one a man, and my brother James, who, with me, had endeavored to escape by running from the house, when we were first attacked. This brother was about fourteen years of age. My oldest brother, whose name was Thomas, wonderfully escaped by land to the Barbican, a point of land on the west side of the river, opposite the fort, where several fishing vessels lay. He got on board one of them and sailed that night.

After doing what mischief they could, they sat down, and made us sit with them. After some time we arose, and the Indians pointed for us to go eastward. We marched about a quarter of a mile, and then made a halt. Here they brought my father to us. They made proposals to him, by old Moxus, who told him that those were strange Indians who shot him,

* The whole company of Indians, according to Charlevoix, was one hundred.—Ed.

† The Indians have a custom of uttering a most horrid howl when they discharge guns, designing thereby to terrify those whom they fight against.

and that he was sorry for it. My father replied that he was a dying man, and wanted no favor of them, but to pray with his children. This being granted him, he recommended us to the protection and blessing of God Almighty; then gave us the best advice, and took his leave for this life, hoping in God that we should meet in a better. He parted with a cheerful voice, but looked very pale, by reason of his great loss of blood, which now gushed out of his shoes. 'The Indians led him aside!—I heard the blows of the hatchet, but neither shriek nor groan! I afterwards heard that he had five or seven shot-holes through his waistcoat or jacket, and that he was covered with some boughs.

The Indians led us, their captives, on the east side of the river, towards the fort, and when we came within a mile and a half of the fort and town, and could see the fort, we saw firing and smoke on all sides. Here we made a short stop, and then moved within or near the distance of three quarters of a mile from the fort, into a thick swamp. There I saw my mother and my two little sisters, and many other captives who were taken from the town. My mother asked me about my father. I told her he was killed, but could say no more for grief. She burst into tears, and the Indians moved me a little farther off, and seized me with cords to a tree.

The Indians came to New Harbor, and sent spies several days to observe how and where the people were employed, &c., who found the men were generally at work at noon, and left about their houses only women and children. Therefore the Indians divided themselves into several parties, some ambushing the way between the fort and the houses, as likewise between them and the distant fields; and then alarming the farthest off first, they killed and took the people, as they moved towards the town and fort, at their pleasure, and very few escaped to it. Mr. Pateshall was taken and killed, as he lay with his sloop near the Barbican.

On the first stir about the fort, my youngest brother was at play near it, and running in, was by God's goodness thus preserved. Captain Weems, with great courage and resolution, defended the weak old fort* two days; when, being much wounded, and the best of his men killed, he beat for a parley, which eventuated in these conditions:

1. That they, the Indians, should give him Mr. Pateshall's sloop. 2. That they should not molest him in carrying off the

---

* I presume Charlevoix was misinformed about the strength of this place. He says, "Ils [the English] y avoient fait un fort bel etablissement, de-féndu par un fort, qui n'étoit a la verité que de pieux, mais assez regulierc-ment construit, avec *vingt canons montés.*"

few people that had got into the fort, and three captives that they had taken. 3. That the English should carry off in their hands what they could from the fort.

On these conditions the fort was surrendered, and Captain Weems went off; and soon after, the Indians set on fire the fort and houses, which made a terrible blast, and was a melancholy sight to us poor captives, who were sad spectators!

After the Indians had thus laid waste Pemmaquid, they moved us to New Harbor, about two miles east of Pemmaquid, a cove much frequented by fishermen. At this place, there were, before the war, about twelve houses. These the inhabitants deserted as soon as the rumor of war reached the place. When we turned our backs on the town, my heart was ready to break! I saw my mother. She spoke to me, but I could not answer her. That night we tarried at New Harbor, and the next day went in their canoes for Penobscot. About noon, the canoe in which my mother was, and that in which I was, came side by side; whether accidentally or by my mother's desire I cannot say. She asked me how I did. I think I said "pretty well," but my heart was so full of grief I scarcely knew whether audible to her. Then she said, "O, my child! how joyful and pleasant it would be, if we were going to old England, to see your uncle Chalker, and other friends there! Poor babe, we are going into the wilderness, the Lord knows where!" Then bursting into tears, the canoes parted. That night following, the Indians with their captives lodged on an island.

A few days after, we arrived at Penobscot fort, where I again saw my mother, my brother and sisters, and many other captives. I think we tarried here eight days. In that time, the Jesuit of the place had a great mind to buy me. My Indian master made a visit to the Jesuit, and carried me with him. And here I will note, that the Indian who takes a captive is accounted his master, and has a perfect right to him, until he gives or sells him to another. I saw the Jesuit show my master pieces of gold, and understood afterwards that he was tendering them for my ransom. He gave me a biscuit, which I put into my pocket, and not daring to eat it, buried it under a log, fearing he had put something into it to make me love him. Being very young, and having heard much of the Papists torturing the Protestants, caused me to act thus; and I hated the sight of a Jesuit.* When my mother heard the

* It is not to be wondered at that antipathy should be so plainly exhibited at this time, considering what had been going on in England up to the latest dates; but that children should have been taught, that Catholics had the power of winning over heretics by any mysterious pow-

7*

talk of my being sold to a Jesuit, she said to me, "Oh, my dear child, if it were God's will, I had rather follow you to your grave, or never see you more in this world, than you should be sold to a Jesuit; for a Jesuit will ruin you, body and soul!"* It pleased God to grant her request, for she never saw me more! Yet she and my two little sisters were, after several years' captivity, redeemed, but she died before I returned. My brother who was taken with me, was, after several years' captivity, most barbarously tortured to death by the Indians.

My Indian master carried me up Penobscot river, to a village called *Madawamkee*, which stands on a point of land between the main river and a branch which heads to the east of it. At home I had ever seen strangers treated with the utmost civility, and being a stranger, I expected some kind treatment here; but I soon found myself deceived, for I presently saw a number of squaws, who had got together in a circle, dancing and yelling. An old grim-looking one took me by the hand, and leading me into the ring, some seized me by my hair, and others by my hands and feet, like so many furies; but my master presently laying down a pledge, they released me.

A captive among the Indians is exposed to all manner of abuses, and to the extremest tortures, unless their master, or some of their master's relations, lay down a ransom; such as a bag of corn, a blanket, or the like, which redeems them from their cruelty for that dance. The next day we went up that eastern branch of Penobscot river many leagues; carried over land to a large pond, and from one pond to another, till, in a few days, we went down a river, called Medocktack, which vents itself into St. John's river. But before we came to the mouth of this river, we passed over a long carrying place, to Medocktack fort, which stands on a bank of St.

ders, or other arts, furnished them by his satanic majesty, is a matter, to say the least, of no little admiration.—Ed.

* It may not be improper to hear how the Jesuits themselves viewed these matters. The settlement here was, according to the French account, in their dominions, and the English settlers "incommoded extremely from thence all the Indians in the adjacent country, who were the avowed friends of the French, and caused the government of Acadia no less inquietude, who feared with reason the effect of their intrigues in detaching the Indians from their alliance. The Indians, who undertook to break up the post at Pemmaquid, were Penobscots, among whom a Jesuit, named M. THURY, a good laborer in the faith, had a numerous mission. The first attention before setting out of these brave Christians was to secure aid of the God of battles, by confessions and the sacrament; and they took care that their wives and children performed the same rites, and raised their pure hands to heaven, while their fathers and mothers went out to battle against the heretics." See Charlevoix.—Ed

John's river. My master went before, and left me with an old Indian, and two or three squaws. The old man often said, (which was all the English he could speak,) "By and by come to a g eat town and fort." I now comforted myself in thinking how finely I should be refreshed when I came to this great town.

After some miles' travel we came in sight of a large cornfield, and soon after of the fort, to my great surprise. Two or three squaws met us, took off my pack, and led me to a large hut or wigwam, where thirty or forty Indians were dancing and yelling round five or six poor captives, who had been taken some months before from Quochech, at the time Major Waldron was so barbarously butchered by them. And before proceeding with my narrative I will give a short account of that action.

Major Waldron's garrison was taken on the night of the 27th of June, 1689.* I have heard the Indians say at a feast that as there was a truce for some days, they contrived to send in two squaws to take notice of the numbers, lodgings and other circumstances of the people in his garrison, and if they could obtain leave to lodge there, to open the gates and whistle. (They said the gates had no locks, but were fastened with pins, and that they kept no watch.) The squaws had a favorable season to prosecute their projection, for it was dull weather when they came to beg leave to lodge in the garrison. They told the major that a great number of Indians were not far from thence, with a considerable quantity of beaver, who would be there to trade with him the next day. Some of the people were very much against their lodging in the garrison, but the major said, "Let the poor creatures lodge by the fire." The squaws went into every apartment, and observing the numbers in each, when all the people were asleep, arose and opened the gates, gave the signal, and the other Indians came to them; and having received an account of the state of the garrison, they divided according to the number of people in each apartment, and soon took and killed them all. The major lodged within an inner room, and when the Indians broke in upon him, he cried out, " What now ! what now !" and jumping out of bed with only his shirt on, seized his sword and drove them before him through two or three doors; but for

* The date stands in the old narrative, "in the beginning of April on the night after a Sabbath," which being an error, I have corrected it. What time in the night of the 27th the place was attacked, is not mentioned, but the accounts of it are chiefly dated the day following, viz. the 28th, when the tragedy was finished. The squaws had taken up their lodging there on the night of the 27th, and if the attack begun before midnight, which it probably did, the date in the text is the true one.—Ed.

some reason, turning about towards the apartment he had just left, an Indian came up behind him, knocked him on the head with his hatchet, which stunned him, and he fell. They now seized upon him, dragged him out, and setting him upon a long table in his hall, bid him "judge Indians again." Then they cut and stabbed him, and he cried out, " O, Lord! O, Lord !" They bid him order his book of accounts to be brought, and to cross out all the Indians' debts,* (he having traded much with them.) After they had tortured him to death, they burned the garrison and drew off. This narration I had from their own mouths, at a general meeting, and have reason to think it true.† But to return to my narrative.

I was whirled in among this circle of Indians, and we prisoners looked on each other with a sorrowful countenance. Presently one of them was seized by each hand and foot, by four Indians, who, swinging him up, let his back fall on the ground with full force. This they repeated, till they had danced, as they called it, round the whole wigwam, which was thirty or forty feet in length. But when they torture a boy they take him up between two. This is one of their customs of torturing captives. Another is to take up a person by the middle, with his head downwards, and jolt him round till one would think his bowels would shake out of his mouth. Sometimes they will take a captive by the hair of the head, and stooping him forward, strike him on the back and shoulder, till the blood gushes out of his mouth and nose. Sometimes an old shrivelled squaw will take up a shovel of hot embers and throw them into a captive's bosom. If he cry out, the Indians will laugh and shout, and say, "What a brave action our old grandmother has done." Sometimes they torture them with whips, &c.

The Indians looked on me with a fierce countenance, as much as to say, it will be your turn next. They champed cornstalks, which they threw into my hat, as I held it in my hand. I smiled on them, though my heart ached. I looked on one, and another, but could not perceive that any eye pitied me. Presently came a squaw and a little girl, and laid down a bag of corn in the ring. The little girl took me by the hand, making signs for me to go out of the circle with them. Not knowing their custom, I supposed they designed to kill me,

* When they gashed his naked breast, they said in derision, " *I cross out my account.*"—Ed.

† In a previous note, to another narrative, I have referred the reader to ____ work, (THE BOOK OF THE INDIANS,) where all the circumstances ____ ____ affair are detailed.—Ed.

and refused to go. Then a grave Indian came and gave me a short pipe, and said in English, " Smoke it ;" then he took me by the hand and led me out. My heart ached, thinking myself near my end. But he carried me to a French hut, about a mile from the Indian fort. The Frenchman was not at home, but his wife, who was a squaw, had some discourse with my Indian friend, which I did not understand. We tarried about two hours, then returned to the Indian village, where they gave me some victuals. Not long after this I saw one of my fellow-captives, who gave me a melancholy account of their sufferings after I left them.

After some weeks had passed, we left this village and went up St. John's river about ten miles, to a branch called *Medockscenecasis*, where there was one wigwam. At our arrival an old squaw saluted me with a yell, taking me by the hair and one hand, but I was so rude as to break her hold and free myself. She gave me a filthy grin, and the Indians set up a laugh, and so it passed over. Here we lived upon fish, wild grapes, roots, &c., which was hard living to me.

When the winter came on we went up the river, till the ice came down, running thick in the river, when, according to the Indian custom, we laid up our canoes till spring. Then we travelled sometimes on the ice, and sometimes on the land, till we came to a river that was open, but not fordable, where we made a raft, and passed over, bag and baggage. I met with no abuse from them in this winter's hunting, though I was put to great hardships in carrying burdens and for want of food. But they underwent the same difficulty, and would often encourage me, saying, in broken English, "*By and by great deal moose*." Yet they could not answer any question I asked them. And knowing little of their customs and way of life, I thought it tedious to be constantly moving from place to place, though it might be in some respects an advantage ; for it ran still in my mind that we were travelling to some settlement ; and when my burden was over-heavy, and the Indians left me behind, and the still evening coming on, I fancied I could see through the bushes, and hear the people of some great town ; which hope, though some support to me in the day, yet I found not the town at night.

Thus we were hunting three hundred miles* from the sea, and knew no man within fifty or sixty miles of us. We were eight or ten in number, and had but two guns, on which we

---

*A pardonable error, perhaps, considering the author's ignorance of the geography of the country. He could hardly have got three hundred miles from the mouth of the Penobscot, in a northerly direction, without crossing the St. Lawrence.—Ed.

wholly depended for food. If any disaster had happened, we must all have perished. Sometimes we had no manner of sustenance for three or four days; but God wonderfully provides for all creatures. In one of these fasts, God's providence was remarkable. Our two Indian men, who had guns, in hunting started a moose, but there being a shallow crusted snow on the ground, and the moose discovering them, ran with great force into a swamp. The Indians went round the swamp, and finding no track, returned at night to the wigwam, and told what had happened. The next morning they followed him on the track, and soon found him lying on the snow. He had, in crossing the roots of a large tree, that had been blown down, broken through the ice made over the water in the hole occasioned by the roots of the tree taking up the ground, and hitched one of his hind legs among the roots, so fast that by striving to get it out he pulled his thigh bone out of its socket at the hip; and thus extraordinarily were we provided for in our great strait. Sometimes they would take a bear, which go into dens in the fall of the year, without any sort of food, and lie there four or five months without food, never going out till spring; in which time they neither lose nor gain in flesh. If they went into their dens fat they came out so, and if they went in lean they came out lean. I have seen some which have come out with four whelps, and both very fat, and then we feasted. An old squaw and a captive, if any present, must stand without the wigwam, shaking their hands and bodies as in a dance, and singing, "WEGAGE OH NELO WOH," which in English is, "Fat is my eating." This is to signify their thankfulness in feasting times. When one supply was spent we fasted till further success.

The way they preserve meat is by taking the flesh from the bones and drying it in smoke, by which it is kept sound months or years without salt. We moved still further up the country after moose when our store was out, so that by the spring we had got to the northward of the Lady mountains.* When the spring came and the rivers broke up, we moved back to the head of St. John's river, and there made canoes of moose hides, sewing three or four together and pitching the seams with balsam mixed with charcoal. Then we went down the river to a place called Madawescook.† There an old man lived and kept a sort of trading house, where

* If these are the same the French called *Monts Notre Dame*, our captive was now on the borders of the St. Lawrence, to the north of the head of the bay of Chaleurs.—Ed.

† Probably the now well-known Madawasca, of " disputed territory" memory.

we tarried several days; then went farther down the river till we came to the greatest falls in these parts, called Checaneke-peag, where we carried a little way over the land, and putting off our canoes we went down-stream still. And as we passed down by the mouths of any large branches, we saw Indians; but when any dance was proposed, I was bought off. At length we arrived at the place where we left our birch canoes in the fall, and putting our baggage into them, went down to the fort.

There we planted corn, and after planting went a fishing, and to look for and dig roots, till the corn was fit to weed. After weeding we took a second tour on the same errand, then returned to hill our corn. After hilling we went some distance from the fort and field, up the river, to take salmon and other fish, which we dried for food, where we continued till corn was filled with milk; some of it we dried then, the other as it ripened. To dry corn when in the milk, they gather it in large kettles and boil it on the ears, till it is pretty hard, then shell it from the cob with clam-shells, and dry it on bark in the sun. When it is thoroughly dry, a kernel is no bigger than a pea, and would keep years, and when it is boiled again it swells as large as when on the ear, and tastes incomparably sweeter than other corn. When we had gathered our corn and dried it in the way already described, we put some into Indian barns, that is, into holes in the ground, lined and covered with bark, and then with dirt. The rest we carried up the river upon our next winter's hunting. Thus God wonderfully favored me, and carried me through the first year of my captivity.

CHAPTER II.—*Of the abusive and barbarous treatment which several captives met with from the Indians.* When any great number of Indians met, or when any captives had been lately taken, or when any captives desert and are retaken, they have a dance, and torture the unhappy people who have fallen into their hands. My unfortunate brother, who was taken with me, after about three years' captivity, deserted with another Englishman, who had been taken from Casco Bay, and was retaken by the Indians at New Harbor, and carried back to Penobscot fort. Here they were both tortured at a stake by fire, for some time; then their noses and ears were cut off, and they made to eat them. After this they were burnt to death at the stake; the Indians at the same time declaring that they would serve all deserters in the same manner. Thus they divert themselves in their dances.

On the second spring of my captivity, my Indian master and

his squaw went to Canada, but sent me down the river with several Indians to the fort, to plant corn. The day before we came to the planting ground, we met two young Indian men, who seemed to be in great haste. After they had passed us, I understood they were going with an express to Canada, and that there was an English vessel at the mouth of the river. I not being perfect in their language, nor knowing that English vessels traded with them in time of war, supposed a peace was concluded on, and that the captives would be released; I was so transported with this fancy, that I slept but little if any that night. Early the next morning we came to the village, where my ecstacy ended; for I had no sooner landed, but three or four Indians dragged me to the great wigwam, where they were yelling and dancing round James Alexander, a Jersey man, who was taken from Falmouth, in Casco Bay. This was occasioned by two families of Cape Sable Indians, who, having lost some friends by a number of English fishermen, came some hundreds of miles to revenge themselves on poor captives. They soon came to me, and tossed me about till I was almost breathless, and then threw me into the ring to my fellow-captive; and taking him out, repeated their barbarities on him. Then I was hauled out again by three Indians, who seized me by the hair of the head; and bending me down by my hair, one beat me on the back and shoulders so long that my breath was almost beat out of my body. Then others put a *tomhake** [tomahawk] into my hands, and ordered me to get up and sing and dance Indian, which I performed with the greatest reluctance, and while in the act, seemed determined to purchase my death, by killing two or three of those monsters of cruelty, thinking it impossible to survive their bloody treatment; but it was impressed on my mind that it was not in their power to take away my life, so I desisted.

Then those Cape Sable Indians came to me again like bears bereaved of their whelps, saying, " Shall we, who have lost relations by the English, suffer an English voice to be heard among us ?" &c. Then they beat me again with the axe.

* The *tomhake* is a warlike club, the shape of which may be seen in cuts of ETOWOHKOAM. one of the four Indian chiefs, which cuts are common amongst us. [Mr. Gyles refers to the four Iroquois chiefs, who visited England in the reign of Queen Anne. About those chiefs I have collected and published the particulars in the Book of the Indians. And I will here remark that the compilers of the ponderous *Indian Biography and History*, now in course of publication, under the names of James Hall and T. L. M'Kenny, have *borrowed* my labors with no sparing hand—they have not even owned it ; having no faith, probably, that *by* so doing they *might* pay half the debt. "He who steals my purse steals trash," but he who robs me of ·ny labors   —Ed.]

Now I repented that I had not sent two or three of them out of the world before me, for I thought I had much rather die than suffer any longer. They left me the second time, and the other Indians put the tomhake into my hands again, and compelled me to sing. Then I seemed more resolute than before to destroy some of them; but a strange and strong impulse that I should return to my own place and people suppressed it, as often as such a motion rose in my breast. Not one of them showed the least compassion, but I saw the tears run down plentifully on the cheeks of a Frenchman who sat behind, though it did not alleviate the tortures that poor James and I were forced to endure for the most part of this tedious day; for they were continued till the evening, and were the most severe that ever I met with in the whole six years that I was a captive with the Indians.

After they had thus inhumanly abused us, two Indians took us up and threw us out of the wigwam, and we crawled away on our hands and feet, and were scarce able to walk for several days. Some time after they again concluded on a merry dance, when I was at some distance from the wigwam dressing leather, and an Indian was so kind as to tell me that they had got James Alexander, and were in search for me. My Indian master and his squaw bid me run for my life into a swamp and hide, and not to discover myself unless they both came to me; for then I might be assured the dance was over. I was now master of their language, and a word or a wink was enough to excite me to take care of one. I ran to the swamp, and hid in the thickest place I could find. I heard hallooing and whooping all around me; sometimes some passed very near me, and I could hear some threaten and others flatter me, but I was not disposed to dance. If they had come upon me, I had resolved to show them a pair of heels, and they must have had good luck to have catched me. I heard no more of them till about evening, for I think I slept, when they came again, calling, "Chon! Chon!" but John would not trust them. After they were gone, my master and his squaw came where they told me to hide, but could not find me; and, when I heard them say, with some concern, they believed the other Indians had frightened me into the woods, and that I was lost, I came out, and they seemed well pleased. They told me James had had a bad day of it; that as soon as he was released he ran away into the woods, and they believed he was gone to the Mohawks. James soon returned, and gave a melancholy account of his sufferings, and the Indians's fright concerning the Mohawks passed over. They often had terrible apprehensions of the incursions of those Indians. They are called also *Ma-*

8

quas, a most ambitious, haughty and blood-thirsty people, from whom the other Indians take their measures and manners, and their modes and changes of dress, &c. One very hot season, a great number gathered together at the village, and being a very droughty [thirsty] people, they kept James and myself night and day fetching water from a cold spring, that ran out of a rocky hill about three quarters of a mile from the fort. In going thither, we crossed a large interval cornfield, and then a descent to a lower interval, before we ascended the hill to the spring. James being almost dead, as well as I, with this continual fatigue, contrived to frighten the Indians. He told me of his plan, but conjured me to secrecy, yet said he knew I could keep counsel! The next dark night, James, going for water, set his kettle down on the descent to the lowest interval, and running back to the fort, puffing and blowing as though in the utmost surprise, told his master that he saw something near the spring that looked like Mohawks, (which were only stumps.) His master, being a most courageous warrior, went with him to make discovery. When they came to the brow of the hill, James pointed to the stumps, and withal touching his kettle with his toe, gave it motion down the hill; at every turn its bail clattered, which caused James and his master to see a Mohawk in every stump, and they lost no time in "turning tail to," and he was the best fellow who could run the fastest. This alarmed all the Indians in the village. They were about thirty or forty in number, and they packed off, bag and baggage, some up the river and others down, and did not return under fifteen days; and then the heat of the weather being finally over, our hard service was abated for this season. I never heard that the Indians understood the occasion of their fright; but James and I had many a private laugh about it.

But my most intimate and dear companion was one John Evans, a young man taken from Quochecho. We, as often as we could, met together, and made known our grievances to each other, which seemed to ease our minds; but, as soon as it was known by the Indians, we were strictly examined apart, and falsely accused of contriving to desert. We were too far from the sea to have any thought of that, and finding our stories agreed, did not punish us. An English captive girl about this time, who was taken by Medocawando, would often falsely accuse us of plotting to desert; but we made the truth so plainly appear, that she was checked and we were released. But the third winter of my captivity, John Evans went into the country, and the Indians imposed a heavy burden on him, while he was extremely weak from long fasting; and as he **was going off** the upland over a place of ice, which was very hollow, he broke through, fell down, and cut his knee very much. Notwithstanding, he travelled for some time, but the wind and cold were so forcible, that they soon overcame him, and he sat or fell down, and all the Indians passed by him. Some of them went back the next day after him, or his pack, and found him, with a dog in his arms, both frozen to death. Thus all of my fellow-captives were dispersed and dead, but through infinite and unmerited goodness I was supported under and carried through all difficulties.

CHAPTER III.—*Of further difficulties and deliverances.* One winter, as we were moving from place to place, our hunters killed some moose. One lying some miles from our wigwams, a young Indian and myself were ordered to fetch part of it. We set out in the morning, when the weather was promising, but it proved a very cold, cloudy day. It was late in the evening before we arrived at the place where the moose lay, so that we had no time to provide materials for fire or shelter. At the same time came on a storm of snow, very thick, which continued until the next morning. We made a small fire with what little rubbish we could find around us. The fire, with the warmth of our bodies, melted the snow upon us as fast as it fell; and so our clothes were filled with water. However, early in the morning we took our loads of moose flesh, and set out to return to our wigwams. We had not travelled far before my moose-skin coat (which was the only garment I had on my back, and the hair chiefly worn off) was frozen stiff round my knees, like a hoop, as were my snowshoes and shoe-clouts to my feet. Thus I marched the whole day without fire or food. At first I was in great pain, then my flesh became numb, and at times I felt extremely sick, and thought I could not travel one foot farther; but I wonderfully revived again.

After long travelling I felt very drowsy, and had thoughts of sitting down, which had I done, without doubt I had fallen on my final sleep, as my dear companion, Evans, had done before. My Indian companion, being better clothed, had left me long before. Again my spirits revived as much as if I had received the richest cordial. Some hours after sunset I reached the wigwam, and crawling in with my snow-shoes on, the Indians cried out, "The captive is frozen to death!" They took off my pack, and the place where that lay against my back was the only one that was not frozen. They cut off my shoes, and stripped off the clouts from my feet, which were as void of feeling as any frozen flesh could be. I had not sat long by the fire before the blood began to circulate, and my feet to my ankles turned black, and swelled with bloody blisters, and were inexpressibly painful. The Indians said one to another, " His feet will rot, and he will die." Yet I slept well at night. Soon after, the skin came off my feet from my ankles, whole, like a shoe, leaving my toes naked, without a nail, and the ends of my great toe bones bare, which, in a little time, turned black, so that I was obliged to cut the first joint off with my knife. The Indians gave me rags to bind up my feet, and advised me to apply fir balsam, but withal added that they believed it was not worth while to use means, for I should certainly die. But, by the use of my elbows, and a stick in each hand, I shoved myself along as I sat upon the ground over the snow from one tree to another, till I got some balsam. This I burned in a clam-shell till it was of a consistence like salve, which I applied to my feet and ankles, and, by the divine blessing, within a week I could go about upon my heels with my staff. And, through God's goodness, we had provisions enough, so that we did not remove under ten or fifteen lays. Then the Indians made two little hoops, something in the form of a snow-shoe, and sewing them to my feet, I was able to follow them in their tracks, on my heels, from place to place, though sometimes half leg deep in snow and water, which gave me the most acute pain imaginable; but I must walk or die. Yet within a year my feet were entirely well; and the nails came on my great toes, so that a very critical eye could scarcely perceive any part missing, or that they had been frozen at all.

In a time of great scarcity of provisions, the Indians chased a large moose into the river, and killed him. They brought the flesh to the village, and raised it on a scaffold, in a large wigwam, in order to make a feast. I was very officious in supplying them with wood and water, which pleased them so well that they now and then gave me a piece of flesh half boiled or roasted, which I ate with eagerness, and I doubt not without due thankfulness to the divine Being who so extraordinarily fed me. At length the scaffold bearing the moose meat broke, and I being under it, a large piece fell, and knocked me on the head.* The Indians said I lay stunned a considerable time. The first I was sensible of was a murmuring noise in my ears, then my sight gradually returned, with an extreme pain in my hand, which was very much bruised; and it was long before I recovered, the weather being very hot.

I was once fishing with an Indian for sturgeon, and the Indian darting one, his feet slipped, and he turned the canoe

---

* Whether he were struck by a timber of the scaffold, or a quantity of the meat on it, we are left to conjecture, and it is not very material.—Ed.

bottom upward, with me under it. I held fast to the cross-bar, as I could not swim, with my face to the bottom of the canoe; but turning myself, I brought my breast to bear on the cross-bar, expecting every minute the Indian to tow me to the bank. But "he had other fish to fry." Thus I continued a quarter of an hour, [though] without want of breath, till the current drove me on a rocky point where I could reach bottom. There I stopped, and turned up my canoe. On looking about for the Indian, I saw him half a mile off up the river. On going to him, I asked him why he had not towed me to the bank, seeing he knew I could not swim. He said he knew I was under the canoe, for there were no bubbles any where to be seen, and that I should drive on the point. So while he was taking care of his fine sturgeon, which was eight or ten feet in length, I was left to sink or swim.

Once, as we were fishing for salmon at a fall of about fifteen feet of water, I came near being drownded in a deep hole at the foot of the fall. The Indians went into the water to wash themselves, and asked me to go with them. I told them I could not swim, but they insisted, and so I went in. They ordered me to dive across the deepest place, and if I fell short of the other side they said they would help me. But, instead of diving across the narrowest part, I was crawling on the bottom into the deepest place. They not seeing me rise, and knowing whereabouts I was by the bubbling of the water, a young girl dived down, and brought me up by the hair, otherwise I had perished in the water. Though the Indians, both male and female, go into the water together, they have each of them such covering on that not the least indecency can be observed, and neither chastity nor modesty is violated.

While at the Indian village, I had been cutting wood and binding it up with an Indian rope, in order to carry it to the wigwam; a stout, ill-natured young fellow, about twenty years of age, threw me backward, sat on my breast, pulled out his knife, and said he would kill me, for he had never yet killed one of the English. I told him he might go to war, and that would be more manly than to kill a poor captive who was doing their drudgery for them. Notwithstanding all I could say, he began to cut and stab me on my breast. I seized him by the hair, and tumbling him off of me, followed him with my fists and knee with such application that he soon cried "enough." But when I saw the blood run from my bosom, and felt the smart of the wounds he had given me, I at him again, and bid him get up, and not lie there like a dog; told him of his former abuses offered to me, and other poor captives, and that if ever he offered the like to me again, I would pay him

8*

double. I sent him before me, and taking up my burden of
wood, came to the Indians, and told them the whole truth,
and they commended me. And I do not remember that ever
he offered me the least abuse afterwards, though he was big
enough to have despatched two of me.

CHAPTER IV.—*Of remarkable events of Providence in the
deaths of several barbarous Indians.* The priest of this river
was of the order of St. Francis, a gentleman of a humane,
generous disposition. In his sermons he most severely repre-
hended the Indians for their barbarities to captives. He would
often tell them that, excepting their errors in religion, the English were a better people than themselves, and that God would
remarkably punish such cruel wretches, and had begun to execute his vengeance upon such already ! He gave an account
of the retaliations of Providence upon those murderous Cape
Sable Indians above mentioned; one of whom got a splinter
into his foot, which festered and rotted his flesh till it killed
him. Another run a fish-bone into her hand or arm, and she
rotted to death, notwithstanding all means that were used to
prevent it. In some such manner they all died, so that not
one of those two families lived to return home.* Were it not
for these remarks of the priest, I had not, perhaps, have noticed
these providences.

There was an old squaw who ever endeavored to outdo all
others in cruelty to captives. Wherever she came into a wigwam, where any poor, naked, starved captives were sitting
near the fire, if they were grown persons, she would stealthily
take up a shovel of hot coals, and throw them into their bosoms. If they were young persons, she would seize them by
the hand or leg, drag them through the fire, &c. The Indians
with whom she lived, according to their custom, left their village in the fall of the year, and dispersed themselves for hunting. After the first or second removal, they all strangely forgot
that old squaw and her grandson, about twelve years of age.
They were found dead in the place where they were left some
months afterwards, and no farther notice was taken of them
by their friends. Of this the priest made special remark, for-
asmuch as it is a thing very uncommon for them to neglect
either their old or young people.

In the latter part of summer, or beginning of autumn, the
Indians were frequently frightened by the appearance of

* Reference is probably had to those Indians, of whom the author has
before spoken, as having come to the fort of those with whom he was
among, to be revenged on any whites for the loss of some of their friends
who had been killed by white fishermen.—Ed.

strange Indians, passing up and down this river in canoes, and about that time the next year died more than one hundred persons, old and young ; all, or most of those who saw those strange Indians ! The priest said it was a sort of plague. A person seeming in perfect health would bleed at the mouth and nose, turn blue in spots, and die in two or three hours.* It was very tedious to me to remove from place to place this cold season. The Indians applied red ochre to my sores, [which had been occasioned by the affray before mentioned,] which by God's blessing cured me. This sickness being at the worst as winter came on, the Indians all scattered ; and the blow was so great to them, that they did not settle or plant at their village while I was on the river, [St. Johns,] and I know not whether they have to this day. Before they thus deserted the village, when they came in from hunting, they would be drunk and fight for several days and nights together, till they had spent most of their skins in wine and brandy, which was brought to the village by a Frenchman called Monsieur *Sigenioncour*.

CHAPTER V.—*Of their familiarity with and frights from the devil,* &c. The Indians are very often surprised with the appearance of ghosts and demons. Sometimes they are encouraged by the devil, for they go to him for success in hunting, &c. I was once hunting with Indians who were not brought over to the Romish faith, and after several days they proposed to inquire, according to their custom, what success they should have. They accordingly prepared many hot stones, and laying them in a heap, made a small hut covered with skins and mats ; then in a dark night two of the powwows went into this hot house with a large vessel of water, which at times they poured on those hot rocks, which raised a thick steam, so that a third Indian was obliged to stand without, and lift up a mat, to give it vent when they were almost suffocated. There was an old squaw who was kind to captives, and never joined with them in their powwowing, to whom I manifested an earnest desire to see their management. She told me that if they knew of my being there they would kill me, and that when she was a girl she had known young persons to be taken away by a hairy man, and therefore she would not advise me to go, lest the hairy man should carry me away. I told

---

* Calamitous mortalities are often mentioned as happening among the Indians, but that the appearance of strange Indians had any thing to do with it, will only excite admiration to the enlightened of this age. It was by a mortality something similar that the country about the coast of Massachusetts was nearly depopulated two or three years before the settlement of Plymouth.—Ed.

her I was not afraid of the hairy man, nor could he hurt me if she would not discover me to the powwows. At length she promised me she would not, but charged me to be careful of myself. I went within three or four feet of the hot house, for it was very dark, and heard strange noises and yellings, such as I never heard before. At times the Indian who tended without would lift up the mat, and a steam would issue which looked like fire. I lay there two or three hours, but saw none of their hairy men, or demons. And when I found they had finished their ceremony, I went to the wigwam, and told the squaw what had passed. She was glad I had escaped without hurt, and never discovered what I had done. After some time inquiry was made of the powwows what success we were likely to have in our hunting. They said they had very likely signs of success, but no real ones as at other times. A few days after we moved up the river, and had pretty good luck.

One afternoon as I was in a canoe with one of the powwows the dog barked, and presently a moose passed by within a few rods of us, so that the waves he made by wading rolled our canoe. The Indian shot at him, but the moose took very little notice of it, and went into the woods to the southward. The fellow said, "I will try if I can't fetch you back for all your haste." The evening following, we built our two wigwams on a sandy point on the upper end of an island in the river, north-west of the place where the moose went into the woods ; and here the Indian powwowed the greatest part of the night following. In the morning we had a fair track of a moose round our wigwams, though we did not see or taste of it. I am of opinion that the devil was permitted to humor those unhappy wretches sometimes, in some things.*

That it may appear how much they were deluded, or under the influence of satan, read the two stories which were related and believed by the Indians. The first, of a boy who was carried away by a large bird called a *Gulloua*, who buildeth her nest on a high rock or mountain. A boy was hunting with his bow and arrow at the foot of a rocky mountain, when the gulloua came diving through the air, grasped the boy in her talons, and although he was eight or ten years of age, she soared aloft and laid him in her nest, food for her young.

---

* Whatever the Indians might have believed about the devil, one thing is pretty clear, that our captive had great faith in his abilities. Quite as easy a way to have accounted for moose tracks about their wigwam, would have been to suppose that that animal might have been attracted by the uncouth noise of the powwow to approach them for the object of discovery. It is very common for wild animals to do so.—Ed.

The boy lay still on his face, but observed two of the young birds in the nest with him, having much fish and flesh to feed upon. The old one seeing they would not eat the boy, took him up in her claws and returned him to the place from whence she took him. I have passed near the mountain in a canoe, and the Indians have said, " There is the nest of the great bird that carried away the boy." Indeed there seemed to be a great number of sticks put together like a nest on the top of the mountain. At another time they said, " There is the bird, but he is now as a boy to a giant to what he was in former days." The bird which we saw was a large and speckled one, like an eagle, though somewhat larger.*

> When from the mountain tops, with hideous cry
> And clattering wings, the hungry harpies fly,
> They snatched   *   *   *   *
> *   *   And whether gods or birds obscene they were,
> Our vows for pardon and for peace prefer.
>
> DRYDEN'S VIRGIL.

The other notion is, that a young Indian in his hunting was belated, and losing his way, was on a sudden introduced to a large wigwam full of dried eels, which proved to be a beaver's house, in which he lived till the spring of the year, when he was turned out of the house, and being set upon a beaver's dam, went home and related the affair to his friends at large.

CHAPTER VI.—*A description of several creatures commonly taken by the Indians on St. John's river.*

I. OF THE BEAVER.—The beaver has a very thick, strong neck ; his fore teeth, which are two in the upper and two in the under jaw, are concave and sharp like a carpenter's gouge. Their side teeth are like a sheep's, for they chew the cud. Their legs are short, the claws something longer than in other creatures. The nails on the toes of their hind feet are flat like an ape's, but joined together by a membrane, as those of the water-fowl, their tails broad and flat like the broad end of a paddle. Near their tails they have four bottles, two of which contain oil, the others gum ; the necks of these meet in one common orifice. The latter of these bottles contain the proper castorum, and not the testicles, as some have fancied, for they are distinct and separate from them, in the males only ;

---

* Not exactly a *fish story*, but it is certainly a *bird story*, and although Mr. Gyles has fortified himself behind " believed by the Indians," yet I fear his reputation for credulity will be somewhat enhanced in the mind of the reader. I think, however, it should not derogate from his character for veracity

whereas the castorum and oil bottles are common to male and female. With this oil and gum they preen themselves, so that when they come out of the water it runs off of them, as it does from a fowl. They have four teats, which are on their breasts, so that they hug up their young and suckle them, as women do their infants. They have generally two, and sometimes four in a litter. I have seen seven or five in the matrix, but the Indians think it a strange thing to find so many in a litter; and they assert that when it so happens the dam kills all but four. They are the most laborious creatures that I have met with. I have known them to build dams across a river, thirty or forty perches wide, with wood and mud, so as to flow many acres of land. In the deepest part of a pond so raised, they build their houses, round, in the figure of an Indian wigwam, eight or ten feet high, and six or eight in diameter on the floor, which is made descending to the water, the parts near the centre about four, and near the circumference between ten and twenty inches above the water. These floors are covered with strippings of wood, like shavings. On these they sleep with their tails in the water;* and if the freshets rise, they have the advantage of rising on their floor to the highest part. They feed on the leaves and bark of trees, and pond lily roots. In the fall of the year they lay in their provision for the approaching winter; cutting down trees great and small. With one end in their mouths they drag their branches near to their house, and sink many cords of it. (They will cut [gnaw] down trees of a fathom in circumference.) They have doors to go down to the wood under the ice. And in case the freshets rise, break down and carry off their store of wood, they often starve. They have a note for conversing, calling and warning each other when at work or feeding; and while they are at labor they keep out a guard, who upon the first approach of an enemy so strikes the water with his tail that he may be heard half a mile. This so alarms the rest that they are all silent, quit their labor, and are to be seen no more for that time. If the male or female die, the survivor seeks a mate, and conducts him or her to their house, and carry on affairs as above.

II. OF THE WOLVERENE. [*Gulo Luscus* of L.] The wolverene is a very fierce and mischievous creature, about the bigness of a middling dog; having short legs, broad feet and

---

* I recollect to have seen a similar statement by that singular genius, THOMAS MORTON, of Mare Mount, in his more singular book, NEW ENGLISH CANAAN, about beavers keeping their tails in the water. Morton, however, tells us the reason they do so, viz. "*which else would overheat and rot off.*"—Ed.

very sharp claws, and in my opinion may be reckoned a species of cat. They will climb trees and wait for moose and other animals which feed below, and when opportunity presents, jump upon and strike their claws in them so fast that they will hang on them till they have gnawed the main nerve in their neck asunder, which causes their death. I have known many moose killed thus. I was once travelling a little way behind several Indians, and hearing them laugh merrily, when I came up I asked them the cause of their laughter. They showed me the track of a moose, and how a wolverene had climbed a tree, and where he had jumped off upon a moose. It so happened, that after the moose had taken several large leaps, it came under the branch of a tree, which striking the wolverene, broke his hold and tore him off; and by his tracks in the snow it appeared he went off another way, with short steps, as if he had been stunned by the blow that had broken his hold. The Indians imputed the accident to the cunning of the moose, and were wonderfully pleased that it had thus outwitted the mischievous wolverene.

These wolverenes go into wigwams which have been left for a time, scatter the things abroad, and most filthily pollute them with ordure. I have heard the Indians say that this animal has sometimes pulled their guns from under their heads while they were asleep, and left them so defiled. An Indian told me that having left his wigwam with sundry things on the scaffold, among which was a birchen flask containing several pounds of powder, he found at his return, much to his surprise and grief, that a wolverene had visited it, mounted the scaffold, hove down bag and baggage. The powder flask happening to fall into the fire, exploded, blowing up the wolverene, and scattering the wigwam in all directions. At length he found the creature, blind from the blast, wandering backward and forward, and he had the satisfaction of kicking and beating him about! This in a great measure made up their loss, and then they could contentedly pick up their utensils and rig out their wigwam.

III.˙ OF THE HEDGEHOG, [*Histrix Dorsata*,] or URCHIN, [*Urson?*] Our hedgehog or urchin is about the bigness of a hog of six months old. His back, sides and tail are full of sharp quills, so that if any creature approach him, he will contract himself into a globular form, and when touched by his enemy, his quills are so sharp and loose in the skin they fix in the mouth of the adversary. They will strike with great force with their tails, so that whatever falls under the lash of them are certainly filled with their prickles; but that they shoot their quills, as some assert they do, is a great mistake, as respects the American hedgehog, and I believe as to the African hedgehog or porcupine, also. As to the former, I have taken them at all seasons of the year.

IV. OF THE TORTOISE. It is needless to describe the fresh-water tortoise, whose form is so well known in all parts; but their manner of propagating their species is not so universally known. I have observed that sort of tortoise whose shell is about fourteen or sixteen inches wide. In their coition they may be heard half a mile, making a noise like a woman washing her linen with a batting staff. They lay their eggs in the sand, near some deep, still water, about a foot beneath the surface of the sand, with which they are very curious in covering them; so that there is not the least mixture of it amongst them, nor the least rising of sand on the beach where they are deposited. I have often searched for them with the Indians, by thrusting a stick into the sand at random, and brought up some part of an egg clinging to it; when, uncovering the place, we have found near one hundred and fifty in one nest. Both their eggs and flesh are good eating when boiled. I have observed a difference as to the length of time in which they are hatching, which is between twenty and thirty days; some sooner than others. Whether this difference ought to be imputed to the various quality or site of the sand in which they are laid, (as to the degree of cold or heat,) I leave to the conjecture of the virtuosi. As soon as they are hatched, the young tortoise breaks through the sand and betake themselves to the water, and, as far as I could discover, without any further care or help of the old ones.

CHAPTER VII.—*Of their feasting.* 1. *Before they go to war.* When the Indians determine on war, or are entering upon a particular expedition, they kill a number of their dogs, burn off their hair and cut them to pieces, leaving only one dog's head whole. The rest of the flesh they boil, and make a fine feast of it. Then the dog's head that was left whole is scorched, till the nose and lips have shrunk from the teeth, leaving them bare and grinning. This done, they fasten it on a stick, and the Indian who is proposed to be chief in the expedition takes the head into his hand, and sings a warlike song, in which he mentions the town they design to attack, and the principal man in it; threatening that in a few days he will carry that man's head and scalp in his hand, in the same manner. When the chief has finished singing, he so places the dog's head as to grin at him who he supposes will go his second, who, if he accepts, takes the head in his hand and sings; but if he refuses to go, he turns the teeth to another;

and thus from one to another till they have enlisted their company.

The Indians imagine that dog's flesh makes them bold and courageous. I have seen an Indian split a dog's head with a hatchet, take out the brains hot, and eat them raw with the blood running down his jaws !

2. *When a relation dies.* In a still evening, a squaw will walk on the highest land near her abode, and with a loud and mournful voice will exclaim, " *Oh hawe, hawe, hawe,*" with a long, mournful tone to each *hawe*, for a long time together. After the mourning season is over, the relations of the deceased make a feast to wipe off tears, and the bereaved may marry freely. If the deceased was a squaw, the relations consult together, and choose a squaw, (doubtless a widow,) and send her to the widower, and if he likes her he takes her to be his wife, if not, he sends her back, and the relations choose and send till they find one that he approves of.

If a young fellow determines to marry, his relations and the Jesuit advise him to a girl. He goes into the wigwam where she is, and looks on her. If he likes her appearance, he tosses a chip or stick into her lap, which she takes, and with a reserved, side look, views the person who sent it; yet handles the chip with admiration, as though she wondered from whence it came. If she likes him she throws the chip to him with a modest smile, and then nothing is wanting but a ceremony with the Jesuit to consummate the marriage. But if she dislikes her suitor, she, with a surly countenance, throws the chip aside, and he comes no more there.

If parents have a daughter marriageable they seek a husband for her who is a good hunter. If she has been educated to make *monoodah,* (Indian bags,) birch dishes, to lace snow-shoes, make Indian shoes, string wampum belts, sew birch canoes, and boil the kettle, she is esteemed a lady of fine accomplishments. If the man sought out for her husband have a gun and ammunition, a canoe, spear, and hatchet, a monoodah, a crooked knife, looking-glass and paint, a pipe, tobacco, and knot-bowl to toss a kind of dice in, he is accounted a gentleman of a plentiful fortune. Whatever the new-married man procures the first year belongs to his wife's parents. If the young pair have a child within a year and nine months, they are thought to be very forward and libidinous persons.

By their play with dice they lose much time, playing whole days and nights together; sometimes staking their whole effects; though this is accounted a great vice by the old men.

A digression.—There is an old story told among the Indians of a family who had a daughter that was accounted a finished

9

beauty, having been adorned with the precious jewel, an Indian education! She was so formed by nature, and polished by art, that they could not find for her a suitable consort. At length, while this family were once residing upon the head of Penobscot river, under the White hills, called *Teddon*, this fine creature was missing, and her parents could learn no tidings of her. After much time and pains spent, and tears showered in quest of her, they saw her diverting herself with a beautiful youth, whose hair, like her own, flowed down below his waist, swimming, washing, &c., in the water; but they vanished upon their approach. This beautiful person, whom they imagined to be one of those kind spirits who inhabit the Teddon, they looked upon as their son-in-law; and, according to their custom, they called upon him for moose, bear, or whatever creature they desired, and if they did but go to the water-side and signify their desire, the animal would come swimming to them! I have heard an Indian say that he lived by the river, at the foot of the Teddon, the top of which he could see through the hole of his wigwam left for the smoke to pass out. He was tempted to travel to it, and accordingly set out on a summer morning, and labored hard in ascending the hill all day, and the top seemed as distant from the place where he lodged at night as from his wigwam, where he began his journey. He now concluded the spirits were there, and never dared to make a second attempt.

I have been credibly informed that several others have failed in like attempts. Once three young men climbed towards its summit three days and a half, at the end of which time they became strangely disordered with delirium, &c., and when their imagination was clear, and they could recollect where they were, they found themselves returned one day's journey. How they came to be thus transported they could not conjecture, unless the genii of the place had conveyed them. These White hills, at the head of Penobscot river, are, by the Indians, said to be much higher than those called Agiockochook, above Saco.[*]

But to return to an Indian feast, of which you may request a bill of fare before you go. If you dislike it, stay at home. The ingredients are fish, flesh, or Indian corn, and beans boiled together; sometimes hasty pudding made of pounded corn, whenever and as often as these are plenty. An Indian boils four or five large kettles full, and sends a messenger to each wigwam door, who exclaims, "*Kuh menscoorebah!*" that is, "I come to conduct you to a feast." The man within demands

---

[*] Some additions to these traditions will be found in the *Book of the Indians* iij. 131.—Ed.

whether he must take a spoon or a knife in his dish, which he always carries with him. They appoint two or three young men to mess it out, to each man his portion, according to the number of his family at home. This is done with the utmost exactness. When they have done eating, a young fellow stands without the door, and cries aloud, "*Mensecommook*," "come and fetch!" Immediately each squaw goes to her husband and takes what he has left, which she carries home and eats with her children. For neither married women, nor any youth under twenty, are allowed to be present; but old widow squaws and captive men may sit by the door. The Indian men continue in the wigwam; some relating their warlike exploits, others something comical, others narrating their hunting exploits. The seniors give maxims of prudence and grave counsel to the young men; and though every one's speech be agreeable to the run of his own fancy, yet they confine themselves to rule, and but one speaks at a time. After every man has told his story, one rises up, sings a feast song, and others succeed alternately as the company sees fit.

Necessity is the mother of invention. If an Indian loses his fire, he can presently take two sticks, one harder than the other, (the drier the better,) and in the softest one make a hollow, or socket, in which one end of the hardest stick being inserted, then holding the softest piece firm between his knees, whirls it round like a drill, and fire will kindle in a few minutes.

If they have lost or left their kettle, it is but putting their victuals into a birch dish, leaving a vacancy in the middle, filling it with water, and putting in hot stones alternately; they will thus thoroughly boil the toughest neck of beef.

CHAPTER VIII.—*Of my three years captivity with the French.*—When about six years of my doleful captivity had passed, my second Indian master died, whose squaw and my first Indian master disputed whose slave I should be. Some malicious persons advised them to end the quarrel by putting a period to my life; but honest father Simon, the priest of the river, told them that it would be a heinous crime, and advised them to sell me to the French. There came annually one or two men of war to supply the fort, which was on the river about 34 leagues from the sea. The Indians having advice of the arrival of a man of war at the mouth of the river, they, about thirty or forty in number, went on board; for the gentlemen from France made a present to them every year, and set forth the riches and victories of their monarch, &c. At this time they presented the Indians with a bag or two of flour with some prunes, as ingredients for a feast. I, who was dressed up in an old greasy blanket, without cap, hat, or shirt, (for I had had no shirt for the six years, except the one I had on at the time I was made prisoner,) was invited into the great cabin, where many well-rigged gentlemen were sitting, who would fain have had a full view of me. I endeavored to hide myself behind the hangings, for I was much ashamed; thinking how I had once worn clothes, and of my living with people who could rig as well as the best of them. My master asked me whether I chose to be sold to the people of the man of war, or to the inhabitants of the country. I replied, with tears, that I should be glad if he would sell me to the English from whom I was taken; but that if I must be sold to the French, I wished to be sold to the lowest inhabitants on the river, or those nearest to the sea, who were about twenty-five leagues from the mouth of the river; for I thought that, if I were sold to the gentlemen in the ship, I should never return to the English. This was the first time I had seen the sea during my captivity, and the first time I had tasted salt or bread.

My master presently went on shore, and a few days after all the Indians went up the river. When we came to a house which I had spoken to my master about, he went on shore with me, and tarried all night. The master of the house spoke kindly to me in Indian, for I could not then speak one word of French. Madam also looked pleasant on me, and gave me some bread. The next day I was sent six leagues further up the river to another French house. My master and the friar tarried with Monsieur Dechouffour, the gentleman who had entertained us the night before. Not long after, father Simon came and said, " Now you are one of us, for you are sold to that gentleman by whom you were entertained the other night. I replied, " Sold!—to a Frenchman!" I could say no more, went into the woods alone, and wept till I could scarce see or stand! The word *sold*, and that to a people of that persuasion which my dear mother so much detested, and in her last words manifested so great fears of my falling into! These thoughts almost broke my heart.

When I had thus given vent to my grief I wiped my eyes, endeavoring to conceal its effects, but father Simon, perceiving my eyes were swollen, called me aside, and bidding me not to grieve, for the gentleman, he said, to whom I was sold, was of a good humor; that he had formerly bought two captives, both of whom had been sent to Boston. This, in some measure, revived me; but he added he did not suppose I would ever wish to go to the English, for the French religion was so much better. He said, also, he should pass that way in about ten days, and if I did not like to live with the French better than with the Indians he would buy me again. On the day following, father Simon and my Indian master went up the river, six and thirty leagues, to their chief village, and I went down the river six leagues with two Frenchmen to my new master. He kindly received me, and in a few days madam made me an osnaburg shirt and French cap, and a coat out of one of my master's old coats. Then I threw away my greasy blanket and Indian flap, and looked as smart as —. And I never more saw the old friar, the Indian village, or my Indian master, till about fourteen years after, when I saw my old Indian master at Port Royal, whither I had been sent by the government with a flag of truce for the exchange of prisoners; and again, about twenty-four years since, he came to St. John's, to fort George, to see me, where I made him very welcome.

My French master held a great trade with the Indians, which suited me very well, I being thorough in the languages of the tribes at Cape Sable and St. Johns.

I had not lived long with this gentleman before he committed to me the keys of his store, &c., and my whole employment was trading and hunting, in which I acted faithfully for my master, and never, knowingly, wronged him to the value of one farthing.

They spoke to me so much in Indian that it was some time before I was perfect in the French tongue. Monsieur generally had his goods from the men-of-war which came there annually from France.

In the year 1696, two men-of-war came to the mouth of the river. In their way they had captured the Newport, Captain Payson, and brought him with them. They made the Indians some presents, and invited them to join in an expedition to Pemmaquid. They accepted it, and soon after arrived there. Capt. Chubb, who commanded that post, delivered it up without much dispute to Monsieur D'Iberville, as I heard the gentleman say, with whom I lived, who was there present.*

Early in the spring I was sent with three Frenchmen to the mouth of the river, for provision, which came from Port Royal. We carried over land from the river to a large bay, where we were driven on an island by a north-east storm, where we were kept seven days, without any sustenance, for we expected a quick passage, and carried nothing with us. The wind con-

---

* The reverend Dr. Mather says, wittily, as he says everything, " This Chubb found opportunity, in a pretty *Chubbish* manner, to kill the famous Edgeremet and Abenquid, a couple of principal Indians, on a Lord's day, the 16th of February, 1695. If there is any unfair dealing in this action

tinuing boisterous, we could not return back, and the ice prevented our going forward.   After seven days the ice broke up
and we went forward, though we were so weak that we could
scarce hear each other speak.   The people at the mouth of the
river were surprised to see us alive, and advised us to be cautious and abstemious in eating.   By this time I knew as much
of fasting as they, and dieted on broth, and recovered very well,
as did one of the others; but the other two would not be
advised, and I never saw any persons in greater distress, till
at length they had action of the bowels, when they recovered.

A friar, who lived in the family, invited me to confession,
but I excused myself as well as I could at that time.   One
evening he took me into his apartment in the dark and advised
me to confess to him what sins I had committed.   I told him I
could not remember a thousandth part of them, they were so
numerous.   Then he bid me remember and relate as many as
I could, and he would pardon them; signifying he had a bag
to put them in.   I told him I did not believe it was in the
power of any but God to pardon sin.   He asked me whether I
had read the Bible.   I told him I had, when I was a little boy,
but it was so long ago I had forgotten most of it.   Then he
told me he did not pardon my sins, but when he knew them he
prayed to God to pardon them; when, perhaps, I was at my
sports and plays.   He wished me well and hoped I should be
better advised, and said he should call for me in a little time.
Thus he dismissed me, nor did he ever call me to confession
afterwards.

The gentleman with whom I lived had a fine field of wheat,
in which great numbers of black-birds continually collected and
made great havoc in it.   The French said a Jesuit would come
and banish them.   He did at length come, and having all
things prepared, he took a basin of holy water, a staff with a
little brush, and having on his white robe, went into the field
of wheat.   I asked several prisoners who had lately been taken
by privateers, and brought in there, viz. Mr. Woodbury, Cocks
[Cox ?] and Morgan, whether they would go and see the ceremony.   Mr. Woodbury asked me whether I designed to go,

of Chubb, there will be another February, not far off, wherein the avenger
of blood will take satisfaction."—Hist. N. E. [Magnalia] B. vii. 79.

Mr. Mather adds, " On the 4th or 5th of August, Chubb, with an uncommon baseness, did surrender the brave fort of Pemmaquid into their
hands."   [For an account of the wretched fate of Chubb as well as that
of the whole transaction, see Book of the Indians, B. iii. 121, 122.]

> Unthinking men no sort of scruples make,
> And some are bad only for mischief's sake,
> But ev'n the best are guilty by mistake.

and I told him yes. He then said I was as bad as a papist, and a d—d fool. I told him I believed as little of it as he did, but that I was inclined to see the ceremony, that I might tell it to my friends.

With about thirty following in procession, the Jesuit marched through the field of wheat, a young lad going before him bearing the holy water. Then the Jesuit, dipping his brush into the holy water, sprinkled the field on each side of him; a little bell jingling at the same time, and all singing the words *Ora pro nobis.* At the end of the field they wheeled to the left about, and returned. Thus they passed and repassed the field of wheat, the black-birds all the while rising before them only to light behind. At their return I told a French lad that the friar had done no service, and recommended them to shoot the birds. The lad left me, as I thought, to see what the Jesuit would say to my observation, which turned out to be the case, for he told the lad that the sins of the people were so great that he could not prevail against those birds. The same friar as vainly attempted to banish the musketoes from Signecto, but the sins of the people there were also too great for him to prevail; but on the other hand, it seemed that more came, which caused the people to suspect that some had come for the sins of the Jesuit also.

Some time after, Col. Hawthorne attempted the taking of the French fort up this river. We heard of him some time before he came up, by the guard which Governor Villebon had stationed at the river's mouth. Monsieur, my master, had gone to France, and madam, his wife, advised with me. She desired me to nail a paper on the door of her house, which paper read as follows:

"I entreat the general of the English not to burn my house or barn, nor destroy my cattle. I don't suppose that such an army comes here to destroy a few inhabitants, but to take the fort above us. I have shown kindness to the English captives, as we were capacitated, and have bought two, of the Indians, and sent them to Boston. We have one now with us, and he shall go also when a convenient opportunity presents, and he desires it."

When I had done this, madam said to me, "Little English," [which was the familiar name she used to call me by,] "we have shown you kindness, and now it lies in your power to serve or disserve us, as you know where our goods are hid in the woods, and that monsieur is not at home. I could have sent you to the fort and put you under confinement, but my respect to you and your assurance of love to us have disposed me to confide in you; persuaded you will not hurt us or our affairs. And, now, if you will not run away to the English, who are coming up the river, but serve our interest, I will acquaint monsieur of it on his return from France, which will be very pleasing to him ; and I now give my word, you shall have liberty to go to Boston on the first opportunity, if you desire it, or any other favor in my power shall not be denied you." I replied :

" Madam, it is contrary to the nature of the English to requite evil for good. I shall endeavor to serve you and your interest. I shall not run to the English, but if I am taken by them I shall willingly go with them, and yet endeavor not to disserve you either in your person or goods."

The place where we lived was called Hagimsack, twenty-five leagues from the river's mouth, as I have before stated.

We now embarked and went in a large boat and canoe two or three miles up an eastern branch of the river that comes from a large pond, and on the following evening sent down four hands to make discovery. And while they were sitting in the house the English surrounded it and took one of the four. The other three made their escape in the dark and through the English soldiers, and coming to us, gave a surprising account of affairs. Upon this news madam said to me, " Little English, now you can go from us, but I hope you will remember your word." I said, " Madam, be not concerned. I will not leave you in this strait." She said, " I know not what to do with my two poor little babes !" I said, " Madam, the sooner we embark and go over the great pond the better." Accordingly we embarked and went over the pond. The next day we spoke with Indians, who were in a canoe, and they gave us an account that Signecto town was taken and burnt. Soon after we heard the great guns at Gov. Villebon's fort, which the English engaged several days. They killed one man, then drew off down the river ; fearing to continue longer, for fear of being frozen in for the winter, which in truth they would have been.

Hearing no report of cannon for several days, I, with two others, went down to our house to make discovery. We found our young lad who was taken by the English when they went up the river. The general had shown himself so honorable, that on reading the note on our door, he ordered it not to be burnt, nor the barn. Our cattle and other things he preserved, except one or two and the poultry for their use. At their return they ordered the young lad to be put on shore. Finding things in this posture, we returned and gave madam an account of it.

She acknowledged the many favors which the English had

showed her, with gratitude, and treated me with great civility. The next spring monsieur arrived from France in the man-of-war. He thanked me for my care of his affairs, and said he would endeavor to fulfil what madam had promised me.

Accordingly, in the year 1698, peace being proclaimed, a sloop came to the mouth of the river with ransom for one Michael Cooms. I put monsieur in mind of his word, telling him there was now an opportunity for me to go and see the English. He advised me to continue with him; said he would do for me as for his own, &c. I thanked him for his kindness, but rather chose to go to Boston, hoping to find some of my relations yet alive. Then he advised me to go up to the fort and take my leave of the governor, which I did, and he spoke very kindly to me. Some days after I took my leave of madam, and monsieur went down to the mouth of the river with me, to see me safely on board. He asked the master, Mr. Starkee, a Scotchman, whether I must pay for my passage, and if so, he would pay it himself rather than I should have it to pay at my arrival in Boston, but he gave me not a penny. The master told him there was nothing to pay, and that if the owner should make any demand he would pay it himself, rather than a poor prisoner should suffer; for he was glad to see any English person come out of captivity.

On the 13th of June, I took my leave of monsieur, and the sloop came to sail for Boston, where we arrived on the 19th of the same, at night. In the morning after my arrival, a youth came on board and asked many questions relating to my captivity, and at length gave me to understand that he was my little brother, who was at play with some other children at Pemmaquid when I was taken captive, and who escaped into the fort at that perilous time. He told me my elder brother, who made his escape from the farm, when it was taken, and our two little sisters, were alive, but that our mother had been dead some years. Then we went on shore and saw our elder brother.

On the 2d of August, 1689, I was taken, and on the 19th of June, 1698, I arrived at Boston; so that I was absent eight years, ten months, and seventeen days. In all which time, though I underwent extreme difficulties, yet I saw much of God's goodness. And may the most powerful and beneficent Being accept of this public testimony of it, and bless my experiences to excite others to confide in his all-sufficiency, through the infinite merits of JESUS CHRIST.

APPENDIX, *containing minutes of the employments, public stations, etc., of* JOHN GYLES, *Esq., commander of the garrison on St. George's river.*

After my return out of captivity, June 28th, 1698, I applied myself to the government for their favor. Soon after I was employed by old father Mitchel, of Malden, to go as his interpreter on trading account to St. John's river.

October 14th, 1698, I was employed by the government, Lieutenant Governor Stoughton commander-in-chief, to go as interpreter, at three pounds per month, with Major Converse and old Capt. Alden to Penobscot to fetch captives. At our return to Boston I was dismissed; but within a few days the governor sent for me to interpret a conference with Bommazeen, and other Indians then in jail.

Some time after I was again put in pay in order to go interpreter with Col. Phillips and Capt. Southack, in the province galley, to Casco bay, to exchange said Indians [Bommazeen and others] for English captives. In December, 1698, we returned to Boston with several captives which we had liberated, and I was dismissed the service, and desired to attend it in the spring. I pleaded to be kept in pay that I might have wherewith to support myself at school. I went into the country, to Rowley, where boarding was cheap, to practise what little I had attained at school.

March, 1699. With the little of my wages that I could reserve, I paid for my schooling and board, and attended the service upon request, and was again put into pay, and went with Col. Phillips and Maj. Converse in a large brigantine up Kennebeck river for captives, and at our return to Boston the province galley being arrived from New York with my lord Bellemont, and the province truck put on board, I was ordered on board the galley. We cruised on the eastern shore; and in November, 1699, I was put out of pay, though I pleaded to be continued in it, seeing I must attend the service in the spring, and be at considerable expense in the winter for my schooling.

In the spring of 1700, I attended the service, and was under pay again. On August 27th, a fort was ordered to be built at Casco bay, which was finished on the 6th of October following, and the province truck landed, and I was ordered to reside there as interpreter, with a captain, &c. Not long after, Gov. Dudley sent me a lieutenant's commission, with a memorandum on its back, " No further pay but as interpreter at three pounds per month."

August 10th, 1703. The French and Indians besieged our fort for six days. (Major March was our commander.) On the 16th of the same month, Capt. Southack arrived in the province galley, and in the night following the enemy withdrew.

May 19th, 1704. I received a few lines from his excellency directing me to leave my post, and accompany Col. Church on an expedition round the bay of Fundy.* September following I returned to my post, without any further wages or encouragement for that service than the beforementioned pay at the garrison.

April, 1706. There was a change of the chief officer at our garrison. I chose to be dismissed with my old officer, which was granted. The same year his excellency Gov. Dudley presented me with a captain's commission, and ordered Colonel Saltonstall to detach fifty effective men to be delivered to me in order for a march. In May, 1707, I entered on an expedition under Col. March, for Port Royal, at the termination of which I was dismissed.

May 12th, 1708, I received orders from his excellency to go to Port Royal with a flag of truce to exchange prisoners, and brought off all. At my return I was dismissed the service.

In 1709, I received a commission, and Colonel Noyes had orders to detach forty men, whom he put under me, with orders to join the forces for Canada. At Hull, August 1st, 1709, I received orders from his excellency to leave my company with my lieutenants, and go to Port Royal with a flag of truce to exchange prisoners. I went in the sloop Hannah and Ruth, Thomas Waters, master. I had nine French prisoners, which were all that were in our governor's hands. These he ordered me to deliver to Gov. Supercass, "and to let him know that he [Gov. Dudley] expected him to deliver all the English prisoners within his power, within six days, which I was ordered to demand and insist upon, agreeably to his promise last year." I was ordered to observe to him that Governor Dudley highly resented his breach of promise in not sending them early this spring, according to his parole of honor, by myself, when we had returned him upwards of forty of his people, and had made provision for bringing home ours; and to make particular inquiry after Capt. Myles, and to demand his and his company's release also.

Accordingly, arriving at Port Royal, I was kindly entertained by Gov. Supercass; brought off above one hundred prisoners. Soon after my return our forces were dismissed, and I received

* A full account of this expedition under Col. Church will be found in Church's History of King Philip's War, &c. ed. 12mo., Boston, 1827, by the editor of this.

no other consideration for my service than pay as captain of my company.

August, 1715. I was desired, and had great promises made me by the proprietors, and received orders from his excellency to build a fort at Pejepscot, [now Brunswick, Me.] Soon after our arrival there the Indians came in the night, and forbid our laying one stone upon another. I told them I came with orders from Governor Dudley to build a fort, and if they disliked it they might acquaint him with it; and that if they came forcibly upon us, they or I should fall on the spot. After such like hot words they left us, and we went on with our building, and finished it, November 25th, 1715, and our carpenters and masons left us. My wages were very small, yet the gentlemen proprietors ordered me only five pounds for my good services, &c.

July 12th, 1722, a number of Indians engaged fort George about two hours, killing one person, and then drew off to killing cattle, &c.

April, 1725, I received orders from his honor Lieut. Gov. Dummer to go ten days' march up Ammiscoggin river, and in my absence the Indians killed two men at our fort. I received no further pay for said service, only the pay of the garrison.

December 12th, 1725, I was dismissed from fort George, and Capt. Woodside received a commission for the command of that place.

December 13th, 1725, I was commissioned for the garrison at St. George river.

September, 1726. I was detained some months from my post, by order of Gov. Dummer, to interpret for the Cape Sable Indians, who were brought in and found guilty.* There was no other person in the province that had their language. His honor and the honorable council presented me with ten pounds for this service, which I gratefully received.

Nov. 28th, 1728, I was commissioned for the peace.

I have had the honor to serve this province under eight commanders in chief, governors, and lieutenant governors, from the year 1698 to the year 1736; and how much longer my services may continue I submit to the Governor of the world, who overrules every circumstance of life, which relates to our happiness and usefulness, as in infinite wisdom he sees meet.

---

* There were five of them belonging to the St. Francis tribe. They had seized on a vessel at Newfoundland belonging to Plymouth. The act being considered piracy, they were all executed at Boston.—(Ed.) *MS. Chronicles of the Indians.*

Be calm, my Delius, and serene,
However fortune change the scene.
In thy most dejected state,
Sink not underneath the weight;
Nor yet when happy days begin,
And the full tide comes rolling in,
Let not a fierce unruly joy
The settled quiet of thy mind destroy.
However fortune change the scene,
Be calm, my Delius, and serene.—HORACE.

THREE NARRATIVES

OF EXCESSIVE DISTRESS OF PERSONS TAKEN AT THE DE-
STRUCTION OF SALMON FALLS, IN THE STATE OF NEW
HAMPSHIRE, ON THE TWENTY-SEVENTH OF MARCH, 1690;
VIZ., THE CRUEL TORTURE OF ROBERT ROGERS, THE FIVE
YEARS' CAPTIVITY OF MEHETABLE GOODWIN, AND THE
FORTUNATE ESCAPE OF THOMAS TOOGOOD. FROM THE
MAGNALIA CHRISTI AMERICANA, OF DOCTOR COTTON
MATHER.

WHEN the news of the destruction of Schenectady reached
New England, it spread great alarm over the whole country.
The wise men gave particular caution to all the frontier posts,
urging them to keep strict watch, and to make strong their
fortifications; but the people in the east did not their duty,
and Salmon Falls, a fine settlement upon a branch of Pascataqua river, fell into the hands of an infuriated and cruel enemy;
the particulars whereof are at large set forth in the work entitled THE BOOK OF THE INDIANS, to which we have before referred.

But, as has been observed, notwithstanding these warnings
the people dreamed, that while the deep snow of the winter
continued, they were safe enough, which proved as vain as a
dream of a dry summer. Near thirty persons were slain, and
more than fifty were led into what the reader will by and by
call the worst captivity in the world. It would be a long story
to tell what a particular share in this calamity fell to the lot of
the family of one Clement Short. This honest man with his
pious wife and three children were killed, and six or seven
others of their children were made prisoners. The most of
these arrived safe at Canada, through a thousand hardships,
and the most of these with more than a thousand mer-

cies afterwards redeemed from Canada, and returned unto
their English friends again.   But as we cannot take notice of
all the individuals, we will pass to the notice of those named
at the commencement of this narrative.

Among the prisoners was one Robert Rogers, with whom as
the Indians journeyed they came to a hill, where this man,
(being through his corpulency called *Robin Pork*) being under
such an intolerable and unsupportable burden of Indian luggage, was not so able to travel as the rest; he therefore,
watching for an opportunity, made his escape.   The wretches
missing him, immediately went in pursuit of him, and it was
not long before they found his burden cast in the way, and the
tracks of his feet going out of the way.   This they followed,
and found him hid in a hollow tree.   They dragged him out,
stripped him, beat and pricked him, pushed him forward with
the points of their swords, until they got back to the hill from
whence he had escaped.   It being almost night, they fastened
him to a tree, with his hands behind him, then made themselves a supper, singing and dancing around him, roaring, and
uttering great and many signs of joy, but with joy little enough
to the poor creature who foresaw what all this tended to.

The Indians next cut a parcel of wood, and bringing it into a
plain place, they cut off the top of a small red-oak tree, leaving
the trunk for a stake, whereunto they bound their sacrifice.
They first made a great fire near this *tree of death*, and
bringing Rogers unto it, bid him take his leave of his friends,
which he did in a doleful manner, such as no pen, though
made of a harpy's quill, were able to describe the dolor of it.
They then allowed him a little time to make his prayers unto
heaven, which he did with an extreme fervency and agony;
whereupon they bound him to the stake, and brought the rest of
the prisoners, with their arms tied each to the other, and seated them round the fire.   This being done, they went behind
the fire, and thrust it forwards upon the man with much laughter and shouting; and when the fire had burnt some time upon
him, even till he was almost suffocated, they pulled away from
him, to prolong his existence.   They now resumed their dancing around him, and at every turn they did with their knives
cut collops of his flesh out of his naked limbs, and throw them
with his blood into his face.   In this manner was their work
continued until he expired.

Being now dead, they set his body down upon the glowing
coals of fire, and thus left him tied with his back to the stake,
where he was found by some English forces soon after, who
were in pursuit of these Indians.

MEHETABLE GOODWIN, another of the captives of this band of Indians, who, it will be proper to notice, were led by the renowned Indian chief Hopehood, had a child with her about five months old. This, through hunger and hardship, she being unable to nourish from her breast, occasioned it to make grievous and distressing ejaculations. Her Indian master told her that if the child were not quiet he would soon dispose of it, which caused her to use all possible means that his *Netopship** might not be offended ; and sometimes she would carry it from the fire out of his hearing, when she would sit down up to her waist in the snow, for several hours together, until it was exhausted and lulled to sleep. She thus for several days preserved the life of her babe, until he saw cause to travel with his own cubs farther afield ; and then, lest he should be retarded in his travel, he violently snatched the babe out of its mother's arms, and before her face knocked out its brains; and having stripped it of its few rags it had hitherto enjoyed, ordered the mother to go and wash them of the blood wherewith they were stained! Returning from this sad and melancholy task, she found the infant hanging by the neck in a forked bough of a tree. She requested liberty to lay it in the earth, but the savage said, "It is better as it is, for now the wild beasts cannot come at it;" [I am sure they had been at it;]† "and you may have the comfort of seeing it again, if ever you come that way."

The journey now before them was like to be very long, as far as Canada, where Mrs. Goodwin's master's purpose was to make merchandise of her, and glad was she to hear such happy tidings. But the desperate length of the way, and want of food, and grief of mind, wherewith she was now encountered, caused her within a few days to faint under her difficulties; when, at length, she sat down for some repose, with many prayers and tears unto God for the salvation of her soul, she found herself unable to rise, until she saw her furious executioner coming towards her with fire in his eyes, the devil in his heart, and his hatchet in his hand, ready to bestow a mercy-stroke of death upon her. Then it was that this poor captive woman, in this extreme misery, got upon her knees, and with weeping and wailing and all expressions of agony and entreaty, prevailed on him to spare her life a little longer, and she did not question but God would enable her to

---

* One of Dr. Mather's miserable misapplications of words. NETOP, among the Indians, signified *friend.*—Ed.

† I need not remind the reader that this is no interpretation of mine.— Ed.

walk a little faster. The merciless tyrant was prevailed with to spare her this time; nevertheless her former weakness quickly returning upon her, he was just going to murder her, when a couple of Indians, just at this moment coming in, called suddenly upon him to hold his hand. At this such a horror surprised his guilty soul, that he ran away from her; but hearing them call his name, he returned, and then permitted these his friends to ransom his prisoner.

After these events, as we were seated by the side of a river, we heard several guns go off on the opposite side, which the Indians concluded was occasioned by a party of Albany Indians, who were their enemies. Whereupon this bold blade [her old master] would needs go in a canoe to discover what they were. They fired upon and shot him through, together with several of his friends, before the discovery could be made. Some days after this, divers of his friends gathered a party to revenge his death on their supposed enemies. With these they soon joined battle, and after several hours' hard fighting were themselves put to the rout. Among the captives which they left in their flight was this poor woman, who was overjoyed, supposing herself now at liberty; but her joy did not last long, for these Indians were of the same sort as the others, and had been by their own friends, thus through a strange mistake, set upon.

However, this crew proved more favorable to her than the former, and went away silently with their booty; being loath to have any noise made of their foul mistake. And yet a few days after, such another mistake happened; for meeting with another party of Indians, which they imagined were in the English interest, they also furiously engaged each other, and many were killed and wounded on both sides; but the conquerors proved to be a party of French Indians this time, who took this poor Mrs. Goodwin and presented her to the French captain of the party, by whom she was carried to Canada, where she continued five years. After which she was brought safely back to New England.

THOMAS TOOGOOD's short narrative is introduced to relieve the reader from the contemplation of blood and misery. At the same time the other captives were taken, three Indians hotly pursued this man, and one of them overtaking him, while the rest perceiving it, staid behind the hill, having seen him quietly yield himself a prisoner. While the Indian was getting out his strings to bind his prisoner, he held his gun under his arm, which Toogood observing, suddenly sprang and wrested it from him; and momentarily presenting it at the

Indian, protested he would shoot him down if he made the least noise. And so away he ran with it unto Quochecho. If my reader be now inclined to smile, when he thinks how simply poor *Isgrim* looked, returning to his mates behind the hill, without either gun or prey, or any thing but strings, to remind him of his own deserts, I am sure his brethren felt not less so, for they derided him with ridicule at his misadventure. The Indians are singularly excessive in the practice of sporting at the misfortunes of one another in any case they are outwitted, or have been guilty of committing any blunder.

MARY PLAISTED was another of the unfortunate captives at that time and place, but only a few particulars of extreme sufferings are related. She had been out of her bed of family sickness but three weeks when she was taken, and like others she was obliged to wade through swamps and snow, when at length she was relieved of the burthen of her infant son by her cruel master, who, after dashing out its brains, threw it into a river !

GOD'S MERCY SURMOUNTING MAN'S CRUELTY,

EXEMPLIFIED IN THE CAPTIVITY AND SURPRISING DELIVERANCE OF ELIZABETH HANSON, WIFE OF JOHN HANSON, OF KNOXMARSH, AT KECHEACHY, IN DOVER TOWNSHIP, WHO WAS TAKEN CAPTIVE WITH HER CHILDREN AND MAID-SERVANT, BY THE INDIANS IN NEW ENGLAND, IN THE YEAR 1724.—The substance of which was taken from her own mouth, and now published for general service. The third edition.—Philadelphia: reprinted; Danvers, near Salem: reprinted and sold by E. Russell, next the Bell Tavern, MDCCLXXX. At the same place may be had a number of new Books, &c., some of which are on the times.—Cash paid for Rags.

☞ This edition of Mrs. Hanson's narrative is copied from that printed at Dover, N. H., in 1824. The above is a copy of the title page of that of 1780. These editions correspond, and I have discovered no disagreements in them. From a MS. extract, in the hand-writing of Mr. John Farmer, upon the cover of a copy of the Dover edition, it seems there was some doubt in his mind about the exact date of the capture of the Hanson family ; for in that memorandum above mentioned, purporting to have been taken from the Boston News-Letter of 1722, it is stated to have happened on the 27th of August of that year. I have not been able to refer to the News-Letter, but I find the event noticed in Pemberton's MS Chronology as happening on the 7th of September, 1724. I have no doubt of the correctness of the date in the narrative, myself, but mention the fact, that some brother antiquary may have the pleasure which may accrue from an investigation.—Ed.

REMARKABLE and many are the providences of God towards his people for their deliverance in a time of trouble, by which we may behold, as in lively characters, the truth of that saying, "That he is a God near at hand, and always ready to help and assist those that fear him and put their confidence in him."

The sacred writings give us instances of the truth hereof in days of old, as in the cases of the Israelites, Job, David, Daniel, Paul, Silas, and many others. Besides which, our modern histories have plentifully abounded with instances of God's fatherly care over his people, in their sharpest trials, deepest distresses, and sorest exercises, by which we may know he is a God that changeth not, but is the same yesterday, to-day and forever.

Among the many modern instances, I think I have not met with a more singular one of the mercy and preserving hand of God, than in the case of ELIZABETH HANSON, wife of JOHN HANSON, of Knoxmarsh,* in Kecheachy, [Cochecho] in Dover township, in New England, who was taken into captivity the twenty-seventh day of the sixth month, called June, 1724, and carried away (with four children and a servant) by the Indians; which relation, as it was taken from her own mouth, by a friend, is as follows:

As soon as the Indians discovered themselves, (having, as we afterwards understood, been skulking in the fields some days, watching their opportunity, when my dear husband, with the rest of our men, were gone out of the way,) two of them came in upon us, and then eleven more, all naked, with their guns and tomahawks, and in a great fury killed one child immediately, as soon as they entered the door, thinking thereby to strike in us the greater terror, and to make us more fearful of them. After which, in like fury, the captain came up to me; but at my request he gave me quarter. There were with me our servant and six of our children; two of the little ones being at play about the orchard, and my youngest child, but fourteen days old, whether in cradle or arms, I now remember not. Being in this condition, I was very unfit for the hardships I after met with, which I shall endeavor briefly to relate.

They went to rifling the house in a great hurry, (fearing, as I suppose, a surprise from our people, it being late in the afternoon,) and packed up some linen, woollen and what other

---

* A name, the use of which was long since discontinued.—Ed.

things pleased them best, and when they had done what they would, they turned out of the house immediately; and while they were at the door, two of my younger children, one six, and the other four years old, came in sight, and being under a great surprise, cried aloud, upon which one of the Indians running to them, took them under the arms, and brought them to us. My maid prevailed with the biggest to be quiet and still; but the other could by no means be prevailed with, but continued shrieking and crying very much, and the Indians, to ease themselves of the noise, and to prevent the danger of a discovery that might arise from it, immediately, before my face, knocked his brains out. I bore this as well as I could, not daring to appear disturbed or to show much uneasiness, lest they should do the same to the others; but should have been exceeding glad if they had kept out of sight until we had gone from the house.

Now having killed two of my children, they scalped them, (a practice common with these people, which is, whenever they kill any enemies, they cut the skin off from the crown of their heads, and carry it with them for a testimony and evidence that they have killed so many, receiving sometimes a reward for every scalp,) and then put forward to leave the house in great haste, without doing any other spoil than taking what they had packed together, with myself and little babe, fourteen days old, the boy six years, and two daughters, the one about fourteen and the other about sixteen years, with my servant girl.

It must be considered, that I having lain in but fourteen days, and being but very tender and weakly, and removed now out of a good room, well accommodated with fire, bedding, and other things suiting a person in my condition, it made these hardships to me greater than if I had been in a strong and healthy frame; yet, for all this, I must go or die. There was no resistance.

In this condition aforesaid we left the house, each Indian having something; and I with my babe and three children that could go of themselves. The captain, though he had as great a load as he could well carry, and was helped up with it, did, for all that, carry my babe for me in his arms, which I took to be a favor from him. Thus we went through several swamps and some brooks, they carefully avoiding all paths of any track like a road, lest by our footsteps we should be followed.

We got that night, I suppose, not quite ten miles from our house in a direct line; then taking up their quarters, lighted a fire, some of them lying down, while others kept watch. I being both wet and weary, and lying on the cold ground in the open woods, took but little rest.

However, early in the morning, we must go just as the day appeared, travelling very hard all that day through sundry rivers, brooks and swamps, they, as before, carefully avoiding all paths for the reason already assigned. At night, I was both wet and tired exceedingly; having the same lodging on the cold ground, in the open woods. Thus, for twenty-six days, day by day we travelled very hard, sometimes a little by water, over lakes and ponds; and in this journey we went up some high mountains, so steep that I was forced to creep up on my hands and knees; under which difficulty, the Indian, my master, would mostly carry my babe for me, which I took as a great favor of God, that his heart was so tenderly inclined to assist me, though he had, as it is said, a very heavy burden of his own; nay, he would sometimes take my very blanket, so that I had nothing to do but to take my little boy by the hand for his help, and assist him as well as I could, taking him up in my arms a little at times, because so small; and when we came to very bad places, he would lend me his hand, or coming behind, would push me before him; in all which, he showed some humanity and civility, more than I could have expected: for which privilege I was secretly thankful to God, as the moving cause thereof.

Next to this we had some very great runs of water and brooks to wade through, in which at times we met with much difficulty, wading often to our middles, and sometimes our girls were up to their shoulders and chins, the Indians carrying my boy on their shoulders. At the side of one of these runs or rivers, the Indians would have my eldest daughter, Sarah, to sing them a song. Then was brought into her remembrance that passage in the 137th Psalm, " By the rivers of Babylon," [&c.] When my poor child had given me this account, it was very affecting, and my heart was very full of trouble, yet on my child's account I was glad that she had so good an inclination, which she yet further manifested in longing for a Bible, that we might have the comfort of reading the holy text at vacant times, for our spiritual comfort under our present affliction.

Next to the difficulties of the rivers, were the prodigious swamps and thickets, very difficult to pass through, in which places my master would sometimes lead me by the hand, a great way together, and give me what help he was capable of, under the straits we went through; and we, passing, one after another, the first made it pretty passable for the hindmost.

But the greatest difficulty, that deserves the first to be named was want of food, having at times nothing to eat but pieces of old beaver-skin match-coats, which the Indians having hid, (for they came naked as is said before,) which in their going back again they took with them, and they were used more for food than raiment. Being cut into long narrow straps, they gave us little pieces, which by the Indians' example we laid on the fire until the hair was singed away, and then we ate them as a sweet morsel, experimentally knowing "that to the hungry soul every bitter thing is sweet."

It is to be considered further, that of this poor diet we had but very scanty allowance; so that we were in no danger of being overcharged. But that which added to my trouble, was the complaints of my poor children, especially the little boy. Sometimes the Indians would catch a squirrel or beaver, and at other times we met with nuts, berries, and roots which they digged out of the ground, with the bark of some trees ; but we had no corn for a great while together, though some of the younger Indians went back and brought some corn from the English inhabitants, (the harvest not being gathered,) of which we had a little allowed us. But when they caught a beaver, we lived high while it lasted ; they allowed me the guts and garbage for myself and children ; but not allowing us to clean and wash them, as they ought, made the food very irksome to us to feed upon, and nothing besides pinching hunger could have made it any way tolerable to be borne.

The next difficulty was no less hard to me ; for my daily travel and hard living made my milk dry almost quite up, and how to preserve my poor babe's life was no small care on my mind ; having no other sustenance for her, many times, but cold water, which I took in my mouth, and let it fall on my breast, when I gave her the teat to suck in, with what it could get from the breast ; and when I had any of the broth of the beaver's guts, or other guts, I fed my babe with it, and as well as I could I preserved her life until I got to Canada, and then I had some other food, of which, more in its place.

Having by this time got considerably on the way, the Indians parted, and we were divided amongst them. This was a sore grief to us all ; but we must submit, and no way to help our-selves. My eldest daughter was first taken away, and carried to another part of the country, far distant from us, where for the present we must take leave of her, though with a heavy heart.

We did not travel far after this, before they divided again, taking my second daughter and servant maid from me, into another part of the country. So, I having now only my babe at my breast, and little boy six years old, we remained with the captain still. But my daughter and servant underwent great hardships after they were parted from me, travelling three days without any food, taking nothing for support but cold water; and the third day, what with the cold, the wet, and hunger, the servant fell down as dead in a swoon, being both very cold and wet, at which the Indians, with whom they were, were surprised, showing some kind of tenderness, being unwilling then to lose them by death, having got them so near home; hoping, if they lived, by their ransom to make considerable profit of them.

In a few days after this, they got near their journey's end, where they had more plenty of corn, and other food. But flesh often fell very short, having no other way to depend on for it but hunting; and when that failed, they had very short commons. It was not long ere my daughter and servant were likewise parted, and my daughter's master being sick, was not able to hunt for flesh; neither had they any corn in that place, but were forced to eat bark of trees for a whole week.

Being almost famished in this distress, Providence so ordered that some other Indians, hearing of their misery, came to visit them, (these people being very kind and helpful to one another, which is very commendable,) and brought to them the guts and liver of a beaver, which afforded them a good repast, being but four in number, the Indian, his wife and daughter, and my daughter.

By this time my master and our company got to our journey's end, where we were better fed at times, having some corn and venison, and wild fowl, or what they could catch by hunting in the woods; and my master having a large family, fifteen in number, we had at times very short commons, more especially when game was scarce.

But here our lodging was still on the cold ground, in a poor wigwam, (which is a kind of little shelter made with the rind of trees, and mats for a covering, something like a tent.) These are so easily set up and taken down, that they often remove them from one place to another. Our shoes and stockings, and our other clothes, being worn out in this long journey through the bushes and swamps, and the weather coming in very hard, we were poorly defended from the cold, for want of necessaries; which caused one of my feet, one of the little babe's, and both of the little boy's, to freeze; and this was no small exercise, yet, through mercy, we all did well.

Now, though we got to our journey's end, we were never long in one place, but very often removed from one place to another, carrying our wigwams with us, which we could do without much difficulty. This, being for the convenience of hunting, made our accommodations much more unpleasant, than if we had continued in one place, by reason the coldness and dampness of the ground, where our wigwams were pitched, made it very unwholesome, and unpleasant lodging.

Having now got to the Indian fort, many of the Indians came to visit us, and in their way welcomed my master home, and held a great rejoicing, with dancing, firing of guns, beating on hollow trees, instead of drums ; shouting, drinking, and feasting after their manner, in much excess, for several days together, which I suppose, in their thoughts, was a kind of thanks to God, put up for their safe return and good success. But while they were in their jollity and mirth, my mind was greatly exercised towards the Lord, that I, with my dear children, separated from me, might be preserved from repining against God under our affliction on the one hand, and on the other we might have our dependence on him, who rules the hearts of men, and can do what he pleases in the kingdoms of the earth, knowing that his care is over them who put their trust in him ; but I found it very hard to keep my mind as I ought, in the resignation which is proper it should be, under such afflictions and sore trials as at that time I suffered in being under various fears and doubts concerning my children, that were separated from me, which helped to add to and greatly increase my troubles. And here I may truly say, my afflictions are not to be set forth in words to the extent of them.

We had not been long at home ere my master went a hunting, and was absent about a week, he ordering me in his absence to get in wood, gather nuts, &c. I was very diligent cutting the wood and putting it in order, not having very far to carry it. But when he returned, having got no prey, he was very much out of humor, and the disappointment was so great that he could not forbear revenging it on us poor captives. However, he allowed me a little boiled corn for myself and child, but with a very angry look threw a stick or corn cob at me with such violence as did bespeak he grudged our eating. At this his squaw and daughter broke out into a great crying. This made me fear mischief was hatching against us. I immediately went out of his presence into another wigwam ; upon which he came after me, and in a great fury tore my blanket off my back, and took my little boy from me, and struck him down as he went along before him ; but the poor child not being hurt, only frightened in the fall, started up and ran away without crying. Then the Indian, my master, left me ; but his wife's mother came and sat down by me, and told me I must sleep there that night. She then going from me a little time, came back with a small skin to cover my feet withal, informing me that my master intended now to kill us, and I, being desirous to know the reason, expostulated, that in his absence I had been diligent to do as I was ordered by him. Thus as well as I could I made her sensible how unreasonable he was. Now, though she could not understand me, nor I her, but by signs, we reasoned as well as we could. She therefore made signs that I must die, advising me, by pointing up with her fingers, in her way, to pray to God, endeavoring by her signs and tears to instruct me in that which was most needful, viz. to prepare for death, which now threatened me : the poor old squaw was so very kind and tender, that she would not leave me all the night, but laid herself down at my feet, designing what she could to assuage her son-in-law's wrath, who had conceived evil against me, chiefly, as I understood, because the want of victuals urged him to it. My rest was little this night, my poor babe sleeping sweetly by me. •

I dreaded the tragical design of my master, looking every hour for his coming to execute his bloody will upon us ; but he being weary with hunting and travel in the woods, having toiled for nothing, went to rest and forgot it. Next morning he applied himself again to hunting in the woods, but I dreaded his returning empty, and prayed secretly in my heart that he might catch some food to satisfy his hunger, and cool his ill humor. He had not been gone but a little time, when he returned with booty, having shot some wild ducks ; and now he appeared in a better temper, ordered the fowls to be dressed with speed ; for these kind of people, when they have plenty, spend it as they get it, using with gluttony and drunkenness, in two days' time, as much as with prudent management might serve a week. Thus do they live for the most part, either in excess of gluttony and drunkenness, or under great straits of want of necessaries. However, in this plentiful time, I felt the comfort of it in part with the family ; having a portion sent for me and my little ones, which was very acceptable. Now, I thinking the bitterness of death was over for this time, my spirits were a little easier.

Not long after this he got into the like ill humor again, threatening to take away my life. But I always observed whenever he was in such a temper, he wanted food, and was pinched with hunger. But when he had success in hunting, to take either bears, bucks, or fowls, on which he could fill his belly, he was better humored, though he was naturally of a very hot and passionate temper, throwing sticks, stones, or whatever lay in his way, on every slight occasion. This made me in continual danger of my life ; but God, whose providence is over all his works, so preserved me that I never received any damage from him, that was of any great consequence to me; for which I ever desire to be thankful to my Maker.

When flesh was scarce we had only the guts and garbage allowed to our part; and not being permitted to cleanse the guts any other wise than emptying the dung [out], without so much as washing them, as before is noted; in that filthy pickle we must boil them and eat them, which was very unpleasant. But hunger made up that difficulty, so that this food, which was very often our lot, became pretty tolerable to a sharp appetite, which otherwise could not have been dispensed with. Thus I considered, none knows what they can undergo until they are tried; for what I had thought in my own family not fit for food, would here have been a dainty dish and sweet morsel.

By this time, what with fatigue of spirits, hard labor, mean diet, and often want of natural rest, I was brought so low, that my milk was dried up, my babe very poor and weak, just skin and bones; for I could perceive all her joints from one end of the back to the other, and how to get what would suit her weak appetite, I was at a loss; on which one of the Indian squaws, perceiving my uneasiness about my child, began some discourse with me, in which she advised me to take the kernels of walnuts, clean them and beat them with a little water, which I did and when I had so done the water looked like milk; then she advised me to add to this water a little of the finest of Indian corn meal, and boil it a little together. I did so, and it became palatable, and was very nourishing to the babe, so that she began to thrive and look well, who was before more like to die than live. I found that with this kind of diet the Indians did often nurse their infants. This was no small comfort to me; but this comfort was soon mixed with bitterness and trouble, which thus happened: my master taking notice of my dear babe's thriving condition, would often look upon her and say when she was fat enough she would be killed, and he would eat her; and pursuant to his pretence, at a certain time, he made me fetch him a stick that he had prepared for a spit to roast the child upon, as he said, which when I had done he made me sit down by him and undress the infant. When the child was naked he felt her arms, legs, and thighs, and told me she was not fat enough yet; I must dress her again until she was better in case.

Now, though he thus acted, I could not persuade myself that he intended to do as he pretended, but only to aggravate and afflict me; neither ever could I think but our lives would be preserved from his barbarous hands, by the overruling power

11

of Him in whose providence I put my trust both day and night.

A little time after this, my master fell sick, and in his sickness, as he lay in his wigwam, he ordered his own son to beat my son; but the old squaw, the Indian boy's grandmother, would not suffer him to do it: then his father, being provoked, caught up a stick, very sharp at one end, and with great violence threw it from him at my son, and hit him on the breast, with which my child was much bruised, and the pain with the surprise made him turn as pale as death; I entreating him not to cry, and the boy, though but six years old, bore it with wonderful patience, not so much as in the least complaining, so that the child's patience assuaged the barbarity of his heart: who, no doubt, would have carried his passion and resentment much higher, had the child cried, as always complaining did aggravate his passion, and his anger grew hotter upon it. Some little time after, on the same day, he got upon his feet, but far from being well. However, though he was sick, his wife and daughter let me know he intended to kill us, and I was under a fear, unless providence now interposed, how it would end. I therefore put down my child, and going out of his presence, went to cut wood for the fire as I used to do, hoping that would in part allay his passion; but withal, ere I came to the wigwam again, I expected my child would be killed in this mad fit, having no other way but to cast my care upon God, who had hitherto helped and cared for me and mine.

Under this great feud, the old squaw, my master's mother-in-law, left him, but my mistress and her daughter abode in the wigwam with my master, and when I came with my wood, the daughter came to me, whom I asked if her father had killed my child, and she made me a sign, no, with a countenance that seemed pleased it was so; for instead of his further venting his passion on me and my children, the Lord in whom I trusted did seasonably interpose, and I took it as a merciful deliverance from him, and the Indian was under some sense of the same, as himself did confess to them about him afterwards.

Thus it was, a little after he got upon his feet, the Lord struck him with great sickness, and a violent pain, as appeared by the complaint he made in a doleful and hideous manner; which when I understood, not having yet seen him, I went to another squaw, that was come to see my master, which could both speak and understand English, and inquired of her if my mistress (for so I always called her, and him master) thought that master would die. She answered yes, it was very likely he would, being worse and worse. Then I told her he struck my boy a dreadful blow without any provocation at all, and had threatened to kill us all in his fury and passion; upon which the squaw told me my master had confessed the above abuse he offered my child, and that the mischief he had done was the cause why God afflicted him with that sickness and pain, and he had promised never to abuse us in such sort more : and after this he soon recovered, but was not so passionate ; nor do I remember he ever after struck either me or my children, so as to hurt us, or with that mischievous intent as before he used to do. This I took as the Lord's doing, and it was marvellous in my eyes.

Some few weeks after this, my master made another remove, having as before made several; but this was the longest ever he made, it being two days' journey, and mostly upon ice. The first day's journey the ice was bare, but the next day, some snow falling, made it very troublesome, tedious, and difficult travelling; and I took much damage in often falling; having the care of my babe, that added not a little to my uneasiness. And the last night when we came to encamp, it being in the night, I was ordered to fetch water; but having sat awhile on the cold ground, I could neither go nor stand; but crawling on my hands and knees, a young Indian squaw came to see our people, being of another family, in compassion took the kettle, and knowing where to go, which I did not, fetched the water for me. This I took as a great kindness and favor, that her heart was inclined to do me this service.

I now saw the design of this journey. My master being, as I suppose, weary to keep us, was willing to make what he could of our ransom; therefore, he went further towards the French, and left his family in this place, where they had a great dance, sundry other Indians coming to our people. This held some time, and while they were in it, I got out of their way in a corner of the wigwam as well [as] I could ; but every time they came by me in their dancing, they would bow my head towards the ground, and frequently kick me with as great fury as they could bear, being sundry of them barefoot, and others having Indian mockosons. This dance held some time, and they made, in their manner, great rejoicings and noise.

It was not many days ere my master returned from the French ; but he was in such a humor when he came back, he would not suffer me in his presence. Therefore I had a little shelter made with some boughs, they having digged through the snow to the ground, it being pretty deep. In this hole I and my poor children were put to lodge; the weather being very sharp, with hard frost, in the month called January, made it more tedious to me and my children. Our stay was not

long in this place before he took me to the French, in order
for a chapman. When we came among them I was exposed
for sale, and he asked for me 80Ʋ livres. But his chapman
not complying with his demand, put him in a great rage,
offering him but 600; he said, in a great passion, if he could
not have his demand, he would make a great fire and burn me
and the babe, in the view of the town, which was named Fort
Royal. The Frenchman bid the Indian make his fire, "and
I will," says he, "help you, if you think that will do you more
good than 600 livres," calling my master fool, and speaking
roughly to him, bid him be gone. But at the same time the
Frenchman was civil to me; and, for my encouragement, bid
me be of good cheer, for I should be redeemed, and not go
back with them again.

Retiring now with my master for this night, the next day I
was redeemed for six hundred livres; and in treating with my
master, the Frenchman queried why he asked so much for the
child's ransom; urging, when she had her belly full, she
would die. My master said, "No, she would not die, having
already lived twenty-six days on nothing but water, believing
the child to be a devil." The Frenchman told him, "No, the
child is ordered for longer life; and it has pleased God to
preserve her to admiration." My master said no, she was a
devil, and he believed she would not die, unless they took a
hatchet and beat her brains out. Thus ended their discourse,
and I was, as aforesaid, with my babe, ransomed for six hundred livres; my little boy, likewise, at the same time, for an
additional sum of livres, was redeemed also.

I now having changed my landlord, my table and diet, as
well as my lodging, the French were civil beyond what I could
either desire or expect. But the next day after I was redeemed, the Romish priest took my babe from me, and according to their custom, they baptized her, urging if she died
before that she would be damned, like some of our modern
pretended reformed priests, and they gave her a name as
pleased them best, which was Mary Ann Frossways, telling
me my child, if she now died, would be saved, being baptized;
and my landlord speaking to the priest that baptized her, said,
"It would be well, now Frossways was baptized, for her to
die, being now in a state to be saved," but the priest said, "No,
the child having been so miraculously preserved through so
many hardships, she may be designed by God for some great
work, and by her life being still continued, may much more
glorify God than if she should now die." ∫A very sensible
remark, and I wish it may prove true. ∖

I having been about five months amongst the Indians, in

about one month after I got amongst the French, my dear husband, to my unspeakable comfort and joy, came to me, who was now himself concerned to redeem his children, two of our daughters being still captives, and only myself and two little ones redeemed ; and, through great difficulty and trouble, he recovered the younger daughter. But the eldest we could by no means obtain from their hands, for the squaw, to whom she was given, had a son whom she intended my daughter should in time be prevailed with to marry. ⋅ The Indians are very civil towards their captive women, not offering any incivility by any indecent carriage, (unless they be much overcome in liquor,) which is commendable in them, so far. ⋅

However, the affections they had for my daughter made them refuse all offers and terms of ransom ; so that, after my poor husband had waited, and made what attempts and endeavors he could to obtain his child, and all to no purpose, we were forced to make homeward, leaving our daughter, to our great grief, behind us, amongst the Indians, and set forward over the lake, with three of our children, and the servant maid, in company with sundry others, and, by the kindness of Providence, we got well home on the 1st day of the 7th month, 1725. From which it appears I had been from home, amongst the Indians and French, about twelve months and six days.

In the series of which time, the many deliverances and wonderful providences of God unto us, and over us, hath been, and I hope will so remain to be, as a continued obligation on my mind, ever to live in that fear, love, and obedience to God, duly regarding, by his grace, with meekness and wisdom, to approve myself by his spirit, in all holiness of life and godliness of conversation, to the praise of him that hath called me, who is God blessed forever.

But my dear husband, poor man ! could not enjoy himself in quiet with us, for want of his dear daughter Sarah, that was left behind ; and not willing to omit anything for her redemption which lay in his power, he could not be easy without making a second attempt ; in order to which, he took his journey about the 19th day of the second month, 1727, in company with a kinsman and his wife, who went to redeem some of their children, and were so happy as to obtain what they went about. But my dear husband being taken sick on the way, grew worse and worse, as we were informed, and was sensible he should not get over it ; telling my kinsman that if it was the Lord's will he must die in the wilderness, he was freely given up to it. He was under a good composure of mind, and sensible to his last moment, and died, as near as we can

11*

judge, in about the half way between Albany and Canada, in my kinsman's arms, and is at rest, I hope, in the Lord : and though my own children's loss is very great, yet I doubt not but his gain is much more ; I therefore desire and pray, that the Lord will enable me patiently to submit to his will in all things he is pleased to suffer to be my lot, while here, earnestly supplicating the God and father of all our mercies to be a father to my fatherless children, and give unto them that blessing, which maketh truly rich, and adds no sorrow with it ; that as they grow in years they may grow in grace, and experience the joy of salvation, which is come by Jesus Christ, our Lord and Savior.   Amen.

Now, though my husband died, by reason of which his labor was ended, yet my kinsman prosecuted the thing, and left no stone unturned, that he thought, or could be advised, was proper to the obtaining my daughter's freedom ; but could by no means prevail ; for, as is before said, she being in another part of the country distant from where I was, and given to an old squaw, who intended to marry her in time to her son, using what persuasion she could to effect her end, sometimes by fair means, and sometimes by severe.

In the mean time a Frenchman interposed, and they by persuasions enticing my child to marry, in order to obtain her freedom, by reason that those captives married by the French are, by that marriage, made free among them, the Indians having then no pretence longer to keep them as captives ; she therefore was prevailed upon, for the reasons afore assigned, to marry, and she was accordingly married to the said Frenchman.

Thus, as well, and as near as I can from my memory, (not being capable of keeping a journal,) I have given a short but a true account of some of the remarkable trials and wonderful deliverances which I never purposed to expose ; but that I hope thereby the merciful kindness and goodness of God may be magnified, and the reader hereof provoked with more care and fear to serve him in righteousness and humility, and then my designed end and purpose will be answered.

                                                    E. H.

A NARRATIVE

OF THE CAPTIVITY OF NEHEMIAH HOW, WHO WAS TAKEN BY THE INDIANS AT THE GREAT MEADOW FORT ABOVE FORT DUMMER, WHERE HE WAS AN INHABITANT, OCTOBER 11th, 1745. Giving an account of what he met with in his travelling to Canada, and while he was in prison there. Together with an account of Mr. How's death at Canada.—Psalm cxxxvii : 1, 2, 3, and 4.—Boston : N. E. Printed and sold opposite to the Prison in Queen Street, 1748.

At the Great Meadow's fort, fourteen miles above fort Dummer, October 11th, 1745, where I was an inhabitant, I went out from the fort about fifty rods to cut wood ; and when I had done, I walked towards the fort, but in my way heard the crackling of fences behind me, and turning about, saw twelve or thirteen Indians, with red painted heads, running after me ; on which I cried to God for help, and ran, and hallooed as I ran, to alarm the fort. But by the time I had run ten rods, the Indians came up with me and took hold of me. At the same time the men at the fort shot at the Indians, and killed one on the spot, wounded another, who died fourteen days after he got home, and likewise shot a bullet through the powder-horn of one that had hold of me. They then led me into the swamp and pinioned me. I then committed my case to God, and prayed that, since it was his will to deliver me into the hands of those cruel men, I might find favor in their eyes ; which request God in his infinite mercy was pleased to grant ; for they were generally kind to me while I was with them. Some of the Indians at that time took charge of me, others ran into the field to kill cattle. They led me about half a mile, where we staid in open sight of the fort, till the Indians who were killing cattle came to us, laden with beef. Then they went a little further to a house, where they staid to cut the meat from the bones, and cut the helve off of my axe, and stuck it into the ground, pointing the way we went.

Then we travelled along the river side, and when we had got about three miles, I espied a canoe coming down on the further side of the river, with David Rugg and Robert Baker, belonging to our fort. I made as much noise as I could, by hammering, &c., that they might see us before the Indians saw them, and so get ashore and escape. But the Indians saw them, and shot across the river, twenty or thirty guns at them, by which the first-mentioned man was killed, but the other, Robert Baker, got ashore and escaped. Then some of the Indians swam across the river and brought the canoe to us :

having stripped and scalped the dead man, and then we went about a mile further, when we came to another house, where we stopped. While there we heard men running by the bank of the river, whom I knew to be Jonathan Thayer, Samuel Nutting and my son Caleb How. Five of the Indians ran to head them. My heart asked for them, and prayed to God to save them from the hands of the enemy. I suppose they hid under the bank of the river, for the Indians were gone some time, but came back without them, blessed be God.

We went about a mile further, where we lodged that night, and roasted the meat they had got. The next day we travelled very slow, by reason of the wounded Indian, which was a great favor to me. We lodged the second night against Number Four [since Charlestown, N. H.] The third day we likewise travelled slowly, and stopped often to rest, and get along the wounded man. We lodged that night by the second small river that runs into the great river against Number Four.

The fourth day morning the Indians held a piece of bark, and bid me write my name, and how many days we had travelled; "for," said they "may be Englishmen will come here." That was a hard day to me, as it was wet and we went over prodigious mountains, so that I became weak and faint; for I had not eaten the value of one meal from the time I was taken, and that being beef almost raw without bread or salt. When I came first to the foot of those hills, I thought it was impossible for me to ascend them, without immediate help from God; therefore my constant recourse was to him for strength, which he was graciously pleased to grant me, and for which I desire to praise him.

We got that day a little before night to a place where they had a hunting house, a kettle, some beer, Indian corn, and salt. They boiled a good mess of it. I drank of the broth, eat of the meat and corn, and was wonderfully refreshed, so that I felt like another man. The next morning we got up early, and after we had eaten, my master said to me, "You must quick walk to day, or I kill you." I told him I would go as fast as I could, and no faster, if he did kill me. At which an old Indian, who was the best friend I had, took care of me. We travelled that day very hard, and over steep hills, but it being a cool, windy day, I performed it with more ease than before; yet I was much tired before night, but dare not complain.

The next day the Indians gave me a pair of their shoes, so that I travelled with abundant more ease than when I wore my own shoes. I ate but very little, as our victuals were almost spent. When the sun was about two hours high, the Indians

scattered to hunt, and they soon killed a fawn, and three small
bears, so that we had again meat enough ; some of which we
boiled and eat heartily of, by which I felt strong.

○ The next day we travelled very hard, and performed it with
ease, insomuch that one of the Indians told me I was a very
strong man. About three o'clock we came to the lake, where
they had five canoes, pork, Indian corn, and tobacco. We got
into the canoes, and the Indians stuck up a pole about eight
feet long with the scalp of David Rugg on the top of it painted
red, with the likeness of eyes and mouth on it. We sailed
about ten miles, and then went on shore, and after we had
made a fire, we boiled a good supper, and eat heartily.

The next day we set sail for Crown Point, but when we were
within a mile of the place, they went on shore, where were
eight or ten French and Indians, two of whom, before I got on
shore, came running into the water, knee deep, and pulled me
out of the canoe. There they sung and danced around me a
while, when one of them bid me sit down, which I did. Then
they pulled off my shoes and buckles, and took them from me.
Soon after we went along to Crown Point. When we got there,
the people, both French and Indians, were very thick by the
water-side. Two of the Indians took me out of the canoe, and
leading me, bid me run, which I did, about twenty rods to the
fort. The fort is large, built with stone and lime. They led
me up to the third loft, where was the captain's chamber. A
chair was brought that I might sit by the fire and warm me.
Soon after, the Indians that I belonged to, and others that were
there, came into the chamber, among whom was one I knew,
named *Pealtomy*. He came and spoke to me, and shook hands
with me, and I was glad to see him. He went out, but soon
returned and brought to me another Indian, named Amrusus,
husband to her who was Eunice Williams, daughter of the late
Rev. John Williams, of Deerfield ; he was glad to see me, and
I to see him. He asked me about his wife's relations, and
showed a great deal of respect to me.

A while after this, the Indians sat in a ring in the chamber,
and Pealtomy came to me, and told me I must go and sing and
dance before the Indians. I told him I could not. He told me
over some Indian words, and bid me sing them. I told him I
could not. With that the rest of the fort who could speak
some English, came to me, and bid me sing it in English, which
was, " I don't know where I go," which I did, dancing round
that ring three times. I then sat down by the fire. The priest
came to me, and gave me a dram of rum, and afterwards the
captain brought me part of a loaf of bread and a plate of butter,
and asked me to eat, which I did heartily, for I had not eaten

any bread from the time I was taken till then. The French priest and all the officers showed me a great deal of respect. The captain gave me a pair of good buck-skin shoes, and the priest fixed them on my feet. We staid there that night, and I slept with the priest, captain and lieutenant. The lieutenant's name was Ballock; he had been a prisoner at Boston, and had been at Northampton and the towns thereabouts. This day, which was the Sabbath, I was well treated by the French officers, with victuals and drink. We tarried there till noon, then went off about a mile, and put on shore, where they staid the most of the day; and having rum with them, most of them were much liquored. Pealtomy and his squaw, and another Indian family, went with us, and by them I found out that William Phips killed an Indian, besides him we wounded before he was killed; for an Indian who was with us asked me if there was one killed near our fort last summer. I told him I did not know. He said he had a brother who went out then, and he had not seen him since, and had heard he was killed at our fort, and wanted to know if it was true. But I did not think it best to tell him any such thing was suspected.

The Indians now got into a frolic, and quarrelled about me, and made me sit in the canoe by the water-side. I was afraid they would hurt if not kill me. They attempted to come to me, but the sober Indians hindered them that were in liquor. Pealtomy seeing the rout, went to the fort, and soon after, Lieut. Ballock, with some soldiers, came to us, and when the Indians were made easy, they went away. We lodged there that night, and the next day was a stormy day of wind, snow and rain, so that we were forced to tarry there that day and the next night. In this time the Indians continued fetching rum from the fort, and kept half drunk. Here I underwent some hardship by staying there so long in a storm without shelter or blanket. They had a great dance that night, and hung up David Rugg's scalp on a pole, dancing round it. After they had done, they lay down to sleep.

The next morning, which was the tenth day from the time of my being taken, we went off in the canoe, and the night after we arrived at the wide lake, and there we staid that night. Some of the Indians went a hunting, and killed a fat deer, so that we had victuals plenty, for we had a full supply of bread given us at the fort at Crown Point.

The next morning the wind being calm, we set out about two hours before day, and soon after came to a schooner lying at anchor. We went on board her, and the French treated us very civilly. They gave each of us a dram of rum, and victuals to eat. As soon as it was day we left the schooner, and two hours before sunset got over the lake, and next day came to Shamballee [Chamblee,*] where we met three hundred French and two hundred Indians, who did the mischief about Mr. Lydin's fort.† I was taken out of the canoe by two Frenchmen, and fled to a house about ten rods off as fast as I could run, the Indians flinging snow-balls at me. As soon as I got to the house, the Indians stood round me very thick, and bid me sing and dance, which I did with them, in their way; then they gave a shout, and left off. Two of them came to me, one of whom smote me on one cheek, the other on the other, which made the blood run plentifully. Then they bid me sing and dance again, which I did with them, and they with me, shouting as before. Then two Frenchmen took me under each arm, and ran so fast that the Indians could not keep up with us to hurt me. We ran about forty rods to another house, where a chair was brought for me to sit down. The house was soon full of French and Indians, and others surrounded it, and some were looking in to the windows. A French gentleman came to me, took me by the hand, and led me into a small room, where none came in but such as he admitted. He gave me victuals and drink. Several French gentlemen and Indians came in and were civil to me. The Indians who came in could speak English, shook hands with me, and called me brother. They told me they were all soldiers, and were going to New England. They said they should go to my town, which was a great damp to my spirits, till I heard of their return, where they had been, and what they had done. A while after this, the Indians whom I belonged to came to me and told me we must go. I went with them. After going down the river about two miles, we came to the thickest of the town, where was a large fort built with stone and lime, and very large and fine houses in it. Here was the general of the army I spoke of before. He asked me what news from London and Boston. I told him such stories as I thought convenient, and omitted the rest, and then went down to the canoes. Some of the Indians went and got a plenty of bread and beef, which they put into the canoes, and then we went into a French house, where we had a good supper. There came in several French gentlemen to see me, who were civil. One of them gave me a crown, sterling. We lodged there till about two hours before day, when we arose, and went down the river. I suppose we

*A fort on a fine river of the same name, about fifteen miles south-west of Montreal.—Ed.

†Nov. 16, 1745, Saratoga, a Dutch village of thirty families, is destroyed by the Indians and French. They burnt a fort, killed many, and carried away others of the inhabitants.—MS. Chronicles of the Indians.

went a hundred miles that day, which brought us into a great river, called Quebec. We lodged that night in a French house, and were civilly treated.

The next day we went down the river, and I was carried before the governor there, which was the Sabbath, and the 16th day after my being taken. We staid there about three hours, and were well treated by the French. The Indians were then ordered to carry me down to Quebec, which was ninety miles further. We went down the river about three miles that night, then going on shore, lodged the remainder of the night.

The next morning we set off, and the second day, which was the 18th from the time I was taken, we arrived at Quebec. The land is inhabited on both sides of the river from the lake to Quebec, which is at least two hundred miles, especially below Chamblee, very thick, so that the houses are within sight of one another all the way.

But to return: After we arrived at Quebec, I was carried up into a large chamber, which was full of Indians, who were civil to me. Many of the French came in to see me, and were also very kind. I staid there about two hours, when a French gentleman, who could speak good English, came in and told me I must go with him to the governor, which I did; and after answering a great many questions, and being treated with as much bread and wine as I desired, I was sent with an officer to the guard-house, and led into a small room, where was an Englishman named William Stroud, a kinsman of the Hon. Judge Lynd,* in New England. He belonged to South Carolina, and had been at Quebec six years. The governor kept him confined for fear he should leave him and go to New England, and discover their strength. Mr. Stroud and I were kept in the guard-house one week, with a sufficiency of food and drink. The French gentlemen kept coming in to see me, and I was very civilly treated by them. I had the better opportunity of discoursing with them, as Mr. Stroud was a good interpreter.

After this we were sent to prison, where I found one James Kinlade, who was taken fourteen days before I was, at Sheepscot, at the eastward, in New England. I was much pleased

---

* Judge Lynd was connected by marriage to the celebrated Gov. Hutchinson. He presided at the trial of Capt. Preston, commander of the British soldiers in Boston, in 1770, who fired upon and killed several citizens. I have a volume of Hutchinson's History of Massachusetts, which belonged to Judge Lynd with the name of the governor in it, in his own hand. In it are numerous notes and corrections throughout, and twenty-four MS. pages of additions at the end, in the judge's hand-writing. It seems to have been presented for this purpose by the governor. Judge Lynd died a few years after the revolution.

with his conversation, esteeming him a man of true piety. We were kept in prison eight days, with liberty to keep in the room with the prison-keeper. We were daily visited by gentlemen and ladies, who showed us great kindness in giving us money and other things, and their behavior towards us was pleasant. ○ Blessed be God therefor, for I desire to ascribe all the favors I have been the partaker of, ever since my captivity, to the abundant grace and goodness of a bountiful God, as the first cause. ○

After this Mr. Kinlade and I were sent to another prison, where were twenty-two seamen belonging to several parts of our king's dominions; three of them captains of vessels, viz. James Southerland of Cape Cod, William Chipman of Marblehead, William Pote of Casco Bay. This prison was a large house, built with stone and lime, two feet thick, and about one hundred and twenty feet long. We had two large stoves in it, and wood enough, so that we could keep ourselves warm in the coldest weather. We had provision sufficient, viz. two pounds of good wheat bread, one pound of beef, and peas answerable, to each man, ready dressed every day.

When I had been there a few days, the captives desired me to lead them in carrying on morning and evening devotion, which I was willing to do. We had a Bible, psalm-book, and some other good books. Our constant practice was to read a chapter in the Bible, and sing part of a psalm, and to pray, night and morning.

When I was at the first prison, I was stripped of all my old and lousy clothes, and had other clothing given me from head to foot, and had many kindnesses shown me by those that lived thereabouts; more especially by one Mr. Corby and his wife, who gave me money there, and brought me many good things at the other prison. But here I was taken ill, as was also most of the other prisoners, with a flux, which lasted near a month, so that I was grown very weak. After that I was healthy, through divine goodness. Blessed be God for it.

I was much concerned for my country, especially for the place I was taken from, by reason that I met an army going thither, as they told me. The 27th day of November we had news come to the prison that this army had returned to Chamblee, and had taken upwards of a hundred captives, which increased my concern; for I expected our fort, and others thereabouts, were destroyed. This news put me upon earnest prayer to God that he would give me grace to submit to his will; after which I was easy in my mind.

About a fortnight after, a Dutchman was brought to prison, who was one of the captives the said army had taken. He told me they had burnt Mr. Lydin's fort, and all the houses at that new township, killed Capt. Schuyler and five or six more, and had brought fifty whites and about sixty negroes to Montreal. I was sorry to hear of so much mischief done, but rejoiced they had not been upon our river, and the towns thereabouts, for which I gave thanks to God for his great goodness in preserving them, and particularly my family.

When Christmas came, the governor sent us twenty-four livres, and the lord-intendant came into the prison and gave us twenty-four more, which was about two guineas. He told us he hoped we should be sent home in a little time. He was a pleasant gentleman, and very kind to captives. Some time after, Mr. Shearsy, a gentleman of quality, came to us, and gave to the three sea captains twenty-four livers, and to me twelve, and the next day sent me a bottle of claret wine. About ten days after he sent me twelve livres more; in all eight pounds, old tenor.

January 20th, 1746, eighteen captives were brought from Montreal to the prison at Quebec, which is 180 miles.

February 22d, seven captives more, who were taken at Albany, were brought to the prison to us, viz. six men and one old woman seventy years old, who had been so infirm for seven years past that she had not been able to walk the streets, yet performed this tedious journey with ease.

March 15th, one of the captives taken at Albany, after fourteen or fifteen days' sickness, died in the hospital at Quebec, —a man of a sober, pious conversation. His name was Lawrence Plaffer, a German born.

May 3d, three captives taken at No. Four, sixteen miles above where I was taken, viz. Capt. John Spafford, Isaac Parker, and Stephen Farnsworth, were brought to prison to us. They informed me my family was well, a few days before they were taken, which rejoiced me much. I was sorry for the misfortune of these my friends, but was glad of their company, and of their being well used by those who took them.

May 14th, two captives were brought into prison, Jacob Read and Edward Cloutman, taken at a new township called Gorhamtown, near Casco Bay. They informed us that one man and four children of one of them were killed, and his wife taken at the same time with them, and was in the hands of the Indians.*

May 16th, two lads, James and Samuel Anderson, brothers, taken at Sheepscot, were brought to prison. On the 17th,

---

* Gorhamtown was attacked in the morning of the 19th April, 1746, by a party of about ten Indians.—*MS. Chronicles of the Indians.*

Samuel Burbank and David Woodwell, who were taken at New Hopkinton, near Rumford, [Concord, N. H.] were brought to prison, and informed us there were taken with them two sons of the said Burbank, and the wife, two sons and a daughter of the said Woodwell, whom they left in the hands of the Indians.

May 24th, Thomas Jones, of Holliston, who was a soldier at Contoocook, was brought to prison, and told us that one Elisha Cook, and a negro belonging to the Rev. Mr. Stevens, were killed when he was taken.

June 1st, William Aikings, taken at Pleasant Point, near fort George, was brought to prison. June 2d, Mr. Shearly brought several letters of deacon Timothy Brown, of Lower Ashuelot, and money, and delivered them to me, which made me think he was killed or taken. A few days after, Mr. Shearly told me he was taken. I was glad to hear he was alive.

June 6th, Timothy Cummings, aged 60, was brought to prison, who informed us he was at work with five other men, about forty rods from the block-house, George's [fort,] when five Indians shot at them, but hurt none. The men ran away, and left him and their guns to the Indians. He told us that the ensign was killed as he stood on the top of the fort, and that the English killed five Indians at the same time.

June 13th, Mr. Shearly brought to the captives some let-ters which were sent from Albany, and among them one from Lieut. Gov. Phips, of the Massachusetts Bay, to the governor of Canada, for the exchange of prisoners, which gave us great hopes of a speedy release.

June 22d, eight men were brought to prison, among whom were deacon Brown and Robert Morse, who informed me that there were six or eight Indians killed, a little before they were taken, at Upper Ashuelot, and that they learnt, by the Indians who took them, there were six more of the English killed at other places near Connecticut river, and several more much wounded; these last were supposed to be the wife and chil-dren of the aforesaid Burbank and Woodwell.

July 5th, we sent a petition to the chief governor that we might be exchanged, and the 7th, Mr. Shearly told us we should be exchanged for other captives in a little time, which caused great joy among us. The same day, at night, John Berran, of Northfield, was brought to prison, who told us that an expedition against Canada was on foot, which much rejoiced us. He also told us of the three fights in No. Four, and who were killed and taken, and of the mischief done in other places near Connecticut river, and that my brother Daniel How's son Daniel was taken with him, and was in the hands of the Indians, who designed to keep him.

July 20th, John Jones, a seaman, was brought into prison, who told us he was going from Cape Breton to Newfoundland with one Englishman and four Frenchmen, who had sworn allegiance to King George, and in the passage they killed the other Englishman, but carried him to the bay of Arb, where there was an army of French and Indians, to whom they delivered him, and by them was sent to Quebec.

July 21st, John Richards and a boy of nine or ten years of age, who belonged to Rochester, in New Hampshire, were brought to prison. They told us there were four Englishmen killed when they were taken.

August 15th, seven captives, who with eight more taken at St. John's Island, were brought to prison. They told us that several were killed after quarters were given, among whom was James Owen, late of Brookfield, in New England. On the 16th, Thomas Jones, late of Sherburne, in New England, after seven or eight days' sickness, died. He gave good satisfaction as to his future state. On the 25th we had a squall of snow.

September 12th, Robert Downing, who had been a soldier at Cape Breton, and was taken at St. Johns, and who was with the Indians two months, and suffered great abuse from them, was brought to prison.

On the 15th, twenty-three of the captives taken at Hoosuck fort were brought to prison, among whom was the Rev. Mr. John Norton. They informed us that after fighting twenty-five hours, with eight hundred French and Indians, they surrendered themselves, on capitulation, prisoners of war; that Thomas Nalton and Josiah Read were killed when they were taken. The names of those now brought in are the Rev. Mr. Norton, John Hawks, John Smead, his wife and six children, John Perry and his wife, Moses Scott, his wife and two children, Samuel Goodman, Jonathan Bridgman, Nathan Eames, Joseph Scott, Amos Pratt, Benjamin Sinconds, Samuel Lovet, David Warren, and Phinehas Furbush. The two last of these informed me that my brother Daniel How's son was taken from the Indians, and now lives with a French gentleman at Montreal. There were four captives more taken at Albany, the last summer, who were brought to prison the same day.

On the 26th (Sept.) 74 men and two women, taken at sea, were brought to prison. October 1st, Jacob Shepard, of Westborough, taken at Hoosuck, was brought to prison. On the 3d, Jonathan Batherick was brought in, and on the 5th, seventeen other men, three of whom were taken with Mr.

Norton and others, viz. Nathaniel Hitchcock, John Aldrick, and Stephen Scott. Richard Subs, who was taken at New Casco, says one man was killed at the same time. Also Pike Gooden, taken at Saco, was brought to prison. He says he had a brother killed at the same time. On the 12th, twenty-four seamen are brought in, and on the 19th, six more. On the 20th, Jacob Read died. On the 23d, Edward Cloutman and Robert Dunbar broke prison and escaped for New England. The 27th, a man was brought into prison, who said the Indians took five more [besides himself], and brought ten scalps to Montreal.

November 1st, John Read died. The 9th, John Davis, taken with Mr. Norman, died. The 17th, Nathan Eames, of Marlborough, died. On the 19th, Mr. Adams, taken at Sheepscot, is brought to prison. He says that James Anderson's father was killed, and his uncle taken at the same time. The 20th, Leonard Lydle and the widow Sarah Briant were married in Canada, by the Rev. Mr. Norton. On the 22d, the abovesaid Anderson's uncle was brought to prison. Two days after, (24th) John Bradshaw died. He had not been well for most of the time he had been a prisoner. It is a very melancholy time with us. There are now thirty sick, and deaths among us daily. Died on the 28th, Jonathan Dunham, and on the 29th, died also Capt. Bailey of Amesbury.

December 1st, an Albany man died, and on the 6th, Pike Gooden, who, we have reason to believe, made a happy change. On the 7th, a girl of ten years died. The 11th, Moses Scott's wife died, and on the 15th, one of Captain Robertson's lieutenants. Daniel Woodwell's wife died on the 18th, a pious woman. John Perry's wife died the 23d. On the 26th, William Dayly, of New York, died.

January 3d, 1747, Jonathan Harthan died. On the 12th, Phinehas Andrews, of Cape Ann, died. He was one of the twenty captives, who, the same night, had been removed to another prison, hoping thereby to get rid of the infection. Jacob Bailey, brother to Capt. Bailey, died the 15th, and the 17th, Giat Braban, Captain Chapman's carpenter, died. On the 23d, Samuel Lovet, son of Major Lovet, of Mendon, in New England, died.

February 10th, William Garwafs died, also the youngest child of Moses Scott. The 15th, my nephew, Daniel How, and six more were brought down from Montreal to Quebec, viz. John Sunderland, John Smith, Richard Smith, William Scott, Philip Scoffil, and Benjamin Tainter, son to Lieutenant Tainter of Westborough in New England. The 23d, Richard Bennet died, and the 25th, Michael Dugon.

12*

March 18th, James Margra died, and on the 22d, Capt. John Fort and Samuel Goodman; the 28th, the wife of John Smead died, and left six children, the youngest of whom was born the second night after the mother was taken.

April 7th, Philip Scaffield, [Scofield ?] and next day John Saneld, the next day Capt. James Jordan and one of his men, died. On the 12th, Amos Pratt, of Shrewsbury, and on the 14th, Timothy Cummings, the 17th, John Dill, of Hull in New England, the 18th, Samuel Venhon, of Plymouth, died. On the 26th, Capt. Jonathan Williamson was brought to prison. He was taken at the new town on Sheepscot river. The same day came in, also, three men who were taken at Albany, three weeks before, and tell us that thirteen were killed, Capt. Trent being one. They were all soldiers for the expedition to Canada. On the 27th, Joseph Denox, and the 28th, Samuel Evans, died. The same night the prison took fire, and was burnt, but the things therein were mostly saved. We were kept that night under a guard.

May 7th, Sarah Lydle, whose name was Braint when she was taken, and married while a captive, died, and the 13th, Mr. Smead's son Daniel died, and Christian Tether the 14th. The same day died also Hezekiah Huntington, a hopeful youth, of a liberal education. He was a son of Colonel Huntington of Connecticut, in New England. On the 15th, Joseph Grey, and on the 19th Samuel Burbank, died. At the same time died two children who were put out to the French to nurse.

At this time I received a letter from Major Willard, dated March 17th, 1747, wherein he informs me my family were well, which was joyful news to me. May 19th, Abraham Fort died.

[Here ends the journal of Mr. How, exceedingly valuable for the many items of exact intelligence therein recorded, relative to so many of the present inhabitants of New England, through those friends who endured the hardships of captivity in the mountain deserts and the damps of loathsome prisons. Had the author lived to have returned, and published his narrative himself, he doubtless would have made it far more valuable, but he was cut off while a prisoner, by the prison fever, in the fifty-fifth year of his age, after a captivity of one year, seven months, and fifteen days. He died May 25th, 1747, in the hospital at Quebec, after a sickness of about ten days. He was a husband and father, and greatly beloved by all who knew him.—Ed.]

PARTICULARS RELATING TO THE CAPTIVITY
OF JOHN FITCH, OF ASHBY, MASS. RELATED BY MR. ENOS JONES, OF ASHBURNHAM.

THE town of Lunenburg, in Massachusetts, was incorporated August 1, 1728, and received its name in compliment to George II., who, the preceding year, came to the British throne, and was styled Duke of Lunenburg, having in his German dominions a town of that name. On the 3d of February, 1764, a part of Lunenburg was detached and incorporated as a distinct town by the name of Fitchburg. In 1767, a part of Fitchburg was disannexed to aid in forming the town of Ashby. Mr. John Fitch lived on the frontiers of the county, in the tract now included in Ashby. After the commencement of the French and Indian war of 1745, Fitch proposed to the government to keep a garrison, with the aid of three soldiers, who were immediately despatched to him. Mr. Fitch was a gentleman of much enterprise, and had had considerable dealings with the Indians in peltries, furs, &c., and was generally well known among them. Soon after the breaking out of the war, they determined to make him a prisoner; and in July, 1746-7, they came into the vicinity to the number of about eighty. The inhabitants of the garrison were Fitch, his wife, five children, and the three soldiers. One of these last left the garrison early in the morning of the disaster, on furlough, to visit a house at the distance of three or four miles. Another went out in quest of game. He had not proceeded far when he discovered the Indians crawling in the high grass between him and the garrison. He attempted to return, but was instantly shot down. One soldier only remained with Fitch and his family; and they determined to defend themselves to the best of their power. The soldier, whose name was Jennings, fired several times, when an Indian shot him through the neck, and he fell. Mrs. Fitch regularly loaded the guns for her husband, and they continued to defend themselves for some time; when the Indians informed them that if they would surrender they should have quarter, but if they refused they should perish in the flames of the garrison. After some consultation with his wife, Fitch concluded to surrender. The Indians then burned the garrison; and after committing various mischiefs in the neighborhood, they took the captive family to Canada. Immediately after the garrison was burnt, Perkins, the soldier on furlough, espied the smoke, and on ascending a hill in the vicinity he could see the ruins.

He immediately gave the alarm, and in the evening nearly an hundred had assembled in arms for the pursuit of the enemy. It being dark, however, they concluded to wait till the following morning, and ere day broke they set out. After proceeding a short distance in the track of the Indians they saw a piece of paper tied to a limb of a tree, which, on examining, they found to be in the hand-writing of Fitch, requesting them by no means to pursue him, as the Indians had assured him of safety if they were not pursued; but would destroy him if his friends should attempt his rescue. Upon this the party returned to their homes. At the close of the war Fitch and his family were liberated; and were crossing the Connecticut on their return home, when Mrs. Fitch took cold and died. The rest of the family returned, and Fitch was afterwards married again. Jennings, who was killed in the garrison, was burnt in the flames. The name of the soldier killed without the garrison was Blodget. The third soldier, whose name was Perkins, escaped.

CAPTIVITY OF MARY FOWLER, OF HOPKINTON.

MARY FOWLER, formerly Mary Woodwell, now living in Canterbury in this state, was born in the town of Hopkinton, in Massachusetts, May 11, 1730. Her parents moved to Hopkinton in this state when she was about twelve years of age, and settled on the westerly side of what is called Putney's Hill.

On the 22d day of April, in the year 1746, while in the garrison at her father's house, six Indians, armed with muskets, tomahawks, knives, &c. broke into the garrison and took eight persons while in their beds, viz. the said Mary, her parents, two of her brothers, Benjamin and Thomas, Samuel Burbank, an aged man, and his two sons, Caleb and Jonathan. They carried them through the wilderness to St. Francis in Canada. Here Mary and Jonathan Burbank were detained for the term of three years, (though not in one family,) and the other six were carried prisoners to Quebec, where Burbank, the aged, and Mary's mother died of the yellow fever in prison. The other four were afterwards exchanged.

The circumstances relative to their being taken were as follows: Ten persons, viz. the eight above mentioned, Samuel Burbank's wife and a soldier, were secluded in the garrison for fear of being attacked by the Indians, who had been frequently scouting through Hopkinton and the other adjacent towns. Early on the morning of their captivity, Samuel Burbank left the garrison and went to the barn in order to feed the cattle before the rest were up, leaving the door unfastened. The Indians, who lay near in ambush, immediately sallied forth and took him. From this affrighted captive they got information that the garrison was weak, whereupon they rushed in, and took them all, except the soldier who escaped, and Burbank's wife, who secreted herself in the cellar. During this attack Mary's mother, being closely embraced by a sturdy Indian, wrested from his side a long knife, with which she was in the act of running him through, when her husband prevailed with her to desist, fearing the fatal consequences. However, she secured the deadly weapon, and before they commenced their march threw it into the well, from whence it was taken after the captives returned. Another Indian presented a musket to Mary's breast, intending to blow her through, when a chief by the name of Pennos, who had previously received numerous kindnesses from her father's family, instantly interfered, and kept him from his cruel design, taking her for his own captive.

After having arrived at St. Francis, Pennos sold Mary to a squaw of another family, while J. Burbank continued in some remote part of the neighborhood under his own master. Mary's father and brothers, after they were exchanged, solicited a contribution for her redemption, which was at last obtained with great difficulty for one hundred livres, through the stratagem of a French doctor; all previous efforts made by her father and brothers having failed. This tender parent, though reduced to poverty by the savages, and having no pecuniary assistance except what he received through the hand of charity from his distant friends, had frequently visited St. Francis in order to have an interview with his only daughter, and to compromise with her mistress, offering her a large sum for Mary's redemption, but all to no effect. She refused to let her go short of her weight in silver. Moreover, Mary had previously been told by her mistress that if she intimated a word to her father that she wanted to go home with him, she should never see his face again; therefore, when interrogated by him on this subject, she remained silent, through fear of worse treatment; yet she could not conceal her grief, for her internal agitation and distress of mind caused the tears to flow profusely from her eyes. Her father, at length, worn out with grief and toil, retired to Montreal, where he contracted with a Frenchman as an agent to effect, if possible, the purchase of his daughter. This agent, after having attempted a compromise several times in vain, employed a French physician, who was in high reputation among the Indians, to assist him. The doctor, under a cloak of friendship, secretly advised Mary to feign herself sick, as the only alternative, and gave her medicine for the purpose. This doctor was soon called upon for medical aid; and although he appeared to exert the utmost of his skill, yet his patient continued to grow worse. After making several visits to no effect, he at length gave her over as being past recovery, advising her mistress, as a real friend, to sell her the first opportunity for what she could get, even if it were but a small sum; otherwise, said he, she will die on your hands, and you must lose her. The squaw, alarmed at the doctor's ceremony, and the dangerous appearance of her captive, immediately contracted with the French agent for one hundred livres; whereupon Mary soon began to amend; and was shortly after conveyed to Montreal, where she continued six months longer among the French waiting for a passport.

Thus after having been compelled to three years' hard labor in planting and hoeing corn, chopping and carrying wood, pounding *samp*, gathering cranberries and other wild fruit for the market, &c., this young woman was at length redeemed from the merciless hands and cruel servitude of the savages, who had not only wrested her from her home, but also from the tender embraces of her parents, and from all social intercourse with her friends.

Jonathan Burbank was redeemed about the same time—became an officer, and was afterwards killed by the Indians in the French war. These sons of the forest supposing him to have been Rogers, their avowed enemy, rushed upon him and slew him without ceremony, after he had given himself up as a prisoner of war.

After six months' detention among the French at Montreal, Mary was conveyed (mostly by water) to Albany by the Dutch, who had proceeded to Canada in order to redeem their black slaves, whom the Indians had previously taken and carried thither; from thence she was conducted to the place of her nativity, where she continued about five years, and was married to one Jesse Corbett, by whom she had two sons. From thence they moved to Hopkinton in this state, to the place where Mary had been taken by the Indians. Corbett, her husband, was drowned in Almsbury river, (now Warner river,) in Hopkinton, in the year 1759, in attempting to swim across the river—was carried down into the Contoocook, thence into the Merrimack, and was finally taken up in Dunstable with his clothes tied fast to his head. Mary was afterwards married to a Jeremiah Fowler, by whom she had five children. She

is now living in Canterbury, in the enjoyment of good health
and remarkable powers of mind, being in the ninety-third year
of her age.   The foregoing narrative was written a few weeks
since as she related it.

_____

NARRATIVE

OF THE CAPTIVITY OF MRS. ISABELLA M'COY, WHO WAS TA-
KEN CAPTIVE AT EPSOM, N. H., IN THE YEAR 1747. COL-
LECTED FROM THE RECOLLECTIONS OF AGED PEOPLE WHO
KNEW HER, BY THE REV. JONATHAN CURTIS, A MINISTER
OF THAT TOWN, ABOUT SEVENTEEN YEARS AGO, AND BY
HIM COMMUNICATED TO THE PUBLISHERS OF THE NEW
HAMPSHIRE HISTORICAL COLLECTIONS.

THE Indians were first attracted to the new settlements in
the town of Epsom, N. H., by discovering M'Coy at Suncook,
now Pembroke.   This, as nearly as can be ascertained, was in
the year 1747.   Reports were spread of the depredations of
the Indians in various places ; and M'Coy had heard that they
had been seen lurking about the woods at Penacook, now Concord.   He went as far as Pembroke ; ascertained that they
were in the vicinity ; was somewhere discovered by them, and
followed home.   They told his wife, whom they afterwards
made prisoner, that they looked through cracks around the
house, and saw what they had for supper that night.   They
however did not discover themselves till the second day after.
They probably wished to take a little time to learn the strength
and preparation of the inhabitants.   The next day, Mrs.
M'Coy, attended by their two dogs, went down to see if any of
the other families had returned from the garrison.   She found
no one.   On her return, as she was passing the block-house,
which stood near the present site of the meeting-house, the
dogs, which had passed round it, came running back growling
and very much excited.   Their appearance induced her to
make the best of her way home.   The Indians afterwards told
her that they then lay concealed there, and saw the dogs, when
they came round.

M'Coy, being now strongly suspicious that the Indians were
actually in the town, determined to set off the next day with
his family for the garrison at Nottingham.   His family now
consisted of himself, his wife, and son John.   The younger
children were still at the garrison.   They accordingly secured
their house as well as they could, and all set off next morning ;

—M'Coy and his son with their guns, though without ammunition, having fired away wha'• they brought with them in hunting.

As they were travelling a little distance east of the place where the meeting-house now stands, Mrs. M'Coy fell a little in the rear of the others. This circumstance gave the Indians a favorable opportunity for separating her from her husband and son. The Indians, three men and a boy, lay in ambush near the foot of Marden's hill, not far from the junction of the mountain road with the main road. Here they suffered M'Coy and his son to pass; but, as his wife was passing them, they reached from the bushes, and took hold of her, charging her to make no noise, and covering her mouth with their hands, as she cried to her husband for assistance. Her husband, hearing her cries, turned, and was about coming to her relief. But he no sooner began to advance, than the Indians, expecting probably that he would fire upon them, began to raise their pieces, which she pushed one side, and motioned to her friends to make their escape, knowing that their guns were not loaded, and that they would doubtless be killed, if they approached. They accordingly ran into the woods and made their escape to the garrison. This took place August 21, 1747.

The Indians then collected together what booty they could obtain, which consisted of an iron trammel, from Mr. George Wallace's, the apples of the only tree which bore in town, which was in the orchard now owned by Mr. David Griffin, and some other trifling articles, and prepared to set off with their prisoner for Canada.

Before they took their departure, they conveyed Mrs. M'Coy to a place near the little Suncook river, where they left her in the care of the young Indian, while the three men, whose names were afterwards ascertained to be Plausawa,* Sabatis, and Christi, went away, and were for some time absent. During their absence, Mrs. M'Coy thought of attempting to make her escape. She saw opportunities, when she thought she might dispatch the young Indian with the trammel, which, with other things, was left with them, and thus perhaps avoid some strange and barbarous death, or a long and distressing captivity. But, on the other hand, she knew not at what distance the others were. If she attempted to kill her young keeper, she might fail. If she effected her purpose in this, she might be pursued and overtaken by a cruel and revengeful foe, and then some dreadful death would be her certain portion.

---

* These were of the Arosaguntacook or St. Francis tribe. See Belknap's Hist. N. H. vol. ii. p. 278.

On the whole, she thought best to endeavor to prepare her mind to bear what might be no more than a period of savage captivity. Soon, however, the Indians returned, and put an end for the present to all thoughts of escape. From the direction in which they went and returned, and from their smutty appearance, she suspected what their business had been. She told them she guessed they had been burning her house. Plausawa, who could speak some broken English, informed her they had.*

They now commenced their long and tedious journey to Canada, in which the poor captive might well expect that great and complicated sufferings would be her lot. She did indeed find the journey fatiguing, and her fare scanty and precarious. But, in her treatment from the Indians, she experienced a very agreeable disappointment. The kindness she received from them was far greater than she had expected from those who were so often distinguished for their cruelties. The apples they had gathered they saved for her, giving her one every day. In this way, they lasted her as far on the way as lake Champlain. They gave her the last, as they were crossing that lake in their canoes. This circumstance gave to the tree, on which the apples grew, the name of " *Isabell's tree*," her name being Isabella. In many ways did they appear desirous of mitigating the distresses of their prisoner while on their tedious journey. When night came on, and they halted to repose themselves in the dark wilderness, Plausawa, the head man, would make a little couch in the leaves a little way from theirs, cover her up with his own blanket; and there she was suffered to sleep undisturbed till morning. When they came to a river, which must be forded, one of them would carry her over on his back. Nothing like insult or indecency did they ever offer her during the whole time she was with them. They carried her to Canada, and sold her as a servant to a French family, whence, at the close of that war, she returned home. But so comfortable was her condition there, and her husband being a man of rather a rough and violent temper, she declared she never should have thought of attempting the journey home, were it not for the sake of her children. O

After the capture of Mrs. M'Coy, the Indians frequently visited the town, but never committed any very great depredations. The greatest damage they ever did to the property of the inhabitants was the spoiling of all the ox-teams in town. At the time referred to, there were but four yoke of oxen in

---

* The writer has a piece of the iron-ware, which was melted down in the burning of the house.

the place, viz. M'Coy's, Capt. M'Clary's, George Wallace's, and Lieut. Blake's. It was a time of apprehension from the Indians; and the inhabitants had therefore all fled to the garrison at Nottingham. They left their oxen to graze about the woods, with a bell upon one of them. The Indians found them, shot one out of each yoke, took out their tongues, made a prize of the bell, and left them.

The ferocity and cruelty of the savages were doubtless very much averted by a friendly, conciliating course of conduct in the inhabitants towards them. This was particularly the case in the course pursued by sergeant Blake. Being himself a curious marksman and an expert hunter, traits of character in their view of the highest order, he soon secured their respect; and, by a course of kind treatment, he secured their friendship to such a degree, that, though they had opportunities, they would not injure him even in time of war.

The first he ever saw of them was a company of them making towards his house, through the opening from the top of Sanborn's hill. He fled to the woods, and there lay concealed, till they had made a thorough search about his house and enclosures, and had gone off. The next time his visitors came, he was constrained to become more acquainted with them, and to treat them with more attention. As he was busily engaged towards the close of the day in completing a yard for his cow, the declining sun suddenly threw along several enormous shadows on the ground before him. He had no sooner turned to see the cause, than he found himself in the company of a number of stately Indians. Seeing his perturbation, they patted him on the head, and told him not to be afraid, for they would not hurt him. They then went with him into his house; and their first business was to search all his bottles to see if he had any "*occapee*," rum. They then told him they were very hungry, and wanted something to eat. He happened to have a quarter of a bear, which he gave them. They took it and threw it whole upon the fire, and very soon began to cut and eat from it half raw. While they were eating, he employed himself in cutting pieces from it, and broiling upon a stick for them, which pleased them very much. After their repast, they wished for the privilege of lying by his fire through the night, which he granted. The next morning, they proposed trying skill with him in firing at a mark. To this he acceded. But in this, finding themselves outdone, they were much astonished and chagrined; nevertheless they highly commended him for his skill, patting him on the head, and telling him *if he would go off with them they would make him their big captain.* They used often to call upon him, and his kindness to them they never forgot even in time of war.

Plausawa had a peculiar manner of doubling his lip, and producing a very shrill piercing whistle, which might be heard a great distance. At a time, when considerable danger was apprehended from the Indians, Blake went off into the woods alone, though considered hazardous, to look for his cow, that was missing. As he was passing along by Sinclair's brook, an unfrequented place, northerly from M'Coy's mountain, a very loud sharp whistle, which he knew to be Plausawa's, suddenly passed through his head, like the report of a pistol. The sudden alarm almost raised him from the ground; and, with a very light step, he soon reached home without his cow. In more peaceable times, Plausawa asked him if he did not remember the time, and laughed very much to think how he ran at the fright, and told him the reason for his whistling. "*Young Indian,*" said he, "*put up gun to shoot Englishman. Me knock it down, and whistle to start you off.*" So lasting is their friendship, when treated well. At the close of the wars, the Indians built several wigwams near the confluence of Wallace's brook with the great Suncook. On a little island in this river, near the place called "short falls," one of them lived for a considerable time. Plausawa and Sabatis were finally both killed in time of peace by one of the whites, after a drunken quarrel, and buried near a certain brook in Boscawen.

A FAITHFUL NARRATIVE

OF THE SUFFERINGS OF PETER WILLIAMSON, WHO SETTLED NEAR THE FORKS OF THE DELAWARE IN PENNSYLVANIA. HAVING BEEN TAKEN BY THE INDIANS IN HIS OWN HOUSE, OCTOBER 2d, 1754.—WRITTEN BY HIMSELF.

I WAS born within ten miles of the town of Aberdeen, in the north of Scotland, of reputable parents. At eight years of age, being a sturdy boy, I was taken notice of by two fellows belonging to a vessel, employed (as the trade then was) by some of the worthy merchants of Aberdeen in that villanous and execrable practice of stealing young children from their parents, and selling them as slaves in the plantations abroad, and on board the ship I was easily cajoled by them, where I was conducted between decks, to some others they had kidnapped in the same manner, and in about a month's time set sail for America. When arrived at Philadelphia, the captain sold us at about sixteen pounds per head. What became of my unhappy companions I never knew; but it was my lot to be sold for seven years, to one of my countrymen, who had in his youth been kidnapped like myself, but from another town.

Having no children of his own, and commiserating my condition, he took care of me, indulged me in going to school, where I went every winter for five years, and made a tolerable proficiency. With this good master I continued till he died, and, as a reward for my faithful service, he left me two hundred pounds currency, which was then about an hundred and twenty pounds sterling, his best horse, saddle, and all his wearing apparel.

Being now seventeen years old, and my own master, having money in my pocket, and all other necessaries, I employed myself in jobbing for near seven years; when I resolved to settle, and married the daughter of a substantial planter. My father-in-law made me a deed of gift of a tract of land that lay (unhappily for me, as it has since proved) on the frontiers of the province of Pennsylvania, near the forks of Delaware, containing about two hundred acres, thirty of which were well cleared and fit for immediate use, on which were a good house and barn. The place pleasing me well, I settled on it. My money I expended in buying stock, household furniture, and implements for out-of-door work; and being happy in a good wife, my felicity was complete: but in 1754, the Indians, who had for a long time before ravaged and destroyed other parts of America unmolested, began now to be very troublesome on the frontiers of our province, where they generally appeared in small skulking parties, committing great devastations.

Terrible and shocking to human nature were the barbarities daily committed by these savages! Scarce did a day pass but some unhappy family or other fell victims to savage cruelty. Terrible, indeed, it proved to me, as well as to many others. I, that was now happy in an easy state of life, blessed with an affectionate and tender wife, became on a sudden one of the most unhappy of mankind: scarce can I sustain the shock which forever recurs on recollecting the fatal second of October, 1754. My wife that day went from home, to visit some of her relations; as I staid up later than usual, expecting her return, none being in the house besides myself, how great was my surprise and terror, when, about eleven o'clock at night, I heard the dismal war-whoop of the savages, and found that my house was beset by them. I flew to my chamber window, and perceived them to be twelve in number. Having my gun loaded, I threatened them with death, if they did not retire. But how vain and fruitless are the efforts of one man against the united force of so many blood-thirsty monsters! One of them that could speak English threatened me in return, "that if I did not come out they would burn me alive," adding, however, "that if I would come out and surrender myself prisoner they would not kill me." In such deplorable circumstances, I chose to rely on their promises, rather than meet death by rejecting them; and accordingly went out of the house, with my gun in my hand, not knowing that I had it. Immediately on my approach they rushed on me like tigers, and instantly disarmed me. Having me thus in their power, they bound me to a tree, went into the house, plundered it of every thing they could carry off, and then set fire to it, and consumed what was left before my eyes. Not satisfied with this, they set fire to my barn, stable, and out-houses, wherein were about two hundred bushels of wheat, six cows, four horses, and five sheep, all which were consumed to ashes.

Having thus finished the execrable business about which they came, one of the monsters came to me with a tomahawk and threatened me with the worst of deaths if I would not go with them. This I agreed to, and then they untied me, and gave me a load to carry, under which I travelled all that night, full of the most terrible apprehensions, lest my unhappy wife should likewise have fallen into their cruel power. At daybreak my infernal masters ordered me to lay down my load, when, tying my hands again round a tree, they forced the blood out at my fingers' ends. And then kindling a fire near the tree to which I was bound, the most dreadful agonies seized me, concluding I was going to be made a sacrifice to their barbarity. The fire being made, they for some time danced round me after their manner, whooping, hollowing and shrieking in a frightful manner. Being satisfied with this sort of mirth, they proceeded in another manner: taking the burning coals, and sticks flaming with fire at the ends, holding them to my face, head, hands, and feet, and at the same time threatening to burn me entirely if I cried out. Thus tortured as I was, almost to death, I suffered their brutalities, without being allowed to vent my anguish otherwise than by shedding silent tears; and these being observed, they took fresh coals and applied them near my eyes, telling me my face was wet, and that they would dry it for me, which indeed they cruelly did. How I underwent these tortures has been matter of wonder to me, but God enabled me to wait with more than common patience for the deliverance I daily prayed for.

At length they sat down round the fire, and roasted the meat, of which they had robbed my dwelling. When they had supped, they offered some to me; though it may easily be imagined

13*

I had but little appetite to eat, after the tortures and miseries I had suffered, yet was I forced to seem pleased with what they offered me, lest by refusing it they should reassume their hellish practices. What I could not eat I contrived to hide, they having unbound me till they imagined I had eat all; but then they bound me as before; in which deplorable condition I was forced to continue the whole day. When the sun was set, they put out the fire, and covered the ashes with leaves, as is their usual custom, that the white people might not discover any traces of their having been there.

Going from thence along the Susquehanna, for the space of six miles, loaded as I was before, we arrived at a spot near the Apalachian mountains, or Blue hills, where they hid their plunder under logs of wood. From thence they proceeded to a neighboring house, occupied by one Jacob Snider and his unhappy family, consisting of his wife, five children, and a young man his servant. They soon got admittance into the unfortunate man's house, where they immediately, without the least remorse, scalped both parents and children; nor could the tears, the shrieks, or cries of poor innocent children prevent their horrid massacre. Having thus scalped them, and plundered the house of every thing that was movable, they set fire to it, and left the distressed victims amidst the flames.

Thinking the young man belonging to this unhappy family would be of service to them in carrying part of their plunder, they spared his life, and loaded him and myself with what they had here got, and again marched to the Blue hills, where they stowed their goods as before. My fellow-sufferer could not support the cruel treatment which we were obliged to suffer, and complaining bitterly to me of his being unable to proceed any farther, I endeavored to animate him, but all in vain, for he still continued his moans and tears, which one of the savages perceiving, as we travelled along, came up to us, and with his tomahawk gave him a blow on the head, which felled the unhappy youth to the ground, whom they immediately scalped and left. The suddenness of this murder shocked me to that degree, that I was in a manner motionless, expecting my fate would soon be the same: however, recovering my distracted thoughts, I dissembled my anguish as well as I could from the barbarians; but still, such was my terror, that for some time I scarce knew the days of the week, or what I did. ◦

They still kept on their course near the mountains, where they lay skulking four or five days, rejoicing at the plunder they had got. When provisions became scarce, they made their way towards Susquehanna, and passing near another house, inhabited by an old man, whose name was John Adams, with his wife and four small children, and meeting with no resistance, they immediately scalped the mother and her children before the old man's eyes. Inhuman and horrid as this was, it did not satisfy them; for when they had murdered the poor woman, they acted with her in such a brutal manner as decency will not permit me to mention. The unhappy husband, not being able to avoid the sight, entreated them to put an end to his miserable being; but they were as deaf to the tears and entreaties of this venerable sufferer as they had been to those of the others, and proceeded to burn and destroy his house, barn, corn, hay, cattle, and every thing the poor man a few hours before was master of. Having saved what they thought proper from the flames, they gave the old man, feeble, weak, and in the miserable condition he then was, as well as myself, burdens to carry, and loading themselves likewise with bread and meat, pursued their journey towards the Great swamp. Here they lay for eight or nine days, diverting themselves, at times, in barbarous cruelties on the old man: sometimes they would strip him naked, and paint him all over with various sorts of colors; at other times they would pluck the white hairs from his head, and tauntingly tell him he was a fool for living so long, and that they should show him kindness in putting him out of the world. In vain were all his tears, for daily did they tire themselves with the various means they tried to torment him; sometimes tying him to a tree, and whipping him; at other times, scorching his furrowed cheek with red-hot coals, and burning his legs quite to the knees. One night, after he had been thus tormented, whilst he and I were condoling each other at the miseries we daily suffered, twenty-five other Indians arrived, bringing with them twenty scalps and three prisoners, who had unhappily fallen into their hands in Conogocheague, a small town near the river Susquehanna, chiefly inhabited by the Irish. These prisoners gave us some shocking accounts of the murders and devastations committed in their parts; a few instances of which will enable the reader to guess at the treatment the provincials have suffered for years past. This party, who now joined us, had it not, I found, in their power to begin their violences so soon as those who visited my habitation; the first of their tragedies being on the 25th of October, 1754, when John Lewis, with his wife and three small children, were inhumanly scalped and murdered, and his house, barn, and every thing he possessed burnt and destroyed. On the 28th, Jacob Miller, with his wife and six of his family, with every thing on his plantations, shared the same fate. The 30th, the house, mill, barn, twenty head of cattle, two teams of horses, and every thing belonging to George Folke, met with the like treatment, himself, wife, and all his miserable family, consisting of nine in number, being scalped, then cut in pieces and given to the swine. One of the substantial traders, belonging to the province, having business that called him some miles up the country, fell into the hands of these ruffians, who not only scalped him, but immediately roasted him before he was dead; then, like cannibals, for want of other food, eat his whole body, and of his head made, what they called, an Indian pudding.

From these few instances of savage cruelty, the deplorable situation of the defenceless inhabitants, and what they hourly suffered in that part of the globe, must strike the utmost horror, and cause in every breast the utmost detestation, not only against the authors, but against those who, through inattention, or pusillanimous or erroneous principles, suffered these savages at first, unrepelled, or even unmolested, to commit such outrages, depredations, and murders.

The three prisoners that were brought with these additional forces, constantly repining at their lot, and almost dead with their excessive hard treatment, contrived at last to make their escape; but being far from their own settlements, and not knowing the country, were soon after met by some others of the tribes or nations at war with us, and brought back. The poor creatures, almost famished for want of sustenance, having had none during the time of their escape, were no sooner in the power of the barbarians than two of them were tied to a tree, and a great fire made round them, where they remained till they were terribly scorched and burnt; when one of the villains with his scalping-knife ripped open their bellies, took out their entrails, and burned them before their eyes, whilst the others were cutting, piercing, and tearing the flesh from their breasts, hands, arms, and legs, with red-hot irons, till they were dead. The third unhappy victim was reserved a few hours longer, to be, if possible, sacrificed in a more cruel manner: his arms were tied close to his body, and a hole being dug deep enough for him to stand upright, he was put into it, and earth rammed and beat in all round his body up to his neck, so that his head only appeared above ground; they then scalped him, and there let him remain for three or four hours in the greatest agonies; after which they made a small fire near his head, causing him to suffer the most excruciating torments; whilst the poor creature could only cry for mercy by killing him immediately, for his brains were boiling in his head. Inexorable to all he said, they continued the fire till his eyes gushed out of their sockets. Such agonizing torments did this unhappy creature suffer for near two hours before he was quite dead. They then cut off his head, and buried it with the other bodies; my task being to dig the graves; which, feeble and terrified as I was, the dread of suffering the same fate enabled me to do.

A great snow now falling, the barbarians were fearful lest the white people should, by their tracks, find out their skulking retreats, which obliged them to make the best of their way to their winter-quarters, about two hundred miles farther from any plantations or inhabitants. After a long and painful journey, being almost starved, I arrived with this infernal crew at Alamingo. There I found a number of wigwams full of their women and children. Dancing, singing, and shouting were their general amusements. And in all their festivals and dances they relate what successes they have had, and what damages they have sustained in their expeditions; in which I now unhappily became a part of their theme. The severity of the cold increasing, they stripped me of my clothes for their own use, and gave me such as they usually wore themselves, being a piece of blanket, and a pair of moccasons, or shoes, with a yard of coarse cloth, to put round me instead of breeches.

At Alamingo I remained near two months, till the snow was off the ground. Whatever thoughts I might have of making my escape, to carry them into execution was impracticable, being so far from any plantations or white people, and the severe weather rendering my limbs in a manner quite stiff and motionless; however, I contrived to defend myself against the inclemency of the weather as well as I could, by making myself a little wigwam with the bark of the trees, covering it with earth, which made it resemble a cave; and, to prevent the ill effects of the cold, I kept a good fire always near the door. My liberty of going about was, indeed, more than I could have expected, but they well knew the impracticability of my escaping from them. Seeing me outwardly easy and submissive, they would sometimes give me a little meat, but my chief food was Indian corn. At length the time came when they were preparing themselves for another expedition against the planters and white people; but before they set out, they were joined by many other Indians.

As soon as the snow was quite gone, they set forth on their journey towards the back parts of the province of Pennsylvania; all leaving their wives and children behind in their wigwams. They were now a formidable body, amounting to near one hundred and fifty. My business was to carry what they thought proper to load me with, but they never intrusted me with a gun. We marched on several days without any thing particular occurring, almost famished for want of provisions; for my part, I had nothing but a few stalks of Indian corn, which I was glad to eat dry; nor did the Indians themselves fare much better, for as we drew near the plantations they were afraid to kill any game, lest the noise of their guns should alarm the inhabitants.

When we again arrived at the Blue hills, about thirty miles from the Irish settlements before mentioned, we encamped for three days, though God knows we had neither tents nor any thing else to defend us from the inclemency of the air, having nothing to lie on by night but the grass; their usual method of lodging, pitching, or encamping, by night, being in parcels of ten or twelve men to a fire, where they lie upon the grass or brush wrapped up in a blanket, with their feet to the fire.

During our stay here, a sort of council of war was held, when it was agreed to divide themselves into companies of about twenty men each; after which every captain marched with his party where he thought proper. I still belonged to my old masters, but was left behind on the mountains with ten Indians, to stay till the rest should return; not thinking it proper to carry me nearer to Conogocheague, or the other plantations.

Here I began to meditate an escape, and though I knew the country round extremely well, yet I was very cautious of giving the least suspicion of any such intention. However, the third day after the grand body left, my companions thought proper to traverse the mountains in search of game for their subsistence, leaving me bound in such a manner that I could not escape. At night, when they returned, having unbound me, we all sat down together to supper on what they had killed, and soon after (being greatly fatigued with their day's excursion) they composed themselves to rest, as usual. I now tried various ways to try whether it was a scheme to prove my intentions or not; but after making a noise and walking about, sometimes touching them with my feet, I found there was no fallacy. Then I resolved, if possible, to get one of their guns, and, if discovered, to die in my defence, rather than be taken. For that purpose I made various efforts to get one from under their heads, (where they always secured them,) but in vain. Disappointed in this, I began to despair of carrying my design into execution; yet, after a little recollection, and trusting myself to the divine protection, I set forwards, naked and defenceless as I was. Such was my terror, however, that in going from them I halted, and paused every four or five yards, looking fearfully towards the spot where I had left them, lest they should awake and miss me; but when I was two hundred yards from them, I mended my pace, and made as much haste as I possibly could to the foot of the mountains; when, on a sudden, I was struck with the greatest terror at hearing the wood cry, as it is called, which the savages I had left were making upon missing their charge. The more my terror increased the faster I pushed on, and, scarce knowing where I trod, drove through the woods with the utmost precipitation, sometimes falling and bruising myself, cutting my feet and legs against the stones in a miserable manner. But faint and maimed as I was, I continued my flight till daybreak, when, without having any thing to sustain nature but a little corn left, I crept into a hollow tree, where I lay very snug, and returned my prayers and thanks to the divine Being that had thus far favored my escape. But my repose was in a few hours destroyed at hearing the voices of the savages near the place where I was hid, threatening and talking how they would use me if they got me again. However, they at last left the spot where I heard them, and I remained in my apartment all that day without further molestation.

At night I ventured forwards again, frightened; thinking each twig that touched me a savage. The third day I concealed myself in like manner as before, and at night travelled, keeping off the main road as much as possible, which lengthened my journey many miles. But how shall I describe the terror I felt on the fourth night, when, by the rustling I made among the leaves, a party of Indians, that lay round a small fire, which I did not perceive, started from the ground, and, seizing their arms, ran from the fire amongst the woods. Whether to move forward or rest where I was, I knew not, when, to my great surprise and joy, I was relieved by a parcel of swine that made towards the place where I guessed the savages to be ; who, on seeing them, imagined they had caused the alarm, very merrily returned to the fire, and lay again down to sleep. Bruised, crippled, and terrified as I was, I pursued my journey till break of day, when, thinking myself safe, I lay down under a great log, and slept till about noon. Before evening I reached the summit of a great hill, and looking out if I could spy any habitations of white people, to my inexpressible joy I saw some, which I guessed to be about ten miles' distance.

In the morning I continued my journey towards the nearest cleared lands I had seen the day before, and, about four o'clock in the afternoon, arrived at the house of John Bell, an old acquaintance, where knocking at the door, his wife, who opened it, seeing me in such a frightful condition, flew from me, screaming, into the house. This alarmed the whole family, who immediately fled to their arms, and I was soon accosted by the master with his gun in his hand. But on making myself known, (for he before took me to be an Indian,) he immediately caressed me, as did all his family, with extraordinary friendship, the report of my being murdered by the savages having reached them some months before. For two days and nights they very affectionately supplied me with all necessaries, and carefully attended me till my spirits and limbs were pretty well recovered, and I thought myself able to ride, when I borrowed of these good people (whose kindness merits my most grateful returns) a horse and some clothes, and set forward for my father-in-law's house in Chester county, about one hundred and forty miles from thence, where I arrived on the 4th of January, 1755, (but scarce one of the family could credit their eyes, believing, with the people I had lately left, that I had fallen a prey to the Indians,) where I was received and embraced by the whole family with great affection. Upon inquiring for my dear wife, I found she had been dead two months! This fatal news greatly lessened the joy I otherwise should have felt at my deliverance from the dreadful state and company I had been in.

A PARTICULAR ACCOUNT OF THE CAPTIVITY AND REDEMPTION OF MRS. JEMIMA HOWE, WHO WAS TAKEN PRISONER BY THE INDIANS AT HINSDALE, NEW HAMPSHIRE, ON THE TWENTY-SEVENTH OF JULY, 1755, AS COMMUNICATED TO DR. BELKNAP BY THE REV. BUNKER GAY.

As Messrs. Caleb Howe, Hilkiah Grout, and Benjamin Gaffield, who had been hoeing corn in the meadow, west of the river, were returning home, a little before sunset, to a place called Bridgman's fort, they were fired upon by twelve Indians, who had ambushed their path. Howe was on horseback, with two young lads, his children, behind him. A ball, which broke his thigh, brought him to the ground. His horse ran a few rods and fell likewise, and both the lads were taken. The Indians, in their savage manner coming up to Howe, pierced his body with a spear, tore off his scalp, stuck a hatchet in his head, and left him in this forlorn condition. He was found alive the morning after, by a party of men from fort Hinsdale; and being asked by one of the party whether he knew him, he answered, " Yes, I know you all." These were his last words, though he did not expire until after his friends had arrived with him at fort Hindsdale. Grout was so fortunate as to escape unhurt. But Gaffield, in attempting to wade through the river, at a certain place which was indeed fordable at that time, was unfortunately drowned. Flushed with the success they had met with here, the savages went directly to Bridgman's fort. There was no man in it, and only three women and some children, viz. Mrs. Jemima Howe, Mrs. Submit Grout, and Mrs. Eunice Gaffield. Their husbands I need not mention again, and their feelings at this juncture I will not attempt to describe. They had heard the enemy's guns, but knew not what had happened to their friends. Extremely anxious for their safety, they stood longing to embrace them, until at length, concluding from the noise they heard without that some of them were come, they unbarred the gate in a hurry to receive them; when, lo! to their inexpressible disappointment and surprise, instead of their husbands, in rushed a number of hideous Indians, to whom they and their tender offspring became an easy prey, and from whom they had nothing to expect but either an immediate death or a long and doleful captivity. The latter of these, by the favor of Providence, turned out to be the lot of these unhappy women and their still more unhappy, because more helpless, children. Mrs. Gaffield had but one, Mrs. Grout had three, and Mrs. Howe seven. The eldest of Mrs. Howe's was eleven years old, and the youngest but six months. The two eldest were daughters, which she had by her first husband, Mr. William Phipps, who was also slain by the Indians, of which I doubt not but you have seen an account in Mr. Doolittle's history. It was from the mouth of this woman that I lately received the foregoing account. She also gave me, I doubt not, a true, though, to be sure, a very brief and imperfect history of her captivity, which I here insert for your perusal. It may perhaps afford you some amusement, and can do no harm, if, after it has undergone your critical inspection, you should not think it (or an abbreviation of it) worthy to be preserved among the records you are about to publish.

The Indians (she says) having plundered and put fire to the fort, we marched, as near as I could judge, a mile and a half into the woods, where we encamped that night. When the morning came, and we had advanced as much farther, six Indians were sent back to the place of our late abode, who collected a little more plunder, and destroyed some other effects that had been left behind; but they did not return until the day was so far spent, that it was judged best to continue where we were through the night. Early the next morning we set off for Canada, and continued our march eight days succes-

14

sively, until we had reached the place where the Indians had left their canoes, about fifteen miles from Crown Point. This was a long and tedious march; but the captives, by divine assistance, were enabled to endure it with less trouble and difficulty than they had reason to expect. From such savage masters, in such indigent circumstances, we could not rationally hope for kinder treatment than we received. Some of us, it is true, had a harder lot than others; and, among the children, I thought my son Squire had the hardest of any. He was then only four years old, and when we stopped to rest our weary limbs, and he sat down on his master's pack, the savage monster would often knock him off; and sometimes, too, with the handle of his hatchet. Several ugly marks, indented in his head by the cruel Indians, at that tender age, are still plainly to be seen.

At length we arrived at Crown Point, and took up our quarters there for the space of near a week. In the mean time some of the Indians went to Montreal, and took several of the weary captives along with them, with a view of selling them to the French. They did not succeed, however, in finding a market for any of them. They gave my youngest daughter, Submit Phipps, to the governor, de Vaudreuil, had a drunken frolic, and returned again to Crown Point with the rest of their prisoners. From hence we set off for St. Johns, in four or five canoes, just as night was coming on, and were soon surrounded with darkness. A heavy storm hung over us. The sound of the rolling thunder was very terrible upon the waters, which, at every flash of expansive lightning, seemed to be all in a blaze. Yet to this we were indebted for all the light we enjoyed. No object could we discern any longer than the flashes lasted. In this posture we sailed in our open, tottering canoes almost the whole of that dreary night. The morning, indeed, had not yet begun to dawn, when we all went ashore; and having collected a heap of sand and gravel for a pillow, I laid myself down, with my tender infant by my side, not knowing where any of my other children were, or what a miserable condition they might be in. The next day, however, under the wing of that ever-present and all-powerful Providence, which had preserved us through the darkness and imminent dangers of the preceding night, we all arrived in safety at St. Johns.

Our next movement was to St. Francois, the metropolis, if I may so call it, to which the Indians, who led us captive, belonged. Soon after our arrival at their wretched capital, a council, consisting of the chief sachem and some principal warriors of the St. Francois tribe, was convened; and after the ceremonies usual on such occasions were over, I was conducted and delivered to an old squaw, whom the Indians told me I must call my mother; my infant still continuing to be the property of its original Indian owners. I was nevertheless permitted to keep it with me a while longer, for the sake of saving them the trouble of looking after it, and of maintaining it with my milk. When the weather began to grow cold, shuddering at the prospect of approaching winter, I acquainted my new mother that I did not think it would be possible for me to endure it, if I must spend it with her, and fare as the Indians did. Listening to my repeated and earnest solicitations, that I might be disposed of among some of the French inhabitants of Canada, she, at length, set off with me and my infant, attended by some male Indians, upon a journey to Montreal, in hopes of finding a market for me there. But the attempt proved unsuccessful, and the journey tedious indeed. Our provisions were so scanty, as well as insipid and unsavory, the weather was so cold, and the travelling so very bad, that it often seemed as if I must have perished on the way. The lips of my poor child were sometimes so benumbed, that when I put it to my breast it could not, till it grew warm, imbibe the nourishment requisite for its support. While we were at Montreal, we went into the house of a certain French gentleman, whose lady, being sent for, and coming into the room where I was, to examine me, seeing I had an infant, exclaimed suddenly in this manner, "Damn it, I will not buy a woman that has a child to look after." There was a swill-pail standing near me, in which I observed some crusts and crumbs of bread swimming on the surface of the greasy liquor it contained; sorely pinched with hunger, I skimmed them off with my hands and eat them; and this was all the refreshment which the house afforded me. Somewhere, in the course of this visit to Montreal, my Indian mother was so unfortunate as to catch the small-pox, of which distemper she died, soon after our return, which was by water, to St. Francois.

And now came on the season when the Indians began to prepare for a winter's hunt. I was ordered to return my poor child to those of them who still claimed it as their property. This was a severe trial. The babe clung to my bosom with all its might; but I was obliged to pluck it thence, and deliver it, shrieking and screaming, enough to penetrate a heart of stone, into the hands of those unfeeling wretches, whose tender mercies may be termed cruel. It was soon carried off by a hunting party of those Indians to a place called Messiskow, at the lower end of lake Champlain, whither, in about a month after, it was my fortune to follow them. I had preserved my milk in hopes of seeing my beloved child again. And here I found it, it is true, but in a condition that afforded me no great satisfaction, it being greatly emaciated, and almost starved. I took it in my arms, put its face to mine, and it instantly bit me with such violence that it seemed as if I must have parted with a piece of my cheek. I was permitted to lodge with it that and the two following nights; but every morning that intervened, the Indians, I suppose on purpose to torment me, sent me away to another wigwam which stood at a little distance, though not so far from the one in which my distressed infant was confined but that I could plainly hear its incessant cries and heart-rending lamentations. In this deplorable condition I was obliged to take my leave of it, on the morning of the third day after my arrival at the place. We moved down the lake several miles the same day; and the night following was remarkable on account of the *great earthquake** which terribly shook that howling wilderness. Among the islands hereabouts we spent the winter season, often shifting our quarters, and roving about from one place to another; our family consisting of three persons only, besides myself, viz. my late mother's daughter, whom therefore I called my sister, her sanhop, and a pappoose. They once left me alone two dismal nights; and when they returned to me again, perceiving them smile at each other, I asked, What is the matter? They replied that two of my children were no more; one of which, they said, died a natural death, and the other was knocked on the head. I did not utter many words, but my heart was sorely pained within me, and my mind exceedingly troubled with strange and awful ideas. I often imagined, for instance, that I plainly saw the naked carcasses of my deceased children hanging upon the limbs of the trees, as the Indians are wont to hang the raw hides of those beasts which they take in hunting.

It was not long, however, before it was so ordered by kind Providence, that I should be relieved in a good measure from those horrid imaginations; for as I was walking one day upon the ice, observing a smoke at some distance upon the land, it must proceed, thought I, from the fire of some Indian hut, and who knows but some one of my poor children may be there? My curiosity, thus excited, led me to the place, and there I found my son Caleb, a little boy between two and three years old, whom I had lately buried, in sentiment at least, or rather imagined to have been deprived of life, and perhaps also denied a decent grave. I found him likewise in tolerable health and circumstances, under the protection of a fond Indian mother; and moreover had the happiness of lodging with him

* November 18, 1755.

in my arms one joyful night. Again we shifted our quarters, and when we had travelled eight or ten miles upon the snow and ice, came to a place where the Indians manufactured sugar, which they extracted from the maple trees. Here an Indian came to visit us, whom I knew, and could speak English. He asked me why I did not go to see my son Squire. I replied that I had lately been informed that he was dead. He assured me that he was yet alive, and but two or three miles off, on the opposite side of the lake. At my request he gave me the best directions he could to the place of his abode. I resolved to embrace the first opportunity that offered of endeavoring to search it out. While I was busy in contemplating this affair, the Indians obtained a little bread, of which they gave me a small share. I did not taste a morsel of it myself, but saved it all for my poor child, if I should be so lucky as to find him. At length, having obtained of my keepers leave to be absent for one day, I set off early in the morning, and steering, as well as I could, according to the directions which the frendly Indian had given me, I quickly found the place which he had so accurately marked out. I beheld, as I drew nigh, my little son without the camp; but he looked, thought I, like a starved and mangy puppy, that had been wallowing in the ashes. I took him in my arms, and he spoke to me these words, in the Indian tongue : "Mother, are you come ?" I took him into the wigwam with me, and observing a number of Indian children in it, I distributed all the bread which I had reserved for my own child, among them all, otherwise I should have given great offence. My little boy appeared to be very fond of his new mother, kept as near me as possible while I staid, and when I told him I must go, he fell as though he had been knocked down with a club. But having recommended him to the care of Him that made him, when the day was far spent, and the time would permit me to stay no longer, I departed, you may well suppose with a heavy load at my heart. The tidings I had received of the death of my youngest child had, a little before, been confirmed to me beyond a doubt, but I could not riourn so heartily for the deceased as for the living child.

When the winter broke up, we removed to St. Johns ; and through the ensuing summer, our principal residence was at no great distance from the fort at that place. In the mean time, however, my sister's husband, having been out with a scouting party to some of the English settlements, had a drunken frolic at the fort, when he returned. His wife, who never got drunk, but had often experienced the ill effects of her husband's intemperance, fearing what the consequence might

14*

prove if he should come home in a morose and turbulent humor, to avoid his insolence, proposed that we should both retire,
and keep out of the reach of it until the storm abated. We ab-
sconded accordingly, but so it happened that I returned and ventured into his presence, before his wife had presumed to come
nigh him. I found him in his wigwam, and in a surly mood;
and not being able to revenge upon his wife, because she was
not at home, he laid hold of me, and hurried me to the fort,
and, for a trifling consideration, sold me to a French gentleman
whose name was Saccapee. 'Tis an ill wind certainly that
blows nobody any good. I had been with the Indians a year
lacking fourteen days; and, if not for my sister, yet for me,
'twas a lucky circumstance indeed, which thus at last, in an
unexpected moment, snatched me out of their cruel hands, and
placed me beyond the reach of their insolent power.

After my Indian master had disposed of me in the manner
related above, and the moment of sober reflection had arrived,
perceiving that the man who bought me had taken the advantage
of him in an unguarded hour, his resentments began to kindle,
and his indignation rose so high, that he threatened to kill me
if he should meet me alone, or if he could not revenge himself
thus that he would set fire to the fort. I was therefore secreted
in an upper chamber, and the fort carefully guarded, until his
wrath had time to cool. My service in the family to which I
was now advanced, was perfect freedom in comparison of what
it had been among the barbarous Indians. My new master
and mistress were both as kind and generous towards me as I
could anyways expect. I seldom asked a favor of either of
them but it was readily granted; in consequence of which I
had it in my power, in many instances, to administer aid and
refreshment to the poor prisoners of my own nation, who were
brought into St. Johns during my abode in the family of the
above-mentioned benevolent and hospitable Saccapee. Yet
even in this family such trials awaited me as I had little reason
to expect, but stood in need of a large stock of prudence, to
enable me to encounter them. Must I tell you then, that even
the good old man himself, who considered me as his property,
and likewise a warm and resolute son of his, at that same time,
and under the same roof, became both excessively fond of my
company; so that between these two rivals, the father and the
son, I found myself in a very critical situation indeed, and was
greatly embarrassed and perplexed, hardly knowing many
times how to behave in such a manner as at once to secure
my own virtue, and the good esteem of the family in which I
resided, and upon which I was wholly dependent for my daily
support. At length, however, through the tender compassion

of a certain English gentleman,* the Governor de Vaudreuil being made acquainted with the condition I had fallen into, immediately ordered the young and amorous Saccapee, then an officer in the French army, from the field of Venus to the field of Mars, and at the same time also wrote a letter to his father, enjoining it upon him by no means to suffer me to be abused, but to make my situation and service in his family as easy and delightful as possible. I was moreover under unspeakable obligations to the governor upon another account. I had received intelligence from my daughter Mary, the purport of which was, that there was a prospect of her being shortly married to a young Indian of the tribe of St. Francois, with which tribe she had continued from the beginning of her captivity. These were heavy tidings, and added greatly to the poignancy of my other afflictions. However, not long after I had heard this melancholy news, an opportunity presented of acquainting that humane and generous gentleman, the commander-in-chief, and my illustrious benefactor, with this affair also, who, in compassion for my sufferings, and to mitigate my sorrows, issued his orders in good time, and had my daughter taken away from the Indians, and conveyed to the same nunnery where her sister was then lodged, with his express injunction that they should both of them together be well looked after, and carefully educated, as his adopted children. In this school of superstition and bigotry they continued while the war in those days between France and Great Britain lasted. At the conclusion of which war, the governor went home to France, took my oldest daughter along with him, and married her then to a French gentleman, whose name is Cron Lewis. He was at Boston with the fleet under Count de Estaing, [1778] and one of his clerks. My other daughter still continuing in the nunnery, a considerable time had elapsed after my return from captivity, when I made a journey to Canada, resolving to use my best endeavors not to return without her. I arrived just in time to prevent her being sent to France. She was to have gone in the next vessel that sailed for that place. And I found it extremely difficult to prevail with her to quit the nunnery and go home with me ; yea, she absolutely refused, and all the persuasions and arguments I could use with her were to no effect, until after I had been to the governor, and obtained a letter from him to the superintendent of the nuns, in which he threatened, if my daughter should not be immediately delivered into my hands, or could not be prevailed with to submit to my paternal author-

---

* Col. Peter Schuyler, then a prisoner.

ity, that he would send a band of soldiers to assist me in bringing her away. Upon hearing this she made no farther resistance. But so extremely bigoted was she to the customs and religion of the place, that, after all, she left it with the greatest reluctance, and the most bitter lamentations, which she continued as we passed the streets, and wholly refused to be comforted. My good friend, Major Small, whom we met with on the way, tried all he could to console her ; and was so very kind and obliging as to bear us company, and carry my daughter behind him on horseback.

But I have run on a little before my story, for I have not yet informed you of the means and manner of my own re-demption, to the accomplishing of which, the recovery of my daughter just mentioned, and the ransoming of some of my other children, several gentlemen of note contributed not a little ; to whose goodness therefore I am greatly indebted, and sincerely hope I shall never be so ungrateful as to forget. Col. Schuyler in particular was so very kind and generous as to advance 2700 livres to procure a ransom for myself and three of my children. He accompanied and conducted us from Montreal to Albany, and entertained us in the most friendly and hospitable manner a considerable time, at his own house, and I believe entirely at his own expense.

I have spun out the above narrative to a much greater length than I at first intended, and shall conclude it with referring you, for a more ample and *brilliant* account of the captive heroine who is the subject of it, to Col. Humphrey's History of the Life of Gen. Israel Putnam, together with some remarks upon a few clauses in it. I never indeed had the pleasure of perusing the whole of said history, but remember to have seen some time ago an extract from it in one of the Boston news-papers, in which the colonel has extolled the beauty and good sense, and rare accomplishments of Mrs. Howe, the person whom he endeavors to paint in the most lively and engaging colors, perhaps a little too highly, and in a style that may ap-pear to those who are acquainted with her to this day romantic and extravagant. And the colonel must needs have been mis-informed with respect to some particulars that he has men-tioned in her history. Indeed, when I read the extract from his history to Mrs. Tute, (which name she has derived from a third husband, whose widow she now remains,) she seemed to be well pleased, and said at first it was all true, but soon after contradicted the circumstance of her lover's being so bereft of his senses, when he saw her moving off in a boat at some dis-tance from the shore, as to plunge into the water after her, in consequence of which he was seen no more. It is true, she said, that as she was returning from Montreal to Albany, she met with young Saccapee on the way; that she was in a boat with Colonel Schuyler; that the French officer came on board the boat, made her some handsome presents, took his final leave of her, and departed, to outward appearance in tolerable good humor.

She moreover says, that when she went to Canada for her daughter, she met with him again, that he showed her a lock of her hair, and her name likewise, printed with vermillion on his arm. As to her being chosen agent to go to Europe, in behalf of the people of Hinsdale, when Colonel Howard obtained from the government of New York a patent of their lands on the west side of Connecticut river, it was never once thought of by Hinsdale people until the above-mentioned extract arrived among them, in which the author has inserted it as a matter of undoubted fact.

NARRATIVE

OF THE CAPTIVITY OF FRANCES NOBLE, WHO WAS, AMONG OTHERS, TAKEN BY THE INDIANS FROM SWAN ISLAND, IN MAINE, ABOUT THE YEAR 1755; COMPILED BY JOHN KELLY, ESQ. OF CONCORD, NEW HAMPSHIRE, FROM THE MINUTES AND MEMORANDA OF PHINEHAS MERRILL, ESQ. OF STRATHAM, IN THE SAME STATE; AND BY THE FORMER GENTLEMAN COMMUNICATED FOR PUBLICATION TO THE EDITORS OF THE HISTORICAL COLLECTIONS OF NEW HAMPSHIRE.

JAMES WHIDDEN, the maternal grandfather of Mrs. Shute, was a captain in the army at the taking of Cape Breton in 1745. He owned a tract of land on Swan Island, in the river Kennebec, where he lived with his family. One of his daughters married Lazarus Noble, of Portsmouth, who lived on the island with her father. The Indians had been accustomed to visit Capt. Whidden for the purposes of trade. There was a garrison on the island to secure the inhabitants from the attacks of the enemy in time of war.

One morning, a little after daybreak, two boys went out of the garrison and left the gate open. The Indians were on the watch, and availing themselves of the opportunity, about ninety entered the garrison. The inhabitants immediately discovered that the enemy was upon them; but there was no escape. Captain Whidden and his wife retreated to the cellar, and concealed themselves. Noble and his hired man met the Indians at the head of the stairs, and fired upon them, wounding one of them in the arm. The Indians did not return the fire, but took Noble, his wife, and seven children, with Timothy Whidden and Mary Holmes, prisoners. The hired man and the two boys escaped. The captives were carried to the water's side and bound; excepting such as could not run away. The Indians then returned to the garrison, burnt the barn and plundered the house, cut open the feather beds, strewed the feathers in the field, and carried off all the silver and gold they could find, and as much of the provisions as they chose. It was supposed they omitted to burn the house from the suspicion that the captain and his wife, from whom they had, in times of peace, received many favors, were concealed in it. Capt. Whidden, after the destruction of his property on the island, returned to Greenland, in this state, which is supposed to have been his native place, and there died.

The Indians also took in a wood on the island an old man by the name of Pomeroy, who was employed in making shingles. Having collected their captives and plunder, they immediately left the island, and commenced their return to Canada to dispose of their prey. Pomeroy was old and feeble, and unable to endure the fatigue of the march, without more assistance than the savages thought fit to render him, and they killed him on the journey. They were more attentive to the children, as for them they undoubtedly expected a higher price or a greater ransom. Abigail, one of the children, died among the Indians. The other captives arrived safe in Canada, and were variously disposed of. Mr. Noble was sold to a baker in Quebec, and his wife to a lady of the same place as a chambermaid. They were allowed to visit each other and to sleep together. Four of the children were also sold in Quebec, as were Timothy Whidden and Mary Holmes. The captives in that city were exchanged within a year, and returned to their homes. Mr. Whidden and Miss Holmes were afterwards united in marriage.

FANNY NOBLE, the principal subject of this memoir, at the time of her captivity, was about thirteen months old. She was carried by a party of Indians to Montreal. In their attempts to dispose of her, they took her one day to the house of Monsieur Louis St. Auge Charlee, an eminent merchant of that place, who was at that time on a journey to Quebec. His lady was called into the kitchen by one of her maids to see a poor infant crawling on the tile floor in dirt and rags, picking apple peelings out of the cracks. She came in, and on kindly noticing the child, Fanny immediately caught hold of the lady's gown, wrapped it over her head, and burst into tears. The lady could not easily resist this appeal to her compassion. She took up the child, who clung about her neck and repeatedly embraced her. The Indians offered to sell her their little captive, but she declined buying, not choosing probably in the absence of her husband to venture on such a purchase. The Indians left the house, and slept that night on the pavements before the door. Fanny, who had again heard the voice of kindness, to which she had not been accustomed from her savage masters, could not be quiet, but disturbed the slumbers and touched the heart of the French lady by her incessant cries. This lady had then lately lost a child by death, and was perhaps more quick to feel for the sufferings of children, and more disposed to love them, than she would otherwise have been. Early the next morning the Indians were called into the house; Fanny was purchased, put into a tub of water, and having been thoroughly washed, was dressed in the clothes of the deceased child, and put to bed. She awoke smiling, and seemed desirous of repaying her mistress' kindness by her infantile prattle and fond caresses. Fanny could never learn for what price she was bought of the Indians, as her French mother declined answering her questions upon that subject, telling her to be a good girl, and be thankful that she was not still in their power.

Mons. and Mad. St. Auge took a lively interest in their little captive, and treated her with much tenderness and affection. She felt for them a filial attachment. When her parents were exchanged, her mother, on her return home, called upon Fanny, and took the child in her arms, but no instinct taught her to rejoice in the maternal embrace, and she fled for protection to her French mamma. Mrs. Noble received many presents from the French lady, and had the satisfaction to see that her little daughter was left in affectionate hands.

Fanny was taught to call and consider Mons. and Mad. St. Auge as her parents. They had her baptized by the name of Eleanor, and educated her in the Roman Catholic religion. She learned her Pater Nosters and Ave Marias, went to mass, crossed herself with holy water, and told her beads with great devotion.

When four or five years old, she was enticed away from her French parents by Wheelwright, who had been employed by the government of Massachusetts to seek for captives in Canada. He carried her to the Three Rivers, where he had several other captives, and left her, as he pretended, with a relation of her French father's for a few days, when she expected to return to Montreal. But she had not been to the Three Rivers more than twenty-four hours, when the old squaw who had sold her to Mad. St. Auge came along in a sleigh, accompanied by a young sanop, seized upon Fanny, and carried her to St. Francois, where they kept her about a fortnight. She had now attained an age when she would be sensible of her misfortunes, and bitterly lamented her separation from her French parents. The Indians endeavored to pacify and please her by drawing on her coat or frock the figures of deers, wolves, bears, fishes, &c.; and once, probably to make her look as handsomely as themselves, they painted her cheeks in the Indian fashion, which very much distressed her, and the old squaw made them wipe off the paint. At one time she got away from the savages, and sought refuge in the best-looking house in the village, which belonged to a French priest, who kissed her, asked her many questions, and treated her kindly, but gave her up to the claim of her Indian masters. While at St. Francois, her brother, Joseph Noble, who had not been sold to the French, but still lived with the Indians, came to see her, but she had a great aversion to him. He was in his Indian dress, and she would not believe him to be a relation, or speak to him if she could avoid it. She was at last turned back by the Indians to Montreal, and to her great satisfaction was delivered to her French father, who rewarded the Indians for returning her. It was doubtless the expectation of much reward which induced the old squaw to seize her at the Three Rivers, as the Indians not unfrequently stole back captives, in order to extort presents for their return from the French gentlemen to whom the same captives had before been sold. Before this time she had been hastily carried from Montreal, hurried over mountains and across waters, and concealed among flags, while those who accompanied her were evidently pursued, and in great apprehension of being overtaken; but the occasion of this flight or its incidents she was too young to understand or distinctly to remember, and she was unable afterwards to satisfy herself whether her French father conveyed her away to keep her out of the reach of her natural friends, or whether she was taken by those friends, and afterwards retaken as at the Three Rivers and returned to Montreal. The French parents cautiously avoided informing her upon this subject, or upon any other which should remind her of her captivity, her country, her parents or her friends, lest she should become discontented with her situation, and desirous of leaving those who had adopted her. They kept her secreted from her natural friends, who were in search of her, and evaded every question which might lead to her discovery. One day, when Mons. St. Auge and most of his family were at mass, she was sent with another captive to the third story of the house, and the domestics were required strictly to watch them, as it was known that some of her relations were then in the place endeavoring to find her. Of this circumstance she was ignorant, but she was displeased with her confinement, and with her little companion found means to escape from their room and went below. While raising a cup of water to her mouth, she saw a man looking at her through the window, and stretching out his arm towards her, at the same time speaking a language which she could not understand. She was very much alarmed, threw down her water, and ran with all possible speed to her room. Little did she suppose that it was her own father, from whom she was flying in such fear and horror. He had returned to Canada to seek those of his children who remained there. He could hear nothing of his Fanny; but watching the house, he perceived her, as was just stated, and joyfully stretching his arms towards her, exclaimed, " There's my daughter! O! that's my daughter!" But she retreated, and he could not gain admittance, for the house was guarded and no stranger permitted to enter. How long he continued hovering about her is now unknown, but he left Canada without embracing her or seeing her again.

Her French parents put her to a boarding school attached to a nunnery in Montreal. where she remained several years, and was taught all branches of needle-work, with geography, music, painting, &c. In the same school were two Misses Johnsons, who were captured at Charlestown, (No. 4) in 1754, and two Misses Phipps, the daughters of Mrs. Howe, who were taken at Hinsdale in 1755. Fanny was in school when Mrs. Howe came for her daughters, and long remembered the grief and lamentations of the young captives when obliged to leave their school and mates to return to a strange, though their native country, and to relatives whom they had long forgotten.

While at school at Montreal, her brother Joseph again visited her. He still belonged to the St. Francois tribe of Indians, and was dressed remarkably fine, having forty or fifty broaches in his shirt, clasps on his arm, and a great variety of knots and bells about his clothing. He brought his little sister Ellen, as she was then called, and who was then not far from seven years old, a young fawn, a basket of cranberries, and a lump of sap sugar. The little girl was much pleased with the fawn, and had no great aversion to cranberries and sugar, but she

15

was much frightened by the appearance of Joseph, and would receive nothing from his hands till, at the suggestion of her friends, he had washed the paint from his face and made some alteration in his dress, when she ventured to accept his offerings, and immediately ran from his presence. The next day, Joseph returned with the Indians to St. Francois, but some time afterwards Mons. St. Auge purchased him of the savages, and dressed him in the French style; but he never appeared so bold and majestic, so spirited and vivacious, as when arrayed in his Indian habit and associating with his Indian friends. He however became much attached to St. Auge, who put him to school; and when his sister parted with him upon leaving Canada, he gave her a strict charge not to let it be known where he was, lest he too should be obliged to leave his friends and return to the place of his birth.

When between eleven and twelve years of age, Fanny was sent to the school of Ursuline nuns in Quebec, to complete her education. Here the discipline was much more strict and solemn than in the school at Montreal. In both places the teachers were called half nuns, who, not being professed, were allowed to go in and out at pleasure; but at Quebec the pupils were in a great measure secluded from the world, being permitted to walk only in a small garden by day, and confined by bolts and bars in their cells at night. This restraint was irksome to Fanny. She grew discontented; and at the close of the year was permitted to return to her French parents at Montreal, and again enter the school in that city.

While Fanny was in the nunnery, being then in her fourteenth year, she was one day equally surprised and alarmed by the entrance of a stranger, who demanded her of the nuns as a redeemed captive. Her father had employed this man, Arnold, to seek out his daughter and obtain her from the French, who had hitherto succeeded in detaining her. Arnold was well calculated for this employment. He was secret, subtle, resolute and persevering. He had been some time in the city without exciting a suspicion of his business. He had ascertained where the captive was to be found—he had procured the necessary powers to secure her, and in his approach to the nunnery was accompanied by a sergeant and a file of men. The nuns were unwilling to deliver up their pupil, and required to know by what right he demanded her. Arnold convinced them that his authority was derived from the governor, and they durst not disobey. They, however, prolonged the time as much as possible, and sent word to Mons. St. Auge, hoping that he would be able in some way or other to detain his adopted daughter. Arnold however was not to be delayed

or trifled with.   He sternly demanded the captive by the name
of Noble in the governor's name, and the nuns were awed
into submission.   Fanny, weeping and trembling, was delivered up by those who wept and trembled too.   She accompanied Arnold to the gate of the nunnery, but the idea of
leaving forever those whom she loved and going with a company of armed men she knew not whither, was too overwhelm-
ing, and she sunk upon the ground.   Her cries and lamentations drew the people around her, and she exclaimed bitterly
against the cruelty of forcing her away, declaring that she could
not and would not go any further as a prisoner with those frightful soldiers.   At this time an English officer appeared in the
crowd ; he reasoned with her, soothed her, and persuaded her
to walk with him, assuring her the guard should be dismissed
and no injury befall her.   As they passed by the door of
Mons. St. Auge, on their way to the inn, her grief and excla-
mations were renewed, and it was with great difficulty that
she could be persuaded to proceed.   But the guard had merely
fallen back, and were too near to prevent a rescue, had an attempt been made.   Capt. M'Clure, the English officer, promised
her that she should be permitted to visit her French parents
the next day.   She found them in tears, but they could not
detain her.   Mons. St. Auge gave her a handful of money,
and embraced her, blessed her, and rushed out of the room.
His lady supplied her with clothes, and their parting was most
affectionate and affecting.   She lived to a considerably advanced age, but she could never speak of this scene without
visible and deep emotion.

   She was carried down the river to Quebec, where she tarried a few days, and then sailed with Captain Wilson for Boston.   She arrived at that port in July, one month before she
was fourteen years of age.   She was joyfully received by
her friends, but her father did not long survive her return.
After his death she resided in the family of Capt. Wilson, at
Boston, until she had acquired the English language, of which
before she was almost entirely ignorant.   She then went to
Newbury, and lived in the family of a relative of her father,
where she found a home, and that peace to which she had long
been a stranger.   Her education had qualified her for the
instruction of youth, and she partially devoted herself to that
employment.   She was engaged in a school at Hampton,
where she formed an acquaintance with Mr. Jonathan Tilton,
a gentleman of good property in Kensington, whom she married about the year 1776.   He died in 1798.   In 1801, she
married Mr. John Shute, of New-Market, and lived in the village of Newfields in that town till her death, in September,

1819.   She was much respected and esteemed in life, and her death was, as her life had been, that of a Christian.

CAPTAIN JONATHAN CARVER'S

NARRATIVE OF HIS CAPTURE, AND SUBSEQUENT ESCAPE FROM THE INDIANS, AT THE BLOODY MASSACRE COMMITTED BY THEM, WHEN FORT WILLIAM HENRY FELL INTO THE HANDS OF THE FRENCH, UNDER GEN. MONTCALM, IN THE YEAR 1757.   WRITTEN BY HIMSELF.

GEN. WEBB, who commanded the English army in North America, which was then encamped at fort Edward, having intelligence that the French troops under Monsieur Montcalm were making some movements towards fort William Henry, he detached a corps of about fifteen hundred men, consisting of English and provincials, to strengthen the garrison.   In this party I went as a volunteer among the latter.

The apprehensions of the English general were not without foundation; for the day after our arrival we saw lake George, (formerly lake Sacrament) to which it lies contiguous, covered with an immense number of boats; and in a few hours we found our lines attacked by the French general, who had just landed with eleven thousand regulars and Canadians, and two thousand Indians.   Colonel Monro, a brave officer, commanded in the fort, and had no more than two thousand three hundred men with him, our detachment included.

With these he made a gallant defence, and probably would have been able at last to preserve the fort, had he been properly supported, and permitted to continue his efforts. On every summons to surrender sent by the French general, who offered the most honorable terms, his answer repeatedly was, that he yet found himself in a condition to repel the most vigorous attacks his besiegers were able to make; and if he thought his present force insufficient, he could soon be supplied with a greater number from the adjacent army.

But the colonel having acquainted General Webb with his situation, and desired he would send him some fresh troops, the general dispatched a messenger to him with a letter, wherein he informed him that it was not in his power to assist him, and therefore gave him orders to surrender up the fort on the best terms he could procure. This packet fell into the hands of the French general, who immediately sent a flag of truce, desiring a conference with the governor.

They accordingly met, attended only by a small guard, in the centre between the lines; when Monsieur Montcalm told the colonel, that he was come in person to demand possession of the fort, as it belonged to the king his master. The colonel replied, that he knew not how that could be, nor should he surrender it up whilst it was in his power to defend it.

The French general rejoined at the same time delivering the packet into the colonel's hand, "By this authority do I make the requisition." The brave governor had no sooner read the contents of it, and was convinced that such were the orders of the commander-in-chief, and not to be disobeyed, than he hung his head in silence, and reluctantly entered into a negotiation.

In consideration of the gallant defence the garrison had made, they were to be permitted to march out with all the honors of war, to be allowed covered wagons to transport their baggage to fort Edward, and a guard to protect them from the fury of the savages.

The morning after the capitulation was signed, as soon as day broke, the whole garrison, now consisting of about two thousand men, besides women and children, were drawn up within the lines, and on the point of marching off, when great numbers of the Indians gathered about, and began to plunder. We were at first in hopes that this was their only view, and suffered them to proceed without opposition. Indeed it was not in our power to make any, had we been so inclined; for though we were permitted to carry off our arms, yet we were not allowed a single round of ammunition. In these hopes however we were disappointed; for presently some of them

15*

began to attack the sick and wounded, when such as were not able to crawl into the ranks, notwithstanding they endeavored to avert the fury of their enemies by their shrieks or groans, were soon dispatched.

Here we were fully in expectation that the disturbance would have concluded; and our little army began to move; but in a short time we saw the front division driven back, and discovered that we were entirely encircled by the savages. We expected every moment that the guard, which the French, by the articles of capitulation, had agreed to allow us, would have arrived, and put an end to our apprehensions; but none appeared. The Indians now began to strip every one without exception of their arms and clothes, and those who made the least resistance felt the weight of their tomahawks.

I happened to be in the rear division, but it was not long before I shared the fate of my companions. Three or four of the savages laid hold of me, and whilst some held their weapons over my head, the others soon disrobed me of my coat, waistcoat, hat and buckles, omitting not to take from me what money I had in my pocket. As this was transacted close by the passage that led from the lines on to the plain, near which a French sentinel was posted, I ran to him and claimed his protection; but he only called me an English dog, and thrust me with violence back again into the midst of the Indians.

I now endeavored to join a body of our troops that were crowded together at some distance; but innumerable were the blows that were made at me with different weapons as I passed on; luckily however the savages were so close together that they could not strike at me without endangering each other. Notwithstanding which one of them found means to make a thrust at me with a spear, which grazed my side, and from another I received a wound, with the same kind of weapon, in my ankle. At length I gained the spot where my countrymen stood, and forced myself into the midst of them. But before I got thus far out of the hands of the Indians, the collar and wristbands of my shirt were all that remained of it, and my flesh was scratched and torn in many places by their savage gripes.

By this time the war-whoop was given, and the Indians began to murder those that were nearest to them without distinction. It is not in the power of words to give any tolerable idea of the horrid scene that now ensued; men, women, and children were dispatched in the most wanton and cruel manner, and immediately scalped. Many of these savages drank the blood of their victims, as it flowed warm from the fatal wound.

We now perceived, though too late to avail us, that we were to expect no relief from the French; and that, contrary to the agreement they had so lately signed to allow us a sufficient force to protect us from these insults, they tacitly permitted them; for I could plainly perceive the French officers walking about at some distance, discoursing together with apparent unconcern. For the honor of human nature I would hope that this flagrant breach of every sacred law proceeded rather from the savage disposition of the Indians, which I acknowledge it is sometimes almost impossible to control, and which might now unexpectedly have arrived to a pitch not easily to be restrained, than to any premeditated design in the French commander. An unprejudiced observer would, however, be apt to conclude, that a body of ten thousand christian troops, most christian troops, had it in their power to prevent the massacre from becoming so general. But whatever was the cause from which it arose, the consequences of it were dreadful, and not to be paralleled in modern history.

As the circle in which I stood inclosed by this time was much thinned, and death seemed to be approaching with hasty strides, it was proposed by some of the most resolute to make one vigorous effort, and endeavor to force our way through the savages, the only probable method of preserving our lives that now remained. This, however desperate, was resolved on, and about twenty of us sprung at once into the midst of them.

In a moment we were all separated, and what was the fate of my companions I could not learn till some months after, when I found that only six or seven of them effected their design. Intent only on my own hazardous situation, I endeavored to make my way through my savage enemies in the best manner possible. And I have often been astonished since, when I have recollected with what composure I took, as I did, every necessary step for my preservation. Some I overturned, being at that time young and athletic, and others I passed by, dexterously avoiding their weapons; till at last two very stout chiefs, of the most savage tribes, as I could distinguish by their dress, whose strength I could not resist, laid hold of me by each arm, and began to force me through the crowd.

I now resigned myself to my fate, not doubting but that they intended to dispatch me, and then to satiate their vengeance with my blood, as I found they were hurrying me towards a retired swamp that lay at some distance. But before we had got many yards, an English gentleman of some distinction, as I could discover by his breeches, the only covering he had on, which were of fine scarlet velvet, rushed close by us. One of the Indians instantly relinquished his hold, and springing on this new object, endeavored to seize him as his prey; but the gentleman being strong, threw him on the ground, and would probably have got away, had not he who held my other arm quitted me to assist his brother. I seized the opportunity, and hastened away to join another party of English troops that were yet unbroken, and stood in a body at some distance. But before I had taken many steps, I hastily cast my eye towards the gentleman, and saw the Indian's tomahawk gash into his back, and heard him utter his last groan. This added both to my speed and desperation.

I had left this shocking scene but a few yards, when a fine boy about twelve years of age, that had hitherto escaped, came up to me, and begged that I would let him lay hold of me, so that he might stand some chance of getting out of the hands of the savages. I told him that I would give him every assistance in my power, and to this purpose bid him lay hold; but in a few moments he was torn from my side, and by his shrieks I judge was soon demolished. I could not help forgetting my own cares for a minute, to lament the fate of so young a sufferer; but it was utterly impossible for me to take any methods to prevent it.

I now got once more into the midst of friends, but we were unable to afford each other any succor. As this was the division that had advanced the furthest from the fort, I thought there might be a possibility (though but a bare one) of my forcing my way through the outer ranks of the Indians, and getting to a neighboring wood, which I perceived at some distance. I was still encouraged to hope by the almost miraculous preservation I had already experienced.

Nor were my hopes in vain, or the efforts I made ineffectual. Suffice to say, that I reached the wood; but by the time I had penetrated a little way into it, my breath was so exhausted that I threw myself into a break, and lay for some minutes apparently at the last gasp. At length I recovered the power of respiration; but my apprehensions returned with all their former force, when I saw several savages pass by, probably in pursuit of me, at no very great distance. In this situation I knew not whether it was better to proceed, or endeavor to conceal myself where I lay till night came on; fearing, however, that they would return the same way, I thought it most prudent to get further from the dreadful scene of my distresses. Accordingly, striking into another part of the wood, I hastened on as fast as the briers and the loss of one of my shoes would permit me; and after a slow progress of some hours, gained a hill that overlooked the plain which I had just left, from whence

I could discern that the bloody storm still raged with unabated fury.

But not to tire my readers, I shall only add, that after passing three days without subsistence, and enduring the severity of the cold dews for three nights, I at length reached fort Edward; where with proper care my body soon recovered its wonted strength, and my mind, as far as the recollection of the late melancholy events would permit, its usual composure.

It was computed that fifteen hundred persons were killed or made prisoners by these savages during this fatal day. Many of the latter were carried off by them and never returned. A few, through favorable accidents, found their way back to their native country, after having experienced a long and severe captivity.

The brave Col. Monro had hastened away, soon after the confusion began, to the French camp, to endeavor to procure the guard agreed by the stipulation; but his application proving ineffectual, he remained there till General Webb sent a party of troops to demand and protect him back to fort Edward. But these unhappy concurrences, which would probably have been prevented had he been left to pursue his own plans, together with the loss of so many brave fellows, murdered in cold blood, to whose valor he had been so lately a witness, made such an impression on his mind that he did not long survive. He died in about three months of a broken heart, and with truth might it be said that he was an honor to his country.

I mean not to point out the following circumstance as the immediate judgment of heaven, and intended as an atonement for this slaughter; but I cannot omit that very few of those different tribes of Indians that shared in it ever lived to return home. The small-pox, by means of their communication with the Europeans, found its way among them, and made an equal havoc to what they themselves had done. The methods they pursued on the first attack of that malignant disorder, to abate the fever attending it, rendered it fatal. Whilst their blood was in a state of fermentation, and nature was striving to throw out the peccant matter, they checked her operations by plunging into the water; the consequence was that they died by hundreds. The few that survived were transformed by it into hideous objects, and bore with them to the grave deep indented marks of this much dreaded disease.

Monsieur Montcalm fell soon after on the plains of Quebec.

That the unprovoked cruelty of this commander was not approved of by the generality of his countrymen, I have since been convinced of by many proofs. One only, however, which

I received from a person who was witness to it, shall I at present give. A Canadian merchant, of some consideration, having heard of the surrender of the English fort, celebrated the fortunate event with great rejoicings and hospitality, according to the custom of that country; but no sooner did the news of the massacre which ensued reach his ears, than he put an immediate stop to the festivity, and exclaimed in the severest terms against the inhuman permission; declaring at the same time that those who had connived at it had thereby drawn down on that part of their king's dominions the vengeance of Heaven. To this he added, that he much feared the total loss of them would deservedly be the consequence. How truly this prediction has been verified we well know.

AN ACCOUNT

OF THE REMARKABLE OCCURRENCES IN THE LIFE AND TRAVELS OF COLONEL JAMES SMITH, (LATE A CITIZEN OF BOURBON COUNTY, KENTUCKY,) DURING HIS CAPTIVITY WITH THE INDIANS, IN THE YEARS 1755, '56, '57, '58, AND '59. In which the Customs, Manners, Traditions, Theological Sentiments, Mode of Warfare, Military Tactics, Discipline and Encampments, Treatment of Prisoners, &c. are better explained, and more minutely related, than has been heretofore done by any author on that subject. Together with a description of the Soil, Timber and Waters, where he travelled with the Indians during his captivity.—To which is added a brief account of some very uncommon occurrences which transpired after his return from captivity; as well as of the different campaigns carried on against the Indians to the westward of fort Pitt, since the year 1755, to the present date, 1799.—Written by himself.

PREFACE.—I was strongly urged to publish the following work immediately after my return from captivity, which was nearly forty years ago; but, as at that time the Americans were so little acquainted with Indian affairs, I apprehended a great part of it would be viewed as fable or romance.

As the Indians never attempted to prevent me either from reading or writing, I kept a journal, which I revised shortly after my return from captivity, and which I have kept ever since; and as I have had but a moderate English education, have been advised to employ some person of liberal education to transcribe and embellish it—but believing that nature always outshines art, have thought, that occurrences truly and plainly stated, as they happened, would make the best history, be better understood, and most entertaining.

In the different Indian speeches copied into this work, I have not only imitated their own style, or mode of speaking, but have also preserved the ideas meant to be communicated in those speeches. In common conversation I have used my own style, but preserved their ideas. The principal advantage that I expect will result to the public, from the publication of the following sheets, is the *observations on the Indian mode of warfare.* Experience has taught the Americans the necessity of adopting their mode; and the more perfect we are in that mode, the better we shall be able to defend ourselves against them, when defence is necessary.

JAMES SMITH.

Bourbon County, June 1st, 1799.

Introduction.—More than thirty years have elapsed since the publication of Col. Smith's journal. The only edition ever presented to the public was printed in Lexington, Kentucky, by John Bradford, in 1799. That edition being in pamphlet form, it is presumed that there is not now a dozen entire copies remaining. A new generation has sprung up, and it is believed the time has now arrived, when a second edition, in a more durable form, will be well received by the public. The character of Colonel Smith is well known in the western country, especially amongst the veteran pioneers of Kentucky and Tennessee. He was a patriot in the strictest sense of the word. His whole life was devoted to the service of his country. Raised, as it were, in the wilderness, he received but a limited education ; yet nature had endowed him with a vigorous constitution, and a strong and sensible mind ; and whether in the camp or the halls of legislation, he gave ample proofs of being, by practice as well as profession, a soldier and a statesman.

During the war of 1811 and 12, being then too old to be serviceable in the field, he made a tender of his experience, and published a treatise on the Indian mode of warfare, with which sad experience had made him so well acquainted. He died shortly afterwards, at the house of a brother-in-law, in Washington county, Kentucky. He was esteemed by all who knew him as an exemplary Christian, and a consistent and unwavering patriot.

By his first marriage, he had several children ; and two of his sons, William and James, it is believed, are now living. The name of his first wife is not recollected.

In the year 1785, he intermarried with Mrs. Margaret Irvin, the widow of Mr. Abraham Irvin. Mrs. Irvin was a lady of a highly cultivated mind ; and had she lived in more auspicious times, and possessed the advantages of many of her sex, she would have made no ordinary figure as a writer, both in prose and verse. And it may not be uninteresting to the friends of Col. Smith to give a short sketch of her life. Her maiden name was Rodgers. She was born in the year 1744, in Hanover county, Virginia. She was of a respectable family ; her father and the Rev. Dr. Rodgers, of New York, were brothers' children. Her mother was sister to the Rev. James Caldwell, who was killed by the British and tories at Elizabeth Point, New Jersey. Her father removed, when she was a child, to what was then called Lunenburg, now Charlotte county, Virginia. She never went to school but three months, and that at the age of five years. At the expiration of that term the school ceased, and she had no opportunity to attend one afterwards. Her mother, however, being an intelligent woman, and an excellent scholar, gave her lessons at home. On the 5th of November, 1764, she was married to Mr. Irvin, a respectable man, though in moderate circumstances. In the year 1777, when every true friend of his country felt it his duty to render some personal service, he and a neighbor, by the name of William Handy, agreed that they would enlist for the term of three years, and each to serve eighteen months; Irvin to serve the first half, and Handy the second. Mr. Irvin entered upon duty, in company with many others from that section of the country. When they had marched to Dumfries, Va., before they joined the main army, they were ordered to halt, and inoculate for the small-pox. Irvin neglected to inoculate, under the impression he had had the disease during infancy. The consequence was, he took the small-pox in the natural way, and died, leaving Mrs. Irvin, and five small children, four sons and a daughter.

In the fall of 1782, Mrs. Irvin removed, in company with a number of enterprising Virginians, to the wilds of Kentucky; and three years afterwards intermarried with Col. Smith, by whom she had no issue. She died about the year 1800, in Bourbon county, Kentucky, in the 56th year of her age. She was a member of the Presbyterian church, and sustained through life an unblemished reputation. In early life she wrote but little, most of her productions being the fruits of her maturer years, and while she was the wife of Col. Smith. But little of her composition has ever been put to press; but her genius and taste were always acknowledged by those who had access to the productions of her pen. She had a happy talent for pastoral poetry, and many fugitive pieces ascribed to her will long be cherished and admired by the children of song.

NARRATIVE.—In May, 1755, the province of Pennsylvania agreed to send out three hundred men, in order to cut a wagon road from fort Loudon, to join Braddock's road, near the Turkey Foot, or three forks of Yohogania. My brother-in-law, William Smith, Esq. of Conococheague, was appointed commissioner, to have the oversight of these road-cutters.

Though I was at that time only eighteen years of age, I had fallen violently in love with a young lady, whom I apprehended was possessed of a large share of both beauty and virtue; but being born between Venus and Mars, I concluded I must also leave my dear fair one, and go out with this company of road-cutters, to see the event of this campaign; but still expecting that some time in the course of this summer I should again return to the arms of my beloved.

We went on with the road, without interruption, until near the Alleghany mountain; when I was sent back, in order to hurry up some provision-wagons that were on the way after us. I proceeded down the road as far as the crossings of Juniata, where, finding the wagons were coming on as fast as possible, I returned up the road again towards the Alleghany mountain, in company with one Arnold Vigoras. About four or five miles above Bedford, three Indians had made a blind of bushes, stuck in the ground, as though they grew naturally, where they concealed themselves, about fifteen yards from the road. When we came opposite to them, they fired upon us, at this short distance, and killed my fellow-traveller, yet their bullets did not touch me: but my horse making a violent start, threw me, and the Indians immediately ran up and took me prisoner. The one that laid hold on me was a Canasatauga, the other two were Delawares. One of them could speak English, and asked me if there were any more white men coming after. I told them not any near that I knew of. Two of these Indians stood by me, whilst the other scalped my comrade; they then set off and ran at a smart rate through the woods, for about fifteen miles, and that night we slept on the Alleghany mountain, without fire.

The next morning they divided the last of their provision which they had brought from fort Du Quesne, and gave me an equal share, which was about two or three ounces of mouldy biscuit; this and a young ground-hog, about as large as a rabbit, roasted, and also equally divided, was all the provision we had until we came to the Loyal Hannan, which was about fifty miles; and a great part of the way we came through exceeding rocky laurel thickets, without any path. When we came to the west side of Laurel hill, they gave the scalp halloo, as usual, which is a long yell or halloo for every scalp or prisoner they have in possession; the last of these scalp halloos were followed with quick and sudden shrill shouts of joy and triumph. On their performing this, we were answered by the firing of a number of guns on the Loyal Hannan, one after another, quicker than one could count, by another party of Indians, who were encamped near where Ligoneer now stands. As we advanced near this party, they increased with repeated shouts of joy and triumph; but I did not share with them in their excessive mirth. When we came to this camp, we found they had plenty of turkeys and other meat there; and though I never before eat venison without bread or salt, yet as I was hungry it relished very well. There we lay that night, and the next morning the whole of us marched on our way for fort Du Quesne. The night after we joined another camp of Indians, with nearly the same ceremony, attended with great noise, and apparent joy, among all except one. The next morning we continued our march, and in the afternoon we came in full view of the fort, which stood on the point, near where fort Pitt now stands. We then made a halt on the bank of the Alleghany, and repeated the scalp halloo, which was answered by the firing of all the firelocks in the hands of both Indians and French who were in and about the fort, in the aforesaid manner, and also the great guns, which were followed by the continued shouts and yells of the different savage tribes who were then collected there.

As I was at this time unacquainted with this mode of firing and yelling of the savages, I concluded that there were thousands of Indians there ready to receive General Braddock; but what added to my surprise, I saw numbers running towards me, stripped naked, excepting breech-clouts, and painted in the most hideous manner, of various colors, though the principal color was vermillion, or a bright red; yet there was annexed to this black, brown, blue, &c. As they approached, they formed themselves into two long ranks, about two or three rods apart. I was told by an Indian that could speak English, that I must run betwixt these ranks, and that they would flog me all the way as I ran; and if I ran quick, it would be so much the better, as they would quit when I got to the end of the ranks. There appeared to be a general rejoicing around me, yet I could find nothing like joy in my breast; but I started to the race with all the resolution and vigor I was capable of exerting, and found that it was as I had been told, for I was flogged the whole way. When I had got near the end of the lines, I was struck with something that appeared to me to be a stick, or the handle of a tomahawk, which caused me to fall to the ground. On my recovering my senses, I endeavored to renew my race; but as I arose, some one cast sand in my eyes, which blinded me so that I could not see where to run. They continued beating me most intolerably, until I was at length insensible; but before I lost my senses, I remember my wishing them to strike the fatal blow, for I thought they intended killing me, but apprehended they were too long about it.

The first thing I remember was my being in the fort amidst the French and Indians, and a French doctor standing by me, who had opened a vein in my left arm: after which the interpreter asked me how I did; I told him I felt much pain. The doctor then washed my wounds, and the bruised places of my body, with French brandy. As I felt faint, and the brandy smelt well, I asked for some inwardly, but the doctor told me, by the interpreter, that it did not suit my case.

When they found I could speak, a number of Indians came around me, and examined me, with threats of cruel death if I did not tell the truth. The first question they asked me was how many men were there in the party that were coming from Pennsylvania to join Braddock? I told them the truth, that there were three hundred. The next question was, were they well armed ? I told them they were all well armed, (meaning the arm of flesh,) for they had only about thirty guns among the whole of them; which if the Indians had known, they would certainly have gone and cut them all off; therefore, I could not in conscience let them know the defenceless situation of these road-cutters. I was then sent to the hospital, and carefully attended by the doctors, and recovered quicker than what I expected.

Some time after I was there, I was visited by the Delaware Indian already mentioned, who was at the taking of me, and could speak some English. Though he spoke but bad English, yet I found him to be a man of considerable understanding. I asked him if I had done any thing that had offended the Indians which caused them to treat me so unmercifully. He said no; it was only an old custom the Indians had, and it was like how do you do; after that, he said, I would be well used. I asked him if I should be admitted to remain with the French. He said no; and told me that, as soon as I recovered, I must not only go with the Indians, but must be made an Indian myself. I asked him what news from Braddock's army. He said the Indians spied them every day, and he showed me, by making marks on the ground with a stick, that Braddock's army was advancing in very close order, and that the Indians would surround them, take trees, and (as he expressed it) *shoot um down all one pigeon.*

Shortly after this, on the 9th day of July, 1755, in the morning, I heard a great stir in the fort. As I could then walk with a staff in my hand, I went out of the door, which was just by the wall of the fort, and stood upon the wall, and viewed the Indians in a huddle before the gate, where were barrels of powder, bullets, flints, &c., and every one taking what suited. I saw the Indians also march off in rank entire; likewise the French Canadians, and some regulars. After viewing the Indians and French in different positions, I computed them to be about four hundred, and wondered that they attempted to go out against Braddock with so small a party. I was then in high hopes that I would soon see them fly before the British troops, and that General Braddock would take the fort and rescue me.

I remained anxious to know the event of this day; and, in the afternoon, I again observed a great noise and commotion in the fort, and though at that time I could not understand French, yet I found that it was the voice of joy and triumph, and feared that they had received what I called bad news.

I had observed some of the old country soldiers speak Dutch: as I spoke Dutch, I went to one of them, and asked him what was the news. He told me that a runner had just arrived, who said that Braddock would certainly be defeated; that the Indians and French had surrounded him, and were concealed behind trees and in gullies, and kept a constant fire upon the English, and that they saw the English falling in heaps, and if they did not take the river, which was the only gap, and make their escape, there would not be one man left alive before sundown. Some time after this I heard a number of scalp halloos, and saw a company of Indians and French coming in. I observed they had a great many bloody scalps, grenadiers' caps, British canteens, bayonets, &c. with them. They brought the news that Braddock was defeated. After that another company came in, which appeared to be about one hundred, and chiefly Indians, and it seemed to me that almost every one of this company was carrying scalps; after this came another company with a number of wagon horses, and also a great many scalps. Those that were coming in, and those that had arrived, kept a constant firing of small arms, and also the great guns in the fort, which were accompanied with the most hideous shouts and yells from all quarters; so that it appeared to me as if the infernal regions had broke loose.

About sundown I beheld a small party coming in with about a dozen prisoners, stripped naked, with their hands tied behind their backs, and their faces and part of their bodies blacked; these prisoners they burned to death on the bank of Alleghany river, opposite to the fort. I stood on the fort wall until I beheld them begin to burn one of these men; they had him tied to a stake, and kept touching him with firebrands, red-hot irons, &c., and he screamed in a most doleful manner; the Indians, in the mean time, yelling like infernal spirits.

As this scene appeared too shocking for me to behold, I retired to my lodgings both sore and sorry.

When I came into my lodgings I saw Russel's Seven Sermons, which they had brought from the field of battle, which a Frenchman made a present to me. From the best information I could receive, there were only seven Indians and four French killed in this battle, and five hundred British lay dead in the field, besides what were killed in the river on their retreat.

The morning after the battle I saw Braddock's artillery brought into the fort; the same day I also saw several Indians in British officers' dress, with sash, half moon, laced hats, &c., which the British then wore.

A few days after this the Indians demanded me, and I was obliged to go with them. I was not yet well able to march, but they took me in a canoe up the Alleghany river to an Indian town, that was on the north side of the river, about forty miles above fort Du Quesne. Here I remained about three weeks, and was then taken to an Indian town on the west branch of Muskingum, about twenty miles above the forks, which was called Tullihas, inhabited by Delawares, Caughne-wagas, and Mohicans. On our route betwixt the aforesaid towns the country was chiefly black oak and white oak land, which appeared generally to be good wheat land, chiefly second and third rate, intermixed with some rich bottoms.

The day after my arrival at the aforesaid town, a number of Indians collected about me, and one of them began to pull the hair out of my head. He had some ashes on a piece of bark, in which he frequently dipped his fingers, in order to take the firmer hold, and so he went on, as if he had been plucking a turkey, until he had all the hair clean out of my head, except a small spot about three or four inches square on my crown; this they cut off with a pair of scissors, excepting three locks, which they dressed up in their own mode. - Two of these they wrapped round with a narrow beaded garter made by themselves for that purpose, and the other they plaited at full length, and then stuck it full of silver brooches. After this they bored my nose and ears, and fixed me off with ear-rings and nose jewels; then they ordered me to strip off my clothes and put on a breech-clout, which I did; they then painted my head, face, and body, in various colors. They put a large belt of wampum on my neck, and silver bands on my hands and right arm; and so an old chief led me out in the street, and gave the alarm halloo, *coo-wigh*, several times repeated quick; and on this, all that were in the town came running and stood round the old chief, who held me by the hand in the midst. As I at that time knew nothing of their mode of adoption, and had seen them put to death all they had taken, and as I never could find that they saved a man alive at Braddock's defeat, I made no doubt but they were about putting me to death in some cruel manner. The old chief, holding me by the hand, made a long speech, very loud, and when he had done, he handed me to three young squaws, who led me by the hand down the bank, into the river, until the water was up to our middle. The squaws then made signs to me to plunge myself into the water, but I did not understand them; I thought that the result of the council was that I should be drowned, and that these young ladies were to be the executioners. They all three laid violent hold of me, and I for some time opposed them with all my might, which occasioned loud laughter by the multitude that were on the bank of the river. At length one of the squaws made out to speak

16*

a little English, (for I believe they began to be afraid of me,) and said *no hurt you.* On this I gave myself up to their ladyships, who were as good as their word; for though they plunged me under water, and washed and rubbed me severely, yet I could not say they hurt me much.

These young women then led me up to the council house, where some of the tribe were ready with new clothes for me. They gave me a new ruffled shirt, which I put on, also a pair of leggins done off with ribbons and beads, likewise a pair of moccasins, and garters dressed with beads, porcupine quills, and red hair—also a tinsel laced cappo. They again painted my head and face with various colors, and tied a bunch of red feathers to one of those locks they had left on the crown of my head, which stood up five or six inches. They seated me on a bearskin, and gave me a pipe, tomahawk, and polecatskin pouch, which had been skinned pocket fashion, and contained tobacco, killegenico, or dry sumach leaves, which they mix with their tobacco; also spunk, flint, and steel. When I was thus seated, the Indians came in dressed and painted in their grandest manner. As they came in they took their seats, and for a considerable time there was a profound silence—every one was smoking; but not a word was spoken among them. At length one of the chiefs made a speech, which was delivered to me by an interpreter, and was as followeth: " My son, you are now flesh of our flesh, and bone of our bone. By the ceremony which was performed this day every drop of white blood was washed out of your veins; you are taken into the Caughnewago nation, and initiated into a warlike tribe; you are adopted into a great family, and now received with great seriousness and solemnity in the room and place of a great man. After what has passed this day, you are now one of us by an old strong law and custom. My son, you have now nothing to fear—we are now under the same obligations to love, support, and defend you that we are to love and to defend one another; therefore, you are to consider yourself as one of our people." At this time I did not believe this fine speech, especially that of the white blood being washed out of me; but since that time I have found that there was much sincerity in said speech; for, from that day, I never knew them to make any distinction between me and themselves in any respect whatever until I left them. If they had plenty of clothing, I had plenty; if we were scarce, we all shared one fate.

After this ceremony was over, I was introduced to my new kin, and told that I was to attend a feast that evening, which I did. And as the custom was, they gave me also a bowl and wooden spoon, which I carried with me to the place, where there was a number of large brass kettles full of boiled venison and green corn; every one advanced with his bowl and spoon, and had his share given him. After this, one of the chiefs made a short speech, and then we began to eat.

The name of one of the chiefs in this town was Tecanyate-righto, alias Pluggy, and the other Asallecoa, alias Mohawk Solomon. As Pluggy and his party were to start the next day to war, to the frontiers of Virginia, the next thing to be performed was the war-dance, and their war-songs. At their war-dance they had both vocal and instrumental music; they had a short hollow gum, closed at one end, with water in it, and parchment stretched over the open end thereof, which they beat with one stick, and made a sound nearly like a muffled drum. All those who were going on this expedition collected together and formed. An old Indian then began to sing, and timed the music by beating on this drum, as the ancients formerly timed their music by beating the tabor. On this the warriors began to advance, or move forward in concert, like well-disciplined troops would march to the fife and drum. Each warrior had a tomahawk, spear, or war-mallet in his hand, and they all moved regularly towards the east, or the way they intended to go to war. At length they all stretched their tomahawks towards the Potomac, and giving a hideous shout or yell, they wheeled quick about, and danced in the same manner back. The next was the war-song. In performing this, only one sung at a time, in a moving posture, with a tomahawk in his hand, while all the other warriors were engaged in calling aloud *he-uh, he-uh*, which they constantly repeated while the war-song was going on. When the warrior that was singing had ended his song, he struck a war-post with his tomahawk, and with a loud voice told what warlike exploits he had done, and what he now intended to do, which were answered by the other warriors with loud shouts of applause. Some who had not before intended to go to war, at this time, were so animated by this performance, that they took up the tomahawk and sung the war-song, which was answered with shouts of joy, as they were then initiated into the present marching company. The next morning this company all collected at one place, with their heads and faces painted with various colors, and packs upon their backs; they marched off, all silent, except the commander, who, in the front, sung the travelling song, which began in this manner: *hoo caughtainte heegana.* Just as the rear passed the end of the town, they began to fire in their slow manner, from the front to the rear, which was accompanied with shouts and yells from all quarters.

This evening I was invited to another sort of dance, which

was a kind of promiscuous dance. The young men stood in
one rank, and the young women in another, about one rod apart,
facing each other. The one that raised the tune, or started
the song, held a small gourd or dry shell of a squash in his
hand, which contained beads or small stones, which rattled.
When he began to sing, he timed the tune with his rattle ; both
men and women danced and sung together, advancing towards
each other, stooping until their heads would be touching together, and then ceased from dancing, with loud shouts, and
retreated and formed again, and so repeated the same thing
over and over, for three or four hours, without intermission.
This exercise appeared to me at first irrational and insipid ;
but I found that in singing their tunes they used *ya ne no hoo
wa ne*, &c., like our *fa sol la*, and though they have no such
thing as jingling verse, yet they can intermix sentences with
their notes, and say what they please to each other, and carry
on the tune in concert. I found that this was a kind of wooing
or courting dance, and as they advanced stooping with their
heads together, they could say what they pleased in each other's ear, without disconcerting their rough music, and the others,
or those near, not hear what they said.

Shortly after this I went out to hunt, in company with Mohawk Solomon, some of the Caughnewagas, and a Delaware
Indian, that was married to a Caughnewaga squaw. We travelled about south from this town, and the first night we killed
nothing, but we had with us green corn, which we roasted and
ate that night. The next day we encamped about twelve
o'clock, and the hunters turned out to hunt, and I went down
the run that we encamped on, in company with some squaws
and boys, to hunt plums, which we found in great plenty. On
my return to camp I observed a large piece of fat meat ; the
Delaware Indian, that could talk some English, observed me
looking earnestly at this meat, and asked me, *what meat you
think that is ?* I said I supposed it was bear meat ; he laughed, and said, *ho, all one fool you, beal now elly pool*, and pointing to the other side of the camp, he said, *look at that skin,
you think that beal skin ?* I went and lifted the skin, which
appeared like an ox-hide ; he then said, *what skin you think
that ?* I replied, that I thought it was a buffalo hide ; he
laughed, and said, *you fool again, you know nothing, you think
buffalo that colo ?* I acknowledged I did not know much about
these things, and told him I never saw a buffalo, and that I
had not heard what color they were. He replied, *by and by
you shall see gleat many buffalo ; he now go to gleat lick.
That skin no buffalo skin, that skin buck-elk skin.* They went

out with horses, and brought in the remainder of this buck-elk, which was the fattest creature I ever saw of the tallow kind.

We remained at this camp about eight or ten days, and killed a number of deer. Though we had neither bread nor salt at this time, yet we had both roast and boiled meat in great plenty, and they were frequently inviting me to eat when I had no appetite.

We then moved to the buffalo lick, where we killed several buffalo, and in their small brass kettles they made about half a bushel of salt. I suppose this lick was about thirty or forty miles from the aforesaid town, and somewhere between the Muskingum, Ohio, and Sciota. About the lick was clear, open woods, and thin white oak land, and at that time there were large roads leading to the lick, like wagon roads. We moved from this lick about six or seven miles, and encamped on a creek.

Though the Indians had given me a gun, I had not yet been admitted to go out from the camp to hunt. At this place Mohawk Solomon asked me to go out with him to hunt, which I readily agreed to. After some time we came upon some fresh buffalo tracks. I had observed before this that the Indians were upon their guard, and afraid of an enemy; for, until now, they and the southern nations had been at war. As we were following the buffalo tracks, Solomon seemed to be upon his guard, went very slow, and would frequently stand and listen, and appeared to be in suspense. We came to where the tracks were very plain in the sand, and I said it is surely buffalo tracks; he said, *hush, you know nothing, may be buffalo tracks, may be Catawba.* He went very cautious until we found some fresh buffalo dung; he then smiled, and said, *Catawba cannot make so.* He then stopped, and told me an odd story about the Catawbas. He said that formerly the Catawbas came near one of their hunting camps, and at some distance from the camp lay in ambush; and in order to decoy them out, sent two or three Catawbas in the night past their camp, with buffalo hoofs fixed on their feet, so as to make artificial tracks. In the morning, those in the camp followed after these tracks, thinking they were buffalo, until they were fired on by the Catawbas, and several of them killed. The others fled, collected a party and pursued the Catawbas; but they, in their subtilty, brought with them rattlesnake poison, which they had collected from the bladder that lieth at the root of the snake's teeth; this they had corked up in a short piece of a cane-stalk. They had also brought with them small cane or reed, about the size of a rye-straw, which they made sharp at the end like a pen, and dipped them in this poison, and stuck them in the ground among the grass, along their own tracks, in such a position that they might stick into the legs of the pursuers, which answered the design; and as the Catawbas had runners behind to watch the motion of the pursuers, when they found that a number of them were lame, being artificially snake bit, and that they were all turning back, the Catawbas turned upon the pursuers, and defeated them, and killed and scalped all those that were lame. When Solomon had finished this story, and found that I understood him, he concluded by saying, *you don't know, Catawba velly bad Indian, Catawba all one devil Catawba.*

Some time after this, I was told to take the dogs with me, and go down the creek, perhaps I might kill a turkey; it being in the afternoon, I was also told not to go far from the creek, and to come up the creek again to the camp, and to take care not to get lost. When I had gone some distance down the creek, I came upon fresh buffalo tracks, and as I had a number of dogs with me to stop the buffalo, I concluded I would follow after and kill one; and as the grass and weeds were rank, I could readily follow the track. A little before sundown I despaired of coming up with them. I was then thinking how I might get to camp before night. I concluded, as the buffalo had made several turns, if I took the track back to the creek it would be dark before I could get to camp; therefore I thought I would take a near way through the hills, and strike the creek a little below the camp; but as it was cloudy weather, and I a very young woodsman, I could find neither creek nor camp. When night came on I fired my gun several times, and hallooed, but could have no answer. The next morning early, the Indians were out after me, and as I had with me ten or a dozen dogs, and the grass and weeds rank, they could readily follow my track. When they came up with me, they appeared to be in very good humor. I asked Solomon if he thought I was running away; he said, *no, no, you go too much clooked.* On my return to camp they took my gun from me, and for this rash step I was reduced to a bow and arrows, for near two years. We were out on this tour for about six weeks.

This country is generally hilly, though intermixed with considerable quantities of rich upland, and some good bottoms.

When we returned to the town, Pluggy and his party had arrived, and brought with them a considerable number of scalps and prisoners from the south branch of the Potomac; they also brought with them an English Bible, which they gave to a Dutch woman who was a prisoner; but as she could not read English, she made a present of it to me, which was very acceptable.

I remained in this town until some time in October, when

my adopted brother, called Tontileaugo, who had married a Wyandot squaw, took me with him to lake Erie. We proceeded up the west branch of Muskingum, and for some distance up the river the land was hilly, but intermixed with large bodies of tolerable rich upland, and excellent bottoms. We proceeded on to the head waters of the west branch of Muskingum. On the head waters of this branch, and from thence to the waters of Canesadooharie, there is a large body of rich, well lying land ; the timber is ash, walnut, sugar-tree, buckeye, honey-locust, and cherry, intermixed with some oak, hickory, &c. This tour was at the time that the black haws were ripe, and we were seldom out of sight of them ; they were common here both in the bottoms and upland.

On this route we had no horses with us, and when we started from the town all the pack I carried was a pouch containing my books, a little dried venison, and my blanket. I had then no gun, but Tontileaugo, who was a first-rate hunter, carried a rifle gun, and every day killed deer, raccoons, or bears. We left the meat, excepting a little for present use, and carried the skins with us until we encamped, and then stretched them with elm bark, in a frame made with poles stuck in the ground, and tied together with lynn or elm bark ; and when the skins were dried by the fire, we packed them up and carried them with us the next day.

As Tontileaugo could not speak English, I had to make use of all the Caughnewaga I had learned, even to talk very imperfectly with him ; but I found I learned to talk Indian faster this way than when I had those with me who could speak English.

As we proceeded down the Canesadooharie waters, our packs increased by the skins that were daily killed, and became so very heavy that we could not march more than eight or ten miles per day. We came to lake Erie about six miles west of the mouth of Canesadooharie. As the wind was very high the evening we came to the lake, I was surprised to hear the roaring of the water, and see the high waves that dashed against the shore, like the ocean. We encamped on a run near the lake, and as the wind fell that night, the next morning the lake was only in a moderate motion, and we marched on the sand along the side of the water, frequently resting ourselves, as we were heavily laden. I saw on the sand a number of large fish, that had been left in flat or hollow places ; as the wind fell and the waves abated, they were left without water, or only a small quantity ; and numbers of bald and grey eagles, &c., were along the shore devouring them.

Some time in the afternoon we came to a large camp of

Wyandots, at the mouth of Canesadooharie, where Tontileau-go's wife was. Here we were kindly received; they gave us a kind of rough, brown potatoes, which grew spontaneously, and were called by the Caughnewagas *ohnenata*. These po-tatoes peeled and dipped in raccoon's fat taste nearly like our sweet potatoes. They also gave us what they call *caneheanta*, which is a kind of homony, made of green corn, dried, and beans, mixed together.

From the head waters of Canesadooharie to this place, the land is generally good; chiefly first or second rate, and, com-paratively, little or no third rate. The only refuse is some swamps that appear to be too wet for use, yet I apprehend that a number of them, if drained, would make excellent meadows. The timber is black oak, walnut, hickory, cherry, black ash, white ash, water ash, buckeye, black-locust, honey-locust, sugar-tree, and elm. There is also some land, though com-paratively but small, where the timber is chiefly white oak, or beech; this may be called third rate. In the bottoms, and also many places in the upland, there is a large quantity of wild apple, plum, and red and black haw trees. It appeared to be well watered, and a plenty of meadow ground, intermixed with upland, but no large prairies or glades that I saw or heard of. In this route deer, bear, turkeys, and raccoons appeared plen-ty, but no buffalo, and very little sign of elks.

We continued our camp at the mouth of Canesadooharie for some time, where we killed some deer, and a great many raccoons; the raccoons here were remarkably large and fat. At length we all embarked in a large birch bark canoe. This vessel was about four feet wide, and three feet deep, and about five and thirty feet long; and though it could carry a heavy burden, it was so artfully and curiously constructed, that four men could carry it several miles, or from one landing place to another, or from the waters of the lake to the waters of the Ohio. We proceeded up Canesadooharie a few miles, and went on shore to hunt; but to my great surprise they carried the vessel we all came in up the bank, and inverted it or turn-ed the bottom up, and converted it to a dwelling-house, and kindled a fire before us to warm ourselves by and cook. With our baggage and ourselves in this house we were very much crowded, yet our little house turned off the rain very well.

We kept moving and hunting up this river until we came to the falls; here we remained some weeks, and killed a num-ber of deer, several bears, and a great many raccoons. From the mouth of this river to the falls is about five and twenty miles. On our passage up I was not much out from the river, but what I saw was good land, and not hilly.

About the falls is thin chesnut land, which is almost the only chesnut timber I ever saw in this country.

While we remained here I left my pouch with my books in camp, wrapt up in my blanket, and went out to hunt chesnuts. On my return to camp my books were missing. I inquired after them, and asked the Indians if they knew where they were; they told me that they supposed the puppies had carried them off. I did not believe them, but thought they were displeased at my poring over my books, and concluded that they had destroyed them, or put them out of my way.

After this I was again out after nuts, and on my return beheld a new erection, composed of two white oak saplings, that were forked about twelve feet high, and stood about fifteen feet apart. They had cut these saplings at the forks, and laid a strong pole across, which appeared in the form of a gallows, and the poles they had shaved very smooth, and painted in places with vermillion. I could not conceive the use of this piece of work, and at length concluded it was a gallows. I thought that I had displeased them by reading my books, and that they were about putting me to death. The next morning I observed them bringing their skins all to this place, and hanging them over this pole, so as to preserve them from being injured by the weather. This removed my fears. They also buried their large canoe in the ground, which is the way they took to preserve this sort of a canoe in the winter season.

As we had at this time no horse, every one got a pack on his back, and we steered an east course about twelve miles and encamped. The next morning we proceeded on the same course about ten miles to a large creek that empties into lake Erie, betwixt Canesadooharie and Cayahaga. Here they made their winter cabin in the following form : they cut logs about fifteen feet long, and laid these logs upon each other, and drove posts in the ground at each end to keep them together; the posts they tied together at the top with bark, and by this means raised a wall fifteen feet long, and about four feet high, and in the same manner they raised another wall opposite to this, at about twelve feet distance ; then they drove forks in the ground in the centre of each end, and laid a strong pole from end to end on these forks ; and from these walls to the poles, they set up poles instead of rafters, and on these they tied small poles in place of laths ; and a cover was made of lynn bark, which will run even in the winter season.

As every tree will not run, they examine the tree first, by trying it near the ground, and when they find it will do they fell the tree, and raise the bark with the tomahawk, near the top of the tree, about five or six inches broad, then put the

17

tomahawk handle under this bark, and pull it along down to the butt of the tree; so that sometimes one piece of bark will be thirty feet long. This bark they cut at suitable lengths in order to cover the hut.

At the end of these walls they set up split timber, so that they had timber all round, excepting a door at each end. At the top, in place of a chimney, they left an open place, and for bedding they laid down the aforesaid kind of bark, on which they spread bear-skins. From end to end of this hut along the middle there were fires, which the squaws made of dry split wood, and the holes or open places that appeared the squaws stopped with moss, which they collected from old logs; and at the door they hung a bear-skin; and notwithstanding the winters are hard here, our lodging was much better than what I expected.

It was some time in December when we finished this winter cabin; but when we had got into this comparatively fine lodging, another difficulty arose, we had nothing to eat. While I was travelling with Tontileaugo, as was before mentioned, and had plenty of fat venison, bear's meat and raccoons, I then thought it was hard living without bread or salt; but now I began to conclude, that if I had any thing that would banish pinching hunger, and keep soul and body together, I would be content.

While the hunters were all out, exerting themselves to the utmost of their ability, the squaws and boys (in which class I was) were scattered out in the bottoms, hunting red haws, black haws and hickory nuts. As it was too late in the year, we did not succeed in gathering haws; but we had tolerable success in scratching up hickory nuts from under a light snow, which we carried with us lest the hunters should not succeed. After our return the hunters came in, who had killed only two small turkeys, which were but little among eight hunters and thirteen squaws, boys, and children; but they were divided with the greatest equity and justice—every one got their equal share.

The next day the hunters turned out again, and killed one deer and three bears.

One of the bears was very large and remarkably fat. The hunters carried in meat sufficient to give us all a hearty supper and breakfast.

The squaws and all that could carry turned out to bring in meat,—every one had their share assigned them, and my load was among the least; yet, not being accustomed to carrying in this way, I got exceeding weary, and told them my load was too heavy, I must leave part of it and come for it again.

They made a halt and only laughed at me, and took part of my load and added it to a young squaw's, who had as much before as I carried.

This kind of reproof had a greater tendency to excite me to exert myself in carrying without complaining than if they had whipped me for laziness. After this the hunters held a council, and concluded that they must have horses to carry their loads; and that they would go to war even in this inclement season, in order to bring in horses.

Tontileaugo wished to be one of those who should go to war; but the votes went against him, as he was one of our best hunters; it was thought necessary to leave him at this winter camp to provide for the squaws and children. It was agreed upon that Tontileaugo and three others should stay and hunt, and the other four go to war.

They then began to go through their common ceremony. They sung their war-songs, danced their war-dances, &c. And when they were equipped they went off singing their marching song, and firing their guns. Our camp appeared to be rejoicing; but I was grieved to think that some innocent persons would be murdered, not thinking of danger.

After the departure of these warriors we had hard times; and though we were not altogether out of provisions, we were brought to short allowance. At length Tontileaugo had considerable success, and we had meat brought into camp sufficient to last ten days. Tontileaugo then took me with him in order to encamp some distance from this winter cabin, to try his luck there. We carried no provisions with us; he said he would leave what was there for the squaws and children, and that we could shift for ourselves. We steered about a south course up the waters of this creek, and encamped about ten or twelve miles from the winter cabin. As it was still cold weather and a crust upon the snow, which made a noise as we walked, and alarmed the deer, we could kill nothing, and consequently went to sleep without supper. The only chance we had under these circumstances was to hunt bear holes; as the bears about Christmas search out a winter lodging place, where they lie about three or four months without eating or drinking. This may appear to some incredible; but it is well known to be the case by those who live in the remote western parts of North America.

The next morning early we proceeded on, and when we found a tree scratched by the bears climbing up, and the hole in the tree sufficiently large for the reception of the bear, we then felled a sapling or small tree against or near the hole; and it was my business to climb up and drive out the bear, while Tontileaugo stood ready with his gun and bow. We went on in this manner until evening, without success. At length we found a large elm scratched, and a hole in it about forty feet up; but no tree nigh, suitable to lodge against the hole. Tontileaugo got a long pole and some dry rotten wood, which he tied in bunches, with bark; and as there was a tree that grew near the elm, and extended up near the hole, but leaned the wrong way, so that we could not lodge it to advantage, to remedy this inconvenience, he climbed up this tree and carried with him his rotten wood, fire and pole. The rotten wood he tied to his belt, and to one end of the pole he tied a hook and a piece of rotten wood, which he set fire to, as it would retain fire almost like spunk, and reached this hook from limb to limb as he went up. When he got up with his pole he put dry wood on fire into the hole; after he put in the fire he heard the bear snuff, and he came speedily down, took his gun in his hand, and waited until the bear would come out; but it was some time before it appeared, and when it did appear he attempted taking sight with his rifle; but it being then too dark to see the sights, he set it down by a tree, and instantly bent his bow, took hold of an arrow, and shot the bear a little behind the shoulder. I was preparing also to shoot an arrow, but he called to me to stop, there was no occasion; and with that the bear fell to the ground.

Being very hungry, we kindled a fire, opened the bear, took out the liver, and wrapped some of the caul fat round, and put it on a wooden spit, which we stuck in the ground by the fire to roast; then we skinned the bear, got on our kettle, and had both roast and boiled, and also sauce to our meat, which appeared to me to be delicate fare. After I was fully satisfied I went to sleep; Tontileaugo awoke me, saying, come, eat hearty, we have got meat plenty now.

The next morning we cut down a lynn tree, peeled bark and made a snug little shelter, facing the south-east, with a large log betwixt us and the north-west; we made a good fire before us, and scaffolded up our meat at one side. When we had finished our camp we went out to hunt, searched two trees for bears, but to no purpose. As the snow thawed a little in the afternoon, Tontileaugo killed a deer, which we carried with us to camp.

The next day we turned out to hunt, and near the camp we found a tree well scratched; but the hole was above forty feet high, and no tree that we could lodge against the hole; but finding that it was very hollow, we concluded that we could cut down the tree with our tomahawks, which kept us working a considerable part of the day. When the tree fell we

ran up, Tontileaugo with his gun and bow, and I with my bow
ready bent. Tontileaugo shot the bear through with his rifle,
a little behind the shoulders ; I also shot, but too far back ; and
not being then much accustomed to the business, my arrow
penetrated only a few inches through the skin. Having killed
an old she bear and three cubs, we hauled her on the snow to
the camp, and only had time afterwards to get wood, make a
fire, cook, &c., before dark.

Early the next morning we went to business, searched several trees, but found no bears. On our way home we took
three raccoons out of a hollow elm, not far from the ground.

We remained here about two weeks, and in this time killed
four bears, three deer, several turkeys and a number of raccoons. We packed up as much meat as we could carry, and
returned to our winter cabin. On our arrival there was great
joy, as they were all in a starving condition, the three hunters that we had left having killed but very little. All that
could carry a pack, repaired to our camp to bring in meat.

Some time in February the four warriors returned, who had
taken two scalps and six horses from the frontiers of Pennsylvania. The hunters could then scatter out a considerable distance from the winter cabin and encamp, kill meat, and bring
it in upon horses ; so that we commonly after this had plenty
of provision.

In this month we began to make sugar. As some of the
elm bark will strip at this season, the squaws, after finding a
tree that would do, cut it down, and with a crooked stick, broad
and sharp at the end, took the bark off the tree, and of this
bark made vessels in a curious manner, that would hold about
two gallons each : they made above one hundred of these kind
of vessels. In the sugar tree they cut a notch, sloping down,
and at the end of the notch stuck in a tomahawk ; in the place
where they stuck the tomahawk they drove a long chip, in
order to carry the water out from the tree, and under this they
set their vessel to receive it. As sugar trees were plenty and
large here, they seldom or never notched a tree that was not
two or three feet over. They also made bark vessels for carrying the water, that would hold about four gallons each.
They had two brass kettles, that held about fifteen gallons
each, and other smaller kettles in which they boiled the water.
But as they could not at times boil away the water as fast as
it was collected, they made vessels of bark, that would hold
about one hundred gallons each, for retaining the water ; and
though the sugar trees did not run every day, they had always
a sufficient quantity of water to keep them boiling during the
whole sugar season.

The way we commonly used our sugar while encamped was by putting it in bear's fat until the fat was almost as sweet as the sugar itself, and in this we dipped our roasted venison. About this time some of the Indian lads and myself were employed in making and attending traps for catching raccoons, foxes, wildcats, &c.

As the raccoon is a kind of water animal, that frequents the runs, or small water courses, almost the whole night, we made our traps on the runs, by laying one small sapling on another, and driving in posts to keep them from rolling. The under sapling we raised about eighteen inches, and set so that on the raccoon's touching a string, or a small piece of bark, the sapling would fall and kill it; and lest the raccoon should pass by, we laid brush on both sides of the run, only leaving the channel open.

The fox traps we made nearly in the same manner, at the end of a hollow log, or opposite to a hole at the root of a hollow tree, and put venison on a stick for bait; we had it so set that when the fox took hold of the meat the trap fell. While the squaws were employed in making sugar, the boys and men were engaged in hunting and trapping.

About the latter end of March, we began to prepare for moving into town, in order to plant corn. The squaws were then frying the last of their bear's fat, and making vessels to hold it: the vessels were made of deer-skins, which were skinned by pulling the skin off the neck, without ripping. After they had taken off the hair, they gathered it in small plaits round the neck and with a string drew it together like a purse; in the centre a pin was put, below which they tied a string, and while it was wet they blew it up like a bladder, and let it remain in this manner until it was dry, when it appeared nearly in the shape of a sugar loaf, but more rounding at the lower end. One of these vessels would hold about four or five gallons. In these vessels it was they carried their bear's oil.

When all things were ready, we moved back to the falls of Canesadooharie. In this route the land is chiefly first and second rate; but too much meadow ground, in proportion to the upland. The timber is white ash, elm, black oak, cherry, buckeye, sugar tree, lynn, mulberry, beech, white oak, hickory, wild apple tree, red haw, black haw, and spicewood bushes. There is in some places spots of beech timber, which spots may be called third rate land. Buckeye, sugar tree and spicewood are common in the woods here. There is in some places large swamps too wet for any use.

On our arrival at the falls, (as we had brought with us on

horseback about two hundred weight of sugar, a large quantity of bear's oil, skins, &c.,) the canoe we had buried was
not sufficient to carry all; therefore we were obliged to make
another one of elm bark. While we lay here, a young Wyandot found my books. On this they collected together; I was
a little way from the camp, and saw the collection, but did not
know what it meant. They called me by my Indian name,
which was Scoouwa, repeatedly. I ran to see what was the
matter; they showed me my books, and said they were glad
they had been found, for they knew I was grieved at the loss
of them, and that they now rejoiced with me because they
were found. As I could then speak some Indian, especially
Caughnewaga, (for both that and the Wyandot tongue were
spoken in this camp,) I told them that I thanked them for the
kindness they had always shown to me, and also for finding
my books. They asked if the books were damaged. I told
them not much. They then showed how they lay, which was
in the best manner to turn off the water. In a deer-skin pouch
they lay all winter. The print was not much injured, though
the binding was. This was the first time that I felt my heart
warm towards the Indians. Though they had been exceedingly kind to me, I still before detested them, on account of
the barbarity I beheld after Braddock's defeat. Neither had I
ever before pretended kindness, or expressed myself in a
friendly manner; but I began now to excuse the Indians on
account of their want of information.

When we were ready to embark, Tontileaugo would not go
to town, but go up the river, and take a hunt. He asked me
if I choosed to go with him. I told him I did. We then got
some sugar, bear's oil bottled up in a bear's gut, and some dry
venison, which we packed up, and went up Canesadooharie,
about thirty miles, and encamped. At this time I did not
know either the day of the week or the month; but I supposed it to be about the first of April. We had considerable
success in our business. We also found some stray horses, or
a horse, mare, and a young colt; and though they had run in
the woods all winter, they were in exceeding good order.
There is plenty of grass here all winter, under the snow, and
horses accustomed to the woods can work it out. These horses
had run in the woods until they were very wild.

Tontileaugo one night concluded that we must run them
down. I told him I thought we could not accomplish it. He
said he had run down bears, buffaloes, and elks; and in the
great plains, with only a small snow on the ground, he had run
down a deer; and he thought that in one whole day he could
tire or run down any four-footed animal except a wolf. I told

him that though a deer was the swiftest animal to run a short distance, yet it would tire sooner than a horse. He said he would at all events try the experiment. He had heard the Wyandots say that I could run well, and now he would see whether I could or not. I told him that I never had run all day, and of course was not accustomed to that way of running. I never had run with the Wyandots more than seven or eight miles at one time. He said that was nothing, we must either catch these horses or run all day.

In the morning early we left camp, and about sunrise we started after them, stripped naked excepting breech-clouts and moccasins. About ten o'clock I lost sight of both Tontileaugo and the horses, and did not see them again until about three o'clock in the afternoon. As the horses run all day in about three or four miles square, at length they passed where I was, and I fell in close after them. As I then had a long rest, I endeavored to keep ahead of Tontileaugo, and after some time I could hear him after me calling *chakoh*, *chakoanaugh*, which signifies, pull away or do your best. We pursued on, and after some time Tontileaugo passed me, and about an hour before sundown we despaired of catching these horses, and returned to camp, where we had left our clothes.

I reminded Tontileaugo of what I had told him; he replied he did not know what horses could do. They are wonderful strong to run; but withal we made them very tired. Tontileaugo then concluded he would do as the Indians did with wild horses when out at war: which is to shoot them through the neck under the mane, and above the bone, which will cause them to fall and lie until they can halter them, and then they recover again. This he attempted to do; but as the mare was very wild, he could not get sufficiently nigh to shoot her in the proper place; however, he shot, the ball passed too low, and killed her. As the horse and colt stayed at this place, we caught the horse, and took him and the colt with us to camp.

We stayed at this camp about two weeks, and killed a number of bears, raccoons, and some beavers. We made a canoe of elm bark, and Tontileaugo embarked in it. He arrived at the falls that night; whilst I, mounted on horseback, with a bear-skin saddle and bark stirrups, proceeded by land to the falls. I came there the next morning, and we carried our canoe and loading past the falls.

The river is very rapid for some distance above the falls, which are about twelve or fifteen feet, nearly perpendicular. This river, called Canesadooharie, interlocks with the West Branch of Muskingum, runs nearly a north course, and empties into the south side of lake Erie, about eight miles east from Sandusky, or betwixt Sandusky and Cayahaga.

On this last route the land is nearly the same as that last described, only there is not so much swampy or wet ground.

We again proceeded towards the lake, I on horseback, and Tontileaugo by water. Here the land is generally good, but I found some difficulty in getting round swamps and ponds. When we came to the lake, I proceeded along the strand, and Tontileaugo near the shore, sometimes paddling, and sometimes poleing his canoe along.

After some time the wind arose, and he went into the mouth of a small creek and encamped. Here we staid several days on account of high wind, which raised the lake in great billows. While we were here, Tontileaugo went out to hunt, and when he was gone a Wyandot came to our camp; I gave him a shoulder of venison which I had by the fire well roasted, and he received it gladly, told me he was hungry, and thanked me for my kindness. When Tontileaugo came home, I told him that a Wyandot had been at camp, and that I gave him a shoulder of roasted venison; he said that was very well, and I suppose you gave him also sugar and bear's oil to eat with his venison. I told him I did not; as the sugar and bear's oil was down in the canoe I did not go for it. He replied, you have behaved just like a Dutchman.* Do you not know that when strangers come to our camp we ought always to give them the best that we have? I acknowledged that I was wrong. He said that he could excuse this, as I was but young; but I must learn to behave like a warrior, and do great things, and never be found in any such little actions.

The lake being again calm,† we proceeded, and arrived safe at Sunyendeand, which was a Wyandot town that lay upon a small creek which empties into the little lake below the mouth of Sandusky.

The town was about eighty rood above the mouth of the creek, on the south side of a large plain, on which timber grew, and nothing more but grass or nettles. In some places there were large flats where nothing but grass grew, about three feet high when grown, and in other places nothing but nettles, very rank, where the soil is extremely rich and loose; here they planted corn. In this town there were also French traders, who purchased our skins and fur, and we all got new clothes, paint, tobacco, &c.

* The Dutch he called Skoharehaugo, which took its derivation from a Dutch settlement called Skoharey.

† The lake, when calm, appears to be of a sky-blue color; though when lifted in a vessel it is like other clear water.

After I had got my new clothes, and my head done off like a red-headed woodpecker, I, in company with a number of young Indians, went down to the corn-field to see the squaws at work. When we came there they asked me to take a hoe, which I did, and hoed for some time. The squaws applauded me as a good hand· at the business; but when I returned to the town the old men, hearing of what I had done, chid me, and said that I was adopted in the place of a great man, and must not hoe corn like a squaw. They never had occasion to reprove me for any thing like this again; as I never was extremely fond of work, I readily complied with their orders.

As the Indians on their return from· their winter hunt bring in with them large quantities of bear's oil, sugar, dried venison, &c., at this time they have plenty, and do not spare eating or giving; thus they make way with their provision as quick as possible. They have no such thing as regular meals, breakfast, dinner, or supper; but if any one, even the town folks, would go to the same house several times in one day, he would be invited to eat of the best; and with them it is bad manners to refuse to eat when it is offered. If they will not eat it is interpreted as a symptom of displeasure, or that the persons refusing to eat were angry with those who invited them.

At this time homony, plentifully mixed with bear's oil and sugar, or dried venison, bear's oil, and sugar, is what they offer to every one who comes in any time of the day; and so they go on until their sugar, bear's oil, and venison are all gone, and then they have to eat homony by itself, without bread, salt, or any thing else; yet still they invite every one that comes in to eat whilst they have any thing to give. It is thought a shame not to invite people to eat while they have any thing; but if they can in truth only say we have got nothing to eat, this is accepted as an honorable apology. All the hunters and warriors continued in town about six weeks after we came in; they spent this time in painting, going from house to house, eating, smoking, and playing at a game resembling dice, or hustle-cap. They put a number of plum-stones in a small bowl; one side of each stone is black, and the other white; they then shake or hustle the bowl, calling, *hits, hits, hits, honesey, honesey; rago, rago;* which signifies calling for white or black, or what they wish to turn up; they then turn the bowl, and count the whites and blacks. Some were beating their kind of drum and singing; others were employed in playing on a sort of flute made of hollow cane; and others playing on the jew's-harp. Some part of this time was also aken up in attending the council house, where the chiefs, and as many others as chose, attended; and at night they were frequently employed in singing and dancing. Towards the last of this time, which was in June, 1756, they were all engaged in preparing to go to war against the frontiers of Virginia. When they were equipped, they went through their ceremonies, sung their war-songs, &c. They all marched off, from fifteen to sixty years of age; and some boys, only twelve years old, were equipped with their bows and arrows, and went to war; so that none were left in town but squaws and children, except myself, one very old man, and another, about fifty years of age, who was lame.

The Indians were then in great hopes that they would drive all the Virginians over the lake, which is all the name they know for the sea. They had some cause for this hope, because, at this time, the Americans were altogether unacquainted with war of any kind, and consequently very unfit to stand their hand with such subtle enemies as the Indians were. The two old Indians asked me if I did not think that the Indians and French would subdue all America, except New England, which they said they had tried in old times. I told them I thought not. They said they had already drove them all out of the mountains, and had chiefly laid waste the great valley betwixt the North and South mountain, from Potomac to James river, which is a considerable part of the best land in Virginia, Maryland, and Pennsylvania, and that the white people appeared to them like fools; they could neither guard against surprise, run, nor fight. These, they said, were their reasons for saying that they would subdue the whites. They asked me to offer my reasons for my opinion, and told me to speak my mind freely. I told them that the white people to the east were very numerous, like the trees, and though they appeared to them to be fools, as they were not acquainted with their way of war, yet they were not fools; therefore, after some time, they will learn your mode of war, and turn upon you, or at least defend themselves. I found that the old men themselves did not believe they could conquer America, yet they were willing to propagate the idea in order to encourage the young men to go to war.

When the warriors left this town, we had neither meat, sugar, or bear's oil left. All that we had then to live on was corn pounded into coarse meal or small homony; this they boiled in water, which appeared like well thickened soup, without salt or any thing else. For some time we had plenty of this kind of homony; at length we were brought to very short allowance, and as the warriors did not return as soon as they expected, we were in a starving condition, and but one

gun in the town, and very little ammunition.   The old lame
Wyandot concluded that he would go a hunting in a canoe,
and take me with him, and try to kill deer in the water, as it
was then watering time.   We went up Sandusky a few miles,
then turned up a creek and encamped.   We had lights prepared, as we were to hunt in the night, and also a piece of
bark and some bushes set up in the canoe, in order to conceal
ourselves from the deer.   A little boy that was with us held
the light; I worked the canoe, and the old man, who had his
gun loaded with large shot, when we came near the deer, fired,
and in this manner killed three deer in part of one night.   We
went to our fire, ate heartily, and in the morning returned to
town in order to relieve the hungry and distressed.

When we came to town the children were crying bitterly on
account of pinching hunger.   We delivered what we had taken,
and though it was but little among so many, it was divided
according to the strictest rules of justice.   We immediately set
out for another hunt, but before we returned a part of the warriors had come in, and brought with them on horseback a
quantity of meat.   These warriors had divided into different
parties, and all struck at different places in Augusta county.
They brought in with them a considerable number of scalps,
prisoners, horses, and other plunder.   One of the parties
brought in with them one Arthur Campbell, that is now Colonel Campbell, who lives on Holston river, near the Royal
Oak.   As the Wyandots at Sunyendeand and those at Detroit were connected, Mr. Campbell was taken to Detroit;
but he remained some time with me in this town.   His company was very agreeable, and I was sorry when he left me.
During his stay at Sunyendeand he borrowed my Bible, and
made some pertinent remarks on what he had read.   One
passage was where it is said, "It is good for man that he
bear the yoke in his youth."   He said we ought to be resigned to the will of Providence, as we were now bearing
the yoke in our youth.   Mr. Campbell appeared to be then
about sixteen or seventeen years of age.

There was a number of prisoners brought in by these
parties, and when they were to run the gauntlet I went and
told them how they were to act.   One John Savage was
brought in, a middle-aged man, or about forty years old.   He
was to run the gauntlet.   I told him what he had to do; and
after this I fell into one of the ranks with the Indians, shouting
and yelling like them; and as they were not very severe on
him, as he passed me, I hit him with a piece of pumpkin,
which pleased the Indians much, but hurt my feelings.

About the time that these warriors came in, the green corn

was beginning to be of use, so that we had either green corn
or venison, and sometimes both, which was, comparatively,
high living. When we could have plenty of green corn, or
roasting ears, the hunters became lazy, and spent their time,
as already mentioned, in singing and dancing, &c. They appeared to be fulfilling the scriptures beyond those who profess
to believe them, in that of taking no thought of to-morrow;
and also in living in love, peace, and friendship together,
without disputes. In this respect they shame those who profess Christianity.

In this manner we lived until October; then the geese,
swans, ducks, cranes, &c., came from the north, and alighted
on this little lake, without number, or innumerable. Sunyendeand is a remarkable place for fish in the spring, and fowl
both in the fall and spring.

As our hunters were now tired with indolence, and fond of
their own kind of exercise, they all turned out to fowling, and
in this could scarce miss of success; so that we had now
plenty of homony and the best of fowls; and sometimes, as a
rarity, we had a little bread, which was made of Indian corn
meal, pounded in a homony block, mixed with boiled beans,
and baked in cakes under the ashes.

This with us was called good living, though not equal to our
fat, roasted, and boiled venison, when we went to the woods
in the fall; or bear's meat and beaver in the winter; or sugar,
bear's oil, and dry venison in the spring.

Some time in October, another adopted brother, older than
Tontileaugo, came to pay us a visit at Sunyendeand, and he
asked me to take a hunt with him on Cayahaga. As they
always used me as a free man, and gave me the liberty of
choosing, I told him that I was attached to Tontileaugo, had
never seen him before, and therefore asked some time to consider of this. He told me that the party he was going with
would not be along, or at the mouth of this little lake, in less
than six days, and I could in this time be acquainted with
him, and judge for myself. I consulted with Tontileaugo on
this occasion, and he told me that our old brother Tecaughretanego (which was his name) was a chief, and a better man
than he was, and if I went with him I might expect to be
well used; but he said I might do as I pleased, and if I staid
he would use me as he had done. I told him that he had
acted in every respect as a brother to me; yet I was much
pleased with my old brother's conduct and conversation; and
as he was going to a part of the country I had never been
in, I wished to go with him. He said that he was perfectly
willing.

18

I then went with Tecaughretanego to the mouth of the little lake, where he met with the company he intended going with, which was composed of Caughnewagas and Ottawas. Here I was introduced to a Caughnewaga sister, and others I had never before seen. My sister's name was Mary, which they pronounced *Maully*. I asked Tecaughretanego how it came that she had an English name. He said that he did not know that it was an English name; but it was the name the priest gave her when she was baptized, which he said was the name of the mother of Jesus. He said there were a great many of the Caughnewagas and Wyandots that were a kind of half Roman Catholics; but as for himself, he said, that the priest and him could not agree, as they held notions that contradicted both sense and reason, and had the assurance to tell him that the book of God taught them these foolish absurdities: but he could not believe the great and good Spirit ever taught them any such nonsense; and therefore he concluded that the Indians' old religion was better than this new way of worshipping God.

The Ottawas have a very useful kind of tents which they carry with them, made of flags, plaited and stitched together in a very artful manner, so as to turn rain or wind well—each mat is made fifteen feet long, and about five feet broad. In order to erect this kind of tent, they cut a number of long straight poles, which they drive in the ground, in form of a circle, leaning inwards; then they spread the mats on these poles, beginning at the bottom and extending up, leaving only a hole in the top uncovered, and this hole answers the place of a chimney. They make a fire of dry split wood in the middle, and spread down bark mats and skins for bedding, on which they sleep in a crooked posture all round the fire, as the length of their beds will not admit of stretching themselves. In place of a door they lift up one end of a mat and creep in, and let the mat fall down behind them.

These tents are warm and dry, and tolerably clear of smoke. Their lumber they keep under birch-bark canoes, which they carry out and turn up for a shelter, where they keep every thing from the rain. Nothing is in the tents but themselves and their bedding.

This company had four birch canoes and four tents. We were kindly received, and they gave us plenty of homony, and wild fowl boiled and roasted. As the geese, ducks, swans, &c., here are well grain-fed, they were remarkably fat, especially the green-necked ducks.

The wild fowl here feed upon a kind of wild rice that

grows spontaneously in the shallow water, or wet places along the sides or in the corners of the lakes.

As the wind was high and we could not proceed on our voyage, we remained here several days, and killed abundance of wild fowl, and a number of raccoons.

When a company of Indians are moving together on the lake, as it is at this time of the year often dangerous sailing, the old men hold a council; and when they agree to embark, every one is engaged immediately in making ready, without offering one word against the measure, though the lake may be boisterous and horrid. One morning, though the wind appeared to me to be as high as in days past, and the billows raging, yet the call was given *yohoh-yohoh*, which was quickly answered by all—*ooh-ooh*, which signifies agreed. We were all instantly engaged in preparing to start, and had considerable difficulties in embarking.

As soon as we got into our canoes we fell to paddling with all our might, making out from the shore. Though these sort of canoes ride waves beyond what could be expected, yet the water several times dashed into them. When we got out about half a mile from shore, we hoisted sail, and as it was nearly a west wind, we then seemed to ride the waves with ease, and went on at a rapid rate. We then all laid down our paddles, excepting one that steered, and there was no water dashed into our canoes until we came near the shore again. We sailed about sixty miles that day, and encamped some time before night.

The next day we again embarked, and went on very well for some time; but the lake being boisterous, and the wind not fair, we were obliged to make to shore, which we accomplished with hard work and some difficulty in landing. The next morning a council was held by the old men.

As we had this day to pass by a long precipice of rocks on the shore about nine miles, which rendered it impossible for us to land, though the wind was high and the lake rough, yet, as it was fair, we were all ordered to embark. We wrought ourselves out from the shore and hoisted sail, (what we used in place of sail-cloth were our tent mats, which answered the purpose very well,) and went on for some time with a fair wind, until we were opposite to the precipice, and then it turned towards the shore, and we began to fear we should be cast upon the rocks. Two of the canoes were considerably farther out from the rocks than the canoe I was in. Those who were farthest out in the lake did not let down their sails until they had passed the precipice; but as we were nearer the rock, we were obliged to lower our sails, and paddle with all our might. With much difficulty we cleared ourselves of the rock, and landed. As the other canoes had landed before us, there were immediately runners sent off to see if we were all safely landed.

This night the wind fell, and the next morning the lake was tolerably calm, and we embarked without difficulty, and paddled along near the shore, until we came to the mouth of Cayahaga, which empties into lake Erie on the south side, betwixt Canesadooharie and Presq' Isle.

We turned up Cayahaga and encamped, where we staid and hunted for several days; and so we kept moving and hunting until we came to the forks of Cayahaga.

This is a very gentle river, and but few ripples, or swift running places, from the mouth to the forks. Deer here were tolerably plenty, large and fat; but bear and other game scarce. The upland is hilly, and principally second and third rate land; the timber chiefly black oak, white oak, hickory, dogwood, &c. The bottoms are rich and large, and the timber is walnut, locust, mulberry, sugar-tree, red haw, black haw, wild apple-trees, &c. The West Branch of this river interlocks with the East Branch of Muskingum, and the East Branch with the Big Beaver creek, that empties into the Ohio about thirty miles below Pittsburgh.

From the forks of Cayahaga to the East Branch of Muskingum there is a carrying place, where the Indians carry their canoes, &c., from the waters of lake Erie into the waters of the Ohio.

From the forks I went over with some hunters to the East Branch of Muskingum, where they killed several deer, a number of beavers, and returned heavy laden with skins and meat, which we carried on our backs, as we had no horses.

The land here is chiefly second and third rate, and the timber chiefly oak and hickory. A little above the forks, on the East Branch of Cayahaga, are considerable rapids, very rocky for some distance, but no perpendicular falls.

About the first of December, 1756, we were preparing for leaving the river: we buried our canoes, and as usual hung up our skins, and every one had a pack to carry. The squaws also packed up their tents, which they carried in large rolls that extended up above their heads, and though a great bulk, yet not heavy. We steered about a south-east course, and could not march over ten miles per day. At night we lodged in our flag tents, which, when erected, were nearly in the shape of a sugar-loaf, and about fifteen feet diameter at the ground.

In this manner we proceeded about forty miles, and wintered in these tents, on the waters of Beaver creek, near a little lake or large pond, which is about two miles long and one broad, and a remarkable place for beaver.

It is a received opinion among the Indians that the geese turn to beavers, and the snakes to raccoons; and though Tecaughretanego, who was a wise man, was not fully persuaded that this was true, yet he seemed in some measure to be carried away with this whimsical notion. He said that this pond had been always a great place for beaver. Though he said he knew them to be frequently all killed, (as he thought,) yet the next winter they would be as plenty as ever. And as the beaver was an animal that did not travel by land, and there being no water communication to or from this pond, how could such a number of beavers get there year after year? But as this pond was also a considerable place for geese, when they came in the fall from the north, and alighted in this pond, they turned beavers, all but the feet, which remained nearly the same.

I said, that though there was no water communication in or out of this pond, yet it appeared that it was fed by springs, as it was always clear, and never stagnated; and as a very large spring rose about a mile below this pond, it was likely that this spring came from this pond. In the fall, when this spring is comparatively low, there would be air under ground sufficient for the beavers to breathe in, with their heads above water, for they cannot live long under water, and so they might have a subterraneous passage by water into this pond. Tecaughretanego granted that it might be so.

About the sides of this pond there grew great abundance of cranberries, which the Indians gathered up on the ice when the pond was frozen over. These berries were about as large as rifle bullets, of a bright red color, an agreeable sour, though rather too sour of themselves, but when mixed with sugar had a very agreeable taste.

In conversation with Tecaughretanego, I happened to be talking of the beavers catching fish. He asked me why I thought that the beaver caught fish. I told him that I had read of the beaver making dams for the conveniency of fishing. He laughed, and made game of me and my book. He said the man that wrote that book knew nothing about the beaver. The beaver never did eat flesh of any kind, but lived on the bark of trees, roots, and other vegetables.

In order to know certainly how this was, when we killed a beaver I carefully examined the intestines, but found no appearance of fish; I afterwards made an experiment on a pet beaver which we had, and found that it would neither eat fish

18*

nor flesh; therefore I acknowledged that the book I had read was wrong.

I asked him if the beaver was an amphibious animal, or if it could live under water. He said that the beaver was a kind of subterraneous water animal that lives in or near the water; but they were no more amphibious than the ducks and geese were, which was constantly proven to be the case, as all the beavers that are caught in steel traps are drowned, provided the trap be heavy enough to keep them under water. As the beaver does not eat fish, I inquired of Tecaughretanego why the beaver made such large dams. He said they were of use to them in various respects—both for their safety and food. For their safety, as by raising the water over the mouths of their holes, or subterraneous lodging places, they could not be easily found; and as the beaver feeds chiefly on the bark of trees, by raising the water over the banks they can cut down saplings for bark to feed upon without going out much upon the land; and when they are obliged to go out on land for this food they frequently are caught by the wolves. As the beaver can run upon land but little faster than a water tortoise, and is no fighting animal, if they are any distance from the water they become an easy prey to their enemies.

I asked Tecaughretanego what was the use of the beavers' stones, or glands, to them; as the she beaver has two pair, which is commonly called the oil stones, and the bark stones. He said that as the beavers are the dumbest of all animals, and scarcely ever make any noise, and as they were working creatures, they made use of this smell in order to work in concert. If an old beaver was to come on the bank and rub his breech upon the ground, and raise a perfume, the others will collect from different places and go to work: this is also of use to them in travelling, that they may thereby search out and find their company. Cunning hunters, finding this out, have made use of it against the beavers, in order to catch them. What is the bait which you see them make use of but a compound of the oil and bark stones? By this perfume, which is only a false signal, they decoy them to the trap.

Near this pond beaver was the principal game. Before the water froze up we caught a great many with wooden and steel traps; but after that, we hunted the beaver on the ice. Some places here the beavers build large houses to live in; and in other places they have subterraneous lodgings in the banks. Where they lodge in the ground we have no chance of hunting them on the ice; but where they have houses, we go with malls and handspikes, and break all the hollow ice, to prevent them from getting their heads above the water under it. Then we break a hole in the house, and they make their escape into the water; but as they cannot live long under water, they are obliged to go to some of those broken places to breathe, and the Indians commonly put in their hands, catch them by the hind leg, haul them on the ice, and tomahawk them. Sometimes they shoot them in the head when they raise it above the water. I asked the Indians if they were not afraid to catch the beavers with their hands. They said no: they were not much of a biting creature; yet if they would catch them by the fore foot they would bite.

I went out with Tecaughretanego and some others a beaver hunting; but we did not succeed, and on our return we saw where several raccoons had passed while the snow was soft, though there was now a crust upon it; we all made a halt, looking at the raccoon tracks. As they saw a tree with a hole in it, they told me to go and see if they had gone in thereat; and if they had to halloo, and they would come and take them out. When I went to that tree, I found they had gone past; but I saw another the way they had gone, and proceeded to examine that, and found they had gone up it. I then began to halloo, but could have no answer.

As it began to snow and blow most violently, I returned and proceeded after my company, and for some time could see their tracks; but the old snow being only about three inches deep, and a crust upon it, the present driving snow soon filled up the tracks. As I had only a bow, arrows, and tomahawk with me, and no way to strike fire, I appeared to be in a dismal situation; and as the air was dark with snow, I had little more prospect of steering my course than I would in the night. At length I came to a hollow tree, with a hole at one side that I could go in at. I went in, and found that it was a dry place, and the hollow about three feet diameter, and high enough for me to stand in. I found that there was also a considerable quantity of soft, dry rotten wood around this hollow; I therefore concluded that I would lodge here, and that I would go to work, and stop up the door of my house. I stripped off my blanket, (which was all the clothes that I had, excepting a breech-clout, leggins and moccasins,) and with my tomahawk fell to chopping at the top of a fallen tree that lay near, and carried wood, and set it up on end against the door, until I had it three or four feet thick all around, excepting a hole I had left to creep in at. I had a block prepared that I could haul after me to stop this hole; and before I went in I put in a number of small sticks that I might more effectually stop it on the inside. When I went in, I took my tomahawk and cut down all the dry rotten wood I could get, and beat it small. With it I made a bed like a goose-nest or hog-bed, and with the small sticks stopped every hole, until my house was almost dark. I stripped off my moccasins, and danced in the centre of my bed, for about half an hour, in order to warm myself. In this time my feet and whole body were agreeably warmed. The snow, in the mean while, had stopped all the holes, so that my house was as dark as a dungeon, though I knew it could not yet be dark out of doors. I then coiled myself up in my blanket, lay down in my little round bed, and had a tolerable night's lodging. When I awoke all was dark—not the least glimmering of light was to be seen. Immediately I recollected that I was not to expect light in this new habitation, as there was neither door nor window in it. As I could hear the storm raging, and did not suffer much cold as I was then situated, I concluded I would stay in my nest until I was certain it was day. When I had reason to conclude that it surely was day, I arose and put on my moccasins, which I had laid under my head to keep from freezing. I then endeavored to find the door, and had to do all by the sense of feeling, which took me some time. At length I found the block, but it being heavy, and a large quantity of snow having fallen on it, at the first attempt I did not move it. I then felt terrified—among all the hardships I had sustained, I never knew before what it was to be thus deprived of light. This, with the other circumstances attending it, appeared grievous. I went straightway to bed again, wrapped my blanket round me, and lay and mused a while, and then prayed to Almighty God to direct and protect me as he had done heretofore. I once again attempted to move away the block, which proved successful; it moved about nine inches. With this a considerable quantity of snow fell in from above, and I immediately received light; so that I found a very great snow had fallen, above what I had ever seen in one night. I then knew why I could not easily move the block, and I was so rejoiced at obtaining the light that all my other difficulties seemed to vanish. I then turned into my cell, and returned God thanks for having once more received the light of heaven. At length I belted my blanket about me, got my tomahawk, bow and arrows, and went out of my den.

I was now in tolerable high spirits, though the snow had fallen above three feet deep, in addition to what was on the ground before; and the only imperfect guide I had in order to steer my course to camp was the trees, as the moss generally grows on the north-west side of them, if they are straight. I proceeded on, wading through the snow, and about twelve o'clock (as it appeared afterwards, from that time to night, for it was yet cloudy) I came upon the creek that our camp was on, about half a mile below the camp; and when I came in sight of the camp, I found that there was great joy, by the shouts and yelling of the boys, &c.

When I arrived, they all came round me, and received me gladly; but at this time no questions were asked, and I was taken into a tent, where they gave me plenty of fat beaver meat, and then asked me to smoke. When I had done, Tecaughretanego desired me to walk out to a fire they had made. I went out, and they all collected round me, both men, women, and boys. Tecaughretanego asked me to give them a particular account of what had happened from the time they left me yesterday until now. I told them the whole of the story, and they never interrupted me; but when I made a stop, the intervals were filled with loud acclamations of joy. As I could not at this time talk Ottawa or Jibewa well, (which is nearly the same,) I delivered my story in Caughnewaga. As my sister Molly's husband was a Jibewa, and could understand Caughnewaga, he acted as interpreter, and delivered my story to the Jibewas and Ottawas, which they received with pleasure. When all this was done, Tecaughretanego made a speech to me in the following manner:

" *Brother*,—You see we have prepared snow-shoes to go after you, and were almost ready to go when you appeared; yet, as you had not been accustomed to hardships in your country, to the east, we never expected to see you alive. Now we are glad to see you in various respects: we are glad to see you on your own account; and we are glad to see the prospect of your filling the place of a great man, in whose room you were adopted. We do not blame you for what has happened, we blame ourselves; because we did not think of this driving snow filling up the tracks, until after we came to camp.

" *Brother*,—Your conduct on this occasion hath pleased us much; you have given us an evidence of your fortitude, skill, and resolution; and we hope you will always go on to do great actions, as it is only great actions that can make a great man."

I told my brother Tecaughretanego that I thanked them for their care of me, and for the kindness I always received. I told him that I always wished to do great actions, and hoped I never would do any thing to dishonor any of those with whom I was connected. I likewise told my Jibewa brother-in-law to tell his people that I also thanked them for their care and kindness.

The next morning some of the hunters went out on snow-shoes, killed several deer, and hauled some of them into camp upon the snow. They fixed their carrying strings (which are broad in the middle and small at each end) in the fore feet and nose of the deer, and laid the broad part of it on their heads or about their shoulders, and pulled it along; and when it is moving, will not sink in the snow much deeper than a snow-shoe; and when taken with the grain of the hair, slips along very easily.

The snow-shoes are made like a hoop-net, and wrought with buckskin thongs. Each shoe is about two feet and a half long, and about eighteen inches broad before, and small behind, with cross-bars, in order to fix or tie them to their feet. After the snow had lain a few days, the Indians tomahawked the deer, by pursuing them in this manner.

About two weeks after this there came a warm rain, and took away the chief part of the snow, and broke up the ice; then we engaged in making wooden traps to catch beavers, as we had but few steel traps. These traps are made nearly in the same manner as the raccoon traps already described.

One day, as I was looking after my traps, I got benighted, by beaver ponds intercepting my way to camp; and as I had neglected to take fireworks with me, and the weather very cold, I could find no suitable lodging place; therefore, the only expedient I could think of to keep myself from freezing was exercise. I danced and hallooed the whole night with all my might, and the next day came to camp. Though I suffered much more this time than the other night I lay out, yet the Indians were not so much concerned, as they thought I had fireworks with me; but when they knew how it was, they did not blame me. They said that old hunters were frequently involved in this place, as the beaver dams were one above another on every creek and run, so that it is hard to find a fording place. They applauded me for my fortitude, and said, as they had now plenty of beaver skins, they would purchase me a new gun at Detroit, as we were to go there the next spring; and then if I should chance to be lost in dark weather, I could make a fire, kill provision, and return to camp when the sun shined. By being bewildered on the waters of Muskingum, I lost repute, and was reduced to the bow and arrow, and by lying out two nights here I regained my credit.

After some time the waters all froze again, and then, as formerly, we hunted beavers on the ice. Though beaver meat, without salt or bread, was the chief of our food this winter, yet we had always plenty, and I was well contented with my diet, as it appeared delicious fare, after the way we had lived the winter before.

Some time in February, we scaffolded up our fur and skins,

and moved about ten miles in quest of a sugar camp, or a suitable place to make sugar, and encamped in a large bottom on the head waters of Big Beaver creek. We had some difficulty in moving, as we had a blind Caughnewaga boy, about fifteen years of age, to lead ; and as this country is very brushy, we frequently had him to carry. We had also my Jibewa brother-in-law's father with us, who was thought by the Indians to be a great conjuror ; his name was Manetohcoa. This old man was so decrepit that we had to carry him this route upon a bier, and all our baggage to pack on our backs.

Shortly after we came to this place, the squaws began to make sugar. We had no large kettles with us this year, and they made the frost, in some measure, supply the place of fire, in making sugar. Their large bark vessels, for holding the stock water, they made broad and shallow ; and as the weather is very cold here, it frequently freezes at night in sugar time ; and the ice they break and cast out of the vessels. I asked them if they were not throwing away the sugar. They said no ; it was water they were casting away ; sugar did not freeze, and there was scarcely any in that ice. They said I might try the experiment, and boil some of it, and see what I would get. I never did try it ; but I observed that, after several times freezing, the water that remained in the vessel changed its color, and became brown and very sweet.

About the time we were done making sugar the snow went off the ground ; and one night a squaw raised an alarm. She said she saw two men with guns in their hands, upon the bank on the other side of the creek, spying our tents ; they were supposed to be Johnston's Mohawks. On this the squaws were ordered to slip quietly out some distance into the bushes, and all who had either guns or bows were to squat in the bushes near the tents ; and if the enemy rushed up, we were to give them the first fire, and let the squaws have an opportunity of escaping. I got down beside Tecaughretanego, and he whispered to me not to be afraid, for he would speak to the Mohawks, and as they spoke the same tongue that we did they would not hurt the Caughnewagas or me ; but they would kill all the Jibewas and Ottawas that they could, and take us along with them. This news pleased me well, and I heartily wished for the approach of the Mohawks.

Before we withdrew from the tents they had carried Manetohcoa to the fire, and gave him his conjuring tools, which were dyed feathers, the bone of the shoulder-blade of a wildcat, tobacco, &c. And while we were in the bushes, Manetohcoa was in a tent at the fire, conjuring away to the utmost of his ability. At length he called aloud for us all to come in, which was quickly obeyed. When we came in he told us that after he had gone through the whole of his ceremony, and expected to see a number of Mohawks on the flat bone when it was warmed at the fire, the pictures of two wolves only appeared. He said, though there were no Mohawks about, we must not be angry with the squaw for giving a false alarm; as she had occasion to go out and happened to see the wolves, though it was moonlight, yet she got afraid, and she conceited it was Indians with guns in their hands. So he said we might all go to sleep, for there was no danger; and accordingly we did.

The next morning we went to the place, and found wolf tracks, and where they had scratched with their feet like dogs; but there was no sign of moccasin tracks. If there is any such thing as a wizard, I think Manetohcoa was as likely to be one as any man, as he was a professed worshipper of the devil. But let him be a conjuror or not, I am persuaded that the Indians believed what he told them upon this occasion, as well as if it had come from an infallible oracle; or they would not, after such an alarm as this, go all to sleep in an unconcerned manner. This appeared to me the most like witchcraft of any thing I beheld while I was with them. Though I scrutinized their proceedings in business of this kind, yet I generally found that their pretended witchcraft was either art or mistaken notions, whereby they deceived themselves. Before a battle they spy the enemy's motions carefully, and when they find that they can have considerable advantage, and the greatest prospect of success, then the old men pretend to conjure, or to tell what the event will be; and this they do in a figurative manner, which will bear something of a different interpretation, which generally comes to pass nearly as they foretold. Therefore the young warriors generally believed these old conjurors, which had a tendency to animate and excite them to push on with vigor.

Some time in March, 1757, we began to move back to the forks of Cayahaga, which was about forty or fifty miles. And as we had no horses, we had all our baggage and several hundred weight of beaver skins, and some deer and bear skins, all to pack on our backs. The method we took to accomplish this was by making short days' journeys. In the morning we would move on, with as much as we were able to carry, about five miles, and encamp, and then run back for more. We commonly made three such trips in the day. When we came to the great pond, we staid there one day to rest ourselves, and to kill ducks and geese.

While we remained here, I went in company with a young Caughnewaga, who was about sixteen or seventeen years of age, Chinnohete by name, in order to gather cranberries. As he was gathering berries at some distance from me, three Jibewa squaws crept up undiscovered, and made at him speedily, but he nimbly escaped, and came to me apparently terrified. I asked him what he was afraid of. He replied, did you not see those squaws? I told him I did, and they appeared to be in a very good humor. I asked him wherefore then he was afraid of them. He said the Jibewa squaws were very bad women, and had a very ugly custom among them. I asked him what that custom was. He said that when two or three of them could catch a young lad, that was betwixt a man and a boy, out by himself, if they could overpower him, they would strip him by force, in order to see whether he was coming on to be a man or not. He said that was what they intended when they crawled up and ran so violently at him; but, said he, I am very glad that I so narrowly escaped. I then agreed with Chinnohete in condemning this as a bad custom, and an exceedingly immodest action for young women to be guilty of.

From our sugar camp on the head waters of Big Beaver creek to this place is not hilly. In some places the woods are tolerably clear, but in most places exceedingly brushy. The land here is chiefly second and third rate. The timber on the upland is white oak, black oak, hickory, and chesnut. There is also in some places walnut upland, and plenty of good water. The bottoms here are generally large and good.

We again proceeded on from the pond to the forks of Caya haga, at the rate of about five miles per day.

The land on this route is not very hilly; it is well watered, and in many places ill timbered, generally brushy, and chiefly second and third rate land, intermixed with good bottoms.

When we came to the forks, we found that the skins we had scaffolded were all safe. Though this was a public place, and Indians frequently passing, and our skins hanging up in view, yet there were none stolen. And it is seldom that Indians do steal any thing from one another. And they say they never did, until the white people came among them, and learned some of them to lie, cheat, and steal; but be that as it may, they never did curse or swear until the whites learned them. Some think their language will not admit of it, but I am not of that opinion. If I was so disposed, I could find language to curse or swear in the Indian tongue.

I remember that Tecaughretanego, when something displeased him, said, God damn it. I asked him if he knew what he then said. He said he did, and mentioned one of their degrading expressions, which he supposed to be the meaning or something like the meaning of what he had said. I told him

19

that it did not bear the least resemblance to it; that what he had said was calling upon the Great Spirit to punish the object he was displeased with.. He stood for some time amazed, and then said, if this be the meaning of these words, what sort of people are the whites? When the traders were among us, these words seemed to be intermixed with all their discourse. He told me to reconsider what I had said, for he thought I must be mistaken in my definition. If I was not mistaken, he said, the traders applied these words not only wickedly, but oftentimes very foolishly and contrary to sense or reason. He said he remembered once of a trader's accidentally breaking his gun-lock, and on that occasion calling out aloud, God damn it; surely, said he, the gun-lock was not an object worthy of punishment for Owaneeyo, or the Great Spirit. He also observed the traders often used this expression when they were in a good humor, and not displeased with any thing. I acknowledged that the traders used this expression very often, in a most irrational, inconsistent, and impious manner; yet I still asserted that I had given the true meaning of these words. He replied, if so, the traders are as bad as Oonasahroona, or the under ground inhabitants, which is the name they give the devils, as they entertain a notion that their place of residence is under the earth.

We took up our birch-bark canoes which we had buried, and found that they were not damaged by the winter; but they not being sufficient to carry all that we now had, we made a large chesnut-bark canoe, as elm bark was not to be found at this place.

We all embarked, and had a very agreeable passage down the Cayahaga, and along the south side of lake Erie, until we passed the mouth of Sandusky; then the wind arose, and we put in at the mouth of the Miami of the lake, at Cedar Point, where we remained several days, and killed a number of turkeys, geese, ducks, and swans. The wind being fair, and the lake not extremely rough, we again embarked, hoisted up sails, and arrived safe at the Wyandot town, nearly opposite to fort Detroit, on the north side of the river. Here we found a number of French traders, every one very willing to deal with us for our beaver.

We bought ourselves fine clothes, ammunition, paint, tobacco, &c., and, according to promise, they purchased me a new gun; yet we had parted with only about one third of our beaver. At length a trader came to town with French brandy; we purchased a keg of it, and held a council about who was to get drunk and who was to keep sober. I was invited to get drunk, but I refused the proposal; then they told me that I must be one of those who were to take care of the drunken people. I did not like this; but of two evils I chose that which I thought was the least—and fell in with those who were to conceal the arms, and keep every dangerous weapon we could out of their way, and endeavor, if possible, to keep the drinking club from killing each other, which was a very hard task. Several times we hazarded our own lives, and got ourselves hurt, in preventing them from slaying each other. Before they had finished this keg, near one third of the town was introduced to this drinking club; they could not pay their part, as they had already disposed of all their skins; but that made no odds—all were welcome to drink.

When they were done with this keg, they applied to the traders, and procured a kettle full of brandy at a time, which they divided out with a large wooden spoon; and so they went on, and never quit while they had a single beaver skin.

When the trader had got all our beaver, he moved off to the Ottawa town, about a mile above the Wyandot town.

When the brandy was gone, and the drinking club sober, they appeared much dejected. Some of them were crippled, others badly wounded, a number of their fine new shirts tore, and several blankets were burned. A number of squaws were also in this club, and neglected their corn-planting.

We could now hear the effects of the brandy in the Ottawa town. They were singing and yelling in the most hideous manner, both night and day; but their frolic ended worse than ours: five Ottawas were killed and a great many wounded.

After this a number of young Indians were getting their ears cut, and they urged me to have mine cut likewise, but they did not attempt to compel me, though they endeavored to persuade me. The principal arguments they used were, its being a very great ornament, and also the common fashion. The former I did not believe, and the latter I could not deny. The way they performed this operation was by cutting the fleshy part of the circle of the ear, close to the gristle, quite through. When this was done they wrapt rags round this fleshy part until it was entirely healed; they then hung lead to it, and stretched it to a wonderful length: when it was sufficiently stretched, they wrapped the fleshy part round with brass wire, which formed it into a semicircle about four inches diameter.

Many of the young men were now exercising themselves in a game resembling foot-ball, though they commonly struck the ball with a crooked stick made for that purpose; also a game something like this, wherein they used a wooden ball, about three inches diameter, and the instrument they moved it with was a strong staff, about five feet long, with a hoop net on the end of it large enough to contain the ball. Before they begin the play, they lay off about half a mile distance in a clear plain, and the opposite parties all attend at the centre, where a disinterested person casts up the ball, then the opposite parties all contend for it. If any one gets it into his net, he runs with it the way he wishes it to go, and they all pursue him. If one of the opposite party overtakes the person with the ball, he gives the staff a stroke, which causes the ball to fly out of the net; then they have another debate for it, and if the one that gets it can outrun all the opposite party, and can carry it quite out, or over the line at the end, the game is won; but this seldom happens. When any one is running away with the ball, and is likely to be overtaken, he commonly throws it, and with this instrument can cast it fifty or sixty yards. Sometimes when the ball is almost at the one end, matters will take a sudden turn, and the opposite party may quickly carry it out at the other end. Oftentimes they will work a long while back and forward before they can get the ball over the line, or win the game.

About the 1st of June, 1757, the warriors were preparing to go to war, in the Wyandot, Pottowatomy, and Ottawa towns; also a great many Jibewas came down from the upper lakes; and after singing their war-songs, and going through their common ceremonies, they marched off against the frontiers of Virginia, Maryland, and Pennsylvania, in their usual manner, singing the travelling song, slow firing, &c.

On the north side of the river St. Lawrence, opposite to fort Detroit, there is an island, which the Indians call the Long Island, and which they say is above one thousand miles long, and in some places above one hundred miles broad. They further say that the great river that comes down by Canesatauga, and that empties into the main branch of St. Lawrence, above Montreal, originates from one source with the St. Lawrence, and forms this island.

Opposite to Detroit, and below it, was originally a prairie, and laid off in lots about sixty rods broad, and a great length; each lot is divided into two fields, which they cultivate year about. The principal grain that the French raised in these fields was spring wheat and peas.

They built all their houses on the front of these lots on the river-side; and as the banks of the river are very low, some of the houses are not above three or four feet above the surface of the water; yet they are in no danger of being disturbed by freshets, as the river seldom rises above eighteen inches;

because it is the communication of the river St. Lawrence, from one lake to another.

As dwelling-houses, barns and stables are all built on the front of these lots, at a distance it appears like a continued row of houses in a town, on each side of the river, for a long way. These villages, the town, the river and the plains, being all in view at once, afford a most delightful prospect.

The inhabitants here chiefly drink the river water; and as it comes from the northward, it is very wholesome.

The land here is principally second rate, and, comparatively speaking, a small part is first or third rate; though about four or five miles south of Detroit there is a small portion that is worse than what I would call third rate, which produces abundance of whortleberries.

There is plenty of good meadow ground here, and a great many marshes that are overspread with water. The timber is elm, sugar-tree, black ash, white ash, abundance of water ash, oak, hickory, and some walnut.

About the middle of June, the Indians were almost all gone to war, from sixteen to sixty; yet Tecaughretanego remained in town with me. Though he had formerly, when they were at war with the southern nations, been a great warrior and an eminent counsellor, and I think as clear and able a reasoner upon any subject that he had an opportunity of being acquainted with as I ever knew; yet he had all along been against this war, and had strenuously opposed it in council. He said, if the English and French had a quarrel, let them fight their own battles themselves; it is not our business to intermeddle therewith.

Before the warriors returned, we were very scarce of provision; and though we did not commonly steal from one another, yet we stole during this time any thing that we could eat from the French, under the notion that it was just for us to do so, because they supported their soldiers; and our squaws, old men and children were suffering on the account of the war, as our hunters were all gone.

Some time in August, the warriors returned, and brought in with them a great many scalps, prisoners, horses and plunder; and the common report among the young warriors was, that they would entirely subdue Tulhasaga, that is the English, or it might be literally rendered the Morning Light inhabitants.

About the first of November, a number of families were preparing to go on their winter hunt, and all agreed to cross the lake together. We encamped at the mouth of the river the first night, and a council was held, whether we should cross through by the three islands, or coast it round the lake. These islands lie in a line across the lake, and are just in sight of each other. Some of the Wyandots, or Ottawas, frequently make their winter hunt on these islands; though, excepting wild fowl and fish, there is scarcely any game here but raccoons, which are amazingly plenty, and exceedingly large and fat, as they feed upon the wild rice, which grows in abundance in wet places round these islands. It is said that each hunter, in one winter, will catch one thousand raccoons.

It is a received opinion among the Indians that the snakes and raccoons are transmigratory, and that a great many of the snakes turn raccoons every fall, and raccoons snakes every spring. This notion is founded on observations made on the snakes and raccoons in this island.

As the raccoons here lodge in rocks, the trappers make their wooden traps at the mouth of the holes; and as they go daily to look at their traps, in the winter season, they commonly find them filled with raccoons; but in the spring, or when the frost is out of the ground, they say, they then find their traps filled with large rattlesnakes; and therefore conclude that the raccoons are transformed. They also say that the reason why they are so remarkably plenty in the winter, is, every fall the snakes turn raccoons again.

I told them that though I had never landed on any of these islands, yet, from the unanimous accounts I had received, I believed that both snakes and raccoons were plenty there; but no doubt they all remained there both summer and winter, only the snakes were not to be seen in the latter; yet I did not believe that they were transmigratory.

These islands are but seldom visited; because early in the spring, and late in the fall, it is dangerous sailing in their bark canoes; and in the summer they are so infested with various kinds of serpents, (but chiefly rattlesnakes,) that it is dangerous landing.

I shall now quit this digression, and return to the result of the council at the mouth of the river. We concluded to coast it round the lake, and in two days we came to the mouth of the Miami of the Lake, and landed on Cedar Point, where we remained several days. Here we held a council, and concluded we would take a driving hunt in concert and in partnership.

The river in this place is about a mile broad, and as it and the lake forms a kind of neck, which terminates in a point, all the hunters (which were fifty-three) went up the river, and we scattered ourselves from the river to the lake. When we first began to move we were not in sight of each other, but as we all raised the yell, we could move regularly together by the noise. At length we came in sight of each other, and appeared to be marching in good order; before we came to the point, both the squaws and boys in the canoes were scattered up the river and along the lake, to prevent the deer from making their escape by water. As we advanced near the point the guns began to crack slowly, and after some time the firing was like a little engagement. The squaws and boys were busy tomahawking the deer in the water, and we shooting them down on the land. We killed in all about thirty deer, though a great many made their escape by water.

We had now great feasting and rejoicing, as we had plenty of homony, venison and wild fowl. The geese at this time appeared to be preparing to move southward. It might be asked what is meant by the geese preparing to move. The Indians represent them as holding a great council at this time concerning the weather, in order to conclude upon a day, that they may all at or near one time leave the northern lakes, and wing their way to the southern bays. When matters are brought to a conclusion, and the time appointed that they are to take wing, then they say a great number of expresses are sent off, in order to let the different tribes know the result of this council, that they may be all in readiness to move at the time appointed. As there is a great commotion among the geese at this time, it would appear by their actions that such a council had been held. Certain it is that they are led by instinct to act in concert, and to move off regularly after their leaders.

Here our company separated. The chief part of them went up the Miami river, which empties into lake Erie at Cedar Point, whilst we proceeded on our journey in company with Tecaughretanego, Tontileaugo, and two families of the Wyandots.

As cold weather was now approaching, we began to feel the doleful effects of extravagantly and foolishly spending the large quantity of beaver we had taken in our last winter's hunt. We were all nearly in the same circumstances; scarcely one had a shirt to his back; but each of us had an old blanket, which we belted round us in the day, and slept in at night, with a deer or bear skin under us for our bed.

When we came to the falls of Sandusky, we buried our birch-bark canoes, as usual, at a large burying-place for that purpose, a little below the falls. At this place the river falls about eight feet over a rock, but not perpendicularly. With much difficulty we pushed up our wooden canoes; some of us went up the river, and the rest by land with the horses, until we came to the great meadows or prairies, that lie between Sandusky and Sciota.

When we came to this place, we met with some Ottawa hunters, and agreed with them to take what they call a ring hunt, in partnership. We waited until we expected rain was near falling to extinguish the fire, and then we kindled a large circle in the prairie. At this time, or before the bucks began to run, a great number of deer lay concealed in the grass, in the day, and moved about in the night; but as the fire burned in towards the centre of the circle, the deer fled before the fire; the Indians were scattered also at some distance before the fire, and shot them down every opportunity, which was very frequent, especially as the circle became small. When we came to divide the deer, there were about ten to each hunter, which were all killed in a few hours. The rain did not come on that night to put out the outside circle of the fire, and as the wind arose, it extended through the whole prairie, which was about fifty miles in length, and in some places nearly twenty in breadth. This put an end to our ring hunting this season, and was in other respects an injury to us in the hunting business; so that upon the whole we received more harm than benefit by our rapid hunting frolic. We then moved from the north end of the glades, and encamped at the carrying place.

This place is in the plains, betwixt a creek that empties into Sandusky and one that runs into Sciota. And at the time of high water, or in the spring season, there is but about one half mile of portage, and that very level, and clear of rocks, timber, or stones; so that with a little digging there may be water carriage the whole way from Sciota to lake Erie.

From the mouth of Sandusky to the falls is chiefly first rate land, lying flat or level, intermixed with large bodies of clear meadows, where the grass is exceedingly rank, and in many places three or four feet high. The timber is oak, hickory, walnut, cherry, black ash, elm, sugar-tree, buckeye, locust and beech. In some places there is wet timber land—the timber in these places is chiefly water ash, sycamore, or button-wood.

From the falls to the prairies, the land lies well to the sun; it is neither too flat nor too hilly, and is chiefly first rate; the timber nearly the same as below the falls, excepting the water ash. There is also here some plats of beech land, that appears to be second rate, as it frequently produces spice-wood. The prairie appears to be a tolerably fertile soil, though in many places too wet for cultivation; yet I apprehend it would produce timber, were it only kept from fire.

The Indians are of the opinion that the squirrels plant all the timber, as they bury a number of nuts for food, and only one at a place. When a squirrel is killed, the various kinds of nuts thus buried will grow.

I have observed that when these prairies have only escaped fire for one year, near where a single tree stood there was a young growth of timber supposed to be planted by the squirrels. But when the prairies were again burned, all this young growth was immediately consumed; as the fire rages in the grass to such a pitch, that numbers of raccoons are thereby burned to death.

On the west side of the prairie, or betwixt that and Sciota, there is a large body of first rate land—the timber, walnut, locust, sugar-tree, buckeye, cherry, ash, elm, mulberry, plum-trees, spice-wood, black haw, red haw, oak, and hickory.

About the time the bucks quit running, Tontileaugo, his wife and children, Tecaughretanego, his son Nunganey and myself, left the Wyandot camps at the carrying place, and crossed the Sciota river at the south end of the glades, and proceeded on about a south-west course to a large creek called Ollentangy, which I believe interlocks with the waters of the Miami, and empties into Sciota on the west side thereof. From the south end of the prairie to Ollentangy there is a large quantity of beech land, intermixed with first rate land. Here we made our winter hut, and had considerable success in hunting.

After some time, one of Tontileaugo's step-sons (a lad about eight years of age) offended him, and he gave the boy a moderate whipping, which much displeased his Wyandot wife. She acknowledged that the boy was guilty of a fault, but thought that he ought to have been ducked, which is their usual mode of chastisement. She said she could not bear to have her son whipped like a servant or slave; and she was so displeased, that when Tontileaugo went out to hunt, she got her two horses, and all her effects, (as in this country the husband and wife have separate interests,) and moved back to the Wyandot camp that we had left.

When Tontileaugo returned, he was much disturbed on hearing of his wife's elopement, and said that he would never go after her, were it not that he was afraid that she would get bewildered, and that his children that she had taken with her might suffer. Tontileaugo went after his wife, and when they met they made up the quarrel; and he never returned, but left Tecaughretanego and his son, (a boy about ten years of age,) and myself, who remained here in our hut all winter.

Tecaughretanego had been a first-rate warrior, statesman and hunter, and though he was now near sixty years of age, was yet equal to the common run of hunters, but subject to the rheumatism, which deprived him of the use of his legs.

Shortly after Tontileaugo left us, Tecaughretanego became lame, and could scarcely walk out of our hut for two months. I had considerable success in hunting and trapping. Though Tecaughretanego endured much pain and misery, yet he bore it all with wonderful patience, and would often endeavor to entertain me with cheerful conversation. Sometimes he would applaud me for my diligence, skill and activity; and at other times he would take great care in giving me instructions concerning the hunting and trapping business. He would also tell me that if I failed of success we would suffer very much, as we were about forty miles from any one living, that we knew of; yet he would not intimate that he apprehended we were in any danger, but still supposed that I was fully adequate to the task.

Tontileaugo left us a little before Christmas, and from that until some time in February we had always plenty of bear meat, venison, &c. During this time I killed much more than we could use, but having no horses to carry in what I killed, I left part of it in the woods. In February, there came a snow, with a crust, which made a great noise when walking on it, and frightened away the deer; and as bear and beaver were scarce here, we got entirely out of provision. After I had hunted two days without eating any thing, and had very short allowance for some days before, I returned late in the evening, faint and weary. When I came into our hut, Tecaughretanego asked what success. I told him not any. He asked me if I was not very hungry. I replied that the keen appetite seemed to be in some measure removed, but I was both faint and weary. He commanded Nunganey, his little son, to bring me something to eat, and he brought me a kettle with some bones and broth. After eating a few mouthfuls, my appetite violently returned, and I thought the victuals had a most agreeable relish, though it was only fox and wildcat bones, which lay about the camp, which the ravens and turkey-buzzards had picked; these Nunganey had collected and boiled, until the sinews that remained on the bones would strip off. I speedily finished my allowance, such as it was, and when I had ended my *sweet* repast, Tecaughretanego asked me how I felt. I told him that I was much refreshed. He then handed me his pipe and pouch, and told me to take a smoke. I did so. He then said he had something of importance to tell me, if I was now composed and ready to hear it. I told him that I was ready to hear him. He said the reason why he deferred his speech till now was because few men are in a right humor to hear good talk when they are extremely hungry, as they are then generally fretful and discomposed, but as you appear now to enjoy calmness and serenity of mind, I will now communicate to you the thoughts of my heart, and those things that I know to be true.

"*Brother*,—As you have lived with the white people, you have not had the same advantage of knowing that the great Being above feeds his people, and gives them their meat in due season, as we Indians have, who are frequently out of provisions, and yet are wonderfully supplied, and that so frequently, that it is evidently the hand of the great Owaneeyo* that doth this. Whereas the white people have commonly large stocks of tame cattle, that they can kill when they please, and also their barns and cribs filled with grain, and therefore have not the same opportunity of seeing and knowing that they are supported by the Ruler of heaven and earth.

"*Brother*,—I know that you are now afraid that we will all perish with hunger, but you have no just reason to fear this.

"*Brother*,—I have been young, but am now old; I have been frequently under the like circumstances that we now are, and that some time or other in almost every year of my life; yet I have hitherto been supported, and my wants supplied in time of need.

"*Brother*,—Owaneeyo sometimes suffers us to be in want, in order to teach us our dependence upon him, and to let us know that we are to love and serve him; and likewise to know the worth of the favors that we receive, and to make us more thankful.

"*Brother*,—Be assured that you will be supplied with food, and that just in the right time; but you must continue diligent in the use of means. Go to sleep, and rise early in the morning and go a hunting; be strong, and exert yourself like a man, and the Great Spirit will direct your way."

The next morning I went out, and steered about an east course. I proceeded on slowly for about five miles, and saw deer frequently; but as the crust on the snow made a great noise, they were always running before I spied them, so that I could not get a shot. A violent appetite returned, and I became intolerably hungry. It was now that I concluded I would run off to Pennsylvania, my native country. As the snow was on the ground, and Indian hunters almost the whole of the way before me, I had but a poor prospect of making my escape, but my case appeared desperate. If I staid here, I thought I would perish with hunger, and if I met with Indians they could but kill me.

I then proceeded on as fast as I could walk, and when I got

---

* This is the name of God, in their tongue, and signifies the owner and ruler of all things.

about ten or twelve miles from our hut, I came upon fresh
buffalo tracks; I pursued after, and in a short time came in
sight of them as they were passing through a small glade.
I ran with all my might and headed them, where I lay in ambush, and killed a very large cow. I immediately kindled a
fire and began to roast meat, but could not wait till it was done;
I ate it almost raw. When hunger was abated, I began to be
tenderly concerned for my old Indian brother and the little boy
I had left in a perishing condition. I made haste and packed
up what meat I could carry, secured what I left from the wolves,
and returned homewards.

I scarcely thought on the old man's speech while I was
almost distracted with hunger, but on my return was much
affected with it, reflected on myself for my hard-heartedness
and ingratitude, in attempting to run off and leave the venerable old man and little boy to perish with hunger. I also considered how remarkably the old man's speech had been verified
in our providentially obtaining a supply. I thought also of
that part of his speech which treated of the fractious dispositions of hungry people, which was the only excuse I had for
my base inhumanity, in attempting to leave them in the most
deplorable situation.

As it was moonlight, I got home to our hut, and found the
old man in his usual good humor. He thanked me for my
exertion, and bid me sit down, as I must certainly be fatigued,
and he commanded Nunganey to make haste and cook. I told
him I would cook for him, and let the boy lay some meat on
the coals for himself; which he did, but ate it almost raw, as
I had done. I immediately hung on the kettle with some water, and cut the beef in thin slices, and put them in. When it
had boiled a while, I proposed taking it off the fire, but the old
man replied, "let it be done enough." This he said in as
patient and unconcerned a manner as if he had not wanted
one single meal. He commanded Nunganey to eat no more
beef at that time, lest he might hurt himself, but told him to
sit down, and after some time he might sup some broth; this
command he reluctantly obeyed.

When we were all refreshed, Tecaughretanego delivered a
speech upon the necessity and pleasure of receiving the necessary supports of life with thankfulness, knowing that Owaneeyo is the great giver. Such speeches from an Indian may be
thought by those who are unacquainted with them altogether
incredible; but when we reflect on the Indian war, we may
readily conclude that they are not an ignorant or stupid sort of
people, or they would not have been such fatal enemies. When
they came into our country they outwitted us; and when we

sent armies into their country, they outgeneralled and beat us with inferior force. Let us also take into consideration that Tecaughretanego was no common person, but was among the Indians as Socrates in the ancient heathen world ; and it may be equal to him, if not in wisdom and in learning, yet perhaps in patience and fortitude. Notwithstanding Tecaughretanego's uncommon natural abilities, yet in the sequel of this history you will see the deficiency of the light of nature, unaided by revelation, in this truly great man.

The next morning Tecaughretanego desired me to go back and bring another load of buffalo beef. As I proceeded to do so, about five miles from our hut I found a bear tree. As a sapling grew near the tree, and reached near the hole that the bear went in at, I got dry dozed or rotten wood, that would catch and hold fire almost as well as spunk. This wood I tied up in bunches, fixed them on my back, and then climbed up the sapling, and with a pole I put them, touched with fire, into the hole, and then came down and took my gun in my hand. After some time the bear came out, and I killed and skinned it, packed up a load of the meat, (after securing the remainder from the wolves,) and returned home before night. On my return, my old brother and his son were much rejoiced at my success. After this we had plenty of provisions.

We remained here until some time in April, 1758. At this time Tecaugretanego had recovered so that he could walk about. We made a birk canoe, embarked, and went down Ollentangy some distance, but the water being low, we were in danger of splitting our canoe upon the rocks ; therefore Tecaughretanego concluded we would encamp on shore, and pray for rain.

When we encamped Tecaughretanego made himself a sweat house, which he did by sticking a number of hoops in the ground, each hoop forming a semicircle ; this he covered all round with blankets and skins. He then prepared hot stones, which he rolled into this hut, and then went into it himself with a little kettle of water in his hand, mixed with a variety of herbs, which he had formerly cured, and had now with him in his pack ; they afforded an odoriferous perfume. When he was in, he told me to pull down the blankets behind him, and cover all up close, which I did, and then he began to pour water upon the hot stones, and to sing aloud. He continued in this vehement hot place about fifteen minutes. All this he did in order to purify himself before he would address the Supreme Being. When he came out of his sweat house, he began to burn tobacco and pray. He began each petition with *oh, ho, ho, ho*, which is a kind of aspiration, and signifies an ardent wish. I observed that all his petitions were only for immediate or present temporal blessings. He began his address by thanksgiving in the following manner:

"O Great Being! I thank thee that I have obtained the use of my legs again; that I am now able to walk about and kill turkeys, &c. without feeling exquisite pain and misery. I know that thou art a hearer and a helper, and therefore I will call upon thee.

"*Oh, ho, ho, ho,*

"Grant that my knees and ankles may be right well, and that I may be able, not only to walk, but to run and to jump logs, as I did last fall.

"*Oh, ho, ho, ho,*

"Grant that on this voyage we may frequently kill bears, as they may be crossing the Sciota and Sandusky.

"*Oh, ho, ho, ho,*

"Grant that we may kill plenty of turkeys along the banks, to stew with our fat bear meat.

"*Oh, ho, ho, ho,*

"Grant that rain may come to raise the Ollentangy about two or three feet, that we may cross in safety down to Sciota, without danger of our canoe being wrecked on the rocks. And now, O Great Being! thou knowest how matters stand; thou knowest that I am a great lover of tobacco, and though I know not when I may get any more, I now make a present of the last I have unto thee, as a free burnt offering; therefore I expect thou wilt hear and grant these requests, and I, thy servant, will return thee thanks, and love thee for thy gifts."

During the whole of this scene I sat by Tecaughretanego, and as he went through it with the greatest solemnity, I was seriously affected with his prayers. I remained duly composed until he came to the burning of the tobacco; and as I knew that he was a great lover of it, and saw him cast the last of it into the fire, it excited in me a kind of merriment, and I insensibly smiled. Tecaughretanego observed me laughing, which displeased him, and occasioned him to address me in the following manner.

"*Brother:* I have somewhat to say to you, and I hope you will not be offended when I tell you of your faults. You know that when you were reading your books in town I would not let the boys or any one disturb you; but now, when I was praying, I saw you laughing. I do not think that you look upon praying as a foolish thing; I believe you pray yourself. But perhaps you may think my mode or manner of praying foolish; if so, you ought in a friendly manner to instruct me, and not make sport of sacred things."

I acknowledged my error, and on this he handed me his

pipe to smoke, in token of friendship and reconciliation, though at this time he had nothing to smoke but red willow bark. I told him something of the method of reconciliation with an offended God, as revealed in my Bible, which I had then in possession. He said that he liked my story better than that of the French priests, but he thought that he was now too old to begin to learn a new religion, therefore he should continue to worship God in the way that he had been taught, and that if salvation or future happiness was to be had in his way of worship, he expected he would obtain it, and if it was inconsistent with the honor of the Great Spirit to accept of him in his own way of worship, he hoped that Owaneeyo would accept of him in the way I had mentioned, or in some other way, though he might now be ignorant of the channel through which favor or mercy might be conveyed. He said that he believed that Owaneeyo would hear and help every one that sincerely waited upon him.

Here we may see how far the light of nature could go; perhaps we see it here almost in its highest extent. Notwithstanding the just views that this great man entertained of Providence, yet we now see him (though he acknowledged his guilt) expecting to appease the Deity, and procure his favor, by burning a little tobacco. We may observe that all heathen nations, as far as we can find out either by tradition or the light of nature, agree with revelation in this, that sacrifice is necessary, or that some kind of atonement is to be made in order to remove guilt and reconcile them to God. This, accompanied with numberless other witnesses, is sufficient evidence of the rationality of the truth of the Scriptures.

A few days after Tecaughretanego had gone through his ceremonies and finished his prayers, the rain came and raised the creek a sufficient height, so that we passed in safety down to Sciota, and proceeded up to the carrying place. Let us now describe the land on this route from our winter hut, and down Ollentangy to the Sciota, and up it to the carrying place.

About our winter cabin is chiefly first and second rate land. A considerable way up Ollentangy, on the south-west side thereof, or betwixt it and the Miami, there is a very large prairie, and from this prairie down Ollentangy to Sciota is generally first rate land. The timber is walnut, sugar-tree, ash, buckeye, locust, wild cherry, and spice-wood, intermixed with some oak and beech. From the mouth of Ollentangy, on the east side of Sciota, up to the carrying place, there is a large body of first and second rate land, and tolerably well watered. The timber is ash, sugar-tree, walnut, locust, oak, and beech. Up near the carrying place the land is a little hilly, but the soil good. We proceeded from this place down Sandusky, and in our passage we killed four bears and a number of turkeys. Tecaughretanego appeared now fully persuaded that all this came in answer to his prayers, and who can say with any degree of certainty that it was not so ?

When we came to the little lake at the mouth of Sandusky, we called at a Wyandot town that was then there, called Sunyendeand. Here we diverted ourselves several days by catching rock fish in a small creek, the name of which is also Sunyendeand, which signifies rock fish. They fished in the night with lights, and struck the fish with gigs or spears. The rock fish here, when they begin first to run up the creek to spawn, are exceedingly fat, sufficiently so to fry themselves. The first night we scarcely caught fish enough for present use for all that was in the town.

The next morning I met with a prisoner at this place by the name of Thompson, who had been taken from Virginia. He told me, if the Indians would only omit disturbing the fish for one night, he could catch more fish than the whole town could make use of. I told Mr. Thompson that if he was certain he could do this, that I would use my influence with the Indians to let the fish alone for one night. I applied to the chiefs, who agreed to my proposal, and said they were anxious to see what the Great Knife (as they called the Virginian) could do. Mr. Thompson, with the assistance of some other prisoners, set to work, and made a hoop-net of elm bark ; they then cut down a tree across the creek, and stuck in stakes at the lower side of it to prevent the fish from passing up, leaving only a gap at the one side of the creek ; here he sat with his net, and when he felt the fish touch the net he drew it up, and frequently would haul out two or three rock fish that would weigh about five or six pounds each. He continued at this until he had hauled out about a wagon load, and then left the gap open in order to let them pass up, for they could not go far on account of the shallow water. Before day Mr. Thompson shut it up, to prevent them from passing down, in order to let the Indians have some diversion in killing them in daylight.

When the news of the fish came to town, the Indians all collected, and with surprise beheld the large heap of fish, and applauded the ingenuity of the Virginian. When they saw the number of them that were confined in the water above the tree, the young Indians ran back to the town, and in a short time returned with their spears, gigs, bows and arrows, &c., and were the chief part of that day engaged in killing rock fish, insomuch that we had more than we could use or preserve. As we had no salt, or any way to keep them, they lay upon the banks, and after some time great numbers of turkey-buzzards and eagles collected together and devoured them.

Shortly after this we left Sunyendeand, and in three days arrived at Detroit, where we remained this summer.

Some time in May we heard that General Forbes, with seven thousand men, was preparing to carry on a campaign against fort Du Quesne, which then stood near where fort Pitt was afterwards erected. Upon receiving this news, a number of runners were sent off by the French commander at Detroit to urge the different tribes of Indian warriors to repair to fort Du Quesne.

Some time in July, 1758, the Ottawas, Jibewas, Potowato-mies, and Wyandots, rendezvoused at Detroit, and marched off to fort Du Quesne, to prepare for the encounter of General Forbes. The common report was that they would serve him as they did General Braddock, and obtain much plunder. From this time until fall, we had frequent accounts of Forbes's army, by Indian runners that were sent out to watch their motion. They espied them frequently from the mountains ever after they left fort Loudon. Notwithstanding their vigilance, Colonel Grant, with his Highlanders, stole a march upon them, and in the night took possession of a hill about eighty rods from fort Du Quesne; this hill is on that account called Grant's Hill to this day. The French and Indians knew not that Grant and his men were there, until they beat the drum and played upon the bagpipes just at daylight. They then flew to arms, and the Indians ran up under cover of the banks of Alleghany and Monongahela for some distance, and then sallied out from the banks of the rivers, and took possession of the hill above Grant; and as he was on the point of it, in sight of the fort, they immediately surrounded him, and as he had his Highlanders in ranks, and in very close order, and the Indians scattered and concealed behind trees, they defeated him with the loss only of a few warriors; most of the Highlanders were killed or taken prisoners.

After this defeat the Indians held a council, but were divided in their opinions. Some said that General Forbes would now turn back, and go home the way that he came, as Dunbar had done when General Braddock was defeated; others supposed he would come on. The French urged the Indians to stay and see the event; but as it was hard for the Indians to be absent from their squaws and children at this season of the year, a great many of them returned home to their hunting. After this, the remainder of the Indians, some French regulars, and a number of Canadians, marched off in quest of General Forbes. They met his army near fort Ligoneer, and attacked them, but were frustrated in their design. They said that Forbes's men were beginning to learn the art of war, and that there were a great number of American riflemen along with the red-coats, who scattered out, took trees, and were good marksmen; therefore they found they could not accomplish their design, and were obliged to retreat. When they returned from the battle to fort Du Quesne, the Indians concluded that they would go to their hunting. The French endeavored to persuade them to stay and try another battle. The Indians said if it was only the red-coats they had to do with, they could soon subdue them, but they could not withstand *Asha-lecoa*, or the Great Knife, which was the name they gave the Virginians. They then returned home to their hunting, and the French evacuated the fort, which General Forbes came and took possession of, without further opposition, late in the year 1758, and at this time began to build fort Pitt.

When Tecaughretanego had heard the particulars of Grant's defeat, he said that he could not well account for his contradictory and inconsistent conduct. He said, as the art of war consists in ambushing and surprising our enemies, and in preventing them from ambushing and surprising us, Grant, in the first place, acted like a wise and experienced warrior in artfully approaching in the night without being discovered; but when he came to the place, and the Indians were lying asleep outside of the fort, between him and the Alleghany river, in place of slipping up quietly, and falling upon them with their broadswords, they beat the drums and played upon the bagpipes. He said he could account for this inconsistent conduct no other way than by supposing that he had made too free with spirituous liquors during the night, and became intoxicated about daylight. But to return.

This year we hunted up Sandusky and down Sciota, and took nearly the same route that we had done the last hunting season. We had considerable success, and returned to Detroit some time in April, 1759.

Shortly after this, Tecaughretanego, his son Nungany and myself, went from Detroit (in an elm-bark canoe) to Caughne-waga, a very ancient Indian town, about nine miles above Montreal, where I remained until about the first of July. I then heard of a French ship at Montreal that had English prisoners on board, in order to carry them over sea and exchange them. I went privately off from the Indians, and got also on board; but as General Wolfe had stopped the river St. Lawrence we were all sent to prison in Montreal, where I remained four months. Some time in November we were all sent off from this place to Crown Point, and exchanged.

Early in the year 1760, I came home to Conococheague, and found that my people could never ascertain whether I was killed or taken until my return. They received me with great joy, but were surprised to see me so much like an Indian both in my gait and gesture.

Upon inquiry, I found that my sweetheart was married a few days before I arrived. My feelings I must leave on this occasion for those of my readers to judge who have felt the pangs of disappointed love, as it is impossible now for me to describe the emotion of soul I felt at that time.

Now there was peace with the Indians, which lasted until the year 1763. Some time in May, this year, I married, and about that time the Indians again commenced hostilities, and were busily engaged in killing and scalping the frontier inhabitants in various parts of Pennsylvania. The whole Conococheague valley, from the North to the South Mountain, had been almost entirely evacuated during Braddock's war. This state was then a Quaker government, and at the first of this war the frontiers received no assistance from the state. As the people were now beginning to live at home again, they thought it hard to be drove away a second time, and were determined, if possible, to make a stand; therefore they raised as much money by collections and subscriptions as would pay a company of riflemen for several months. The subscribers met, and elected a committee to manage the business. The committee appointed me captain of this company of rangers, and gave me the appointment of my subalterns. I chose two of the most active young men that I could find, who had also been long in captivity with the Indians. As we enlisted our men, we dressed them uniformly in the Indian manner, with breech-clouts, leggins, moccasins, and green shrouds, which we wore in the same manner that the Indians do, and nearly as the Highlanders wear their plaids. In place of hats we wore red handkerchiefs, and painted our faces red and black like Indian warriors. I taught them the Indian discipline, as I knew of no other at that time, which would answer the purpose much better than British. We succeeded beyond expectation in defending the frontiers, and were extolled by our employers. Near the conclusion of this expedition I accepted of an ensign's commission in the regular service, under King George, in what was then called the Pennsylvania line. Upon my resignation, my lieutenant succeeded me in command the rest of the time they were to serve. In the fall (the same year) I went on the Susquehanna campaign against the Indians, under the command of General Armstrong. In this route we burnt the Delaware and Monsey towns, on the west branch of the Susquehanna, and destroyed all their corn.

In the year 1764 I received a lieutenant's commission, and went out on General Bouquet's campaign against the Indians on the Muskingum. Here we brought them to terms, and promised to be at peace with them, upon condition that they would give up all our people that they had then in captivity among them. They then delivered unto us three hundred of the prisoners, and said that they could not collect them all at this time, as it was now late in the year, and they were far scattered; but they promised that they would bring them all into fort Pitt early next spring, and as security that they would do this, they delivered to us six of their chiefs as hostages. Upon this we settled a cessation of arms for six months, and promised, upon their fulfilling the aforesaid condition, to make with them a permanent peace.

A little below fort Pitt the hostages all made their escape. Shortly after this the Indians stole horses and killed some people on the frontiers. The king's proclamation was then circulating and set up in various public places, prohibiting any person from trading with the Indians until further orders.

Notwithstanding all this, about the first of March, 1765, a number of wagons, loaded with Indian goods and warlike stores, were sent from Philadelphia to Henry Pollens, Conococheague, and from thence seventy pack horses were loaded with these goods, in order to carry them to fort Pitt. This alarmed the country, and Mr. William Duffield raised about fifty armed men, and met the pack horses at the place where Mercersburg now stands. Mr. Duffield desired the employers to store up their goods, and not proceed until further orders. They made light of this, and went over the North Mountain, where they lodged in a small valley called the Great Cove. Mr. Duffield and his party followed after, and came to their lodging, and again urged them to store up their goods; he reasoned with them on the impropriety of the proceedings, and the great danger the frontier inhabitants would be exposed to, if the Indians should now get a supply: he said, as it was well known that they had scarcely any ammunition, and were almost naked, to supply them now would be a kind of murder, and would be illegally trading at the expense of the blood and treasure of the frontiers. Notwithstanding his powerful reasoning, these traders made game of what he said, and would only answer him by ludicrous burlesque.

When I beheld this, and found that Mr. Duffield would not compel them to store up their goods, I collected ten of my old warriors, that I had formerly disciplined in the Indian way, went off privately after night, and encamped in the woods. The next day, as usual, we blacked and painted, and waylaid them near Sidelong Hill. I scattered my men about forty rod along the side of the road, and ordered every two to take a tree, and about eight or ten rod between each couple, with orders to keep a reserve fire, one not to fire until his comrade had loaded his gun ; by this means we kept up a constant, slow fire upon them, from front to rear. We then heard nothing of these traders' merriment or burlesque. When they saw their pack-horses falling close by them, they called out, *pray, gentlemen, what would you have us to do ?* The reply was, *collect all your loads to the front, and unload them in one place ; take your private property, and immediately retire.* When they were gone, we burnt what they left, which consisted of blankets, shirts, vermillion, lead beads, wampum, tomahawks, scalping-knives, &c.

The traders went back to fort Loudon, and applied to the commanding officer there, and got a party of Highland soldiers, and went with them in quest of the robbers, as they called us; and without applying to a magistrate, or obtaining any civil authority, but barely upon suspicion, they took a number of creditable persons prisoners, (who were chiefly not any way concerned in this action,) and confined them in the guard-house in fort Loudon. I then raised three hundred riflemen, marched to fort Loudon, and encamped on a hill in sight of the fort. We were not long there, until we had more than double as many of the British troops prisoners in our camp as they had of our people in the guard-house. Captain Grant, a Highland officer, who commanded fort Loudon, then sent a flag of truce to our camp, where we settled a cartel, and gave them above two for one, which enabled us to redeem all our men from the guard-house, without further difficulty.

After this, Captain Grant kept a number of rifle guns which the Highlanders had taken from the country people, and refused to give them up. As he was riding out one day, we took him prisoner, and detained him until he delivered up the arms ; we also destroyed a large quantity of gunpowder that the traders had stored up, lest it might be conveyed privately to the Indians. The king's troops and our party had now got entirely out of the channel of the civil law, and many unjustifiable things were done by both parties. This convinced me more than ever I had been before of the absolute necessity of the civil law in order to govern mankind.

About this time the following song was composed by Mr. George Campbell, (an Irish gentleman, who had been edu-

cated in Dublin,) and was frequently sung to the tune of the
Black Joke.

> Ye patriot souls, who love to sing,
> Who serve your country and your king,
>   In wealth, peace and royal estate ;
> Attention give whilst I rehearse
> A modern fact in jingling verse,
> How party interest strove what it could
> To profit itself by public blood,
>   But justly met its merited fate.
>
> Let all those Indian traders claim
> Their just reward, inglorious fame,
>   For vile, base and treacherous ends.
> To Pollens, in the spring, they sent
> Much warlike stores, with an intent
> To carry them to our barbarous foes,
> Expecting that nobody dare oppose,
>   A present to their Indian friends.
>
> Astonish'd at the wild design,
> Frontier inhabitants combin'd
>   With brave souls to stop their career,
> Although some men apostatiz'd,
> Who first the grand attempt advis'd,
> The bold frontiers they bravely stood,
> To act for their king and their country's good
>   In joint league, and strangers to fear.
>
> On March the fifth, in sixty-five,
> The Indian presents did arrive,
>   In long pomp and cavalcade,
> Near Sidelong Hill, where in disguise
> Some patriots did their train surprise,
> And quick as lightning tumbled their loads,
> And kindled them bonfires in the woods,
>   And mostly burnt their whole brigade.
>
> At Loudon when they heard the news,
> They scarcely knew which way to choose,
>   For blind rage and discontent ;
> At length some soldiers they sent out,
> With guides for to conduct the route,
> And seized some men that were trav'ling there,
> And hurried them into Loudon, where
>   They laid them fast with one consent.
>
> But men of resolution thought
> Too much to see their neighbors caught
>   For no crime but false surmise ;
> Forthwith they join'd a warlike band,
> And march'd to Loudon out of hand,
> And kept the jailers pris'ners there,
> Until our friends enlarged were,
>   Without fraud or any disguise.

> Let mankind censure or commend
> This rash performance in the end,
>   Then both sides will find their account.
> 'Tis true no law can justify
> To burn our neighbor's property,
> But when this property is design'd
> To serve the enemies of mankind,
>   It's high treason in the amount.

After this, we kept up a guard of men on the frontiers, for several months, to prevent supplies being sent to the Indians, until it was proclaimed that Sir William Johnson had made peace with them, and then we let the traders pass unmolested.

In the year 1766, I heard that Sir William Johnson, the king's agent for settling affairs with the Indians, had purchased from them all the land west of the Appalachian Mountains that lay between the Ohio and Cherokee river ; and as I knew by conversing with the Indians in their own tongue that there was a large body of rich land there, I concluded I would take a tour westward and explore that country.

I set out about the last of June, 1766, and went in the first place to Holstein river, and from thence I travelled westward in company with Joshua Horton, Uriah Stone, William Baker and James Smith, who came from near Carlisle. There were only four white men of us, and a mulatto slave about eighteen years of age, that Mr. Horton had with him. We explored the country south of Kentucky, and there was no more sign of white men there then than there is now west of the head waters of the Missouri. We also explored Cumberland and Tennessee rivers, from Stone's* river down to the Ohio.

When we came to the mouth of Tennessee, my fellow-travellers concluded that they would proceed on to the Illinois, and see some more of the land to the west ; this I would not agree to. As I had already been longer from home than what I expected, I thought my wife would be distressed, and think I was killed by the Indians ; therefore I concluded that I would return home. I sent my horse with my fellow-travellers to the Illinois, as it was difficult to take a horse through the mountains. My comrades gave me the greatest part of the ammunition they then had, which amounted only to half a pound of powder, and lead equivalent. Mr. Horton also lent me his mulatto boy, and I then set off through the wilderness for Carolina.

---

* Stone's river is a south branch of Cumberland, and empties into it above Nashville. We first gave it this name in our journal, in May, 1767, after one of my fellow-travellers, Mr. Uriah Stone, and I am told that it retains the same name unto this day.

About eight days after I left my company at the mouth of Tennessee, on my journey eastward, I got a cane stab in my foot, which occasioned my leg to swell, and I suffered much pain. I was now in a doleful situation; far from any of the human species, excepting black Jamie, or the savages, and I knew not when I might meet with them. My case appeared desperate, and I thought something must be done. All the surgical instruments I had was a knife, a moccasin awl, and a pair of bullet-moulds; with these I determined to draw the snag from my foot, if possible. I stuck the awl in the skin, and with the knife I cut the flesh away from around the cane, and then I commanded the mulatto fellow to catch it with the bullet-moulds, and pull it out, which he did. When I saw it, it seemed a shocking thing to be in any person's foot; it will therefore be supposed that I was very glad to have it out. The black fellow attended upon me, and obeyed my directions faithfully. I ordered him to search for Indian medicine, and told him to get me a quantity of bark from the root of a lynn tree, which I made him beat on a stone, with a tomahawk, and boil it in a kettle, and with the ooze I bathed my foot and leg; what remained when I had finished bathing I boiled to a jelly and made poultices thereof. As I had no rags, I made use of the green moss that grows upon logs, and wrapped it round with elm bark; by this means, (simple as it may seem,) the swelling and inflammation in a great measure abated. As stormy weather appeared, I ordered Jamie to make us a shelter, which he did by erecting forks and poles, and covering them over with cane tops, like a fodder house. It was about one hundred yards from a large buffalo road. As we were almost out of provision, I commanded Jamie to take my gun, and I went along as well as I could, concealed myself near the road, and killed a buffalo. When this was done, we jerked* the lean, and fried the tallow out of the fat meat, which we kept to stew with our jerk as we needed it.

While I lay at this place, all the books I had to read was a psalm-book and Watts upon Prayer. Whilst in this situation, I composed the following verses, which I then frequently sung.

> Six weeks I've in this desert been,
> 　With one mulatto lad :
> Excepting this poor stupid slave,
> 　No company I had.

---

* Jerk is a name well known by the hunters and frontier inhabitants for meat cut in small pieces and laid on a scaffold, over a slow fire, whereby it is roasted until it is thoroughly dry.

In solitude I here remain,
  A cripple very sore,
No friend or neighbor to be found,
  My case for to deplore.

I'm far from home, far from the wife
  Which in my bosom lay,
Far from the children dear, which used
  Around me for to play.

This doleful circumstance cannot
  My happiness prevent,
While peace of conscience I enjoy,
  Great comfort and content.

I continued in this place until I could walk slowly, without crutches. As I now lay near a great buffalo road, I was afraid that the Indians might be passing that way, and discover my fire-place, therefore I moved off some distance, where I remained until I killed an elk. As my foot was yet sore, I concluded that I would stay here until it was healed, lest by travelling too soon it might again be inflamed.

In a few weeks after I proceeded on, and in October I arrived in Carolina. I had now been eleven months in the wilderness, and during this time I neither saw bread, money, women, nor spirituous liquors; and three months of which I saw none of the human species, except Jamie.

When I came into the settlement, my clothes were almost worn out, and the boy had nothing on him that ever was spun. He had buckskin leggins, moccasins, and breech-clout; a bear-skin dressed with the hair on, which he belted about him, and a raccoon-skin cap. I had not travelled far after I came in before I was strictly examined by the inhabitants. I told them the truth, and where I came from, &c.; but my story appeared so strange to them that they did not believe me. They said that they had never heard of any one coming through the mountains from the mouth of Tennessee, and if any one would undertake such a journey, surely no man would lend him his slave. They said that they thought that all I had told them were lies, and on suspicion they took me into custody, and set a guard over me.

While I was confined here, I met with a reputable old acquaintance, who voluntarily became my voucher, and also told me of a number of my acquaintances that now lived near this place, who had moved from Pennsylvania; on this being made public I was liberated. I went to a magistrate and obtained a pass, and one of my old acquaintances made me a present of a shirt. I then cast away my old rags; and all the

clothes I now had was an old beaver hat, buckskin leggins, moccasins, and a new shirt; also an old blanket, which I commonly carried on my back in good weather. Being thus
equipped, I marched on with my white shirt loose, and Jamie
with his bear-skin about him; myself appearing white, and
Jamie very black, alarmed the dogs wherever we came, so that
they barked violently. The people frequently came out and
asked me where we came from, &c. I told them the truth, but
they for the most part suspected my story, and I generally
had to show them my pass. In this way I came on to fort
Chissel, where I left Jamie at Mr. Horton's negro quarter,
according to promise. I went from thence to Mr. George
Adams's, on Reed Creek, where I had lodged, and where I
had left my clothes as I was going out from home. When I
dressed myself in good clothes, and mounted on horseback, no
man ever asked me for a pass; therefore I concluded that a
horse-thief, or even a robber, might pass without interruption,
provided he was only well dressed, whereas the shabby villian
would be immediately detected.

I returned home to Conococheague in the fall of 1767.
When I arrived, I found that my wife and friends had despaired of ever seeing me again, as they had heard that I was killed
by the Indians, and my horse brought into one of the Cherokee towns.

In the year 1769, the Indians again made incursions on the
frontiers; yet the traders continued carrying goods and warlike
stores to them. The frontiers took the alarm, and a number
of persons collected, destroyed and plundered a quantity of
their powder, lead, &c., in Bedford county. Shortly after this,
some of these persons, with others, were apprehended and laid
in irons in the guard-house in fort Bedford, on suspicion of
being the perpetrators of this crime.

Though I did not altogether approve of the conduct of this
new club of black boys, yet I concluded that they should not
lie in irons in the guard-house, or remain in confinement, by
arbitrary or military power. I resolved, therefore, if possible,
to release them, if they even should be tried by the civil law
afterwards. I collected eighteen of my old black boys, that I
had seen tried in the Indian war, &c. I did not desire a large
party, lest they should be too much alarmed at Bedford, and
accordingly prepared for us. We marched along the public
road in daylight, and made no secret of our design. We told
those whom we met that we were going to take fort Bedford,
which appeared to them a very unlikely story. Before this, I
made it known to one William Thompson, a man whom I
could trust, and who lived there. Him I employed as a spy,

and sent him along on horseback before, with orders to meet me at a certain place near Bedford, one hour before day. The next day a little before sunset, we encamped near the crossings of Juniata, about fourteen miles from Bedford, and erected tents, as though we intended staying all night, and not a man in my company knew to the contrary, save myself. Knowing that they would hear this in Bedford, and wishing it to be the case, I thought to surprise them by stealing a march.

As the moon rose about eleven o'clock, I ordered my boys to march; and we went on at the rate of five miles an hour, until we met Thompson at the place appointed. He told us that the commanding officer had frequently heard of us by travellers, and had ordered thirty men upon guard. He said they knew our number, and only made game of the notion of eighteen men coming to rescue the prisoners, but they did not expect us until towards the middle of the day. I asked him if the gate was open. He said it was then shut, but he expected they would open it as usual at daylight, as they apprehended no danger. I then moved my men privately up under the banks of Juniata, where we lay concealed about one hundred yards from the fort gate. I had ordered the men to keep a profound silence until we got into it. I then sent off Thompson again to spy. At daylight he returned, and told us that the gate was open, and three sentinels were standing on the wall; that the guards were taking a morning dram, and the arms standing together in one place. I then concluded to rush into the fort, and told Thompson to run before me to the arms. We ran with all our might, and as it was a misty morning, the sentinels scarcely saw us until we were within the gate, and took possession of the arms. Just as we were entering, two of them discharged their guns, though I do not believe they aimed at us. We then raised a shout, which surprised the town, though some of them were well pleased with the news. We compelled a blacksmith to take the irons off the prisoners, and then we left the place. This, I believe, was the first British fort in America that was taken by what they called American rebels.

Some time after this I took a journey westward, in order to survey some located land I had on and near the Youhogany. As I passed near Bedford, while I was walking and leading my horse, I was overtaken by some men on horseback, like travellers. One of them asked my name, and on telling it, they immediately pulled out their pistols, and presented them at me, calling upon me to deliver myself, or I was a dead man. I stepped back, presented my rifle, and told them to stand off. One of them snapped a pistol at me, and another was preparing to shoot, when I fired my piece. One of them also fired near the same time, and one of my fellow-travellers fell. The assailants then rushed up, and as my gun was empty, they took and tied me. I charged them with killing my fellow-traveller, and told them he was a man that I had accidentally met with on the road, that had nothing to do with the public quarrel. They asserted that I had killed him. I told them that my gun blowed, or made a slow fire; that I had her from my face before she went off, or I would not have missed my mark; and from the position my piece was in when it went off, it was not likely that my gun killed this man, yet I acknowledged I was not certain that it was not so. They then carried me to Bedford, laid me in irons in the guard-house, summoned a jury of the opposite party, and held an inquest. The jury brought me in guilty of wilful murder. As they were afraid to keep me long in Bedford, for fear of a rescue, they sent me privately through the wilderness to Carlisle, where I was laid in heavy irons.

Shortly after I came here, we heard that a number of my old black boys were coming to tear down the jail. I told the sheriff that I would not be rescued, as I knew that the indictment was wrong; therefore I wished to stand my trial. As I had found the black boys to be always under good command, I expected I could prevail on them to return, and therefore wished to write to them; to this the sheriff readily agreed. I wrote a letter to them, with irons on my hands, which was immediately sent; but as they had heard that I was in irons, they would come on. When we heard they were near the town, I told the sheriff I would speak to them out of the window, and if the irons were off I made no doubt but I could prevail on them to desist. The sheriff ordered them to be taken off, and just as they were taking off my bands the black boys came running up to the jail. I went to the window and called to them, and they gave attention. I told them, as my indictment was for wilful murder, to admit of being rescued would appear dishonorable. I thanked them for their kind intentions, and told them the greatest favor they could confer upon me would be to grant me this one request, *to withdraw from the jail and return in peace;* to this they complied, and withdrew. While I was speaking, the irons were taken off my feet, and never again put on.

Before this party arrived at Conococheague, they met about three hundred more on the way, coming to their assistance, and were resolved to take me out; they then turned, and all came together to Carlisle. The reason they gave for coming again was, because they thought that government was so enraged at

me, that I would not get a fair trial. But my friends and
myself together again prevailed on them to return in peace.

At this time the public papers were partly filled with these
occurrences. The following is an extract from the Pennsylvania Gazette, No. 2132, Nov. 2d, 1769.

"*Conococheague, October* 16*th,* 1769.

" MESSRS. HALL & SELLERS,

" Please to give the following narrative a place in your Gazette, and you will much oblige

" Your humble servant,

" WILLIAM SMITH."

"Whereas, in this Gazette of September 28th, 1769, there
appeared an extract of a letter from Bedford, September 12th,
1769, relative to James Smith, as being apprehended on suspicion of being a black boy, then killing his companion, &c., I
took upon myself, as bound by all the obligations of truth, justice to character, and to the world, to set that matter in a true
light; by which I hope the impartial world will be enabled to
obtain a more just opinion of the present scheme of acting in
this end of the country, as also to form a true idea of the truth,
candor, and ingenuity of the author of the said extract, in
stating that matter in so partial a light. The state of the case
(which can be made appear by undeniable evidence) was this.
James Smith, (who is styled the principal ringleader of the
black boys, by the said author,) together with his younger
brother and brother-in-law, were going out in order to survey
and improve their land on the waters of Youghoghany, and as
the time of their return was long, they took with them their
arms, and horses loaded with the necessaries of life; and as
one of Smith's brothers-in-law was an artist in surveying, he
had also with him the instruments for that business. Travelling on the way, within about nine miles of Bedford, they
overtook and joined company with one Johnson and Moorhead,
who likewise had horses loaded, part of which loading was
liquor, and part seed wheat, their intentions being to make
improvements on their lands. When they arrived at the parting of the road on this side-Bedford, the company separated.
One part going through the town, in order to get a horse shod,
were apprehended, and put under confinement, but for what
crime they knew not, and treated in a manner utterly inconsistent with the laws of their country and the liberties of
Englishmen; whilst the other part, viz. James Smith, Johnson, and Moorhead, taking along the other road, were met by

John Holmes, Esq., to whom James Smith spoke in a friendly manner, but received no answer. Mr. Holmes hasted, and gave an alarm in Bedford, from whence a party of men were sent in pursuit of them; but Smith and his companions not having the least thought of any such measures being taken, (why should they?) travelled slowly on. After they had gained the place where the roads joined, they delayed until the other part of their company should come up. At this time a number of men came riding. like men travelling; they asked Smith his name, which he told them; on which they immediately assaulted him as a highwayman, and with presented pistols commanded him to surrender or he was a dead man; upon which Smith stepped back, asked them if they were highwaymen, charging them at the same time to stand off, when immediately Robert George (one of the assailants) snapped a pistol at Smith's head, and that before Smith offered to shoot, (which said George himself acknowledged upon oath;) whereupon Smith presented his gun at another of the assailants, who was preparing to shoot him with his pistol. The said assailant having a hold of Johnson by the arm, two shots were fired, one by Smith's gun, the other from a pistol, so quick as just to be distinguishable, and Johnson fell. After which, Smith was taken and carried into Bedford, where John Holmes, Esq., the informer, held an inquest on the corpse, one of the assailants being as an evidence, (nor was there any other troubled about the matter.) Smith was brought in guilty of wilful murder, and so committed to prison. But a jealousy arising in the breasts of many, that the inquest, either through inadvertency, ignorance, or some other default, was not so fair as it ought to be, William Deny, coroner of the county, upon requisition made, thought proper to re-examine the matter, and summoning a jury of unexceptionable men out of three townships —men whose candor, probity, and honesty, is unquestionable with all who are acquainted with them, and having raised the corpse, held an inquest in a solemn manner during three days. In the course of their scrutiny they found Johnson's shirt blacked about the bullet-hole by the powder of the charge by which he was killed, whereupon they examined into the distance Smith stood from Johnson when he shot, and one of the assailants, being admitted to oath, swore to the respective spots of ground they both stood on at that time, which the jury measured, and found to be twenty-three feet nearly; then, trying the experiment of shooting at the same shirt, both with and against the wind, and at the same distance, found no effects, nor the least stain from the powder on the shirt. And let any person that pleases make the experiment, and I will venture to affirm he shall find that powder will not stain at half the distance above mentioned, if shot out of a rifle gun, which Smith's was. Upon the whole, the jury, after the most accurate examination and mature deliberation, brought in their verdict that some one of the assailants themselves must necessarily have been the perpetrators of the murder.

"I have now represented the matter in its true and genuine colors, and which I will abide by. I only beg liberty to make a few remarks and reflections on the above-mentioned extract. The author says, 'James Smith, with two others in company, passed round the town, without touching,' by which it is plain he would insinuate, and make the public believe, that Smith, and that part of the company, had taken some by-road, which is utterly false, for it was the king's highway, and the straightest, that through Bedford being something to the one side ; nor would the other part of the company have gone through the town but for the reason already given. Again, the author says that 'four men were sent in pursuit of Smith and his companions, who overtook them about five miles from Bedford, and commanded them to surrender, on which Smith presented his gun at one of the men, who was struggling with his companion, fired it at him, and shot his companion through the back.' Here I would just remark, again, the unfair and partial account given of this matter by the author. Not a word mentioned of George snapping his pistol before Smith offered to shoot, or of another of the assailants actually firing his pistol, though he confessed himself afterwards he had done so; not the least mention of the company's baggage, which, to men in the least open to a fair inquiry, would have been sufficient proof of the innocence of their intentions. Must not an effusive blush overspread the face of the partial representer of facts, when he finds the veil he had thrown over truth thus pulled aside, and she exposed to naked view? Suppose it should be granted that Smith shot the man, (which is not, and I presume never can be proved to be the case,) I would only ask, was he not on his own defence ? Was he not publicly assaulted ? Was he not charged, at the peril of his life, to surrender, without knowing for what? no warrant being shown him, or any declaration made of their authority. And seeing these things are so, would any judicious man, any person in the least acquainted with the laws of the land, or morality, judge him guilty of wilful murder ? But I humbly presume every one who has an opportunity of seeing this will, by this time, be convinced that the proceedings against Smith were truly unlawful and tyrannical, perhaps unparalleled by any instance in a civilized nation ;— for to endeavor to kill a man in the apprehending of him, in

order to bring him to trial for a fact, and that too on a supposed one, is undoubtedly beyond all bounds of law or government.

"If the author of the extract thinks I have treated him unfair, or that I have advanced any thing he can controvert, let
him come forward, as a fair antagonist, and make his defence,
and I will, if called upon, vindicate all that I have advanced
against him or his abettors.

"WILLIAM SMITH."

I remained in prison four months, and during this time I
often thought of those that were confined in the time of the
persecution, who declared their prison was converted into a pal-
ace. I now learned what this meant, as I never since or before
experienced four months of equal happiness.

When the supreme court sat, I was severely prosecuted.
At the commencement of my trial the judges, in a very unjust
and arbitrary manner, rejected several of my evidences ; yet,
as Robert George (one of those who was in the affray when I
was taken) swore in court that he snapped a pistol at me
before I shot, and a concurrence of corroborating circumstances amounted to strong presumptive evidence that it could
not possibly be my gun that killed Johnson, the jury, without
hesitation, brought in their verdict, NOT GUILTY. One of the
judges then declared that not one of this jury should ever hold
an office above a constable. Notwithstanding this proud, ill-
natured declaration, some of these jurymen afterwards filled
honorable places, and I myself was elected the next year, and
sat on the board* in Bedford county, and afterwards I served
in the board three years in Westmoreland county.

In the year 1774, another Indian war commenced, though
at this time the white people were the aggressors. The prospect of this terrified the frontier inhabitants, insomuch that
the great part on the Ohio waters either fled over the mountains eastward or collected into forts. As the state of Pennsylvania apprehended great danger, they at this time appointed me captain over what was then called the Pennsylvania
line. As they knew I could raise men that would answer
their purpose, they seemed to lay aside their former inveteracy.

In the year 1776, I was appointed a major in the Pennsylvania association. When American independence was declared, I was elected a member of the convention in Westmoreland county, state of Pennsylvania, and of the Assembly,
as long as I proposed to serve.

---

* A board of commissioners was annually elected in Pennsylvania to
regulate taxes and lay the county levy.

While I attended the Assembly in Philadelphia, in the year 1777, I saw in the street some of my old boys, on their way to the Jerseys, against the British, and they desired me to go with them; I petitioned the house for leave of absence, in order to head a scouting party, which was granted me. We marched into the Jerseys, and went before General Washington's army, waylaid the road at Rocky Hill, attacked about two hundred of the British, and with thirty-six men drove them out of the woods, into a large open field. After this, we attacked a party that were guarding the officers' baggage, and took the wagon and twenty-two Hessians; and also retook some of our continental soldiers, which they had with them. In a few days we killed and took more of the British than was of our party. At this time I took the camp fever, and was carried in a stage wagon to Burlington, where I lay until I recovered. When I took sick, my companion, Major James M'Common, took the command of the party, and had greater success than I had. If every officer, and his party, that lifted arms against the English, had fought with the same success that Major M'Common did, we would have made short work of the British war.

When I returned to Philadelphia, I applied to the Assembly for leave to raise a battalion of riflemen, which they appeared very willing to grant, but said they could not do it, as the power of raising men and commissioning officers were at that time committed to General Washington; therefore they advised me to apply to his excellency. The following is a true copy of a letter of recommendation which I received at this time from the council of safety:

"IN COUNCIL OF SAFETY.
"Philadelphia, February 10th, 1777.

"SIR—Application has been made to us by James Smith, Esq., of Westmoreland, a gentleman well acquainted with the Indian customs and their manner of carrying on war, for leave to raise a battalion of marksmen, expert in the use of rifles, and such as are acquainted with the Indian method of fighting, to be dressed entirely in their fashion, for the purpose of annoying and harassing the enemy in their marches and encampments. We think two or three hundred men in that way might be very useful. Should your excellency be of the same opinion, and direct such a corps to be formed, we will take proper measures for raising the men on the frontiers of this state, and follow such other directions as your excellency shall give in this matter.

"To his Excellency, General Washington."

"The foregoing is a copy of a letter to his excellency, General Washington, from the council of safety.

*"*JACOB S. HOWELL, *Secretary."*

After this I received another letter of recommendation, which is as follows:—

"We, whose names are underwritten, do certify that James Smith, (now of the county of Westmoreland,) was taken prisoner by the Indians in an expedition before General Braddock's defeat, in the year 1755, and remained with them until the year 1760; and also that he served as ensign, in the year 1763, under the pay of the province of Pennsylvania, and as lieutenant in the year 1764, and as captain in the year 1774; and as a military officer he has sustained a good character; and we do recommend him as a person well acquainted with the Indians' method of fighting, and, in our humble opinion, exceedingly fit for the command of a ranging or scouting party, which we are also humbly of opinion he could, (if legally authorized,) soon raise. Given under our hands at Philadelphia, this 13th day of March, 1777.

THOMAS PAXTON, Capt.	JONATHAN HODGE, Esq.
WILLIAM DUFFIELD, Esq.	WILLIAM PARKER, Capt.
DAVID ROBB, Esq.	ROBERT ELLIOT,
JOHN PIPER, Col.	JOSEPH ARMSTRONG, Col.
WILLIAM M'COMB,	ROBERT PEEBLES, Lt. Col.
WILLIAM PEPPER, Lt. Col.	SAMUEL PATTON, Capt.
JAMES M'LANE, Esq.	WILLIAM LYON, Esq."
JOHN PROCTOR, Col.	

With these and some other letters of recommendation, which I have not now in my possession, I went to his excellency, who lay at Morristown. Though General Washington did not fall in with the scheme of white men turning Indians, yet he proposed giving me a major's place in a battalion of riflemen already raised. I thanked the general for his proposal, but as I entertained no high opinion of the colonel I was to serve under, and with whom I had no prospect of getting my old boys again, I thought I would be of more use in the cause we were then struggling to support to remain with them as a militia officer; therefore I did not accept this offer.

In the year 1778, I received a colonel's commission, and after my return to Westmoreland the Indians made an attack upon our frontiers. I then raised men and pursued them, and the second day we overtook and defeated them. We likewise took four scalps, and recovered the horses and plunder which they were carrying off. At the time of this attack, Captain John Hinkston pursued an Indian, both their guns being empty, and after the fray was over he was missing. While we were inquiring about him, he came walking up, seemingly unconcerned, with a bloody scalp in his hand; he had pursued the Indian about a quarter of a mile, and tomahawked him.

Not long after this, I was called upon to command four hundred riflemen on an expedition against the Indian town on French Creek. It was some time in November before I received orders from General M'Intosh to march, and then we were poorly equipped and scarce of provision. We marched in three columns, forty rod from each other. There were also flankers on the outside of each column, that marched abreast in the rear, in scattered order; and even in the columns the men were one rod apart; and in the front the volunteers marched abreast in the same manner of the flankers, scouring the woods. In case of an attack, the officers were immediately to order the men to face out and take trees; in this position, the Indians could not avail themselves by surrounding us, or have an opportunity of shooting a man from either side of the tree. If attacked, the centre column was to reinforce whatever part appeared to require it most. When we encamped, our encampment formed a hollow square, including about thirty or forty acres; on the outside of the square, there were sentinels placed, whose business it was to watch for the enemy, and see that neither horses nor bullocks went out; and when encamped, if any attacks were made by an enemy, each officer was immediately to order the men to face out and take trees, as before mentioned; and in this form, they could not take the advantage by surrounding us, as they commonly had done when they fought the whites.

The following is a copy of general orders, given at this time, which I have found among my journals:

"AT CAMP—OPPOSITE FORT PITT.

"*November 29th*, 1778.

"GENERAL ORDERS.

"*A copy thereof is to be given to each Captain and Subaltern, and to be read to each Company.*

"You are to march in three columns, with flankers on the front and rear, and to keep a profound silence, and not to fire a gun, except at the enemy, without particular orders for that purpose; and in case of an attack, let it be so ordered that every other man only is to shoot at once, excepting on extraordinary occasions; the one half of the men to keep a reserve fire until their comrades load; and let every one be particularly careful not to fire at any time without a view of the enemy, and that not at too great a distance. I earnestly urge the above caution, as I have known very remarkable and grievous errors of this kind. You are to encamp on the hollow square, except the volunteers, who, according to their own request, are to encamp on the front of the square. A sufficient number of sentinels are to be kept round the square at a proper distance. Every man is to be under arms at the break of day, and to parade opposite to their fire-places, facing out, and when the officers examine their arms, and find them in good order, and give necessary directions, they are to be dismissed, with orders to have their arms near them, and be always in readiness.

"Given by

"JAMES SMITH, *Colonel.*"

In this manner, we proceeded on to French Creek, where

we found the Indian town evacuated. I then went on further than my orders called for, in quest of Indians; but our provision being nearly exhausted, we were obliged to return. On our way back we met with considerable difficulties, on account of high waters and scarcity of provision; yet we never lost one horse, excepting some that gave out.

After peace was made with the Indians, I met with some of them in Pittsburg, and inquired of them in their own tongue concerning this expedition, not letting them know I was there. They told me that they watched the movements of this army ever after they had left fort Pitt, and as they passed through the glades or barrens they had a full view of them from the adjacent hills, and computed their number to be about one thousand. They said they also examined their camps, both before and after they were gone, and found they could not make an advantageous attack, and therefore moved off from their town and hunting ground before we arrived.

In the year 1788, I settled in Bourbon county, Kentucky, seven miles above Paris, and in the same year was elected a member of the convention that sat at Danville to confer about a separation from the state of Virginia; and from that year until the year 1799, I represented Bourbon county either in convention or as a member of the General Assembly, except two years that I was left a few votes behind.

ON THE MANNERS AND CUSTOMS OF THE INDIANS.

The Indians are a slovenly people in their dress. They seldom ever wash their shirts, and in regard to cookery they are exceedingly filthy. When they kill a buffalo they will sometimes lash the paunch of it round a sapling, and cast it into the kettle, boil it, and sup the broth; though they commonly shake it about in cold water, then boil and eat it. Notwithstanding all this, they are very polite in their own way, and they retain among them the essentials of good manners; though they have few compliments, yet they are complaisant to one another, and when accompanied with good humor and discretion, they entertain strangers in the best manner their circumstances will admit. They use but few titles of honor. In the military line the titles of great men are only captains or leaders of parties. In the civil line, the titles are only counsellors, chiefs, or the old wise men. These titles are never made use of in addressing any of their great men. The language commonly made use of in addressing them is grandfather, father, or uncle. They have no such thing in use among them as Sir, Mr., Madam, or Mistress. The common mode of address is, my friend, brother, cousin, or mother, sister, &c. They pay great respect to age, or to the aged fathers and mothers among them of every rank. No one can arrive at any place of honor among them but by merit. Either some exploit in war must be performed before any one can be advanced in the military line, or become eminent for wisdom before they can obtain a seat in council. It would appear to the Indians a most ridiculous thing to see a man lead on a company of warriors, as an officer, who had himself never been in a battle in his life. Even in case of merit they are slow in advancing any one, until they arrive at or near middle age.

They invite every one that comes to their house or camp to eat, while they have any thing to give; and it is accounted bad manners to refuse eating when invited. They are very tenacious of their old mode of dressing and painting, and do not change their fashions as we do. They are very fond of tobacco, and the men almost all smoke it mixed with sumach leaves or red willow bark, pulverized, though they seldom use it in any other way. They make use of the pipe also as a token of love and friendship.

In courtship they also differ from us. It is a common thing among them for a young woman, if in love, to make suit to a young man; though the first address may be by the man, yet

22

the other is the most common. The squaws are generally
very immodest in their words and actions, and will often put the
young men to the blush. The men commonly appear to be
possessed of much more modesty than the women; yet I have
been acquainted with some young squaws that appeared really
modest: genuine it must be, as they were under very little
restraint in the channel of education or custom.

When the Indians meet one another, instead of saying how
do you do, they commonly salute in the following manner:
you are my friend—the reply is, truly friend, I am your friend;
or, cousin, you yet exist—the reply is, certainly I do. They
have their children under tolerable command; seldom ever
whip them, and their common mode of chastising is by duck-
ing them in cold water; therefore their children are more
obedient in the winter season than they are in the summer,
though they are then not so often ducked. They are a peaceable
people, and scarcely ever wrangle or scold, when sober; but
they are very much addicted to drinking, and men and women
will become basely intoxicated, if they can by any means procure
or obtain spirituous liquor, and then they are commonly either
extremely merry and kind, or very turbulent, ill-humored and
disorderly.

ON THEIR TRADITIONS AND RELIGIOUS SENTIMENTS.

As the family that I was adopted into was intermarried with
the Wyandots and Ottawas, three tongues were commonly
spoken, viz.: Caughnewaga, or what the French call Iroque,
also the Wyandot and Ottawa. By this means I had an opportunity of learning these three tongues; and I found that these
nations varied in their traditions and opinions concerning religion; and even numbers of the same nation differed widely in
their religious sentiments. Their traditions are vague, whimsical, romantic, and many of them scarce worth relating, and
not any of them reach back to the creation of the world. The
Wyandots come the nearest to this. They tell of a squaw
that was found when an infant in the water, in a canoe, made
of bulrushes. This squaw became a great prophetess, and did
many wonderful things: she turned water into dry land, and at
length made this continent, which was at that time only a very
small island, and but a few Indians in it. Though they were
then but few, they had not sufficient room to hunt; therefore
this squaw went to the water-side, and prayed that this little
island might be enlarged. The Great Being then heard her
prayer, and sent great numbers of water tortoises and muskrats, which brought with them mud and other materials for

enlarging this island, and by this means, they say, it was increased to the size that it now remains; therefore, they say, that the white people ought not to encroach upon them, or take their land from them, because their great grandmother made it. They say that about this time the angels or heavenly inhabitants, as they call them, frequently visited them and talked with their forefathers, and gave directions how to pray, and how to appease the Great Being when he was offended. They told them they were to offer sacrifice, burn tobacco, buffalo and deer bones; but they were not to burn bear's or raccoon's bones in sacrifice.

The Ottawas say that there are two Great Beings that govern and rule the universe, who are at war with each other; the one they call *Maneto*, and the other *Matchemaneto*. They say that Maneto is all kindness and love, and that Matchemaneto is an evil spirit, that delights in doing mischief; and some of them think that they are equal in power, and therefore worship the evil spirit out of a principle of fear. Others doubt which of the two may be the most powerful, and therefore endeavor to keep in favor with both, by giving each of them some kind of worship. Others say that Maneto is the first great cause, and therefore must be all powerful and supreme, and ought to be adored and worshipped, whereas Matchemaneto ought to be rejected and despised.

Those of the Ottawas that worship the evil spirit pretend to be great conjurors. I think if there is any such thing now in the world as witchcraft it is among these people. I have been told wonderful stories concerning their proceedings, but never was eye-witness to any thing that appeared evidently supernatural.

Some of the Wyandots and Caughnewagas profess to be Roman Catholics; but even these retain many of the notions of their ancestors. Those of them who reject the Roman Catholic religion hold that there is one great first cause, whom they call *Owaneeyo*, that rules and governs the universe, and takes care of all his creatures, rational and irrational, and gives them their food in due season, and hears the prayers of all those that call upon him; therefore it is but just and reasonable to pray, and offer sacrifice to this Great Being, and to do those things that are pleasing in his sight; but they differ widely in what is pleasing or displeasing to this Great Being. Some hold that following nature or their own propensities is the way to happiness, and cannot be displeasing to the Deity, because he delights in the happiness of his creatures, and does nothing in vain, but gave these dispositions with a design to lead to happiness, and therefore they ought to be followed.

Others reject this opinion altogether, and say that following their own propensities in this manner is neither the means of happiness nor the way to please the Deity.

Tecaughretanego was of opinion that following nature in a limited sense was reasonable and right. He said that most of the irrational animals, by following their natural propensities, were led to the greatest pitch of happiness that their natures and the world they lived in would admit of. He said that mankind and the rattlesnakes had evil dispositions, that led them to injure themselves and others. He gave instances of this. He said he had a puppy that he did not intend to raise, and in order to try an experiment he tied this puppy on a pole, and held it to a rattlesnake, which bit it several times; that he observed the snake shortly after rolling about apparently in great misery, so that it appeared to have poisoned itself as well as the puppy. The other instance he gave was concerning himself. He said that when he was a young man he was very fond of the women, and at length got the venereal disease, so that, by following this propensity, he was led to injure himself and others. He said our happiness depends on our using our reason, in order to suppress these evil dispositions; but when our propensities neither lead us to injure ourselves nor others we might with safety indulge them, or even pursue them as the means of happiness.

The Indians, generally, are of opinion that there are great numbers of inferior deities, which they call *Carreyagaroona*, which signifies the heavenly inhabitants. These beings they suppose are employed as assistants in managing the affairs of the universe, and in inspecting the actions of men; and that even the irrational animals are engaged in viewing their actions, and bearing intelligence to the gods. The eagle, for this purpose, with her keen eye, is soaring about in the day, and the owl, with her nightly eye, perched on the trees around their camp in the night; therefore, when they observe the eagle or the owl near they immediately offer sacrifice, or burn tobacco, that they may have a good report to carry to the gods. They say that there are also great numbers of evil spirits, which they call *Onasahroona*, which signifies the inhabitants of the lower region. These, they say, are employed in disturbing the world, and the good spirits are always going after them, and setting things right, so that they are constantly working in opposition to each other. Some talk of a future state, but not with any certainty; at best their notions are vague and unsettled. Others deny a future state altogether, and say that, after death, they neither think nor live.

As the Caughnewagas and the Six Nations speak nearly

the same language, their theology is also nearly alike. When I met with the Shawanees, or Delawares, as I could not speak their tongue, I spoke Ottawa to them, and as it bore some resemblance to their language, we understood each other in some common affairs; but, as I could only converse with them very imperfectly, I cannot from my own knowledge, with certainty, give any account of their theological opinions.

ON THEIR POLICE, OR CIVIL GOVERNMENT.

I have often heard of Indian kings, but never saw any. How any term used by the Indians in their own tongue, for the chief man of a nation, could be rendered king, I know not. The chief of a nation is neither a supreme ruler, monarch, or potentate; he can neither make war or peace, leagues or treaties; he cannot impress soldiers, or dispose of magazines; he cannot adjourn, prorogue, or dissolve a general assembly, nor can he refuse his assent to their conclusions, or in any manner control them. With them there is no such thing as hereditary succession, title of nobility, or royal blood, even talked of. The chief of a nation, even with the consent of his assembly, or council, cannot raise one shilling of tax off the citizens, but only receive what they please to give as free and voluntary donations. The chief of a nation has to hunt for his living as any other citizen. How then can they, with any propriety, be called kings? I apprehend that the white people were formerly so fond of the name of kings, and so ignorant of their power, that they concluded the chief man of a nation must be a king.

As they are illiterate, they consequently have no written code of laws. What they execute as laws are either old customs, or the immediate result of new councils. Some of their ancient laws or customs are very pernicious, and disturb the public weal. Their vague law of marriage is a glaring instance of this, as the man and his wife are under no legal obligation to live together if they are both willing to part. They have little form or ceremony among them in matrimony, but do like the Israelites of old; the man goes in unto the woman, and she becomes his wife. The years of puberty, and the age of consent, is about fourteen for the women, and eighteen for the men. Before I was taken by the Indians, I had often heard that in the ceremony of marriage the man gave the woman a deer's leg, and she gave him a red ear of corn, signifying that she was to keep him in bread, and he was to keep her in meat. I inquired of them concerning the truth of this, and they said they knew nothing of it, further than

22*

that they had heard it was the ancient custom among some nations. Their frequent changing of partners prevents propagation, creates disturbances, and often occasions murder and bloodshed, though this is commonly committed under the pretence of being drunk. Their impunity to crimes committed when intoxicated with spirituous liquors, or their admitting one crime as an excuse for another, is a very unjust law or custom.

The extremes they run into in dividing the necessaries of life are hurtful to the public weal; though their dividing meat when hunting may answer a valuable purpose, as one family may have success one day, and the other the next; but their carrying this custom to the town, or to agriculture, is striking at the root of industry, as industrious persons ought to be rewarded, and the lazy suffer for their indolence.

They have scarcely any penal laws; the principal punishment is degrading; even murder is not punished by any formal law, only the friends of the murdered are at liberty to slay the murderer if some atonement is not made. Their not annexing penalties to their laws is perhaps not as great a crime, or as unjust and cruel, as the bloody laws of England, which we have so long shamefully practised, and which are to be in force in this state until our penitentiary house is finished, which is now building, and then they are to be repealed.

Let us also take a view of the advantages attending Indian police: They are not oppressed or perplexed with expensive litigation; they are not injured by legal robbery; they have no splendid villains that make themselves grand and great upon other people's labor; they have neither church nor state erected as money-making machines.

ON THEIR DISCIPLINE AND METHOD OF WAR.

I have often heard the British officers call the Indians the undisciplined savages, which is a capital mistake, as they have all the essentials of discipline. They are under good command, and punctual in obeying orders; they can act in concert, and when their officers lay a plan and give orders, they will cheerfully unite in putting all their directions into immediate execution; and by each man observing the motion or movement of his right-hand companion, they can communicate the motion from right to left, and march abreast in concert, and in scattered order, though the line may be more than a mile long, and continue, if occasion requires, for a considerable distance, without disorder or confusion. They can perform various necessary manœuvres, either slowly, or as fast as they can run; they can form a circle or semicircle. The circle they make use of in order to surround their enemy, and the semicircle if the enemy has a river on one side of them. They can also form a large hollow square, face out and take trees; this they do if their enemies are about surrounding them, to prevent being shot from either side of the tree. When they go into battle they are not loaded or encumbered with many clothes, as they commonly fight naked, save only breech-clout, leggins, and moccasins. There is no such thing as corporeal punishment used in order to bring them under such good discipline; degrading is the only chastisement, and they are so unanimous in this that it effectually answers the purpose. Their officers plan, order, and conduct matters until they are brought into action, and then each man is to fight as though he was to gain the battle himself. General orders are commonly given in time of battle either to advance or retreat, and is done by a shout or yell, which is well understood, and then they retreat or advance in concert. They are generally well equipped, and exceedingly expert and active in the use of arms. Could it be supposed that undisciplined troops could defeat Generals Braddock, Grant, &c. ? It may be said by some that the French were also engaged in this war. True, they were; yet I know it was the Indians that laid the plan, and with small assistance put it into execution. The Indians had no aid from the French, or any other power, when they besieged fort Pitt in the year 1763, and cut off the communication for a considerable time between that post and fort Loudon, and would have defeated General Bouquet's army (who were on the way to raise the siege) had it not been for the assistance of the Virginia volunteers. They had no British troops with them when they defeated Colonel Crawford, near the Sandusky, in the time of the American war with Great Britain; or when they defeated Colonel Loughrie, on the Ohio, near the Miami, on his way to meet General Clarke: this was also in the time of the British war. It was the Indians alone that defeated Colonel Todd, in Kentucky, near the Blue Licks, in the year 1782; and Colonel Harmer, betwixt the Ohio and lake Erie, in the year 1790, and General St. Clair, in the year 1791; and it is said that there were more of our men killed at this defeat than there were in any one battle during our contest with Great Britain. They had no aid when they fought even the Virginia riflemen, almost a whole day, at the Great Kenhawa, in the year 1774; and when they found they could not prevail against the Virginians they made a most artful retreat. Notwithstanding they had the Ohio to cross, some continued firing whilst others were crossing the river; in this manner they proceeded, until they all got over, before the Virginians knew that they had retreated, and in this retreat they carried off all their wounded. In the most of the foregoing defeats they fought with an inferior number, though in this, I believe, it was not the case.

Nothing can be more unjustly represented than the different accounts we have had of their number, from time to time, both by their own computations, and that of the British. While I was among them I saw the account of the number that they, in those parts, gave to the French, and kept it by me. When they, in their own council-house, were taking an account of their number, with a piece of bark, newly stripped, and a small stick, which answered the end of a slate and pencil, I took an account of the different nations and tribes, which I added together, and found there were not half the number which they had given the French; and though they were then their allies, and lived among them, it was not easy finding out the deception, as they were a wandering set, and some of them almost always in the woods hunting. I asked one of the chiefs what was their reason for making such different returns. He said it was for political reasons, in order to obtain greater presents from the French, by telling them they could not divide such and such quantities of goods among so many.

In the year of General Bouquet's last campaign, 1764, I saw the official return made by the British officers of the number of Indians that were in arms against us that year, which amounted to thirty thousand. As I was then a lieutenant in the British service, I told them I was of opinion that there was not above one thousand in arms against us, as they were divided by Broadstreet's army, being then at lake Erie. The British officers hooted at me, and said they could not make England sensible of the difficulties they labored under in fighting them, as England expected that their troops could fight the undisciplined savages in America five to one, as they did the East Indians, and therefore my report would not answer their purpose, as they could not give an honorable account of the war but by augmenting their number. I am of opinion that from Braddock's war until the present time there never were more than three thousand Indians, at any time, in arms against us west of fort Pitt, and frequently not half that number. According to the Indians' own accounts, during the whole of Braddock's war, or from 1755 till 1758, they killed or took fifty of our people for one that they lost. In the war that commenced in the year 1763 they killed comparatively few of our people, and lost more of theirs, as the frontiers (especially the Virginians) had learned something of their method of war; yet they, in this war, according to their own accounts, (which I believe to be true,) killed or took ten of our people for one they lost.

Let us now take a view of the blood and treasure that was spent in opposing comparatively a few Indian warriors, with only some assistance from the French, the first four years of the war. Additional to the amazing destruction and slaughter that the frontiers sustained from James river to Susquehanna, and about thirty miles broad, the following campaigns were also carried on against the Indians: General Braddock's, in the year 1755; Colonel Armstrong's, against the Cattanyan town on the Alleghany, 1757; Gen. Forbes's, in 1758; Gen. Stanwick's, in 1759; General Monkton's, in 1760; Colonel Bouquet's, in 1761 and 1763, when he fought the battle of Brushy Run, and lost above one hundred men, but, by the assistance of the Virginia volunteers, drove the Indians; Col. Armstrong's, up the west branch of Susquehanna, in 1763; General Broadstreet's, up lake Erie, in 1764; Gen. Bouquet's against the Indians at Muskingum, 1764; Lord Dunmore's, in 1774; Gen. M'Intosh's, in 1778; Colonel Crawford's, shortly after his; Gen. Clarke's, in 1778, 1780; Colonel Bowman's, in 1779; General Clarke's, in 1782, against the Wabash in 1786; Gen. Logan's, against the Shawanees, in 1786; Gen. Wilkinson's, in ——; Colonel Harmer's, in 1790; and Gen. St. Clair's, in 1791; which, in all, are twenty-two campaigns, besides smaller expeditions; such as the French Creek expedition, Colonel Edwards's, Loughrie's, &c. All these were exclusive of the number of men that were internally employed as scouting parties, and in erecting forts, guarding stations, &c. When we take the foregoing occurrences into consideration, may we not reasonably conclude, that they are the best disciplined troops in the known world? Is it not the best discipline that has the greatest tendency to annoy the enemy and save their own men? I apprehend that the Indian discipline is as well calculated to answer the purpose in the woods of America, as the British discipline in Flanders; and British discipline in the woods is the way to have men slaughtered, with scarcely any chance of defending themselves.

Let us take a view of the benefits we have received by what little we have learned of their art of war, which cost us dear, and the loss we have sustained for want of it, and then see if it will not be well worth our while to retain what we have, and also to endeavor to improve in this necessary branch of business. Though we have made considerable proficiency in this line, and in some respects outdo them, viz. as marksmen, and in cutting our rifles, and keeping them in good order; yet I apprehend we are far behind in their manœuvres, or in being able to surprise, or prevent a surprise. May we not conclude, that the progress we had made in their art of war contributed considerably towards our success, in various respects, when contending with Great Britain for liberty? Had the British king attempted to enslave us before Braddock's war, in all probability he might readily have done it, because, except the New Englanders, who had formerly been engaged in war with the Indians, we were unacquainted with any kind of war. But after fighting such a subtle and barbarous enemy as the Indians, we were not terrified at the approach of British red-coats. Was not Burgoyne's defeat accomplished, in some measure, by the Indian mode of fighting? And did not General Morgan's riflemen, and many others, fight with greater success in consequence of what they had learned of their art of war? Kentucky would not have been settled at the time it was, had the Virginians been altogether ignorant of this method of war.

In Braddock's war the frontiers were laid waste for above three hundred miles long, and generally about thirty broad, excepting some that were living in forts, and many hundreds, or perhaps thousands, killed or made captives, and horses, and all kinds of property carried off. But, in the next Indian war, though we had the same Indians to cope with, the frontiers almost all stood their ground, because they were by this time, in some measure, acquainted with their manœuvres; and the want of this in the first war was the cause of the loss of many hundreds of our citizens, and much treasure.

Though large volumes have been written on morality, yet it may be all summed up in saying, do as you would wish to be done by. So the Indians sum up the art of war in the following manner.

The business of the private warriors is to be under command, or punctually to obey orders; to learn to march abreast in scattered order, so as to be in readiness to surround the enemy, or to prevent being surrounded; to be good marksmen, and active in the use of arms; to practise running; to learn to endure hunger or hardships with patience and fortitude; to tell the truth at all times to their officers, but more especially when sent out to spy the enemy.

Concerning Officers.—They say that it would be absurd to appoint a man an officer whose skill and courage had never been tried; that all officers should be advanced only according to merit; that no one man should have the absolute command of an army; that a council of officers are to determine when and how an attack is to be made; that it is the business of the officers to lay plans to take every advantage of the enemy; to ambush and surprise them, and to prevent being ambushed and surprised themselves. It is the duty of officers to prepare and deliver speeches to the men, in order to animate and encourage them ; and on the march, to prevent the men, at any time, from getting into a huddle, because if the enemy should surround them in this position they would be exposed to the enemy's fire. It is likewise their business at all times to endeavor to annoy their enemy, and save their own men, and therefore ought never to bring on an attack without considerable advantage, or without what appeared to them the sure prospect of victory, and that with the loss of few men ; and if at any time they should be mistaken in this, and are like to lose many men by gaining the victory, it is their duty to retreat, and wait for a better opportunity of defeating their enemy, without the danger of losing so many men. Their conduct proves that they act upon these principles ; therefore it is that, from Braddock's war to the present time, they have seldom ever made an unsuccessful attack. The battle at the mouth of the Great Kenhawa is the greatest instance of this ; and even then, though the Indians killed about three for one they lost, yet they retreated. The loss of the Virginians in this action was seventy killed, and the same number wounded. The Indians lost twenty killed on the field, and eight who died afterwards of their wounds. This was the greatest loss of men that I ever knew the Indians to sustain in any one battle. They will commonly retreat if their men are falling fast ; they will not stand cutting like the Highlanders or other British troops ; but this proceeds from a compliance with their rules of war rather than cowardice. If they are surrounded they will fight while there is a man of them alive, rather than surrender. When Colonel John Armstrong surrounded the Cattanyan town, on the Alleghany river, Captain Jacobs, a Delaware chief, with some warriors, took possession of a house, defended themselves for some time, and killed a number of our men. As Jacobs could speak English, our people called on him to surrender. He said that he and his men were warriors, and they would all fight while life remained. He was again told that they should be well used if they would only surrender ; and if not, the house should be burned down over their heads. Jacobs replied, he could eat fire ; and when the house was in a flame, he, and they that were with him, came out in a fighting position, and were all killed. As they are a sharp, active kind of people, and war is their principal study, in this they have arrived at considerable perfection. We may learn of the Indians what is useful and laudable, and at the same time lay aside their barbarous proceedings. It is much to be lamented, that some of our frontier riflemen are too prone to imitate them in their inhumanity. During the British war, a considerable number of men from below fort Pitt crossed the Ohio, and marched into a town of friendly Indians, chiefly Delawares, who professed the Moravian religion. As the Indians apprehended no danger, they neither lifted arms nor fled. After these riflemen were some time in the town, and the Indians altogether in their power, in cool blood they massacred the whole town, without distinction of age or sex. This was an act of barbarity beyond any thing I ever knew to be committed by the savages themselves.

Why have we not made greater proficiency in the Indian art of war? Is it because we are too proud to imitate them, even though it should be a means of preserving the lives of many of our citizens? No! We are not above borrowing language from them, such as homony, pone, tomahawk, &c., which is of little or no use to us. I apprehend, that the reasons why we have not improved more in this respect are as follow: no important acquisition is to be obtained but by attention and diligence; and as it is easier to learn to move and act in concert in close order in the open plain, than to act in concert in scattered order in the woods, so it is easier to learn our discipline than the Indian manœuvres. They train up their boys in the art of war from the time they are twelve or fourteen years of age; whereas, the principal chance our people had of learning was by observing their manœuvres when in action against us. I have been long astonished that no one has written upon this important subject, as their art of war would not only be of use to us in case of another rupture with them; but were only part of our men taught this art, accompanied with our continental discipline, I think no European power, after trial, would venture to show its head in the American woods.

If what I have written should meet the approbation of my countrymen, perhaps I may publish more upon this subject in a future edition.

A FAITHFUL NARRATIVE

OF THE MANY DANGERS AND SUFFERINGS, AS WELL AS WONDERFUL AND SURPRISING DELIVERANCES, OF ROBERT EASTBURN, DURING HIS LATE CAPTIVITY AMONG THE INDIANS. WRITTEN BY HIMSELF. Published at the earnest request of many persons, for the benefit of the Public. With a recommendatory Preface by the Rev. Gilbert Tennent.—Psalms 24, 6, 7, and 193, 2, 4. Philadelphia: Printed. Boston: Reprinted and sold by Green & Russell, opposite the Probate Office in Queen street, 1758.

PREFACE.—Candid Reader: The author (and subject) of the ensuing narrative (who is a deacon of our church, and has been so for many years) is of such an established good character, that he needs no recommendation of others where he is known; a proof of which was the general joy of the inhabitants of this city, occasioned by his return from a miserable captivity; together with the readiness of divers persons to contribute to the relief of himself and necessitous family, without any request of his, or the least motion of that tendency. But seeing the following sheets are like to spread into many places where he is not known, permit me to say that, upon long acquaintance, I have found him to be a person of candor, integrity, and sincere piety, whose testimony may with safety be depended upon; which give his narrative the greater weight, and may induce to read it with the greater pleasure. The design of it is evidently pious; the matters contained in

23

it, and manner of handling them, will, I hope, be esteemed by the impartial to be entertaining and improving. I wish it may, by the divine benediction, be of great and durable service. I am thy sincere servant in the gospel of Jesus Christ.

GILBERT TENNENT.

Philadelphia, January 19th, 1758.

KIND READERS: On my return from my captivity I had no thoughts of publishing any observations of mine to the world in this manner. As I had no opportunity to keep a journal, and my memory being broken and capacity small, I was disinclined to undertake it. But a number of friends were pressing in their persuasions that I should do it; with whose motions I complied, from a sincere regard to God, my king and country, so far as I know my own heart. The following pages contain, as far as I can remember, the most material passages that happened within the compass of my observation while a prisoner in Canada. The facts therein related are certainly true, but the way of representing some things especially, is not so regular, clear and strong as I could wish; but I trust it will be some apology, that I am not so much acquainted with performances of this kind as many others, who may be hereby excited to give better representations of things, far beyond my knowledge. I remain your unfeigned well-wisher and humble servant,

ROBERT EASTBURN.

Philadelphia, January 19, 1758.

————

A FAITHFUL NARRATIVE, &c.—About thirty tradesmen and myself arrived at Captain Williams' fort, at the carrying place, in our way to Oswego, the 26th of March, 1756. Captain Williams informed me that he was like to be cumbered in the fort, and therefore advised us to take the Indian house for our lodging. About ten o'clock next day, a negro man came running down the road and reported that our slaymen were all taken by the enemy. Captain Williams, on hearing this, sent a sergeant and about twelve men to see if it were true. I being at the Indian house, and not thinking myself safe there, in case of an attack, and being also sincerely willing to serve my king and country, in the best manner I could in my present circumstances, asked him if he would take company. He replied, with all his heart! hereupon I fell into the rear with my arms, and marched after them. When we had advanced about a quarter of a mile, we heard a shot, followed with doleful cries of a dying man, which excited me to advance, in order to discover the enemy, who I soon perceived were prepared to receive us. In this difficult situation, seeing a large pine tree near, I repaired to it for shelter; and while the enemy were viewing our party, I, having a good chance of killing two at a shot, quickly discharged at them, but could not certainly know what execution was done till some time after. Our company likewise discharged and retreated. Seeing myself in danger of being surrounded, I was obliged to retreat a different course, and to my great surprise fell into a deep mire, which the enemy by following my track in a light snow soon discovered, and obliged me to surrender, to prevent a cruel death; they standing ready to drive their darts into my body, in case I refused to deliver up my arms. Presently after I was taken, I was surrounded by a great number, who stripped me of my clothing, hat and neckcloth, so that I had nothing left but a flannel vest without sleeves, put a rope on my neck, bound my arms fast behind me, put a long band round my body, and a large pack on my back, struck me a severe blow on the head, and drove me through the woods before them. It is not easy to conceive how distressing such a condition is. In the mean time I endeavored with all my little remaining strength to lift up my eyes to God, from whom alone I could with reason expect relief.

Seventeen or eighteen prisoners were soon added to our number, one of whom informed me that the Indians were angry with me, reported to some of their chiefs that I had fired on them, wounded one and killed another; for which he doubted not they would kill me.

I had not as yet learned what number the enemy's parties consisted of; there being only about one hundred Indians who had lain in ambush on the road to kill or take into captivity all that passed between the two forts. Here an interpreter came to me to inquire what strength Captain Williams had to defend his fort. After a short pause I gave such a discouraging answer, (yet consistent with truth,)* as prevented their attacking it, and of consequence the effusion of much blood. Hereby it evidently appeared that I was suffered to fall into the hands of the enemy to promote the good of my countrymen, to better purpose than I could by continuing with them.

In the mean time the enemy determined to destroy Bull's

---

* It is a great pity that our modern managers of Indian affairs had not indulged in such scrupulous veracity. They would probably say our captive was "more nice than wise." But perhaps he was like an old acquaintance of mine, who used to say sometimes that "he *al-most told a lie*," though *not quite.*—Ed

fort, (at the head of Wood Creek,) which they soon effected ; all being put to the sword, except five persons, the fort burnt, the provisions and powder destroyed, (saving only a little for their own use.) Then they retired to the woods and joined their main body, including which, consisted of four hundred French and three hundred Indians, commanded by one of the principal gentlemen of Quebec. As soon as they got together, (having a priest with them,) they fell on their knees and returned thanks for their victory. An example this, worthy of imitation! an example which may make profane, pretended Protestants blush, if they are not lost to all sense of shame,* who, instead of acknowledging a God, or providence, in their military undertakings, are continually reproaching him with oaths and curses. Is it any wonder the attempts of such are blasted with disappointment and disgrace ?

The enemy had several wounded men, both French and Indians, among them, whom they carried on their backs ; besides these, about fifteen of their number were killed, and of us about forty. It being by this time near dark, and some Indians drunk, they only marched about four miles and encamped. The Indians untied my arms, cut hemlock boughs and strewed round the fire, tied my band to two trees, with my back on the green boughs, (by the fire,) covered me with an old blanket, and lay down across my band, on each side, to prevent my escape while they slept.

Sunday the 28th, we rose early ; the commander ordered a hasty retreat towards Canada, for fear of General Johnson. In the mean time, one of our men said he understood the French and Indians designed to join a strong party, and fall on Oswego, before our forces at that place could get any provision or succor ; having, as they thought, put a stop to our relieving them for a time. When encamped in the evening, the commanding officer ordered the Indians to bring me to his tent, and asked me by an interpreter if I thought General Johnson would follow them. I told him I judged not, but rather thought he would proceed to Oswego, (which was indeed my sentiment, grounded upon prior information, and then expressed to prevent the execution of their design.) He further inquired what my trade was. I told him, that of a smith. He then persuaded me, when I got to Canada, to send for my wife, "for," said he, "you can get a rich living there." But when he saw that he could not prevail, he asked me no more ques-

---

* What would Captain Gyles have said to such praise of Catholics and their religion ? and by a Protestant too. He would no doubt have said that the devil had helped them, inasmuch as no good spirit would have heard the prayers of "wicked papists."—Ed.

tions, but commanded me to my Indian master. Having this opportunity of conversation, I informed the general that his Indian warriors had stripped me of my clothing, and would be glad if he would be good enough to order me some relief; to which he replied, " I should get clothes when I came to Canada," which was cold comfort to one almost frozen. On my return, the Indians, perceiving I was unwell and could not eat their coarse food, ordered some chocolate, which they had brought from the carrying place, to be boiled for me, and seeing me eat that appeared pleased. A strong guard was kept every night. One of our men being weakened by his wounds, and rendered unable to keep pace with them, was killed and scalped on the road ! I was all this time almost naked, travelling through deep snow, and wading through rivers, cold as ice !

After seven days' march, we arrived at lake Ontario, where I eat some horse flesh, which tasted very agreeably, for to a hungry man, as Solomon observes, every bitter thing is sweet. On the Friday before we arrived at the lake, the Indians killed a porcupine. The Indians threw it on a large fire, burnt off the hair and quills, roasted and eat of it, with whom I had a part.

The French carried several of their wounded men all the way upon their backs ; many of whom wore no breeches in their travels in this cold season, being strong hardy men. The Indians had three of their party wounded, which they likewise carried on their backs. I wish there was more of this hardiness, so necessary for war, in our nation, which would open a more encouraging scene than appears at present. The prisoners were so divided, that but few could converse together on the march, and what was still more disagreeable and distressing, an Indian who had a large bunch of green scalps, taken off our men's heads, marched before me, and another with a sharp spear behind, to drive me after him, by which means the scalps were often close to my face. And as we marched, they frequently every day gave the dead shout, which was repeated as many times as there were captives and scalps taken.

I may with justice and truth observe, that our enemies leave no stone unturned to compass our ruin. They pray, work, and travel to bring it about, and are unwearied in the pursuit, while many among us sleep in a storm which has laid a good part of our country desolate, and threatens the whole with destruction.

April 4th, several French batteaux met us, and brought a large supply of provision, the sight of which caused great joy, for we were in great want. Then a place was soon erected to

23*

celebrate mass in, which being ended, we all went over the mouth of a river, where it empties itself into the east end of lake Ontario. A great part of our company set off on foot towards Oswegatchy, while the rest were ordered into batteaux and carried towards the extreme of St. Lawrence, (where that river takes its beginning,) but by reason of bad weather, wind, rain, and snow, whereby the waters of the lake were troubled, we were obliged to lie by, and haul our batteaux on shore. Here I lay on the cold shore two days. Tuesday set off, and entered the head of St. Lawrence in the afternoon; came too late at night, made fires, but did not lie down to sleep. Embarking long before day, and after some miles' progress down the river, saw many fires on our right hand, which were made by the men who left us and went by land. With them we staid till day, then again embarked in our batteaux. The weather was very bad, (it snowed fast all day;) near night we arrived at Oswegatchy. I was almost starved to death, but hoped to stay in this Indian town till warm weather; slept in an Indian wigwam, rose early in the morning, (being Thursday,) and soon to my grief discovered my disappointment. Several of the prisoners had leave to tarry here, but I must go two hundred miles further down stream, to another Indian town. The moving being extremely cold, I applied to a French merchant or trader for some old rags of clothing, for I was almost naked, but to no purpose.

About ten o'clock, I was ordered into a boat, to go down the river, with eight or nine Indians, one of whom was the man wounded in the skirmish before mentioned.* At night we went on shore; the snow being much deeper than before, we cleared it away and made a large fire. Here, when the wounded Indian cast his eyes upon me, his old grudge revived; he took my blanket from me and commanded me to dance round the fire barefoot, and sing the prisoner's song, which I utterly refused. This surprised one of my fellow-prisoners, who told me they would put me to death, for he understood what they said. He therefore tried to persuade me to comply, but I desired him to let me alone, and was through great mercy enabled to reject his importunity with abhorrence. This Indian also continued urging, saying, you shall dance and sing; but apprehending my compliance sinful, I determined to persist in declining it at all adventures, and leave the issue to the divine disposal. The Indian, perceiving his orders disobeyed, was fired with indignation, and endeavored to push me into the fire, which I leaped over, and he, being weak with his wounds, and

---

* The author probably refers to the time he was taken.—Ed

not being assisted by any of his brethren, was obliged to desist. For this gracious interposure of Providence, in preserving me both from sin and danger, I desire to bless God while I live.

Friday morning I was almost perished with cold. Saturday we proceeded on our way, and soon came in sight of the upper part of the inhabitants of Canada. Here I was in great hopes of some relief, not knowing the manner of the Indians, who do not make many stops among the French in their return from war till they get home. However, when they came near some rapid falls of water, one of my fellow-prisoners and several Indians, together with myself, were put on shore to travel by land, which pleased me well; it being much warmer running on the snow than to lie still in the batteau. We passed by several French houses, but stopped at none; the vessel going down a rapid stream, it required haste to keep pace with her, and we crossed over a point of land and found the batteau waiting for us, as near the shore as the ice would permit. Here we left the St. Lawrence and turned up Conasadauga river, but it being frozen up, we hauled our batteau on shore, and each of us took our share of her loading on our backs, and marched towards Conasadauga, an Indian town, which was our designed port, but could not reach it that night. We came to a French house, cold, weary, and hungry. Here my old friend, the wounded Indian, again appeared, and related to the Frenchman the affair of my refusing to dance, who immediately assisted him to strip me of my flannel vest, which was my all. Now they were resolved to compel me to dance and sing. The Frenchman was as violent as the Indian in promoting this imposition; but the woman belonging to the house seeing the rough usage I had, took pity on me and rescued me out of their hands, till their heat was over, and prevailed with the Indian to excuse me from dancing, but he insisted that I must be shaved, and then he would let me alone. (I had at that time a long beard, which the Indians hate.) With this motion I readily complied, and then they seemed contented.

Sunday, April 11th, we set off towards Conasadauga, and travelled about two hours, when we saw the town over a great river, which was still frozen. The Indians stopped, and we were soon joined with a number of our own company, which we had not seen for several days. The prisoners, in number eight, were ordered to lay down their packs, and be painted. The wounded Indian painted me, and put a belt of wampum round my neck, instead of the rope I had worn four hundred miles. Then we set off for the town on the ice, which was four miles over. Our heads were not allowed to be covered, lest our fine paint should be hid, the weather in the mean time very cold, like to freeze our ears. After we had advanced nearer to the town, the Indian women came out to meet us, and relieved their husbands of their packs.

As soon as we landed at Conasadauga a large body of Indians came and encompassed us round, and ordered the prisoners to dance and sing the prisoner's song, (which I was still enabled to decline.) At the conclusion they gave a shout, and opened the ring to let us run, and then fell on us with their fists, and knocked several down. In the mean time, one ran before to direct us to an Indian house which was open, and as soon as we got in we were safe from beating. My head was sore with bruises, and pained me several days. The squaws were kind to us, gave us boiled corn and beans to eat, and fire to warm us, which was a great mercy, for I was both cold and hungry. This town lies about thirty miles north-west of Montreal. I staid here till the ice was gone, which was about ten days, and then was sent to Cohnewago, in company with some Indians, who, when they came within hearing, gave notice by their way of shouting that they had a prisoner, on which the whole town rose to welcome me, which was the more distressing as there was no other prisoner in their hands. When we came near shore, a stout Indian took hold of me, and hauled me into the water, which was knee deep, and very cold. As soon as I got ashore the Indians gathered round me, ordered me to dance and sing, although I was stiff with cold and wet, and lying long in the canoe. I only stamped to prepare for my race, and was encompassed with about five hundred Indians, who danced and sung, and at last gave a shout and opened the circle. About one hundred and fifty Indian lads made ready to pelt me with dirt and gravel-stones, and on my starting off gave me a smart volley, but from which I did not suffer much hurt. An Indian seeing me running, met me, seized and held me fast, till the boys had stored themselves again with small stones, and then let me go. Now I fared much worse than before, for a small stone among the mud hit my right eye, and my head and face were so covered with the dirt that I could scarce see my way; but discovering the door of an Indian house standing open, I ran in. From this retreat I was soon dragged to be pelted more, but the Indian women, being more merciful, interposed, took me into a house, brought me water to wash, and gave me boiled corn and beans to eat. The next day I was brought to the centre of the town and cried according to the Indian custom, in order to be sent to a family of Indians two hundred miles up stream, at Oswegatchy, and there to be adopted and abused no more. To this end I was delivered to three young men, who said I was their brother, and set forward on our way to the aforesaid town, with about twenty more, but by reason of bad weather we were obliged to encamp on a cold, stony shore three days, and then proceeded on. We called at Conasadauga, staid there about a week, in which time I went and viewed four houses at a distance from the town, about a quarter of a mile from each other, in which are represented in large paintings the sufferings of our Savior, designed to draw the Indians to the papist's religion. The work is curiously done. A little further stand three houses near together, on a high hill, which they call mount Calvary, with three large crosses before them, which completes the whole representation. To all these houses the papists and Indians repair, in performing their grand processions, which takes up much time.

The pains the papists take to propagate such a bloody religion is truly surprising; and the zeal they employ to propagate superstition and idolatry should make Protestants ashamed of their lukewarmness. A priest asked me "if I was a Catholic." I answered him, "no;" to which he replied, "no bon." When I told a fellow-captive of this, he said by my answer the priest understood that I was not a Christian. Shortly after another asked me the same question, and I answered, "yes, but not a Roman Catholic;" but he too said "no bon! no bon!"

We next set off on our journey for Oswegatchy, against a rapid stream, and being long in it, and our provisions growing short, the Indians put to shore a little before night. My lot was to get wood, others were ordered to get fires, and some to hunt. Our kettle was put over the fire with some pounded Indian corn, and after it had boiled about two hours my oldest Indian brother returned with a she beaver, big with young, which he soon cut to pieces and threw into the kettle, together with the guts, and took the four young beavers whole as they were found in embryo, and put them likewise into the kettle, and when all was well boiled, gave each of us a large dish full of the broth, of which we eat freely, and then part of the old beaver; the tail of which was divided equally among us, there being eight at our fire. The four young beavers were cut in the middle, and each of us got half a beaver. I watched for an opportunity to hide my share, (having satisfied myself before that tender dish came to hand,) which if they had seen would have much displeased them.* The other Indians catch-

---

* The reader will observe here a parallel custom to that in practice a hundred years before among the Indians who carried off Stockwell. They compelled him to drink raccoon fat because he wished to save some of the flesh of one for another time. See Stockwell's Narrative.—Ed.

ed young muskrats, thrust a stick through their bodies, and roasted it without skinning or dressing, and so eat them. Next morning we hastened on our journey, which continued several days, till we came near Oswegatchy, where we landed about three miles from the town on the contrary side of the river. Here I was to be adopted. My father and mother, whom I had never seen before, were waiting, and ordered me into an Indian house, where we were directed to sit down silent for a considerable time. The Indians appeared very sad, and my mother began to cry, and continued to cry aloud for some time, and then dried up her tears and received me for her son, and took me over the river to the Indian town. The next day I was ordered to go to mass with them, but I refused once and again; yet they continued their importunities several days. Seeing they could not prevail with me, they seemed much displeased with their new son. I was then sent over the river to be employed in hard labor, as a punishment for not going to mass, and not allowed a sight of or any conversation with my fellow-prisoners. The old Indian man with whom I was ordered to work had a wife and children. He took me into the woods with him, and made signs for me to chop, and he soon saw that I could handle the axe. Here I tried to reconcile myself to this employ, that they might have no occasion against me, except concerning the law of my God. The old man began to appear kind, and his wife gave me milk and bread when we came home, and when she got fish, gave me the gills to eat, out of real kindness; but perceiving I did not like them, gave me my own choice, and behaved lovingly. When we had finished our fence, which had employed us about a week, I showed the old squaw my shirt, (having worn it from the time I was first taken prisoner, which was about seven weeks,) all in rags, dirt and lice. She said it was not good, and brought me a new one with ruffled sleeves, saying "that is good," which I thankfully accepted. The next day they carried me back to the Indian town, and permitted me to converse with my fellow-prisoners. They told me we were all to be sent to Montreal, which accordingly came to pass.

On our arrival at Montreal we had our lodgings first in the Jesuits' convent, where I saw a great number of priests and people who came to confession. After some stay we were ordered to attend with the Indians in a grand council, held before the head general, Vaudreuil. We prisoners sat in our rank, (surrounded with our fathers and brethren,) but were asked no questions. The general had a number of officers to attend him in council, where a noted priest, called Picket, sat at his right hand, who understands the Indian tongue well and does more hurt to the English than any other of his order in Canada. His dwelling is at Oswegatchy. Here I was informed that some measures were concerted to destroy Oswego, which had been long in agitation. We met on our journey many batteaux going up stream, with provision and men for an attack on our frontiers, which confirmed the report. The council adjourned to another day, and then broke up. My Indian father and mother took me with them to several of their old acquaintances, who were French, to show them their lately adopted son. These persons had been concerned with my father and other Indians in destroying many English families in their younger days, and, (as one standing by who understood their language said,) were boasting of their former murders! After some days the council was again called, before which several of the Oneida chiefs appeared and offered some complaints against the French's attacking our carrying place, it being their land. But the general labored to make them easy, and gave them sundry presents of value, which they accepted. The French are exceedingly careful to prevent spirituous liquors being sold among the Indians, and if any inhabitant is proved guilty of it, their temporal interest is quite broken, and corporal punishment is inflicted on such offenders. Herein the French are vastly superior to us. The Indians do not fear our numbers, (which they deride,) because of our unhappy divisions, in consequence of which they expect to conquer us entirely.

Knowing these Oneidas were acquainted with Capt. Williams, at the carrying place, I sent a letter by them to let my family and friends know that I was yet alive, and lodged for redemption; but it never came to hand. The treaty being ended, the general sent about ten gallons of red wine to the Indians, which they divided among us. Afterwards came the presents, consisting of coats, blankets, shirts, skins, (to make Indian shoes,) cloth, (for stockings,) powder, lead-shot, and to each a bag of paint for their own use, &c.

After we prisoners had our share my mother came to me with an interpreter, and told me I might stay in the town at a place she had found for me, if I pleased. This proposal I almost agreed to, but one of my fellow-prisoners, with whom I had had before some discourse about making our escape, opposed the motion, and said, "Pray do not stay, for, if you do, we shall not be able to form a plan for our deliverance." So I told her I chose to go home with her, and soon set off by land, in our way thither, to Laschene, distant from Montreal about nine miles. Here we left our canoes, and proceeded without delay on our journey, in which I saw, to my sorrow, great numbers of soldiers and much provisions in motion towards lake Ontario. After a painful and distressing journey, we arrived at Oswegatchy, where we likewise saw many batteaux, with provisions and soldiers, daily passing by in their way to Frontenac, which greatly distressed me for Oswego. Hence I resolved, if possible, to give our people notice of their danger. To this end, I told two of my fellow-prisoners tha it was not a time to sleep, and asked them if they would go with me, to which they heartily agreed. But we had no provision, and were closely eyed by the enemy, so that we could not lay up a stock out of our allowance. However, at this time, Mr. Picket had concluded to dig a large trench round the town. I therefore went to a negro, the principal manager of this work, (who could speak English, French, and Indian well,) and asked him if he could get employ for two others and myself, which he soon did. For this service we were to have meat, [board,] and wages. Here we had a prospect of procuring provision for our flight. This, after some time, I obtained for myself, and then asked my brethren if they were ready. They said "they were not yet, but that Ann Bowman (our fellow-prisoner) had brought one hundred and thirty dollars from Bull's fort, [when it was destroyed, as has been related,] and would give them all they needed." I told them it was not safe to disclose such a secret to her, but they blamed me for entertaining such fears, and applied to her for provisions, letting her know our intention. She immediately informed the priest of it! We were forthwith apprehended, the Indians informed of it, and a court called. Four of us were ordered by this court to be confined in a room, under a strong guard, within the fort, for several days. From hence, another and myself were sent to Cohnewago, under a strong guard of sixty Indians, to prevent my plotting any more against the French, and to banish all hope of my escape!

When we arrived at this place, it pleased God to incline the captain of the guard to show me great kindness in giving me liberty to walk or work where I pleased, within any small distance. I went to work with a French smith for six livres and five sous per week. This sum the captain let me have to myself, and further favored me with the privilege of lodging at his mother's house, (an English woman named Mary Harris, taken captive when a child from Deerfield, in New England,) who told me she was my grandmother, and was kind; but the wages being small, and not sufficient to procure such clothing as I was in want of, I proceeded no farther with the smith, but went to my uncle Peter, and told him I wanted clothes, and that it would be better to let me go to Montreal, and work there, where I could clothe myself better than by staying with him. He after some reasoning consented.

I set off on my journey to Montreal, and on my entering the city met an English smith, who took me to work with him. After some time we settled to work in a shop opposite the general's door, where we had an opportunity of seeing a great part of the forces of Canada, both French and Indians, who were commonly brought there before their going out to war, and likewise all prisoners. By this means we got intelligence how our people were preparing for defence; but no good news from Oswego, which made me fear, knowing that great numbers of French had gone out against it, and hearing there were but few to defend it.

Prayers were put up in all the churches of Canada, and great processions made, in order to procure success to their arms against poor Oswego; but our people knew little of their danger till it was too late. For, to my surprise, the dismal news came that the French had taken one of the Oswego forts. In a few hours, in confirmation of this news, I saw the English standards, the melancholy trophies of victory, and the French rejoicing at our downfall, and mocking us, poor prisoners, in our exile and extremity, which was no great argument either of humanity or true greatness of mind. Great joy appeared in all their faces, which they expressed in loud shouts, firing of cannon, and returning thanks in their churches. But our faces were covered with shame, and our hearts filled with grief!*

Soon after, I saw several of the officers brought in prisoners in small parties, and soldiers in the same manner, who were confined within the walls [of the fort] in a starving condition, in order to make them work, which some complied with, while others bravely refused; and last of all came the tradesmen, among whom was my son, who, looking round, saw me, to his great surprise, for he had supposed I was dead. This joyful sight so affected him that he wept; nor could I refrain from the expression of a father's tenderness, in the same kind, upon so extraordinary an occasion; it was far more than I can disclose in writing, and therefore must cover it with a veil of silence. But he, with all my Philadelphia friends, being guarded by soldiers, with fixed bayonets, we could not come near each other. They were sent to the common pound, but I hastened to the interpreter to try to get my son set at liberty, which was soon effected. When we had the happiness of an interview, he gave me some information of the state of our

* Oswego was taken July 15th, 1756, and 1400 English were made prisoners.—Ed.

family, and told me that, as soon as the news reached home that I was killed or taken, his mother was not allowed any further wages of mine, which grieved me much, and added to my other afflictions.

In the mean time it gave me some pleasure in this situation to see an expression of equal affection and prudence in my son's conduct, who, though young in years, (about seventeen,) that he, in such a confused state of things, had taken care to bring, with much labor and fatigue, a large bundle, of considerable value to me, of clothing, &c., of which I was in great need. He likewise saved a quantity of wampum which we brought from New York, and afterwards sold it here for one hundred and fifty livres. He travelled with me part of the journey towards Oswego, but not being so far on his way as I was when taken, did not fall into the enemy's hands until that place was taken. At that time he was delivered in a remarkable manner from a wretched captivity among distant Indians. His escape was in this manner: fifteen young white prisoners were selected out to be delivered into their power, who, from a well-known custom among the Indians, there was no doubt, were to supply the places of those they had lost in the war. Of this number was my son. The French artfully concealed their destination, and pretended they were designed to labor in the batteaux. My son, seeing that most of the selection were small lads, doubted their pretensions, for they were not equal to such performance. Watching his opportunity, he slipped from his place in the ranks unnoticed, and lay concealed until his place was filled by another. The other unhappy youths were delivered up a sacrifice to the Indian enemy, to be instructed in popish principles, and be employed in murdering their countrymen, yea, perhaps, their own fathers, mothers, and brethren! O horrible! O lamentable!

The insatiable thirst of the French for empire* is heightened, doubtless, from the pardons they receive from the pope and their priests, [as will appear from the following facts:] On a Sabbath day I went to see what was the occasion of a great concourse of people at a chapel. I found a kind of fair, at which were sold cakes, wine, brandy, &c. Numbers of people were going in and out of the chapel, over the door of which was a board hanging, and on it was written, in large capital letters, "Indulgence plenary, or full pardon." To return to my narrative.

---

* The author wished probably to convey the idea that the French might commit any crimes in the acquisition of empire, without fear of future punishment, so long as they availed themselves of absolution, which it appears, from his next paragraph, was very prominently held forth.—Ed.

When the people taken at Oswego were setting out on their way to Quebec, I made application for liberty to go with them, but the interpreter said I was an Indian prisoner, and the general would not suffer it till the Indians were satisfied; and as they lived two hundred miles from Montreal, it could not be done at that time. Finding that all arguments on that head would not avail, because I was not included in the capitulation, I told the interpreter my son must go and leave me, to be ready at Quebec to go home when the Oswego people went, which probably would be soon. He replied, "It would be better to keep him with me, for it might be a mean to get me clear much sooner."

The officers belonging to Oswego would gladly have had me with them, but found it impracticable. This was an instance of kindness and condescension for which I was greatly obliged. Capt. Bradley gave me a good coat, vest, and shirt, and a young gentleman, who formerly lived in Philadelphia, (by name James Stone, doctor at Oswego,) gave me four pistoles. These expressions of kindness I remember with gratitude, and, if ever in my power, will requite. This money, with what my son brought me, I was in hopes would go far towards procuring my release from my Indian masters. But seeing a number of prisoners in sore distress, among whom were Capt. Grant and Capt. Shepherd, and about seven more in company, I thought it my duty to relieve them, and commit my release to the disposal of Providence, nor was this suffered to turn to my disadvantage in the issue, for my deliverance was brought about in due time, in another and unexpected way. This company informed me of their intention to escape; accordingly I gave them all the help in my power, saw them clear of the town on a Saturday evening, before the sentries were set at the gates, and advised them not to part from each other, and delivered to Capt. Shepherd two pocket compasses; but, contrary to this counsel, they parted, and saw each other no more. By their separating, Captain Grant and Sergeant Newel were deprived of the benefit of a compass; the others got safe to fort William Henry, as I was informed by Sergeant Henry, who was brought in prisoner, being taken in a battle, when the gallant and indefatigable Capt. Rogers made a brave stand against more than twice his number.* But I have not heard

---

* About the 21st of May, 1756, Capt. Rogers, with only eleven men, ambushed the carrying place between lakes George and Champlain, fired on a party of twenty-two Frenchmen, and killed six. He had let another party of 118 men pass only "a few minutes before," who immediately returned and rescued the others, and obliged the English to fly. Rogers says nothing about having any of his men taken, but took one himself.— *Rogers' Journal.*—Ed.

any account of Capt. Grant. I was enabled, through much mercy, to continue communicating relief to other prisoners out of the wages I received for my labors, which was forty livres per month.

In the latter part of winter, coal and iron were so scarce that it was difficult to get work. I then offered to work for my board, rather than to be thrust into a stinking dungeon, or sent among the Indians. The interpreter took some pains, which I thankfully acknowledge, without success, in my behalf. However, as I offered to work without wages, a Frenchman took me and my son in upon these terms. Here we staid one week, and hearing of no other chance, our employer offered us thirty livres a month to blow the bellows and strike, which I did for about two months, and then was discharged, and travelled about, from place to place, having no fixed abode. In this dilemma I was obliged to spend my little earnings for food to live upon, and my lodging was the hay-loft. I then made my case known to the kind interpreter, and requested him to consider of some means for my relief. He said he would.

Meanwhile, as I was taking a walk in the city, I met an Indian prisoner [a prisoner among them] that belonged to the town where my father lived. He reported that a great part of the Indians there had just arrived with the resolution to carry me back with them; and knowing him to be a very honest fellow, I believed him, and fled from the town, and concealed myself from the Indians. Schemes were now formed for an escape, and well prosecuted to a fortunate issue. General Vaudreuil gave me and my son liberty (under his hand) to go to Quebec, and to work there at our pleasure, without confinement, as prisoners of war. By this means I was freed from paying a ransom.

The commissary, Monsieur Portwee, [?] being about to set off for Quebec, my son informed me I must come to town in the evening, a passage being provided for us. I waited till near dark, and then entered the town with great caution, to escape the Indians, who kept watch for me, and had done so for some time, which made it very difficult and dangerous to move; but as they had no knowledge of my son, he could watch their motions without suspicion. In the morning, upon seeing an Indian set to watch for me over against the house I was in, I quickly made my escape through the back part of the house, over some high pickets, and so out of the city to the river-side, and fled. A friend, knowing my scheme for deliverance, kindly assisted me to conceal myself. The commissary had now got ready for his voyage, of which my son gave me notice. With no lingering motion I repaired to the boat, was received on board, got off undiscovered, and saw the Indians no more! A very narrow and surprising escape from a violent death! for they had determined to kill me if ever I attempted to leave them.

I arrived at Quebec May 1st. The honorable Col. Peter Schuyler, hearing of my coming there, kindly sent for me, and after inquiries about my welfare generously told me I should be supplied, and need not trouble myself for support. This public-spirited gentleman, who is indeed an honor to his country, did in like manner nobly relieve many other poor prisoners at Quebec. Here I had full liberty to walk where I pleased to view the city, which is well situated for strength, but far from being impregnable.

Here, I hope, it will not be judged improper to give a short hint of the French governor's conduct. Even in time of peace he gives the Indians great encouragement to murder and captivate the poor inhabitants on our frontiers.* An honest good man, named William Ross, was taken prisoner twice in time of peace. When he was first taken he learned a little of the French language, was afterwards redeemed, and got to his place of abode. Some years after, he, with two sons, was again taken, and brought to Quebec. The governor seeing the poor man was lame, and that one of his legs was smaller than the other, reproved the Indians for not killing him, asking them "what they brought a lame man there for who could do nothing but eat! You should have brought his scalp!" However, another of his countrymen, more merciful than his excellency, knowing the poor prisoner to be a quiet, hardworking man, redeemed him from the Indians, and two other Frenchmen bought his two sons. Here they had been slaves more than three years when I first arrived at Quebec. This account I had from Mr. Ross himself, who further added, that the governor gave the Indians presents to encourage them to proceed in that kind of work, which is a scandal to any civilized nation, and what many pagans would abhor. Here, also, I saw one Mr. Johnson, who was taken in a time of peace, with his wife and three small children. A fourth was born on the way, whom Mrs. Johnson named Captive.† All of these had been prisoners between three and four years. Several

---

* The author certainly discovers great care for veracity in the course of his narrative, but he may have erred here. We hope he has.—Ed.

† On Mrs. Johnson's return out of captivity she had published a very full and excellent account of it, which has gone through at least four editions since 1796. The last (Lowell, 1834) is quite imperfect.—Ed.

young men, and Mr. Johnson's wife's sister, were likewise
taken with them, and made slaves.

Our cartel being ready, I obtained liberty to go to England
in her. We set sail the 23d of July, 1757, in the morning,
and discharged our pilot about four o'clock in the afternoon.
After that we neither cast anchor nor lead till we got clear of
the great river St. Lawrence ; from which I conclude the navigation to be much safer than the French have reported. In
28 days we arrived at Plymouth, which occasioned great joy
[to us], for we were ragged, lousy, sick, and in a manner
starved ; and many of the prisoners, (who were in all about
three hundred,) were sick of the small-pox. Myself and son
having each a blanket coat, (which we bought in Canada to
keep us warm,) and now expecting relief, gave them to poor
sick men, almost naked. We were not allowed to go on
shore, but were removed to a king's ship, and sent to Portsmouth, where we were still confined on board near two weeks,
and then removed to the Mermaid, to be sent to Boston. We
now repented our well-meant though rash charity in giving
our coats away, as we were not to get any more ; all applica-
tions to the captain for any kind of covering being in vain.
Our joy was turned into sorrow at the prospect of coming on a
cold coast, in the beginning of winter, almost naked, which was
not a little increased by a near view of our mother country ;
the soil and comforts of which we were not suffered to touch
or taste.*

September the 6th we sailed for Boston, with a fleet in con-
voy, at which we arrived on the 7th of November, in the
evening. It being dark, and we strangers and poor, it was difficult to get a lodging. I had no shoes, and but pieces of
stockings, and the weather very cold. We were indeed
directed to a tavern, but found cold entertainment there ; the
master of the house, seeing a ragged and lousy company,
turned us out to wander in the dark. He was suspicious of
us, and feared we came from Halifax, where the small-pox
then was, and told us he was ordered not to receive such as
came from thence. We soon met a young man who said he
could find lodgings for us, but still detained us by asking
many questions. I told him we were in no condition to
answer them till we came to a more comfortable place, which

---

* Such barbarous treatment of poor prisoners, by a government like
that of England, who had hazarded their lives in its cause, is almost
incredible. Thus brutes might treat men, but *men* will not deal so with
men. A miserable old cartel hulk may contain germs destined to shake
the thrones of tyrants.—Ed.

be quickly found, where we were used well; but as we were lousy, we could not expect beds.

The next morning we made application for clothing. Mr. Erving, son-in-law to the late General Shirley, gave us relief, not only in respect of apparel, but also three dollars per man, to bear our charges to Newport. When I put on fresh clothes I was seized with a cold fit, which was followed by a high fever, and in that condition obliged to travel on foot as far as Providence, in our way to Rhode Island. In this journey I was exceedingly distressed. Our comforts in this life are often embittered with miseries, which are doubtless great mercies when they are suitably improved. At Newport we met with Captain Gibbs, and agreed with him for our passage to New York, where we arrived, November 21st, and met with many friends, who expressed much satisfaction at our return, and treated us kindly, particularly Mr. Livingston and Mr. Waldron.

November the 26th, 1757, I arrived at Philadelphia, to the great joy of all my friends, and particularly of my poor afflicted wife and family, who thought they should never see me again, till we met beyond the grave. Being returned, sick and weak in body, and empty-handed, not having any thing for my family's and my own support, several humane and generous persons, of different denominations, in this city, without any application of mine, have freely given seasonable relief. For which may God grant them blessings in this world, and in the world to come everlasting life, for Christ's sake!

But to hasten to the conclusion, suffer me with humility and sorrow to observe that our enemies seem to make a better use of a bad religion than we do of a good one. They rise up long before day in winter and go through the snow in the coldest seasons to perform their devotions in the churches. When these are over they return, to be ready for their work as soon as daylight appears. The Indians are as zealous in religion as the French. They oblige their children to pray morning and evening, particularly at Canasadauga.

Our case appears to me indeed gloomy, notwithstanding our enemies are inconsiderable in numbers, compared with us; yet they are united as one man, while we may justly be compared to a house divided against itself, and therefore cannot stand long in our present situation. May Almighty God graciously incline us to look to him for deliverance, to repent of our sins, reform our lives, and unite in the vigorous and manly use of all proper means to this end. AMEN.

NARRATIVE

OF THE DESTRUCTION OF THE SETTLEMENT OF GREEN-
BRIER, VIRGINIA, TOGETHER WITH THE CAPTURE AND
SURPRISING CONDUCT OF MRS. CLENDENIN, WHO WAS
AMONG THOSE WHO ESCAPED THE TOMAHAWK OF THE
INDIANS AT THAT MASSACRE.

[Whether the following narrative was ever in print, except as it stands
in Mr. Martin's Gazetteer of Virginia, I have never learned. It would seem
from the following note accompanying it in that work, "that it was
extracted from memoirs of Indian wars on the western frontiers of Virginia, communicated to the Philosophical Society of Virginia, by Charles
A. Stuart, Esq., of Augusta Co."—Ed.]

AFTER peace was confirmed between England and France in
the year 1761, the Indians commenced hostilities in 1763,*
when all the inhabitants in Greenbrier were totally cut off by
a party of Indians, headed by the chief warrior Cornstalk.†
The principal settlements were on Muddy Creek. These
Indians, in number about sixty, introduced themselves into the
people's houses under the mask of friendship, where every
civility was offered them by the people, providing them with

* Hostilities had *not* ceased between the whites and the Indians, as will
be seen by a reference to the CHRONICLES OF THE INDIANS for this and the
preceding years.—Ed.

† The life and barbarous death of this great chief are given at length
in the BOOK OF THE INDIANS, v. 42, 44.—Ed.

victuals and other accommodations for their entertainment, when, on a sudden, they fall upon and kill the men, and make prisoners of the women and children. From thence they passed over into the Levels, where some families were collected at the house of Archibald Clendenin, where the Honorable Balard Smith now lives. There are between fifty and one hundred persons, men, women and children. There the Indians were entertained, as at Muddy Creek, in the most hospitable manner. Mr. Clendenin had just arrived from a hunt, with three fat elks, upon which they were feasted in a bountiful manner.

In the mean time an old woman, with a sore leg, was showing her distress to an Indian, and inquiring if he could administer to her any relief. He said he thought he could, and drawing his tomahawk, instantly killed her, and all the men, almost, that were in the house. One, named Conrad Yolkom, only escaped. He, being at some distance from the house, was alarmed by the cries and shrieks of the women and children, fled with all his might to Jackson's river, and alarmed the people there. They however were loath to believe his tale until they saw the Indians approaching. All fled before them; and they pursued on to Carr's Creek, in Rockbridge county, where many families were killed and taken by them. At Clendenin's a scene of much cruelty was performed, not only by the Indians, but some such as the terrors of their approach influenced thereto. In this I refer to an act committed by a negro woman, who in escaping from the Indians killed her own child, whose cries she had reason to fear would lead to her capture!

Mrs. Clendenin did not fail to abuse the Indians with her tongue, with the most reproachful epithets she could command, although the tomahawk was brandishing at the same moment overhead; but instead of bringing it down upon her, the less effectual means of silencing her clamors was resorted to, namely, lashing her in the face and eyes with the bleeding scalp of her dead husband!

The provisions were all taken over to Muddy Creek, and a party of Indians retained them there till the return of the others from Carr's Creek, when the whole were marched off together. On the day they started from the foot of Kenney's Knob, going over the mountain, Mrs. Clendenin gave her infant child to another female prisoner, to carry, to relieve her for a few paces, and in a few moments after, a favorable opportunity offering for escape, she improved it with such alacrity into a dense thicket which they were at the time passing, that not an Indian saw her or could tell which way she went. The opportunity was rendered more favorable by the

manner in which the Indians at the time were marching
They had placed the prisoners in the centre, and dividing
themselves into two companies, one marched before them and
the other followed in their rear, having each flank open, and
this gave her the desired chance of escape.

It was not until all had left the place that the cries of Mrs.
Clendenin's child caused the Indians to inquire for its mother.
When they found she had made her escape, a monster Indian
observed " he would bring the cow to her calf," and taking the
infant by the heels, dashed out its brains against a tree ! and
as though this was not enough, the miscreant throwing it down
into the van, the whole company marched over it, the hoofs of
the horses tearing out its bowels, and the feet of the Indians
tracked the ground as they went with its blood !

Mrs. Clendenin returned that night to her own house, a distance of more than ten miles. Here she found her husband's
dead body, which she covered with rails. She found him as
he had been killed, with one of his children in his arms. He
was shot down as he was making his escape over a fence.
She now returned to her friends ; and thus ends the remarkable, though short captivity of a woman, more to be admired
for her courage than some other qualities not less desirable in
the female character.

NARRATIVE

OF THE CAPTIVITY OF ALEXANDER HENRY, ESQ., WHO, IN
THE TIME OF PONTIAK'S WAR, FELL INTO THE HANDS OF
THE HURON INDIANS. DETAILING A FAITHFUL ACCOUNT
OF THE CAPTURE OF THE GARRISON OF MICHILIMACKI-
NAC, AND THE MASSACRE OF ABOUT NINETY PEOPLE.—
WRITTEN BY HIMSELF.

[Mr. Henry was an Indian trader in America for about sixteen years.
He came to Canada with the army of General Amherst, and previous to his being made prisoner by the Indians experienced a variety of
fortune. His narrative, as will be seen, is written with great candor as
well as ability, and to the discriminating reader needs no encomium.
He was living in Montreal in 1809, as appears from the date of his preface to his Travels, which he published in New York that year, with a dedi-
cation to Sir Joseph Banks.—Ed.]

WHEN I reached Michilimackinac I found several other
traders, who had arrived before me, from different parts of the
country, and who, in general, declared the dispositions of the
Indians to be hostile to the English, and even apprehended

some attack. M. Laurent Ducharme distinctly informed
Major Etherington that a plan was absolutely conceived
for destroying him, his garrison and all the English in the
upper country ; but the commandant believing this and other
reports to be without foundation, proceeding only from idle or
ill-disposed persons, and of a tendency to do mischief, expressed much displeasure against M. Ducharme, and threatened to
send the next person who should bring a story of the same
kind, a prisoner, to Detroit.

The garrison, at this time, consisted of ninety privates, two
subalterns and the commandant ; and the English merchants
at the fort were four in number. Thus strong, few entertained
anxiety concerning the Indians, who had no weapons but small
arms.

Meanwhile, the Indians, from every quarter, were daily
assembling, in unusual numbers, but with every appearance of
friendship, frequenting the fort, and disposing of their peltries,
in such a manner as to dissipate almost every one's fears. For
myself, on one occasion, I took the liberty of observing to
Major Etherington that, in my judgment, no confidence ought
to be placed in them, and that I was informed no less than four
hundred lay around the fort.

In return the major only rallied me on my timidity ; and it
is to be confessed that if this officer neglected admonition, on
his part, so did I on mine. Shortly after my first arrival at
Michilimackinac, in the preceding year, a Chippeway, named
Wawatam. began to come often to my house, betraying in his
demeanor strong marks of personal regard. After this had
continued some time, he came on a certain day, bringing with
him his whole family, and at the same time a large present,
consisting of skins, sugar and dried meat. Having laid these
in a heap, he commenced a speech, in which he informed me
that some years before he had observed a fast, devoting himself, according to the custom of his nation, to solitude, and to
the mortification of his body, in the hope to obtain, from the
Great Spirit, protection through all his days; that on this
occasion he had dreamed of adopting an Englishman as his
son, brother and friend; that from the moment in which he
first beheld me he had recognised me as the person whom the
Great Spirit had been pleased to point out to him for a brother;
that he hoped that I would not refuse his present; and that he
should forever regard me as one of his family.

I could do no otherwise than accept the present, and declare
my willingness to have so good a man as this appeared to be for
my friend and brother. I offered a present in return for that
which I had received, which Wawatam accepted, and then,

thanking me for the favor which he said that I had rendered him, he left me, and soon after set out on his winter's hunt.

Twelve months had now elapsed since the occurrence of this incident, and I had almost forgotten the person of my *brother*, when, on the second day of June, Wawatam came again to my house, in a temper of mind visibly melancholy and thoughtful. He told me that he had just returned from his *wintering ground*, and I asked after his health ; but without answering my question, he went on to say, that he was sorry to find me returned from the Sault ; that he intended to go to that place himself, immediately after his arrival at Michili-mackinac ; and that he wished me to go there along with him and his family the next morning. To all this he joined an inquiry, whether or not the commandant had heard bad news, adding that during the winter he had himself been frequently disturbed with the *noise of evil birds ;* and further suggesting that there were numerous Indians near the fort, many of whom had never shown themselves within it. Wawatam was about forty-five years of age, of an excellent character among his nation, and a chief.

Referring much of what I heard to the peculiarities of the Indian character, I did not pay all the attention which they will be found to have deserved to the entreaties and remarks of my visitor. I answered that I could not think of going to the Sault so soon as the next morning, but would follow him there after the arrival of my clerks. Finding himself unable to prevail with me, he withdrew for that day ; but early the next morning he came again, bringing with him his wife, and a present of dried meat. At this interview, after stating that he had several packs of beaver, for which he intended to deal with me, he expressed a second time his apprehensions, from the numerous Indians who were round the fort, and earnestly pressed me to consent to an immediate departure for the Sault. As a reason for this particular request, he assured me that all the Indians proposed to come in a body, that day, to the fort, to demand liquor of the commandant, and that he wished me to be gone before they should grow intoxicated.

I had made, at the period to which I am now referring, so much progress in the language in which Wawatam addressed me, as to be able to hold an ordinary conversation in it ; but the Indian manner of speech is so extravagantly figurative that it is only for a perfect master to follow and comprehend it entirely. Had I been further advanced in this respect, I think that I should have gathered so much information, from this my friendly monitor, as would have put me into possession of the design of the enemy, and enabled me to save as well others as myself; as it was, it unfortunately happened that I turned a deaf ear to every thing, leaving Wawatam and his wife, after long and patient, but ineffectual efforts, to depart alone, with dejected countenances, and not before they had each let fall some tears.

In the course of the same day, I observed that the Indians came in great numbers into the fort, purchasing tomahawks, (small axes of one pound weight,) and frequently desiring to see silver arm-bands, and other valuable ornaments, of which I had a large quantity for sale. The ornaments, however, they in no instance purchased, but, after turning them over, left them, saying that they would call again the next day. Their motive, as it afterward appeared, was no other than the very artful one of discovering, by requesting to see them, the particular places of their deposit, so that they might lay their hands on them in the moment of pillage with the greater certainty and dispatch.

At night, I turned in my mind the visits of Wawatam ; but, though they were calculated to excite uneasiness, nothing induced me to believe that serious mischief was at hand. The next day, being the fourth of June, was the king's birth-day.

The morning was sultry. A Chippeway came to tell me that his nation was going to play at *baggatiway,* with the Sacs or Saäkies, another Indian nation, for a high wager. He invited me to witness the sport, adding that the commandant was to be there, and would bet on the side of the Chippeways. In consequence of this information, I went to the commandant, and expostulated with him a little, representing that the Indians might possibly have some sinister end in view ; but the commandant only smiled at my suspicions.

Baggatiway, called by the Canadians *le jeu de la crosse,* is played with a bat and ball. The bat is about four feet in length, curved, and terminating in a sort of racket. Two posts are planted in the ground, at a considerable distance from each other, as a mile or more. Each party has its post, and the game consists in throwing the ball up to the post of the adversary. The ball at the beginning is placed in the middle of the course, and each party endeavors as well to throw the ball out of the direction of its own post, as into that of the adversary's.

I did not go myself to see the match which was now to be played without the fort, because, there being a canoe prepared to depart, on the following day, for Montreal, I employed myself in writing letters to my friends ; and even when a fellow-trader, Mr. Tracy, happened to call upon me, saying that another canoe had just arrived from Detroit, and proposing that I
25

should go with him to the beach, to inquire the news, it so happened that I still remained, to finish my letters ; promising to follow Mr. Tracy in the course of a few minutes. Mr. Tracy had not gone more than twenty paces from the door, when I heard an Indian war-cry, and a noise of general confusion.

Going instantly to my window, I saw a crowd of Indians, within the fort, furiously cutting down and scalping every Englishman they found. In particular, I witnessed the fate of Lieutenant Jemette.

I had in the room in which I was a fowling-piece, loaded with swan-shot. This I immediately seized, and held it for a few minutes, waiting to hear the drum beat to arms. In this dreadful interval I saw several of my countrymen fall, and more than one struggling between the knees of an Indian, who, holding him in this manner, scalped him while yet living.

At length, disappointed in the hope of seeing resistance made to the enemy, and sensible of course that no effort of my own unassisted arm could avail against four hundred Indians, I thought only of seeking shelter. Amid the slaughter which was raging, I observed many of the Canadian inhabitants of the fort calmly looking on, neither opposing the Indians nor suffering injury; and from this circumstance I conceived a hope of finding security in their houses.

Between the yard-door of my own house and that of M. Langlade, my next neighbor, there was only a low fence, over which I easily climbed. At my entrance I found the whole family at the windows, gazing at the scene of blood before them. I addressed myself immediately to M. Langlade, begging that he would put me into some place of safety, until the heat of the affair should be over; an act of charity by which he might perhaps preserve me from the general massacre; but while I uttered my petition, M. Langlade, who had looked for a moment at me, turned again to the window, shrugging his shoulders, and intimating that he could do nothing for me :— " *Que voudriez-vous que j'en ferais?* "

This was a moment for despair; but the next, a Pani woman,* a slave of M. Langlade's, beckoned to me to follow her. She brought me to a door, which she opened, desiring me to enter, and telling me that it led to the garret, where I must go and conceal myself. I joyfully obeyed her directions; and she, having followed me up to the garret-door, locked it after me, and with great presence of mind took away the key.

This shelter obtained, if shelter I could hope to find it, I was

---

* The Panies are an Indian nation of the south

naturally anxious to know what might still be passing without. Through an aperture, which afforded me a view of the area of the fort, I beheld, in shapes the foulest and most terrible, the ferocious triumphs of barbarian conquerors. The dead were scalped and mangled; the dying were writhing and shrieking under the unsatiated knife and tomahawk; and from the bodies of some, ripped open, their butchers were drinking the blood, scooped up in the hollow of joined hands, and quaffed amid shouts of rage and victory. I was shaken not only with horror, but with fear. The sufferings which I witnessed, I seemed on the point of experiencing. No long time elapsed before, every one being destroyed who could be found, there was a general cry of "All is finished!" At the same instant I heard some of the Indians enter the house in which I was.

The garret was separated from the room below only by a layer of single boards, at once the flooring of the one and the ceiling of the other. I could therefore hear every thing that passed; and the Indians no sooner came in than they inquired whether or not any Englishman were in the house. M. Langlade replied that "he could not say; he did not know of any;" answers in which he did not exceed the truth; for the Pani woman had not only hidden me by stealth, but kept my secret and her own. M. Langlade was therefore, as I presume, as far from a wish to destroy me as he was careless about saving me, when he added to these answers, that "they might examine for themselves, and would soon be satisfied as to the object of their question." Saying this, he brought them to the garret-door.

The state of my mind will be imagined. Arrived at the door, some delay was occasioned by the absence of the key, and a few moments were thus allowed me in which to look around for a hiding-place. In one corner of the garret was a heap of those vessels of birch-bark used in maple-sugar making, as I have recently described.

The door was unlocked and opening, and the Indians ascending the stairs, before I had completely crept into a small opening which presented itself at one end of the heap. An instant after, four Indians entered the room, all armed with tomahawks, and all besmeared with blood upon every part of their bodies.

The die appeared to be cast. I could scarcely breathe; but I thought that the throbbing of my heart occasioned a noise loud enough to betray me. The Indians walked in every direction about the garret, and one of them approached me so closely that at a particular moment, had he put forth his hand, he must have touched me. Still I remained undiscovered; a circumstance to which the dark color of my clothes, and the

want of light in a room which had no window, and in the
corner in which I was, must have contributed. In a word, after
taking several turns in the room, during which they told M.
Langlade how many they had killed, and how many scalps
they had taken, they returned down stairs, and I, with sensations not to be expressed, heard the door, which was the barrier
between me and my fate, locked for the second time.

There was a feather-bed on the floor ; and on this, exhausted
as I was by the agitation of my mind, I threw myself down
and fell asleep. In this state I remained till the dusk of the
evening, when I was awakened by a second opening of the
door. The person that now entered was M. Langlade's wife,
who was much surprised at finding me, but advised me not to
be uneasy, observing that the Indians had killed most of the
English, but that she hoped I might myself escape. A shower
of rain having begun to fall, she had come to stop a hole in the
roof. On her going away, I begged her to send me a little
water to drink ; which she did.

As night was now advancing, I continued to lie on the bed,
ruminating on my condition, but unable to discover a resource
from which I could hope for life. A flight to Detroit had no
probable chance of success. The distance from Michilimackinac was four hundred miles ; I was without provisions ; and
the whole length of the road lay through Indian countries,
countries of an enemy in arms, where the first man whom I
should meet would kill me. To stay where I was threatened
nearly the same issue. As before, fatigue of mind, and not
tranquillity, suspended my cares, and procured me further
sleep.

The game of baggatiway, as from the description above will
have been perceived, is necessarily attended with much violence and noise. In the ardor of contest, the ball, as has been
suggested, if it cannot be thrown to the goal desired, is struck
in any direction by which it can be diverted from that designed
by the adversary. At such a moment, therefore, nothing could
be less liable to excite premature alarm, than that the ball
should be tossed over the pickets of the fort, nor that, having
fallen there, it should be followed on the instant by all engaged
in the game, as well the one party as the other, all eager, all
struggling, all shouting, all in the unrestrained pursuit of a
rude athletic exercise. Nothing could be less fitted to excite
premature alarm ; nothing, therefore, could be more happily
devised, under the circumstances, than a stratagem like this ;
and this was, in fact, the stratagem which the Indians had employed, by which they had obtained possession of the fort, and
by which they had been enabled to slaughter and subdue its

garrison, and such of its other inhabitants as they pleased. To be still more certain of success, they had prevailed upon as many as they could, by a pretext the least liable to suspicion, to come voluntarily without the pickets; and particularly the commandant and garrison themselves.

The respite which sleep afforded me, during the night, was put an end to by the return of morning. I was again on the rack of apprehension. At sunrise, I heard the family stirring; and presently after Indian voices, informing M. Langlade that they had not found my hapless self among the dead, and that they supposed me to be somewhere concealed. M. Langlade appeared, from what followed, to be by this time acquainted with the place of my retreat, of which, no doubt, he had been informed by his wife. The poor woman, as soon as the Indians mentioned me. declared to her husband, in the French tongue, that he should no longer keep me in his house, but deliver me up to my pursuers; giving as a reason for this measure, that, should the Indians discover his instrumentality in my concealment, they might revenge it on her children, and that it was better that I should die than they. M. Langlade resisted at first this sentence of his wife's, but soon suffered her to prevail, informing the Indians that he had been told I was in his house, that I had come there without his knowledge, and that he would put me into their hands. This was no sooner expressed than he began to ascend the stairs, the Indians following upon his heels.

I now resigned myself to the fate with which I was menaced; and regarding every attempt at concealment as vain, I arose from the bed, and presented myself full in view to the Indians who were entering the room. They were all in a state of intoxication, and entirely naked, except about the middle. One of them, named Wenniway, whom I had previously known, and who was upward of six feet in height, had his entire face and body covered with charcoal and grease, only that a white spot, of two inches in diameter, encircled either eye. This man, walking up to me, seized me with one hand by the collar of the coat, while in the other he held a large carving knife, as if to plunge it into my breast; his eyes meanwhile were fixed steadfastly on mine. At length, after some seconds of the most anxious suspense, he dropped his arm, saying, "I won't kill you!" To this he added, that he had been frequently engaged in wars against the English, and had brought away many scalps; that on a certain occasion he had lost a brother, whose name was Musinigon, and that I should be called after him.

A reprieve upon any terms placed me among the living, and

gave me back the sustaining voice of hope ; but **Wenniway** ordered me down stairs, and there informing me that I was to be taken to his cabin, where, and indeed everywhere else, the Indians were all mad with liquor, death again was threatened, and not as possible only, but as certain. I mentioned my fears on this subject to M. Langlade, begging him to represent the danger to my master. M. Langlade, in this instance, did not withhold his compassion, and Wenniway immediately consented that I should remain where I was, until he found another opportunity to take me away.

Thus far secure, I re-ascended my garret-stairs, in order to place myself the furthest possible out of the reach of insult from drunken Indians ; but I had not remained there more than an hour, when I was called to the room below, in which was an Indian, who said that I must go with him out of the fort, Wenniway having sent him to fetch me. This man, as well as Wenniway himself, I had seen before. In the preceding year, I had allowed him to take goods on credit, for which he was still in my debt ; and some short time previous to the surprise of the fort he had said, upon my upbraiding him with want of honesty, that "he would pay me before long !" This speech now came fresh into my memory, and led me to suspect that the fellow had formed a design against my life. I communicated the suspicion to M. Langlade ; but he gave for answer that "I was not now my own master, and must do as I was ordered."

The Indian, on his part, directed that before I left the house I should undress myself, declaring that my coat and shirt would become him better than they did me. His pleasure in this respect being complied with, no other alternative was left me than either to go out naked, or to put on the clothes of the Indian, which he freely gave me in exchange. His motive for thus stripping me of my own apparel was no other, as I afterward learned, than this, that it might not be stained with blood when he should kill me.

I was now told to proceed ; and my driver followed me close, until I had passed the gate of the fort, when I turned toward the spot where I knew the Indians to be encamped. This, however, did not suit the purpose of my enemy, who seized me by the arm, and drew me violently in the opposite direction, to the distance of fifty yards above the fort. Here, finding that I was approaching the bushes and sand-hills, I determined to proceed no farther, but told the Indian that I believed he meant to murder me, and that if so he might as well strike where I was as at any greater distance. He replied, with coolness, that my suspicions were just, and that he meant to pay me in this manner for my goods.   At the same time he produced a knife, and held me in a position to receive the intended blow.   Both this and that which followed were necessarily the affair of a moment.   By some effort, too sudden and too little dependent on thought to be explained or remembered, I was enabled to arrest his arm, and give him a sudden push, by which I turned him from me, and released myself from his grasp.   This was no sooner done than I ran toward the fort, with all the swiftness in my power, the Indian following me, and I expecting every moment to feel his knife.   I succeeded in my flight; and, on entering the fort, I saw Wenniway standing in the midst of the area, and to him I hastened for protection.   Wenniway desired the Indian to desist; but the latter pursued me round him, making several strokes at me with his knife, and foaming at the mouth with rage at the repeated failure of his purpose.   At length Wenniway drew near to M. Langlade's house; and the door being open, I ran into it.   The Indian followed me; but, on my entering the house, he voluntarily abandoned the pursuit.

Preserved so often, and so unexpectedly, as it had now been my lot to be, I returned to my garret, with a strong inclination to believe that, through the will of an overruling power, no Indian enemy could do me hurt; but new trials, as I believed, were at hand, when, at ten o'clock in the evening, I was roused from sleep, and once more desired to descend the stairs.   Not less, however, to my satisfaction than surprise, I was summoned only to meet Major Etherington, Mr. Bostwick and Lieutenant Lesslie, who were in the room below.

These gentlemen had been taken prisoners, while looking at the game, without the fort, and immediately stripped of all their clothes.   They were now sent into the fort, under the charge of Canadians, because, the Indians having resolved on getting drunk, the chiefs were apprehensive that they would be murdered if they continued in the camp.   Lieutenant Jemette and seventy soldiers had been killed; and but twenty Englishmen, including soldiers, were still alive.   These were all within the fort, together with nearly three hundred Canadians belonging to the canoes, &c.

These being our numbers, myself and others proposed to Maj. Etherington to make an effort for regaining possession of the fort, and maintaining it against the Indians.   The Jesuit missionary was consulted on the project; but he discouraged us, by his representations, not only of the merciless treatment which we must expect from the Indians, should they regain their superiority, but of the little dependence which was to be placed upon our Canadian auxiliaries.   Thus the fort and prisoners remained in the hands of the Indians, though, through the whole night, the prisoners and whites were in actual possession, and they were without the gates.

That whole night, or the greater part of it, was passed in mutual condolence; and my fellow-prisoners shared my garret. In the morning, being again called down, I found my master Wenniway, and was desired to follow him. He led me to a small house, within the fort, where, in a narrow room, and almost dark, I found Mr. Ezekiel Solomons, an Englishman from Detroit, and a soldier, all prisoners. With these, I remained in painful suspense, as to the scene that was next to present itself, till ten o'clock in the forenoon, when an Indian arrived, and presently marched us to the lake-side, where a canoe appeared ready for departure, and in which we found that we were to embark.

Our voyage, full of doubt as it was, would have commenced immediately, but that one of the Indians, who was to be of the party, was absent. His arrival was to be waited for; and this occasioned a very long delay, during which we were exposed to a keen north-east wind. An old shirt was all that covered me; I suffered much from the cold; and in this extremity, M. Langlade coming down to the beach, I asked him for a blanket, promising if I lived to pay him for it, at any price he pleased; but the answer I received was this, that he could let me have no blanket unless there were some one to be security for the payment. For myself, he observed, I had no longer any property in that country. I had no more to say to M. Langlade; but presently seeing another Canadian, named John Cuchoise, I addressed to him a similar request, and was not refused. Naked as I was and rigorous as was the weather, but for the blanket I must have perished. At noon, our party was all collected, the prisoners all embarked, and we steered for the Isles du Castor, [Beaver Island,] in lake Michigan.

The soldier who was our companion in misfortune was made fast to a bar of the canoe, by a rope tied round his neck, as is the manner of the Indians in transporting their prisoners. The rest were left unconfined; but a paddle was put into each of our hands, and we were made to use it. The Indians in the canoe were seven in number, the prisoners four. I had left, as it will be recollected, Major Etherington, Lieutenant Lesslie and Mr. Bostwick, at M. Langlade's, and was now joined in misery with Mr. Ezekiel Solomons, the soldier, and the Englishman who had newly arrived from Detroit. This was on the sixth day of June. The fort was taken on the fourth; I surrendered myself to Wenniway on the fifth; and this was the third day of our distress.

We were bound, as I have said, for the Isles du Castor, which lie in the mouth of lake Michigan; and we should have crossed the lake, but that a thick fog came on, on account of which the Indians deemed it safer to keep the shore close under their lee. We therefore approached the lands of the Ottawas, and their village of L'Arbre Croche, already mentioned as lying about twenty miles to the westward of Michilimackinac, on the opposite side of the tongue of land on which the fort is built.

Every half hour, the Indians gave their war-whoops, one for every prisoner in their canoe. This is a general custom, by the aid of which all other Indians, within hearing, are apprized of the number of prisoners they are carrying.

In this manner, we reached Wagoshense, Fox-point, a long point, stretching westward into the lake, and which the Ottawas make a carrying place, to avoid going round it. It is distant eighteen miles from Michilimackinac. After the Indians had made their war-whoop, as before, an Ottawa appeared upon the beach, who made signs that we should land. In consequence, we approached. The Ottawa asked the news, and kept the Chippeways in further conversation, till we were within a few yards of the land, and in shallow water. At this moment, a hundred men rushed upon us, from among the bushes, and dragged all the prisoners out of the canoes, amid a terrifying shout.

We now believed that our last sufferings were approaching; but no sooner were we fairly on shore, and on our legs, than the chiefs of the party advanced, and gave each of us their hands, telling us that they were our friends, and Ottawas, whom the Chippeways had insulted, by destroying the English without consulting with them on the affair. They added that what they had done was for the purpose of saving our lives, the Chippeways having been carrying us to the Isles du Castor only to kill and devour us.

The reader's imagination is here distracted by the variety of our fortunes, and he may well paint to himself the state of mind of those who sustained them, who were the sport or the victims of a series of events, more like dreams than realities, more like fiction than truth! It was not long before we were embarked again, in the canoes of the Ottawas, who, the same evening, relanded us at Michilimackinac, where they marched us into the fort, in view of the Chippeways, confounded at beholding the Ottawas espouse a side opposite to their own.

The Ottawas, who had accompanied us in sufficient numbers, took possession of the fort. We, who had changed masters, but were still prisoners, were lodged in the house of the commandant, and strictly guarded.

Early the next morning, a general council was held, in which the Chippeways complained much of the conduct of the Ottawas in robbing them of their prisoners ; alleging that all the Indians, the Ottawas alone excepted, were at war with the English ; that Pontiac had taken Detroit ; that the king of France had awoke, and repossessed himself of Quebec and Montreal ; and that the English were meeting destruction, not only at Michilimackinac, but in every other part of the world.   From all this they inferred that it became the Ottawas to restore the prisoners, and to join in the war ; and the speech was followed by large presents, being part of the plunder of the fort, and which was previously heaped in the centre of the room.   The Indians rarely make their answers till the day after they have heard the arguments offered.   They did not depart from their custom on this occasion ; and the council therefore adjourned.

We, the prisoners, whose fate was thus in controversy, were unacquainted at the time with this transaction ; and therefore enjoyed a night of tolerable tranquillity, not in the least suspecting the reverse which was preparing for us.   Which of the arguments of the Chippeways, or whether or not all were deemed valid by the Ottawas, I cannot say ; but the council was resumed at an early hour in the morning, and, after several speeches had been made in it, the prisoners were sent for, and returned to the Chippeways.

The Ottawas, who now gave us into the hands of the Chippeways, had themselves declared that the latter designed no other than to kill us, and *make broth of us.*   The Chippeways, as soon as we were restored to them, marched us to a village of their own, situate on the point which is below the fort, and put us into a lodge, already the prison of fourteen soldiers, tied two and two, with each a rope about his neck, and made fast to a pole which might be called the supporter of the building.

I was left untied ; but I passed a night sleepless and full of wretchedness.   My bed was the bare ground, and I was again reduced to an old shirt, as my entire apparel ; the blanket which I had received, through the generosity of M. Cuchoise, having been taken from me among the Ottawas, when they seized upon myself and the others, at Wagoshense. I was, besides, in want of food, having for two days eaten nothing.

I confess that in the canoe with the Chippeways I was offered bread ; but, bread, with what accompaniment !   They had a loaf, which they cut with the same knives that they had employed in the massacre—knives still covered with blood. The blood they moistened with spittle, and rubbing it on the bread, offered this for food to their prisoners, telling them to eat the blood of their countrymen.

Such was my situation on the morning of the seventh of June, in the year one thousand seven hundred and sixty-three; but a few hours produced an event which gave still a new color to my lot.

Toward noon, when the great war-chief, in company with Wenniway was seated at the opposite end of the lodge, my friend and brother, Wawatam, suddenly came in. During the four days preceding, I had often wondered what had become of him. In passing by he gave me his hand, but went immediately toward the great chief, by the side of whom and Wenniway, he sat himself down. The most uninterrupted silence prevailed; each smoked his pipe; and this done, Wawatam arose, and left the lodge, saying to me, as he passed, " Take courage !"

An hour elapsed, during which several chiefs entered, and preparations appeared to be making for a council. At length, Wawatam re-entered the lodge, followed by his wife, and both loaded with merchandise, which they carried up to the chiefs, and laid in a heap before them. Some moments of silence followed, at the end of which Wawatam pronounced a speech, every word of which, to me, was of extraordinary interest :

" Friends and relations," he began, " what is it that I shall say ? You know what I feel. You all have friends and brothers and children, whom as yourselves you love ; and you, what would you experience, did you, like me, behold your dearest friend—your brother—in the condition of a slave ; a slave, exposed every moment to insult, and to menaces of death ? This case, as you all know, is mine. See there (*pointing to myself*) my friend and brother among slaves, himself a slave !

" You all well know that long before the war began I adopted him as my brother. From that moment he became one of my family, so that no change of circumstances could break the cord which fastened us together.

" He is my brother ; and, because I am your relation, he is therefore your relation too :—and how, being your relation, can he be your slave ?

" On the day on which the war began, you were fearful, lest on this very account I should reveal your secret. You requested, therefore, that I would leave the fort, and even cross the lake. I did so, but did it with reluctance.

I did it with reluctance, notwithstanding that you, Meneh-wehna, who had the command in this enterprise, gave me your promise that you would protect my friend, delivering him from all danger, and giving him safely to me.

" The performance of this promise I now claim. I come not with empty hands to ask it. You, Menehwehna, best know whether or not, as it respects yourself, you have kept your word, but I bring these goods, to buy off every claim which any man among you all may have on my brother, as his prisoner."

Wawatam having ceased, the pipes were again filled; and, after they were finished, a further period of silence followed. At the end of this, Menehwehna arose, and gave his reply:

" My relation and brother," said he, " what you have spoken is the truth. We were acquainted with the friendship which subsisted between yourself and the Englishman, in whose behalf you have now addressed us. We knew the danger of having our secret discovered, and the consequences which must follow; and you say truly that we requested you to leave the fort. This we did out of regard for you and your family; for, if a discovery of our design had been made, you would have been blamed, whether guilty or not; and you would thus have been involved in difficulties from which you could not have extricated yourself.

" It is also true that I promised you to take care of your friend; and this promise I performed, by desiring my son, at the moment of assault, to seek him out, and bring him to my lodge. He went accordingly, but could not find him. The day after I sent him to Langlade's, when he was informed that your friend was safe; and had it not been that the Indians were then drinking the rum which had been found in the fort, he would have brought him home with him, according to my orders.

" I am very glad to find that your friend has escaped. We accept your present; and you may take him home with you."

Wawatam thanked the assembled chiefs, and taking me by the hand, led me to his lodge, which was at the distance of a few yards only from the prison-lodge. My entrance appeared to give joy to the whole family; food was immediately prepared for me; and I now ate the first hearty meal which I had made since my capture. I found myself one of the family; and but that I had still my fears, as to the other Indians, I felt as happy as the situation could allow.

In the course of the next morning, I was alarmed by a noise in the prison-lodge; and looking through the openings of the lodge in which I was, I saw seven dead bodies of white men dragged forth. Upon my inquiry into the occasion, I was informed that a certain chief, called by the Canadians Le Grand Sable, had not long before arrived from his winter's hunt; and that he, having been absent when the war begun, and being now desirous of manifesting to the Indians at large his hearty concurrence in what they had done, had gone into the prison-lodge, and there with his knife put the seven men whose bodies I had seen to death.

Shortly after, two of the Indians took one of the dead bodies, which they chose as being the fattest, cut off the head, and divided the whole into five parts, one of which was put into each of five kettles, hung over as many fires kindled for this purpose, at the door of the prison-lodge. Soon after things were so far prepared, a message came to our lodge, with an invitation to Wawatam to assist at the feast.

An invitation to a feast is given by him who is the master of it. Small cuttings of cedar wood, of about four inches in length, supply the place of cards; and the bearer by word of mouth states the particulars.

Wawatam obeyed the summons, taking with him, as is usual, to the place of entertainment, his dish and spoon.

After an absence of about half an hour, he returned, bringing in his dish a human hand, and a large piece of flesh. He did not appear to relish the repast, but told me that it was then, and always had been the custom among all the Indian nations, when returning from war, or on overcoming their enemies, to make a war-feast from among the slain. This he said inspired the warrior with courage in attack, and bred him to meet death with fearlessness.

In the evening of the same day, a large canoe, such as those which came from Montreal, was seen advancing to the fort. It was full of men, and I distinguished several passengers. The Indian cry was made in the village; a general muster ordered; and to the number of two hundred they marched up to the fort, where the canoe was expected to land. The canoe, suspecting nothing, came boldly to the fort, where the passengers, as being English traders, were seized, dragged through the water, beat, reviled, marched to the prison-lodge, and there stripped of their clothes and confined.

Of the English traders that fell into the hands of the Indians at the capture of the fort, Mr. Tracy was the only one who lost his life. Mr. Ezekiel Solomons and Mr. Henry Bostwick were taken by the Ottawas, and after the peace carried down to Montreal, and there ransomed. Of ninety troops, about seventy were killed; the rest, together with those of the posts

26

in the Bay des Puants, and at the river Saint Joseph, were also kept in safety by the Ottawas till the peace, and then either freely restored, or ransomed at Montreal. The Ottawas never overcame their disgust at the neglect with which they had been treated, in the beginning of the war, by those who afterward desired their assistance as allies.

In the morning of the ninth of June, a general council was held, at which it was agreed to remove to the island of Michilimackinac, as a more defensible situation in the event of an attack by the English. The Indians had begun to entertain apprehensions of want of strength. No news had reached them from the Potawatamies, in the Bay des Puants; and they were uncertain whether or not the Monomins* would join them. They even feared that the Sioux would take the English side.

This resolution fixed, they prepared for a speedy retreat. At noon the camp was broken up, and we embarked, taking with us the prisoners that were still undisposed of. On our passage we encountered a gale of wind, and there were some appearances of danger. To avert it, a dog, of which the legs were previously tied together, was thrown into the lake; an offering designed to soothe the angry passions of some offended Manito.

As we approached the island, two women in the canoe in which I was began to utter melancholy and hideous cries. Precarious as my condition still remained, I experienced some sensations of alarm from these dismal sounds, of which I could not then discover the occasion. Subsequently, I learned that it is customary for the women, on passing near the burial-places of relations, never to omit the practice of which I was now a witness, and by which they intend to denote their grief.

By the approach of evening we reached the island in safety, and the women were not long in erecting our cabins. In the morning, there was a muster of the Indians, at which there were found three hundred and fifty fighting men.

In the course of the day there arrived a canoe from Detroit, with ambassadors, who endeavored to prevail on the Indians to repair thither to the assistance of Pontiac; but fear was now the prevailing passion. A guard was kept during the day, and a watch by night, and alarms were very frequently spread. Had an enemy appeared, all the prisoners would have been put to death; and I suspected that, as an Englishman, I should share their fate.

* Manomines, or Malomines. In the first syllable, the substitution of *l* for *n*, and *n* for *l*, marks one of the differences in the Chippeway and Algonquin dialects. In the mouth of an Algonquin, it is *Michilimackinac*, in that of a Chippeway, *Michinimackinac*.

Several days had now passed, when one morning a contin-ued alarm prevailed, and I saw the Indians running in a con-fused manner toward the beach. In a short time I learned that two large canoes from Montreal were in sight.

All the Indian canoes were immediately manned, and those from Montreal were surrounded and seized, as they turned a point behind which the flotilla had been concealed. The goods were consigned to a Mr. Levy, and would have been saved if the canoe men had called them French property; but they were terrified and disguised nothing.

In the canoes was a large proportion of liquor, a dangerous acquisition, and which threatened disturbance among the In-dians, even to the loss of their dearest friends. Wawatam, always watchful of my safety, no sooner heard the noise ot drunkenness, which in the evening did not fail to begin, than he represented to me the danger of remaining in the village, and owned that he could not himself resist the temptation of joining his comrades in the debauch. That I might escape all mischief, he therefore requested that I would accompany him to the mountain, where I was to remain hidden till the liquor should be drank.

We ascended the mountain accordingly. It is this mountain which constitutes that high land in the middle of the island, of which I have spoken before, as of a figure considered as resembling a *turtle*, and therefore called *Michilimackinac*. It is thickly covered with wood, and very rocky toward the top. After walking more than half a mile, we came to a large rock, at the base of which was an opening, dark within, and appear-ing to be the entrance of a cave.

Here, Wawatam recommended that I should take up my lodging, and by all means remain till he returned.

On going into the cave, of which the entrance was nearly ten feet wide, I found the further end to be rounded in its shape, like that of an oven, but with a further aperture, too small, however, to be explored.

After thus looking around me, I broke small branches from the trees, and spread them for a bed; then wrapped myself in my blanket, and slept till daybreak.

On awaking I felt myself incommoded by some object upon which I lay; and removing it, found it to be a bone. This I supposed to be that of a deer, or some other animal, and what might very naturally be looked for in the place in which it was; but, when daylight visited my chamber, I discovered, with some feelings of horror, that I was lying on nothing less than a heap of human bones and skulls, which covered all the floor!

The day passed without the return of Wawatam, and without food. As night approached, I found myself unable to meet its darkness in the charnel-house, which, nevertheless, I had viewed free from uneasiness during the day. I chose, therefore, an adjacent bush for this night's lodging, and slept under it as before; but in the morning, I awoke hungry and dispirited, and almost envying the dry bones, to the view of which I returned: At length the sound of a foot reached me, and my Indian friend appeared, making many apologies for his long absence, the cause of which was an unfortunate excess in the enjoyment of his liquor.

This point being explained, I mentioned the extraordinary sight that had presented itself in the cave to which he had commended my slumbers. He had never heard of its existence before; and, upon examining the cave together, we saw reason to believe that it had been anciently filled with human bodies.

On returning to the lodge, I experienced a cordial reception from the family, which consisted of the wife of my friend, his two sons, of whom the eldest was married, and whose wife, and a daughter of thirteen years of age, completed the list.

Wawatam related to the other Indians the adventure of the bones. All of them expressed surprise at hearing it, and declared that they had never been aware of the contents of this cave before. After visiting it, which they immediately did, almost every one offered a different opinion as to its history.

Some advanced, that at a period when the waters overflowed the land, (an event which makes a distinguished figure in the history of their world,) the inhabitants of this island had fled into the cave, and been there drowned; others, that those same inhabitants, when the Hurons made war upon them, (as tradition says they did,) hid themselves in the cave, and being discovered, were there massacred. For myself, I am disposed to believe that this cave was an ancient receptacle of the bones of prisoners, sacrificed and devoured at war-feasts. I have always observed that the Indians pay particular attention to the bones of sacrifices, preserving them unbroken, and depositing them in some place kept exclusively for that purpose.

A few days after the occurrence of the incidents recorded above, Menehwehna, whom I now found to be the great chief of the village of Michilimackinac, came to the lodge of my friend; and when the usual ceremony of smoking was finished, he observed that Indians were now daily arriving from Detroit, some of whom had lost relations or friends in the war, and who would certainly retaliate on any Englishman they found; upon which account, his errand was to advise that I should be dressed like an Indian, an expedient whence I might hope to escape all future insult.

I could not but consent to the proposal, and the chief was so kind as to assist my friend and his family in effecting that very day the desired metamorphosis. My hair was cut off, and my head shaved, with the exception of a spot on the crown, of about twice the diameter of a crown-piece. My face was painted with three or four different colors; some parts of it red, and others black. A shirt was provided for me, painted with vermilion, mixed with grease. A large collar of wampum was put round my neck, and another suspended on my breast. Both my arms were decorated with large bands of silver above the elbow, besides several smaller ones on the wrists; and my legs were covered with *mitases*, a kind of hose, made, as is the favorite fashion, of scarlet cloth. Over all, I was to wear a scarlet blanket or mantle, and on my head a large bunch of feathers. I parted, not without some regret, with the long hair which was natural to it, and which I fancied to be ornamental; but the ladies of the family, and of the village in general, appeared to think my person improved, and now condescended to call me handsome, even among Indians.

Protected, in a great measure, by this disguise, I felt myself more at liberty than before; and the season being arrived in which my clerks, from the interior, were to be expected, and some part of my property, as I had a right to hope, recovered, I begged the favor of Wawatam that he would enable me to pay a short visit to Michilimackinac. He did not fail to comply, and I succeeded in finding my clerks; but, either through the disturbed state of the country, as they represented to be the case, or through their misconduct, as I had reason to think, I obtained nothing; and nothing, or almost nothing, I now began to think would be all that I should need during the rest of my life. To fish and to hunt, to collect a few skins, and exchange them for necessaries, was all that I seemed destined to do, and to acquire, for the future.

I returned to the Indian village, where at this time much scarcity of food prevailed. We were often for twenty-four hours without eating; and when in the morning we had no victuals for the day before us, the custom was to black our faces with grease and charcoal, and exhibit, through resignation, a temper as cheerful as if in the midst of plenty.

A repetition of the evil, however, soon induced us to leave the island in search of food; and accordingly we departed for the Bay of Boutchitaouy, distant eight leagues, and where we found plenty of wild-fowl and fish.

While in the bay, my guardian's daughter-in-law was taken in labor of her first child. She was immediately removed out of the common lodge; and a small one, for her separate accommodation, was begun and finished by the women in less than half an hour.

The next morning we heard that she was very ill, and the family began to be much alarmed on her account; the more so, no doubt, because cases of difficult labor are very rare among Indian women. In this distress, Wawatam requested me to accompany him into the woods; and on our way informed me that if he could find a snake, he should soon secure relief to his daughter-in-law.

On reaching some wet ground, we speedily obtained the object of our search, in a small snake, of the kind called the garter-snake. Wawatam seized it by the neck, and, holding it fast, while it coiled itself round his arm, he cut off its head, catching the blood in a cup that he had brought with him. This done, he threw away the snake, and carried home the blood, which he mixed with a quantity of water. Of this mixture he administered first one table-spoonful, and shortly after a second. Within an hour the patient was safely delivered of a fine child; and Wawatam subsequently declared that the remedy, to which he had resorted, was one that never failed.

On the next day, we left the Bay of Boutchitaouy; and the young mother, in high spirits, assisted in loading the canoe, barefooted, and knee-deep in the water.

The medical information, the diseases and the remedies of the Indians, often engaged my curiosity during the period through which I was familiar with these nations; and I shall take this occasion to introduce a few particulars connected with their history.

The Indians are in general free from disorders; and an instance of their being subject to dropsy, gout, or stone, never came within my knowledge. Inflammations of the lungs are among their most ordinary complaints, and rheumatism still more so, especially with the aged. Their mode of life, in which they are so much exposed to the wet and cold, sleeping on the ground, and inhaling the night air, sufficiently accounts for their liability to these diseases. The remedies on which they most rely are emetics, cathartics, and the lancet; but especially the last. Bleeding is so favorite an operation among the women that they never lose an occasion of enjoying it, whether sick or well. I have sometimes bled a dozen women in a morning as they sat in a row, along a fallen tree, beginning with the first, opening the vein, then proceeding to the second, and so on, having three or four individuals bleeding at the same time.

In most villages, and particularly in those of the Chippeways, this service was required of me; and no persuasion of mine could ever induce a woman to dispense with it.

In all parts of the country, and among all the nations that I have seen, particular individuals arrogate to themselves the art of healing, but principally by means of pretended sorcery; and operations of this sort are always paid for by a present made before they are begun. Indeed, whatever, as an impostor, may be the demerits of the operator, his reward may generally be said to be fairly earned by dint of corporal labor.

I was once present at a performance of this kind, in which the patient was a female child of about twelve years of age. Several of the elder chiefs were invited to the scene; and the same compliment was paid to myself, on account of the medical skill for which it was pleased to give me credit.

The physician (so to call him) seated himself on the ground; and before him, on a new stroud blanket, was placed a basin of water, in which were three bones, the larger ones, as it appeared to me, of a swan's wing. In his hand he had his *shishiquoi*, or rattle, with which he beat time to his *medicine-song*. The sick child lay on a blanket, near the physician. She appeared to have much fever, and a severe oppression of the lungs, breathing with difficulty, and betraying symptoms of the last stage of consumption.

After singing for some time, the physician took one of the bones out of the basin: the bone was hollow; and one end being applied to the breast of the patient, he put the other into his mouth, in order to remove the disorder by suction. Having persevered in this as long as he thought proper, he suddenly seemed to force the bone into his mouth, and swallow it. He now acted the part of one suffering severe pain; but, presently, finding relief, he made a long speech, and after this returned to singing, and to the accompaniment of his rattle. With the latter, during his song, he struck his head, breast, sides, and back; at the same time straining, as if to vomit forth the bone.

Relinquishing this attempt, he applied himself to suction a second time, and with the second of the three bones; and this also he soon seemed to swallow.

Upon its disappearance, he began to distort himself in the most frightful manner, using every gesture which could convey the idea of pain; at length he succeeded, or pretended to succeed, in throwing up one of the bones. This was handed about to the spectators, and strictly examined; but nothing remarkable could be discovered. Upon this, he went back to his song and rattle; and after some time threw up the second of the two bones. In the groove of this, the physician, upon examination, found, and displayed to all present, a small white substance, resembling a piece of the quill of a feather, It was passed round the company from one to the other; and declared, by the physician, to be the thing causing the disorder of his patient.

The multitude believe that these physicians, whom the French call *jongleurs*, or jugglers, can inflict as well as remove disorders. They believe that by drawing the figure of any person in sand or ashes, or on clay, or by considering any object as the figure of a person, and then pricking it with a sharp stick, or other substance, or doing, in any other manner, that which done to a living body would cause pain or injury, the individual represented, or supposed to be represented, will suffer accordingly. On the other hand, the mischief being done, another physician, of equal pretensions, can by suction remove it. Unfortunately, however, the operations which I have described were not successful in the instance referred to; for, on the day after they had taken place, the girl died.

With regard to flesh-wounds, the Indians certainly effect astonishing cures. Here, as above, much that is fantastic occurs; but the success of their practice evinces something solid.

At the Sault de Sainte-Marie I knew a man who, in the result of a quarrel, received the stroke of an axe in his side. The blow was so violent, and the axe driven so deep, that the wretch who held it could not withdraw it, but left it in the wound, and fled. Shortly after, the man was found, and brought into the fort, where several other Indians came to his assistance. Among these, one, who was a physician, immediately withdrew, in order to fetch his *penegusan*, or medicine-bag, with which he soon returned. The eyes of the sufferer were fixed, his teeth closed, and his case apparently desperate.

The physician took from his bag a small portion of a very white substance, resembling that of a bone; this he scraped into a little water, and forcing open the jaws of the patient with a stick, he poured the mixture down his throat. What followed was, that in a very short space of time the wounded man moved his eyes; and beginning to vomit, threw up a small lump of clotted blood.

The physician now, and not before, examined the wound, from which I could see the breath escape, and from which a part of the omentum depended. This the physician did not set about to restore to its place, but, cutting it away, minced it into small pieces, and made his patient swallow it.

The man was then carried to his lodge, where I visited him daily. By the sixth day he was able to walk about; and within a month he grew quite well, except that he was troubled with a cough. Twenty years after his misfortune he was still alive.

Another man, being on his wintering-ground, and from home, hunting beaver, was crossing a lake, covered with smooth ice, with two beavers on his back, when his foot slipped, and he fell. At his side, in his belt, was his axe, the blade of which came upon the joint of his wrist; and, the weight of his body coming upon the blade, his hand was completely separated from his arm, with the exception of a small piece of the skin. He had to walk three miles to his lodge, which was thus far away. The skin, which alone retained his hand to his arm, he cut through, with the same axe which had done the rest; and fortunately having on a shirt, he took it off, tore it up, and made a strong ligature above the wrist, so as in some measure to avoid the loss of blood. On reaching his lodge, he cured the wound himself, by the mere use of simples. I was a witness to its perfect healing.

I have said that these physicians, jugglers, or practitioners of pretended sorcery, are supposed to be capable of inflicting diseases; and I may add, that they are sometimes themselves sufferers on this account. In one instance I saw one of them killed, by a man who charged him with having brought his brother to death by malefic arts. The accuser, in his rage, thrust his knife into the belly of the accused, and ripped it open. The latter caught his bowels in his arms, and thus walked toward his lodge, gathering them up, from time to time, as they escaped his hold. His lodge was at no considerable distance, and he reached it alive, and died in it.

Our next encampment was on the island of Saint-Martin, off Cape Saint-Ignace, so called from the Jesuit mission of Saint Ignatius to the Hurons, formerly established there. Our object was to fish for sturgeon, which we did with great success; and here, in the enjoyment of a plentiful and excellent supply of food, we remained until the twentieth day of August. At this time, the autumn being at hand, and a sure prospect of increased security from hostile Indians afforded, Wawatam proposed going to his intended wintering-ground. The removal was a subject of the greatest joy to myself, on account of the frequent insults, to which I had still to submit, from the Indians of our band or village, and to escape from which I would freely have gone almost anywhere. At our wintering-ground we were to be alone; for the Indian families, in the countries of which I write, separate in the winter season, for the convenience as well of subsistence as of the chase, and re-associate in the spring and summer.

In preparation, our first business was to sail for Michilimackinac, where, being arrived, we procured from a Canadian trader, on credit, some trifling articles, together with ammunition, and two bushels of maize. This done, we steered directly for lake Michigan. At L'Arbre Croche we stopped one day on a visit to the Ottawas, where all the people, and particularly Okinochumaki, the chief, the same who took me from the Chippeways, behaved with great civility and kindness. The chief presented me with a bag of maize. It is the Ottawas, it will be remembered, who raise this grain for the market of Michilimackinac.

Leaving L'Arbre Croche, we proceeded direct to the mouth of the river Aux Sables, on the south side of the lake, and distant about a hundred and fifty miles from fort Michilimackinac. On our voyage, we passed several deep bays and rivers, and I found the banks of the lake to consist in mere sands, without any appearance of verdure; the sand drifting from one hill to another, like snow in winter. Hence, all the rivers, which here entered the lake, are as much entitled to the epithet of *sandy* as that to which we were bound. They are also distinguished by another particularity, always observable in similar situations. The current of the stream being met, when the wind is contrary, by the waves of the lake, it is driven back, and the sands of the shore are at the same time washed into its mouth. In consequence, the river is able to force a passage into the lake, broad only in proportion to its utmost strength; while it hollows for itself, behind the sandbanks, a basin of one, two, or three miles across. In these rivers we killed many wild-fowl and beaver.

To kill beaver, we used to go several miles up the rivers, before the approach of night, and after the dusk came on suffer the canoe to drift gently down the current, without noise. The beaver in this part of the evening come abroad to procure food, or materials for repairing their habitations; and as they are not alarmed by the canoe, they often pass it within gun-shot.

While we thus hunted along our way, I enjoyed a personal freedom of which I had been long deprived, and became as expert in the Indian pursuits as the Indians themselves.

On entering the river Aux Sables, Wawatam took a dog, tied its feet together, and threw it into the stream, uttering, at the same time, a long prayer, which he addressed to the Great Spirit, supplicating his blessing on the chase, and his aid in the support of the family, through the dangers of a long winter. Our lodge was fifteen miles above the mouth of the stream. The principal animals which the country afforded were the stag or red deer, the common American deer, the bear, raccoon, beaver and marten.

The beaver feeds in preference on young wood of the birch, aspen and poplar tree, (*populus nigra*, called by the Canadians *liard*,) but in defect of these on any other tree, those of the pine and fir kinds excepted. These latter it employs only for building its dams and houses. In wide meadows, where no wood is to be found, it resorts, for all its purposes, to the roots of the rush and water lily. It consumes great quantities of food, whether of roots or wood; and hence often reduces itself to the necessity of removing into a new quarter. Its house has an arched dome-like roof, of an elliptical figure, and rises from three to four feet above the surface of the water. It is always entirely surrounded by water; but, in the banks adjacent, the animal provides holes or *washes*, of which the entrance is below the surface, and to which it retreats on the first alarm.

The female beaver usually produces two young at a time, but not unfrequently more. During the first year the young remain with their parents. In the second they occupy an adjoining apartment, and assist in building, and in procuring food. At two years old, they part, and build houses of their own; but often rove about for a considerable time, before they fix upon a spot. There are beavers, called by the Indians *old bachelors*, who live by themselves, build no houses, and work at no dams, but shelter themselves in holes. The usual method of taking these is by traps, formed of iron, or logs, and baited with branches of poplar.

According to the Indians, the beaver is much given to jealousy. If a strange male approaches the cabin, a battle immediately ensues. Of this the female remains an unconcerned spectator, careless to which party the law of conquest may assign her. Among the beaver which we killed, those who were with me pretended to show demonstrations of this fact; some of the skins of the males, and almost all of the older ones, bearing marks of violence, while none were ever to be seen on the skins of the females.

The Indians add, that the male is as constant as he is jealous, never attaching himself to more than one female; while the female, on her side, is always fond of strangers.

The most common way of taking the beaver is that of breaking up its house, which is done with trenching-tools, during the winter, when the ice is strong enough to allow of approaching them; and when, also, the fur is in its most valuable state.

Breaking up the house, however, is only a preparatory step.

During this operation, the family make their escape to one or more of their *washes*. These are to be discovered by striking the ice along the bank, and where the holes are a hollow sound is returned. After discovering and searching many of these in vain, we often found the whole family together, in the same wash. I was taught occasionally to distinguish a full wash from an empty one, by the motion of the water above its entrance, occasioned by the breathing of the animals concealed in it. From the washes they must be taken out with the hands; and in doing this, the hunter sometimes receives severe wounds from their teeth. While a hunter, I thought, with the Indians, that the beaver flesh was very good; but after that of the ox was again within my reach, I could not relish it. The tail is accounted a luxurious morsel.

Beavers, say the Indians, were formerly a people endowed with speech, not less than with the other noble faculties they possess; but the Great Spirit has taken this away from them, lest they should grow superior in understanding to mankind.

The raccoon was another object of our chase. It was my practice to go out in the evening, with dogs, accompanied by the youngest son of my guardian, to hunt this animal. The raccoon never leaves its hiding-place till after sunset.

As soon as a dog falls on a fresh track of the raccoon, he gives notice by a cry, and immediately pursues. His barking enables the hunter to follow. The raccoon, which travels slowly, and is soon overtaken, makes for a tree, on which he remains till shot.

After the falling of the snow, nothing more is necessary, for taking the raccoon, than to follow the track of his feet. In this season, he seldom leaves his habitation; and he never lays up any food. I have found six at a time, in the hollow of one tree, lying upon each other, and nearly in a torpid state. In more than one instance, I have ascertained that they have lived six weeks without food. The mouse is their principal prey.

Raccoon hunting was my more particular and daily employ. I usually went out at the first dawn of day, and seldom returned till sunset, or till I had laden myself with as many animals as I could carry. By degrees I became familiarized with this kind of life; and had it not been for the idea, of which I could not divest my mind, that I was living among savages, and for the whispers of a lingering hope, that I should one day be released from it—or if I could have forgotten that I had ever been otherwise than as I then was—I could have enjoyed as much happiness in this as in any other situation.

One evening, on my return from hunting, I found the fire

put out, and the opening in the top of the lodge covered over with skins; by this means excluding, as much as possible, external light. I further observed that the ashes were removed from the fire-place, and that dry sand was spread where they had been. Soon after, a fire was made withoutside the cabin, in the open air, and a kettle hung over it to boil.

I now supposed that a feast was in preparation. I supposed so only, for it would have been indecorous to inquire into the meaning of what I saw. No person, among the Indians themselves, would use this freedom. Good breeding requires that the spectator should patiently wait the result.

As soon as the darkness of night had arrived, the family, including myself, were invited into the lodge. I was now requested not to speak, as a feast was about to be given to the dead, whose spirits delight in uninterrupted silence.

As we entered, each was presented with his wooden dish and spoon, after receiving which we seated ourselves. The door was next shut, and we remained in perfect darkness.

The master of the family was the master of the feast. Still in the dark, he asked every one, by turn, for his dish, and put into each two boiled ears of maize. The whole being served, he began to speak. In his discourse, which lasted half an hour, he called upon the manes of his deceased relations and friends, beseeching them to be present, to assist him in the chase, and to partake of the food which he had prepared for them. When he had ended, we proceeded to eat our maize, which we did without other noise than what was occasioned by our teeth. The maize was not half boiled, and it took me an hour to consume my share. I was requested not to break the spikes, [cob,] as this would be displeasing to the departed spirits of their friends.

When all was eaten, Wawatam made another speech, with which the ceremony ended. A new fire was kindled, with fresh sparks, from flint and steel; and the pipes being smoked, the spikes were carefully buried, in a hole made in the ground for that purpose, within the lodge. This done, the whole family began a dance, Wawatam singing, and beating a drum. The dance continued the greater part of the night, to the great pleasure of the lodge. The night of the feast was that of the first day of November.

On the twentieth of December, we took an account of the produce of our hunt, and found that we had a hundred beaver skins, as many raccoons, and a large quantity of dried venison; all which was secured from the wolves, by being placed upon a scaffold.

A hunting excursion, into the interior of the country, was

resolved on; and early the next morning the bundles were made up by the women for each person to carry. I remarked that the bundle given to me was the lightest, and those carried by the women the largest and heaviest of the whole.

On the first day of our march, we advanced about twenty miles, and then encamped. Being somewhat fatigued, I could not hunt; but Wawatam killed a stag, not far from our encampment. The next morning we moved our lodge to the carcass. At this station we remained two days, employed in drying the meat. The method was to cut it into slices, of the thickness of a steak, and then hang it over the fire in the smoke. On the third day we removed, and marched till two o'clock in the afternoon.

While the women were busy in erecting and preparing the lodges, I took my gun and strolled away, telling Wawatam that I intended to look out for some fresh meat for supper. He answered, that he would do the same; and on this we both left the encampment, in different directions.

The sun being visible, I entertained no fear of losing my way; but in following several tracks of animals, in momentary expectation of falling in with the game, I proceeded to a considerable distance, and it was not till near sunset that I thought of returning. The sky, too, had become overcast, and I was therefore left without the sun for my guide. In this situation, I walked as fast as I could, always supposing myself to be approaching our encampment, till at length it became so dark that I ran against the trees.

I became convinced that I was lost; and I was alarmed by the reflection that I was in a country entirely strange to me, and in danger from strange Indians. With the flint of my gun I made a fire, and then laid me down to sleep. In the night, it rained hard. I awoke cold and wet; and as soon as light appeared, I recommenced my journey, sometimes walking and sometimes running, unknowing where to go, bewildered, and like a madman.

Toward evening, I reached the border of a large lake, of which I could scarcely discern the opposite shore. I had never heard of a lake in this part of the country, and therefore felt myself removed further than ever from the object of my pursuit. To tread back my steps appeared to be the most likely means of delivering myself; and I accordingly determined to turn my face directly from the lake, and keep this direction as nearly as I could.

A heavy snow began to descend, and night soon afterward came on. On this, I stopped and made a fire; and stripping a tree of its sheet of bark, lay down under it to shelter me from the snow. All night, at small distances, the wolves howled around, and to me seemed to be acquainted with my misfortune.

Amid thoughts the most distracted, I was able at length to fall asleep ; but it was not long before I awoke, refreshed, and wondering at the terror to which I had yielded myself. That I could really have wanted the means of recovering my way, appeared to me almost incredible, and the recollection of it like a dream, or as a circumstance which must have proceeded from the loss of my senses. Had this not happened, I could never, as I now thought, have suffered so long, without calling to mind the lessons which I had received from my Indian friend, for the very purpose of being useful to me in difficulties of this kind. These were, that, generally speaking, the tops of pine trees lean toward the rising of the sun ; that moss grows toward the roots of trees on the side which faces the north ; and that the limbs of trees are most numerous, and largest, on that which faces the south.

Determined to direct my feet by these marks, and persuaded that I should thus, sooner or later, reach lake Michigan, which I reckoned to be distant about sixty miles, I began my march at break of day. I had not taken, nor wished to take, any nourishment since I left the encampment ; I had with me my gun and ammunition, and was therefore under no anxiety in regard to food. The snow lay about half a foot in depth.

My eyes were now employed upon the trees. When their tops leaned different ways, I looked to the moss, or to the branches ; and by connecting one with another, I found the means of travelling with some degree of confidence. At four o'clock in the afternoon, the sun, to my inexpressible joy, broke from the clouds, and I had now no further need of examining the trees.

In going down the side of a lofty hill, I saw a herd of red deer approaching. Desirous of killing one of them for food, I hid myself in the bushes, and on a large one coming near, presented my piece, which missed fire, on account of the priming having been wetted. The animals walked along, without taking the least alarm ; and, having reloaded my gun, I followed them, and presented a second time. But now a disaster of the heaviest kind had befallen me ; for, on attempting to fire, I found that I had lost the cock. I had previously lost the screw by which it was fastened to the lock ; and to prevent this from being lost also, I had tied it in its place, with a leather string. The lock, to prevent its catching in the boughs, I had carried under my molton coat.

Of all the sufferings which I had experienced, this seemed

to me the most severe. I was in a strange country, and knew not how far I had to go. I had been three days without food; I was now without the means of procuring myself either food or fire. Despair had almost overpowered me; but I soon resigned myself into the hands of that Providence, whose arm had so often saved me, and returned on my track, in search of what I had lost. My search was in vain, and I resumed my course, wet, cold and hungry, and almost without clothing.

The sun was setting fast, when I descended a hill, at the bottom of which was a small lake, entirely frozen over. On drawing near, I saw a beaver lodge in the middle, offering some faint prospect of food; but I found it already broken up. While I looked at it, it suddenly occurred to me that I had seen it before; and turning my eyes round the place, I discovered a small tree which I had myself cut down, in the autumn, when, in company with my friends, I had taken the beaver. I was no longer at a loss, but knew both the distance and the route to the encampment. The latter was only to follow the course of a small stream of water, which ran from the encampment to the lake on which I stood. An hour before, I had thought myself the most miserable of men; and now I leaped for joy, and called myself the happiest.

The whole of the night, and through all the succeeding day, I walked up the rivulet, and at sunset reached the encampment, where I was received with the warmest expressions of pleasure by the family, by whom I had been given up for lost, after a long and vain search for me in the woods.

Some days elapsed, during which I rested myself, and recruited my strength; after this, I resumed the chase, secure that, as the snow had now fallen, I could always return by the way I went.

In the course of the month of January, I happened to observe that the trunk of a very large pine tree was much torn by the claws of a bear, made both in going up and down. On further examination, I saw that there was a large opening in the upper part, near which the smaller branches were broken. From these marks, and from the additional circumstance that there were no tracks on the snow, there was reason to believe that a bear lay concealed in the tree.

On returning to the lodge, I communicated my discovery; and it was agreed that all the family should go together in the morning, to assist in cutting down the tree, the girth of which was not less than three fathom. The women at first opposed the undertaking, because our axes, being only of a pound and a half weight, were not well adapted to so heavy a labor; but the hope of finding a large bear, and obtaining from its fat a great quantity of oil, an article at the time much wanted, at length prevailed.

Accordingly, in the morning, we surrounded the tree, both men and women, as many at a time as could conveniently work at it; and here we toiled like beaver till the sun went down. This day's work carried us about half way through the trunk; and the next morning we renewed the attack, continuing it till about two o'clock in the afternoon, when the tree fell to the ground. For a few minutes, everything remained quiet, and I feared that all our expectations were disappointed; but as I advanced to the opening, there came out, to the great satisfaction of all our party, a bear of extraordinary size, which, before she had proceeded many yards, I shot.

The bear being dead, all my assistants approached, and all, but more particularly my old mother, (as I was wont to call her,) took his head in their hands, stroking and kissing it several times; begging a thousand pardons for taking away her life; calling her their relation and grandmother; and requesting her not to lay the fault upon them, since it was truly an Englishman that had put her to death.

This ceremony was not of long duration; and if it was I that killed their grandmother, they were not themselves behindhand in what remained to be performed. The skin being taken off, we found the fat in several places six inches deep. This, being divided into two parts, loaded two persons; and the flesh parts were as much as four persons could carry. In all, the carcass must have exceeded five hundred weight.

As soon as we reached the lodge, the bear's head was adorned with all the trinkets in the possession of the family, such as silver arm-bands and wrist-bands, and belts of wampum, and then laid upon a scaffold, set up for its reception, within the lodge. Near the nose was placed a large quantity of tobacco.

The next morning no sooner appeared than preparations were made for a feast to the manes. The lodge was cleaned and swept; and the head of the bear lifted up, and a new stroud blanket, which had never been used before, spread under it. The pipes were now lit; and Wawatam blew tobacco smoke into the nostrils of the bear, telling me to do the same, and thus appease the anger of the bear, on account of my having killed her. I endeavored to persuade my benefactor and friendly adviser that she no longer had any life, and assured him that I was under no apprehension from her displeasure; but the first proposition obtained no credit, and the second gave but little satisfaction.

At length, the feast being ready, Wawatam commenced a
27*

speech, resembling in many things his address to the manes of his relations and departed companions; but having this peculiarity, that he here deplored the necessity under which men labored thus to destroy their *friends.* He represented, however, that the misfortune was unavoidable, since without doing so they could by no means subsist. The speech ended, we all ate heartily of the bear's flesh; and even the head itself, after remaining three days on the scaffold, was put into the kettle.

It is only the female bear that makes her winter lodging in the upper parts of trees, a practice by which her young are secured from the attacks of wolves and other animals. She brings forth in the winter season; and remains in her lodge till the cubs have gained some strength.

The male always lodges in the ground, under the roots of trees. He takes to this habitation as soon as the snow falls, and remains there till it has disappeared. The Indians remark that the bear comes out in the spring with the same fat which he carried in in the autumn, but after exercise of only a few days becomes lean. Excepting for a short part of the season, the male lives constantly alone.

The fat of our bear was melted down, and the oil filled six porcupine skins. A part of the meat was cut into strips and fire-dried, after which it was put into the vessels containing the oil, where it remained in perfect preservation until the middle of summer.

February, in the country and by the people where and among whom I was, is called the Moon of Hard or Crusted Snow; for now the snow can bear a man, or at least dogs, in pursuit of animals of the chase. At this season, the stag is very successfully hunted, his feet breaking through at every step, and the crust upon the snow cutting his legs with its sharp edges to the very bone. He is consequently, in this distress, an easy prey; and it frequently happened that we killed twelve in the short space of two hours. By this means we were soon put into possession of four thousand weight of dried venison, which was to be carried on our backs, along with all the rest of our wealth, for seventy miles, the distance of our encampment from that part of the lake shore at which in the autumn we left our canoes. This journey it was our next business to perform.

Our venison and furs and peltries were to be disposed of at Michilimackinac, and it was now the season for carrying them to market. The women therefore prepared our loads; and the morning of departure being come, we set off at daybreak, and continued our march till two o'clock in the afternoon.

Where we stopped we erected a scaffold, on which we deposited the bundles we had brought, and returned to our encampment, which we reached in the evening. In the morning, we carried fresh loads, which being deposited with the rest, we returned a second time in the evening. This we repeated, till all was forwarded one stage. Then, removing our lodge to the place of deposit, we carried our goods, with the same patient toil, a second stage; and so on, till we were at no great distance from the shores of the lake.

Arrived here, we turned our attention to sugar-making, the management of which, as I have before related, belongs to the women, the men cutting wood for the fires, and hunting and fishing. In the midst of this, we were joined by several lodges of Indians, most of whom were of the family to which I belonged, and had wintered near us. The lands belonged to this family, and it had therefore the exclusive right to hunt on them. This is according to the custom of the people; for each family has its own lands. I was treated very civilly by all the lodges.

Our society had been a short time enlarged by this arrival of our friends, when an accident occurred which filled all the village with anxiety and sorrow. A little child, belonging to one of our neighbors, fell into a kettle of boiling syrup. It was instantly snatched out, but with little hope of its recovery.

So long, however, as it lived, a continual feast was observed; and this was made to the Great Spirit and Master of Life, that he might be pleased to save and heal the child. At this feast I was a constant guest; and often found difficulty in eating the large quantity of food which, on such occasions as these, is put upon each man's dish. The Indians accustom themselves both to eat much and to fast much with facility.

Several sacrifices were also offered; among which were dogs, killed and hung upon the tops of poles, with the addition of stroud blankets and other articles. These also were given to the Great Spirit, in humble hope that he would give efficacy to the medicines employed.

The child died. To preserve the body from the wolves, it was placed upon a scaffold, where it remained till we went to the lake, on the border of which was the burial-ground of the family.

On our arrival there, which happened in the beginning of April, I did not fail to attend the funeral. The grave was made of a large size, and the whole of the inside lined with birch bark. On the bark was laid the body of the child, accompanied with an axe, a pair of snow-shoes, a small kettle, several pairs of common shoes, its own strings of beads, and because it was a girl, a carrying-belt and a paddle. The kettle was filled with meat.

All this was again covered with bark; and at about two feet nearer the surface, logs were laid across, and these again covered with bark, so that the earth might by no means fall upon the corpse.

The last act before the burial performed by the mother, crying over the dead body of her child, was that of taking from it a lock of hair for a memorial. While she did this I endeavored to console her, by offering the usual arguments: that the child was happy in being released from the miseries of this present life, and that she should forbear to grieve, because it would be restored to her in another world, happy and everlasting. She answered that she knew it, and that by the lock of hair she should discover her daughter, for she would take it with her. In this she alluded to the day when some pious hand would place in her own grave, along with the carrying-belt and paddle, this little relic, hallowed by maternal tears.

I have frequently inquired into the ideas and opinions of the Indians in regard to futurity, and always found that they were somewhat different in different individuals.

Some suppose their souls to remain in this world, although invisible to human eyes; and capable, themselves, of seeing and hearing their friends, and also of assisting them, in moments of distress and danger.

Others dismiss from the mortal scene the unembodied spirit, and send it to a distant world or country, in which it receives reward or punishment, according to the life which it has led in its prior state. Those who have lived virtuously are transported into a place abounding with every luxury, with deer and all other animals of the woods and water, and where the earth produces, in their greatest perfection, all its sweetest fruits. While, on the other hand, those who have violated or neglected the duties of this life, are removed to a barren soil, where they wander up and down, among rocks and morasses, and are stung by gnats as large as pigeons.

While we remained on the border of the lake a watch was kept every night, in the apprehension of a speedy attack from the English, who were expected to avenge the massacre of Michilimackinac. The immediate grounds of this apprehension were the constant dreams, to this effect, of the more aged women. I endeavored to persuade them that nothing of the kind would take place; but their fears were not to be subdued.

Amid these alarms, there came a report concerning a real though less formidable enemy discovered in our neighborhood. This was a panther, which one of our young men had seen, and which animal sometimes attacks and carries away the Indian children. Our camp was immediately on the alert, and we set off into the woods, about twenty in number. We had not proceeded more than a mile before the dogs found the panther, and pursued him to a tree, on which he was shot. He was of a large size.

On the twenty-fifth of April we embarked for Michilimackinac. At La Grande Traverse we met a large party of Indians, who appeared to labor, like ourselves, under considerable alarm; and who dared proceed no further, lest they should be destroyed by the English. Frequent councils of the united bands were held; and interrogations were continually put to myself as to whether or not I knew of any design to attack them. I found that they believed it possible for me to have a foreknowledge of events, and to be informed by dreams of all things doing at a distance.

Protestations of my ignorance were received with but little satisfaction, and incurred the suspicion of a design to conceal my knowledge. On this account, therefore, or because I saw them tormented with fears which had nothing but imagination to rest upon, I told them, at length, that I knew there was no enemy to insult them; and that they might proceed to Michilimackinac without danger from the English. I further, and with more confidence, declared that if ever my countrymen returned to Michilimackinac I would recommend them to their favor, on account of the good treatment which I had received from them. Thus encouraged, they embarked at an early hour the next morning. In crossing the bay we experienced a storm of thunder and lightning.

Our port was the village of L'Arbre Croche, which we reached in safety, and where we staid till the following day. At this village we found several persons who had been lately at Michilimackinac, and from them we had the satisfaction of learning that all was quiet there. The remainder of our voyage was therefore performed with confidence.

In the evening of the twenty-seventh we landed at the fort, which now contained only two French traders. The Indians who had arrived before us were very few in number; and by all, who were of our party, I was used very kindly. I had the entire freedom both of the fort and camp.

Wawatam and myself settled our stock, and paid our debts; and this done, I found that my share of what was left consisted in a hundred beaver-skins, sixty raccoon-skins, and six otter, of the total value of about one hundred and sixty dollars. With these earnings of my winter's toil I proposed to purchase clothes, of which I was much in need, having been six months without a shirt; but, on inquiring into the prices of goods, I found that all my funds would not go far. I was able, however, to buy two shirts, at ten pounds of beaver each; a pair of *leggins*, or pantaloons, of scarlet cloth, which, with the ribbon to garnish them *fashionably*, cost me fifteen pounds of beaver; a blanket, at twenty pounds of beaver; and some other articles, at proportionable rates. In this manner my wealth was soon reduced; but not before I had laid in a good stock of ammunition and tobacco. To the use of the latter I had become much attached during the winter. It was my principal recreation after returning from the chase; for my companions in the lodge were unaccustomed to pass the time in conversation. Among the Indians the topics of conversation are but few, and limited, for the most part, to the transactions of the day, the number of animals which they have killed, and of those which have escaped their pursuit, and other incidents of the chase. Indeed, the causes of taciturnity among the Indians may be easily understood, if we consider how many occasions of speech, which present themselves to us, are utterly unknown to them: the records of history, the pursuits of science, the disquisitions of philosophy, the systems of politics, the business and the amusements of the day, and the transactions of the four corners of the world.

Eight days had passed in tranquillity, when there arrived a band of Indians from the Bay of Saguenaum. They had assisted at the siege of Detroit, and came to muster as many recruits for that service as they could. For my own part, I was soon informed that, as I was the only Englishman in the place, they proposed to kill me, in order to give their friends a mess of English broth to raise their courage.

This intelligence was not of the most agreeable kind; and in consequence of receiving it, I requested my friend to carry me to the Sault de Sainte-Marie, at which place I knew the Indians to be peaceably inclined, and that M. Cadotte enjoyed a powerful influence over their conduct. They considered M. Cadotte as their chief; and he was not only my friend, but a friend to the English. It was by him that the Chippeways of lake Superior were prevented from joining Pontiac.

Wawatam was not slow to exert himself for my preservation, but, leaving Michilimackinac in the night, transported myself and all his lodge to Point Saint-Ignace, on the opposite side of the strait. Here we remained till daylight, and then went into the Bay of Boutchitaouy, in which we spent three days in fishing and hunting, and where we found plenty of wild-fowl. Leaving the bay, we made for the Isle aux Outardes, where we were obliged to put in, on account of the wind's coming ahead. We proposed sailing for the Sault the next morning.

But when the morning came, Wawatam's wife complained that she was sick, adding, that she had had bad dreams, and knew that if we went to the Sault we should all be destroyed. To have argued, at this time, against the infallibility of dreams, would have been extremely unadvisable, since I should have appeared to be guilty not only of an odious want of faith, but also of a still more odious want of sensibility to the possible calamities of a family which had done so much for the alleviation of mine. I was silent; but the disappointment seemed to seal my fate. No prospect opened to console me. To return to Michilimackinac could only ensure my destruction; and to remain at the island was to brave almost equal danger, since it lay in the direct route between the fort and the Missisaki, along which the Indians from Detroit were hourly expected to pass on the business of their mission. I doubted not but, taking advantage of the solitary situation of the family, they would carry into execution their design of killing me.

Unable therefore to take any part in the direction of our course, but a prey at the same time to the most anxious thoughts as to my own condition, I passed all the day on the highest part to which I could climb of a tall tree, and whence the lake, on both sides of the island, lay open to my view. Here I might hope to learn, at the earliest possible, the approach of canoes, and by this means be warned in time to conceal myself.

On the second morning I returned, as soon as it was light, to my watch-tower, on which I had not been long before I discovered a sail coming from Michilimackinac.

The sail was a white one, and much larger than those usually employed by the Northern Indians. I therefore indulged a hope that it might be a Canadian canoe, on its voyage to Montreal; and that I might be able to prevail upon the crew to take me with them, and thus release me from all my troubles.

My hopes continued to gain ground; for I soon persuaded myself that the manner in which the paddles were used, on board the canoe, was Canadian, and not Indian. My spirits were elated; but disappointment had become so usual with me that I could not suffer myself to look to the event with any strength of confidence.

Enough, however, appeared at length to demonstrate itself to induce me to descend the tree, and repair to the lodge, with my tidings and schemes of liberty. The family congratulated me on the approach of so fair an opportunity of escape; and

my father and brother (for he was alternately each of these)
lit his pipe, and presented it to me, saying, "My son, this
may be the last time that ever you and I shall smoke out of
the same pipe! I am sorry to part with you. You know the
affection which I have always borne you, and the dangers to
which I have exposed myself and family, to preserve you from
your enemies; and I am happy to find that my efforts promise
not to have been in vain." At this time a boy came into the
lodge, informing us that the canoe had come from Michilimackinac, and was bound to the Sault de Sainte-Marie. It
was manned by three Canadians, and was carrying home
Madame Cadotte, the wife of M. Cadotte, already mentioned.

My hopes of going to Montreal being now dissipated, I
resolved on accompanying Madame Cadotte, with her permission, to the Sault. On communicating my wishes to Madame
Cadotte, she cheerfully acceded to them. Madame Cadotte,
as I have already mentioned, was an Indian woman of the
Chippeway nation, and she was very generally respected.

My departure fixed upon, I returned to the lodge, where I
packed up my wardrobe, consisting of my two shirts, pair of
leggins, and blanket. Besides these, I took a gun and ammunition, presenting what remained further to my host. I also
returned the silver arm-bands with which the family had
decorated me the year before.

We now exchanged farewells with an emotion entirely
reciprocal. I did not quit the lodge without the most grateful
sense of the many acts of goodness which I had experienced
in it, nor without the sincerest respect for the virtues which I
had witnessed among its members. All the family accompanied me to the beach; and the canoe had no sooner put off
than Wawatam commenced an address to the Kichi Manito,
beseeching him to take care of me, his brother, till we should
next meet. This he had told me would not be long, as he
intended to return to Michilimackinac for a short time only,
and would then follow me to the Sault. We had proceeded
to too great a distance to allow of our hearing his voice before
Wawatam had ceased to offer up his prayers.

Being now no longer in the society of the Indians, I laid
aside the dress, putting on that of a Canadian : a molton or
blanket coat, over my shirt; and a handkerchief about my
head, hats being very little worn in this country.

At daybreak, on the second morning of our voyage, we
embarked, and presently perceived several canoes behind us.
As they approached, we ascertained them to be the fleet,
bound for the Missisaki, of which I had been so long in dread.
It amounted to twenty sail.

On coming up with us, and surrounding our canoe, and amid general inquiries concerning the news, an Indian challenged me for an Englishman, and his companions supported him, by declaring that I looked very like one; but I affected not to understand any of the questions which they asked me, and Madame Cadotte assured them that I was a Canadian, whom she had brought on his first voyage from Montreal.

The following day saw us safely landed at the Sault, where I experienced a generous welcome from M. Cadotte. There were thirty warriors at this place, restrained from joining in the war only by M. Cadotte's influence.

Here, for five days, I was once more in possession of tranquillity; but on the sixth a young Indian came into M. Cadotte's, saying that a canoe full of warriors had just arrived from Michilimackinac; that they had inquired for me; and that he believed their intentions to be bad. Nearly at the same time, a message came from the good chief of the village, desiring me to conceal myself until he should discover the views and temper of the strangers.

A garret was the second time my place of refuge; and it was not long before the Indians came to M. Cadotte's. My friend immediately informed Mutchikiwish, their chief, who was related to his wife, of the design imputed to them, of mischief against myself. Mutchikiwish frankly acknowledged that they had had such a design; but added that if displeasing to M. Cadotte, it should be abandoned. He then further stated, that their errand was to raise a party of warriors to return with them to Detroit; and that it had been their intention to take me with them

In regard to the principal of the two objects thus disclosed, M. Cadotte proceeded to assemble all the chiefs and warriors of the village; and these, after deliberating for some time among themselves, sent for the strangers, to whom both M. Cadotte and the chief of the village addressed a speech. In these speeches, after recurring to the designs confessed to have been entertained against myself, who was now declared to be under the immediate protection of all the chiefs, by whom any insult I might sustain would be avenged, the ambassadors were peremptorily told that they might go back as they came, none of the young men of this village being foolish enough to join them.

A moment after, a report was brought, that a canoe had just arrived from Niagara. As this was a place from which every one was anxious to hear news, a message was sent to these fresh strangers, requesting them to come to the council.

The strangers came accordingly, and being seated, a long silence ensued. At length, one of them, taking up a belt of wampum, addressed himself thus to the assembly: "My friends and brothers, I am come, with this belt, from our great father, Sir William Johnson. He desired me to come to you as his ambassador, and tell you that he is making a great feast at fort Niagara ; that his kettles are all ready, and his fires lit. He invites you to partake of the feast, in common with your friends, the Six Nations,.which have all made peace with the English. He advises you to seize this opportunity of doing the same, as you cannot otherwise fail of being destroyed; for the English are on their march, with a great army, which will be joined by different nations of Indians. In a word, before the fall of the leaf, they will be at Michilimackinac, and the Six Nations with them."

The tenor of this speech greatly alarmed the Indians of the Sault, who, after a very short consultation, agreed to send twenty deputies to Sir William Johnson, at Niagara. This was a project highly interesting to me, since it offered me the means of leaving the country. I intimated this to the chief of the village, and received his promise that I should accompany the deputation.

Very little time was proposed to be lost, in setting forward on the voyage ; but the occasion was of too much magnitude not to call for more than human knowledge and discretion ; and preparations were accordingly made for solemnly invoking and consulting the GREAT TURTLE.

For invoking and consulting the Great Turtle, the first thing to be done was the building of a large house or wigwam, within which was placed a species of tent, for the use of the priest and reception of the spirit. The tent was formed of moose-skins, hung over a frame-work of wood. Five poles, or rather pillars, of five different species of timber, about ten feet in height, and eight inches in diameter, were set in a circle of about four feet in diameter. The holes made to receive them were about two feet deep ; and the pillars being set, the holes were filled up again, with the earth which had been dug out. At top the pillars were bound together by a circular hoop, or girder. Over the whole of this edifice were spread the moose-skins, covering it at top and round the sides, and made fast with thongs of the same ; except that on one side a part was left unfastened, to admit of the entrance of the priest.

The ceremonies did not commence but with the approach of night. To give light within the house, several fires were kindled round the tent. Nearly the whole village assembled in the house, and myself among the rest. It was not long before the priest appeared, almost in a state of nakedness. As he approached the tent the skins were lifted up, as much as was necessary to allow of his creeping under them, on his hands and knees. His head was scarcely withinside, when the edifice, massy as it has been described, began to shake; and the skins were no sooner let fall, than the sounds of numerous voices were heard beneath them, some yelling, some barking as dogs, some howling like wolves, and in this horrible concert were mingled screams and sobs, as of despair, anguish and the sharpest pain. Articulate speech was also uttered, as if from human lips, but in a tongue unknown to any of the audience.

After some time, these confused and frightful noises were succeeded by a perfect silence; and now a voice, not heard before, seemed to manifest the arrival of a new character in the tent. This was a low and feeble voice, resembling the cry of a young puppy. The sound was no sooner distinguished, than all the Indians clapped their hands for joy, exclaiming, that this was the Chief Spirit, the Turtle, the spirit that never lied! Other voices, which they had discriminated from time to time, they had previously hissed, as recognising them to belong to evil and lying spirits, which deceive mankind.

New sounds came from the tent. During the space of half an hour, a succession of songs were heard, in which a diversity of voices met the ear. From his first entrance, till these songs were finished, we heard nothing in the proper voice of the priest; but now, he addressed the multitude, declaring the presence of the Great Turtle, and the spirit's readiness to answer such questions as should be proposed.

The questions were to come from the chief of the village, who was silent, however, till after he had put a large quantity of tobacco into the tent, introducing it at the aperture. This was a sacrifice offered to the spirit; for spirits are supposed by the Indians to be as fond of tobacco as themselves. The tobacco accepted, he desired the priest to inquire whether or not the English were preparing to make war upon the Indians; and whether or not there were at fort Niagara a large number of English troops.

These questions having been put by the priest, the tent instantly shook; and for some seconds after it continued to rock so violently that I expected to see it levelled with the ground. All this was a prelude, as I supposed, to the answers to be given; but a terrific cry announced, with sufficient intelligibility, the departure of the Turtle.

A quarter of an hour elapsed in silence, and I waited impatiently to discover what was to be the next incident in this scene of imposture. It consisted in the return of the spirit, whose voice was again heard, and who now delivered a continued speech. The language of the GREAT TURTLE, like that which we had heard before, was wholly unintelligible to every ear, that of his priest excepted; and it was, therefore, not till the latter gave us an interpretation, which did not commence before the spirit had finished, that we learned the purport of this extraordinary communication.

The spirit, as we were now informed by the priest, had, during his short absence, crossed lake Huron, and even proceeded as far as fort Niagara, which is at the head of lake Ontario, and thence to Montreal. At fort Niagara, he had seen no great number of soldiers; but on descending the St. Lawrence, as low as Montreal, he had found the river covered with boats, and the boats filled with soldiers, in number like the leaves of the trees. He had met them on their way up the river, coming to make war upon the Indians.

The chief had a third question to propose, and the spirit, without a fresh journey to fort Niagara, was able to give an instant and most favorable answer. "If," said the chief, "the Indians visit Sir William Johnson, will they be received as friends?"

"Sir William Johnson," said the spirit, (and after the spirit the priest,) "Sir William Johnson will fill their canoes with presents, with blankets, kettles, guns, gunpowder and shot, and large barrels of rum, such as the stoutest of the Indians will not be able to lift; and every man will return in safety to his family."

At this, the transport was universal; and, amid the clapping of hands, a hundred voices exclaimed, "I will go, too! I will go too!"

The questions of public interest being resolved, individuals were now permitted to seize the opportunity of inquiring into the condition of their absent friends, and the fate of such as were sick. I observed that the answers, given to these questions, allowed of much latitude of interpretation.

Amid this general inquisitiveness, I yielded to the solicitations of my own anxiety for the future; and having first, like the rest, made my offering of tobacco, I inquired whether or not I should ever revisit my native country. The question being put by the priest, the tent shook as usual; after which I received this answer: "That I should take courage, and fear no danger, for that nothing would happen to hurt me; and that I should, in the end, reach my friends and country in safety."

These assurances wrought so strongly on my gratitude, that I presented an additional and extra offering of tobacco.

The Great Turtle continued to be consulted till near midnight, when all the crowd dispersed to their respective lodges. I was on the watch, through the scene I have described, to detect the particular contrivances by which the fraud was carried on ; but such was the skill displayed in the performance, or such my deficiency of penetration, that I made no discoveries, but came away as I went, with no more than those general surmises which will naturally be entertained by every reader.*

On the 10th of June, I embarked with the Indian deputation, composed of sixteen men. Twenty had been the number originally designed ; and upward of fifty actually engaged themselves to the council for the undertaking ; to say nothing of the general enthusiasm, at the moment of hearing the GREAT TURTLE's promises. But exclusively of the degree of timidity which still prevailed, we are to take into account the various domestic calls, which might supersede all others, and detain many with their families.

In the evening of the second day of our voyage, we reached the mouth of the Missisaki, where we found about forty Indians, by whom we were received with abundant kindness, and at night regaled at a great feast, held on account of our arrival. The viand was a preparation of the roe of the sturgeon, beat up, and boiled, and of the consistence of porridge.

After eating, several speeches were made to us, of which the general topic was a request that we should recommend the village to Sir William Johnson. This request was also specially addressed to me, and I promised to comply with it.

On the 14th of June, we passed the village of La Cloche, of which the greater part of the inhabitants were absent, being already on a visit to Sir William Johnson. This circumstance greatly encouraged the companions of my voyage, who now saw that they were not the first to run into danger.

The next day, about noon, the wind blowing very hard, we were obliged to put ashore at Point aux Grondines, a place of

---

* M. de Champlain has left an account of an exhibition of the nature here described, which may be seen in Charlevoix's Histoire et Description Generale de la Nouvelle France, livre IV. This took place in the year 1609, and was performed among a party of warriors, composed of Algonquins, Montagnez and Hurons. Carver witnessed another, among the Christinaux. In each case, the details are somewhat different, but the outline is the same. M. de Champlain mentions that he saw the *jongleur* shake the stakes or pillars of the tent. I was not so fortunate ; but this is the obvious explanation of that part of the mystery to which it refers. Captain Carver leaves the whole in darkness.

which some description has been given above. While the Indians erected a hut, I employed myself in making a fire. As I was gathering wood, an unusual sound fixed my attention for a moment; but, as it presently ceased, and as I saw nothing from which I could suppose it to proceed, I continued my employment, till, advancing further, I was alarmed by a repetition. I imagined that it came from above my head; but after looking that way in vain, I cast my eyes on the ground, and there discovered a rattlesnake, at not more than two feet from my naked legs. The reptile was coiled, and its head raised considerably above its body. Had I advanced another step before my discovery, I must have trodden upon it.

I no sooner saw the snake than I hastened to the canoe, in order to procure my gun; but the Indians, observing what I was doing, inquired the occasion, and being informed, begged me to desist. At the same time they followed me to the spot, with their pipes and tobacco-pouches in their hands. On returning, I found the snake still coiled.

The Indians, on their part, surrounded it, all addressing it by turns and calling it their *grandfather*; but yet keeping at some distance. During this part of the ceremony they filled their pipes; and now each blew the smoke toward the snake, who, as it appeared to me, really received it with pleasure. In a word, after remaining coiled, and receiving incense, for the space of half an hour, it stretched itself along the ground in visible good humor. Its length was between four and five feet. Having remained outstretched for some time, at last it moved slowly away, the Indians following it, and still addressing it by the title of grandfather, beseeching it to take care of their families during their absence, and to be pleased to open the heart of Sir William Johnson, so that he might *show them charity*, and fill their canoe with rum.

One of the chiefs added a petition that the snake would take no notice of the insult which had been offered him by the Englishman, who would even have put him to death but for the interference of the Indians, to whom it was hoped he would impute no part of the offence. They further requested that he would remain and inhabit their country, and not return among the English, that is, go eastward.

After the rattlesnake was gone, I learned that this was the first time that an individual of the species had been seen so far to the northward and westward of the river Des Français; a circumstance, moreover, from which my companions were disposed to infer that this *manito* had come or been sent on purpose to meet them; that his errand had been no other than to stop them on their way; and that consequently it would be most advisable to return to the point of departure. I was so fortunate, however, as to prevail with them to embark; and at six o'clock in the evening we again encamped. Very little was spoken of through the evening, the rattlesnake excepted.

Early the next morning we proceeded. We had a serene sky and very little wind, and the Indians therefore determined on steering across the lake to an island which just appeared in the horizon; saving, by this course, a distance of thirty miles, which would be lost in keeping the shore. At nine o'clock, A. M. we had a light breeze astern, to enjoy the benefit of which we hoisted sail. Soon after the wind increased, and the Indians, beginning to be alarmed, frequently called on the rattlesnake to come to their assistance. By degrees the waves grew high; and at eleven o'clock it blew a hurricane, and we expected every moment to be swallowed up. From prayers the Indians now proceeded to sacrifices, both alike offered to the god rattlesnake, or *manito kinibic.* One of the chiefs took a dog, and after tying its fore legs together threw it overboard, at the same time calling on the snake to preserve us from being drowned, and desiring him to satisfy his hunger with the carcass of the dog. The snake was unpropitious, and the wind increased. Another chief sacrificed another dog, with the addition of some tobacco. In the prayer which accompanied these gifts, he besought the snake, as before, not to avenge upon the Indians the insult which he had received from myself, in the conception of a design to put him to death. He assured the snake that I was absolutely an Englishman, and of kin neither to him nor to them.

At the conclusion of this speech, an Indian who sat near me observed, that if we were drowned it would be for my fault alone, and that I ought myself to be sacrificed, to appease the angry manito; nor was I without apprehensions that in case of extremity this would be my fate; but, happily for me, the storm at length abated, and we reached the island safely.

The next day was calm, and we arrived at the entrance* of the navigation which leads to lake Aux Claies.† We presently passed two short carrying-places, at each of which were several lodges of Indians,‡ containing only women and children, the men being gone to the council at Niagara. From this, as from a former instance, my companions derived new courage.

* This is the bay of Matchedash, or Matchitashk.

† This lake, which is now called lake Simcoe, lies between lakes Huron and Ontario.

‡ These Indians are Chippeways, of the particular description called Missisakies; and from their residence at Matchedash, or Matchitashk, also called Matchedash or Matchitashk Indians.

On the 18th of June, we crossed lake Aux Claies, which appeared to be upward of twenty miles in length. At its further end we came to the carrying-place of Toranto.* Here the Indians obliged me to carry a burden of more than a hundred pounds weight. The day was very hot, and the woods and marshes abounded with mosquitoes; but the Indians walked at a quick pace, and I could by no means see myself left behind. The whole country was a thick forest, through which our only road was a foot-path, or such as, in America, is exclusively termed an *Indian path.*

Next morning at ten o'clock we reached the shore of lake Ontario. Here we were employed two days in making canoes out of the bark of the elm tree, in which we were to transport ourselves to Niagara. For this purpose the Indians first cut down a tree; then stripped off the bark in one entire sheet of about eighteen feet in length, the incision being lengthwise. The canoe was now complete as to its top, bottom, and sides. Its ends were next closed by sewing the bark together; and a few ribs and bars being introduced, the architecture was finished. In this manner we made two canoes, of which one carried eight men and the other nine.

On the 21st, we embarked at Toranto, and encamped in the evening four miles short of fort Niagara, which the Indians would not approach till morning.

At dawn, the Indians were awake, and presently assembled in council, still doubtful as to the fate they were to encounter. I assured them of the most friendly welcome; and at length, after painting themselves with the most lively colors, in token of their own peaceable views, and after singing the song which is in use among them on going into danger, they embarked, and made for point Missisaki, which is on the north side of the mouth of the river or strait of Niagara, as the fort is on the south. A few minutes after I crossed over to the fort; and here I was received by Sir William Johnson, in a manner for which I have ever been gratefully attached to his person and memory.

Thus was completed my escape from the sufferings and dangers which the capture of fort Michilimackinac brought upon me; but the property which I had carried into the upper country was left behind. The reader will therefore be far from attributing to me any idle or unaccountable motive, when he finds me returning to the scene of my misfortunes.

* Toranto, or Toronto, is the name of a French trading-house on lake Ontario, built near the site of the present town of York, the capital of the province of Upper Canada. [It is one of the most important places in that province at this time.—Ed.]

NARRATIVE

OF THE CAPTIVITY OF FREDERICK MANHEIM.

FREDERICK MANHEIM, an industrious German, with his family, consisting of his wife, a daughter of eighteen years of age, and Maria and Christina, his youngest children, (twins,) about sixteen, resided near the river Mohawk, eight miles west of Johnston. On the 19th of October, 1779, the father being at work at some distance from his habitation, and the mother and eldest daughter on a visit at a neighbor's, two hostile Canasadaga Indians rushed in and captured the twin sisters.

The party to which these savages belonged consisted of fifty warriors, who, after securing twenty-three of the inhabitants of that neighborhood, (among whom was the unfortunate Frederick Manheim,) and firing their houses, retired for four days with the utmost precipitancy, till they were quite safe from pursuit. The place where they halted on the evening of the day of rest was a thick pine swamp, which rendered the darkness of an uncommonly gloomy night still more dreadful. The Indians kindled a fire, which they had not done before, and ordered their prisoners, whom they kept together, to refresh themselves with such provisions as they had. The Indians eat by themselves. After supper the appalled captives observed their enemies, instead of retiring to rest, busied in operations which boded nothing good. Two saplings were pruned clear of branches up to the very top, and all the brush cleared away for several rods around them. While this was doing, others were splitting pitch-pine billets into small splinters about five inches in length, and as small as one's little finger, sharpening one end, and dipping the other in melted turpentine.

At length, with countenances distorted by infernal fury, and hideous yells, the two savages who had captured the hapless Maria and Christina leaped into the midst of the circle of prisoners, and dragged those ill-fated maidens, shrieking, from the embraces of their companions. These warriors had disagreed about whose property the girls should be, as they had jointly seized them; and, to terminate the dispute agreeably to the abominable custom of the savages, it was determined by the chiefs of the party that the prisoners who had given rise to the contention should be destroyed, and that their captors should be the principal agents in the execrable business. These furies, assisted by their comrades, stripped the forlorn girls, convulsed with apprehensions, and tied each to a sapling, with their hands as high extended above their heads as possible; and then pitched them from their knees to their shoulders, with upwards of six hundred of the sharpened splinters above described, which, at every puncture, were attended with screams of distress, that echoed through the wilderness. And then, to complete the infernal tragedy, the splinters, all standing erect on the bleeding victims, were set on fire, and exhibited a scene of extreme misery, beyond the power of speech to describe, or even the imagination to conceive. It was not until near three hours had elapsed from the commencement of their torments, and that they had lost almost every resemblance of the human form, that these helpless virgins sunk down in the arms of their deliverer, death.

SIGNAL PROWESS OF A WOMAN, IN A COMBAT
WITH SOME INDIANS. IN A LETTER TO A LADY OF PHILADELPHIA.

Westmoreland, April 26, 1779.

MADAM,—I have written an account of a very particular affair between a white man and two Indians.* I am now to give you a relation in which you will see how a person of your sex acquitted herself in defence of her own life, and that of her husband and children.

---

* Reference is probably made to the desperate encounter of one Morgan and two Indians.—Ed.

The lady who is the burthen of this story is named Experience Bozarth. She lives on a creek called Dunkard creek, in the south-west corner of this county. About the middle of March last, two or three families, who were afraid to stay at home, gathered to her house and there stayed; looking on themselves to be safer than when all scattered about at their own houses.

On a certain day some of the children thus collected came running in from play in great haste, saying there were ugly red men. One of the men in the house stepped to the door, where he received a ball in the side of his breast, which caused him to fall back into the house. The Indian was immediately in over him, and engaged with another man who was in the house. The man tossed the Indian on a bed, and called for a knife to kill him. (Observe these were all the men that were in the house.) Now Mrs. Bozarth appears the only defence, who, not finding a knife at hand, took up an axe that lay by, and with one blow cut out the brains of the Indian. At that instant, (for all was instantaneous,) a second Indian entered the door, and shot the man dead who was engaged with the Indian on the bed. Mrs. Bozarth turned to this second Indian, and with her axe gave him several large cuts, some of which let his entrails appear. He bawled out, murder, murder. On this sundry other Indians (who had hitherto been fully employed, killing some children out of doors) came rushing to his relief; one of whose heads Mrs. Bozarth clove in two with her axe, as he stuck it in at the door, which laid him flat upon the soil. Another snatched hold of the wounded bellowing fellow, and pulled him out of doors, and Mrs. Bozarth, with the assistance of the man who was first shot in the door, and by this time a little recovered, shut the door after them, and made it fast, where they kept garrison for several days, the dead white man and dead Indian both in the house with them, and the Indians about the house besieging them. At length they were relieved by a party sent for that purpose.

This whole affair, to shutting the door, was not perhaps more than three minutes in acting.

REV. JOHN CORBLY'S NARRATIVE.

If, after perusing the annexed melancholy narrative, you deem it worthy a place in your publication, it is at your service. Such communications, founded on fact, have a tendency on one hand to make us feel for the persons afflicted, and on the other to impress our hearts with gratitude to the Sovereign Disposer of all events for that emancipation which the United States have experienced from the haughty claims of Britain—a power, at that time, so lost to every human affection, that, rather than not subdue and make us slaves, they basely chose to encourage, patronize and reward, as their most faithful and beloved allies, the savages of the wilderness; who, without discrimination, barbarously massacred the industrious husbandman, the supplicating female, the prattling child and tender infant, vainly sheltered within the encircling arms of maternal fondness. Such transactions, as they come to our knowledge well authenticated, ought to be recorded, that our posterity may not be ignorant of what their ancestors underwent at the trying period of our national exertions for American independence.

The following account was, at my request, drawn up by the unfortunate sufferer. Respecting the author, suffice it to say, that he is an ordained minister of the Baptist faith and order, and held in high estimation by all our associated churches.

I am, sir, yours, &c.,

WILLIAM ROGERS.

Muddy Creek, Washington County, July 8, 1785.

Dear Sir,—The following is a just and true account of the tragical scene of my family's falling by the savages, which I related when at your house in Philadelphia, and you requested me to forward in writing.

On the second Sabbath in May, in the year 1782, being my appointment at one of my meeting-houses about a mile from my dwelling-house, I set out with my dear wife and five children, for public worship. Not suspecting any danger, I walked behind two hundred yards, with my Bible in my hand, meditating; as I was thus employed, all on a sudden I was greatly alarmed with the frightful shrieks of my dear family before me. I immediately ran with all the speed I could, vainly hunting a club as I ran, till I got within forty yards of them. My poor wife, seeing me, cried to me to make my escape; an Indian ran up to shoot me. I had to strip, and by so doing outran him. My dear wife had a sucking child in her arms; this little infant they killed and scalped. They then struck my wife at sundry times, but not getting her down, the Indian who had aimed to shoot me ran to her, shot her through the body, and scalped her. My little boy, an only son, about six years old, they sunk the hatchet into his brains, and thus dispatched him. A daughter, besides the infant, they also killed and **scalped**. My eldest daughter, who is yet alive, was hid in a

tree about twenty yards from the place where the rest were
killed, and saw the whole proceedings. She, seeing the Indians all go off, as she thought, got up and deliberately crept
out from the hollow trunk ; but one of them espying her, ran
hastily up, knocked her down and scalped her ; also her only
surviving sister, on whose head they did not leave more than
one inch round, either of flesh or skin, besides taking a piece
out of her skull. She and the before-mentioned one are still
miraculously preserved, though, as you must think, I have had,
and still have, a great deal of trouble and expense with them,
besides anxiety about them, insomuch that I am, as to worldly
circumstances, almost ruined. I am yet in hopes of seeing
them cured ; they still, blessed be God, retain their senses, notwithstanding the painful operations they have already and must
yet pass through. At the time I ran round to see what was
become of my family, and found my dear and affectionate wife
with five children all scalped in less than ten minutes from the
first outset. No one, my dear brother, can conceive how I felt ;
this you may well suppose was killing to me. I instantly
fainted away, and was borne off by a friend, who by this time
had found us out. When I recovered, oh the anguish of my
soul ! I cried, would to God I had died for them ! would to
God I had died with them ! O how dark and mysterious did
this trying providence then appear to me ! but—

> ' Why should I grieve, when, grieving, I must bear ?"

This, dear sir, is a faithful, though short narrative of that
fatal catastrophe ; and my life amidst it all, for what purpose
Jehovah only knows, redeemed from surrounding death. Oh,
may I spend it to the praise and glory of his grace, who work-
eth all things after the council of his own will. The government of the world and of the church is in his hands. May it
be taught the important lesson of acquiescing in all his dispensations. I conclude with wishing you every blessing, and
subscribe myself your affectionate, though afflicted friend and
unworthy brother in the gospel ministry,

JOHN CORBLY.

A TRUE AND WONDERFUL NARRATIVE OF THE SURPRISING CAPTIVITY AND REMARKABLE DELIVERANCE OF MRS. FRANCIS SCOTT, AN INHABITANT OF WASHINGTON COUNTY, VIRGINIA, WHO WAS TAKEN BY THE INDIANS ON THE EVENING OF THE 29th OF JUNE, 1785.

On Wednesday, the 29th day of June, 1785, late in the evening, a large company of armed men passed the house on their way to Kentucky, some part of whom encamped within two miles. Mr. Scott's living on a frontier part generally made the family watchful; but on this calamitous day, after so large a body of men had passed, he lay down in his bed, and imprudently left one of the doors of his house open; the children were also in bed and asleep. Mrs. Scott was nearly undressed, when, to her unutterable astonishment and horror, she saw rushing in through the door, that was left open, painted savages, with their arms presented at the same time, raising a hideous shriek. Mr. Scott, being awake, instantly jumped from his bed, and was immediately fired at. He forced his way through the midst of the enemy, and got out of the house, but fell a few paces from the door. An Indian seized Mrs. Scott, and ordered her to a particular place, charging her not to move. Others stabbed and cut the throats of the three youngest children in their bed, and afterwards lifted them up, and dashed them on the floor near their mother. The eldest, a beautiful girl, eight years of age, awoke, and jumping out of bed, ran to her mother, and with the most plaintive accents cried, " O mamma! mamma! save me!" The mother, in the deepest anguish of spirit, and with a flood of tears, entreated the Indians to spare her life; but, with that awfully revolting brutality, they tomahawked and stabbed her in her mother's arms!!

Adjacent to Mr. Scott's dwelling-house another family lived of the name of Ball. The Indians also attacked them at the same time, but the door being shut, they fired into the house through an opening between the logs which composed its walls, and killed a lad, and then essayed to force open the door; but a brother of the lad which had been shot down fired at the Indians through the door, and they relinquished the attack. In the mean time the remaining part of the family ran out of the house and escaped.

In the house of Mr. Scott were four good rifles, well loaded, belonging to people that had left them as they were going to Kentucky. The Indians, thirteen in number, seized these, and all the plunder they could lay their hands on besides, and hastily began a retreat into the wilderness. It was now late in the evening, and they travelled all the following night. The next morning, June the 30th, the chief of the party allotted to each of his followers his share of the plunder and prisoners, at the same time detaching nine of his party to go on a horse-stealing expedition on Clinch river.

The eleventh day after Mrs. Scott's captivity, four Indians that had her in charge stopped at a place fixed on for rendez-vous, and to hunt, being now in great want of provisions. Three of these four set out on the hunting expedition, leaving their chief, an old man, to take care of the prisoner, who now had, to all appearances, become reconciled to her situation, and expressed a willingness to proceed to the Indian towns, which seemed to have the desired effect of lessening her keeper's watchfulness. In the daytime, while the old man was graining a deer-skin, Mrs. Scott, pondering on her situa-tion, began anxiously to look for an opportunity to make an escape. At length, having matured her resolution in her own mind for the accomplishment of this object, the first opportunity she goes to the old chief with great confidence, and in the most disinterested manner asked him for liberty to go to a small stream, a little distance off, to wash the blood from her apron, that had remained upon it since the fatal night, caused by the murder of her child in her arms, before related. He replied, in the English tongue, " go along." She then passed by him, his face being in a contrary direction from that she was going, and he very busy in dressing his skin, passed on, seemingly unnoticed by him.

After arriving at the water, instead of stopping to wash her apron, as she pretended, she proceeded on without a moment's delay. She laid her course for a high barren mountain which was in sight, and travelled until late at night, when she came down into the valley in search of the track she had been taken along in by the Indians a few days before, hoping thereby to find the way back to the settlement without the imminent peril, which now surrounded her, of being lost and perishing with hunger in this unknown region.

On coming across the valley to the side of a river which skirted it, supposed to be the easterly branch of Kentucky river, she observed in the sand tracks of two men that had gone up the river, and had just returned. She concluded these to have been her pursuers, which excited in her breast emotions of gratitude and thankfulness to divine Providence for so timely a deliverance. Being without any provisions, having no kind of weapon or tool to assist her in getting any, and almost destitute of clothing; also knowing that a vast tract of rugged high mountains intervened between where she was and the inhabitants easterly, and she almost as ignorant as a child of the method of steering through the woods, excited painful sensations. But certain death, either by hunger or wild beasts, seemed to be better than to be in the power of beings who excited in her mind such horror. She addressed Heaven, and taking courage, proceeded onward.

After travelling three days, she had nearly met with the Indians, as she supposed, that had been sent to Clinch river to steal horses, but providentially hearing their approach, concealed herself among the cane until they had passed by her. This giving her a fresh alarm, and her mind being filled with consternation, she got lost, proceeded backwards and forwards for several days. At length she came to a river that seemed to come from the east. Concluding it was Sandy river, she accordingly resolved to trace it to its source, which is adjacent to the Clinch settlement. After proceeding up the same several days she came to the point where it runs through the great Laurel mountain, where there is a prodigious waterfall and high craggy cliffs along the water's edge; that way seemed impassable, the mountain steep and difficult; however, our mournful traveller concluded the latter way was best. She therefore ascended for some time, but coming to a lofty range of inaccessible rocks, she turned her course towards the foot of the mountain and the river-side. After getting into a deep gully, and passing over several high steep rocks, she reached the river-side, where, to her inexpressible affliction, she found that a perpendicular rock, or rather one that hung over, to the height of fifteen or twenty feet, formed the bank. Here a solemn pause ensued. She essayed to return, but the height of the steeps and rocks she had descended over prevented her. She then returned to the edge of the precipice, and viewing the bottom of it as the certain spot to end all her troubles, or remain on the top to pine away with hunger, or be devoured by wild beasts.

After serious meditation and devout exercises, she determined on leaping from the height, and accordingly jumped off. Now, although the place she had to alight upon was covered with uneven rocks, not a bone was broken, but being exceedingly stunned by the fall, she remained unable to proceed for some time.

The dry season had caused the river to be shallow. She travelled in it, and, where she could, by its edge, until she got through the mountain, which she thought was several miles. After this, as she was travelling along the bank of the river, a

venomous snake bit her on the ankle. She had strength to
kill it, and knowing its kind, concluded death must soon overtake her.

By this time Mrs. Scott was reduced to a mere skeleton
with fatigue, hunger, and grief. Probably this reduced state
of her system saved her from the effects of the poison fangs of
the snake; be that as it may, so it was, that very little pain
succeeded the bite, and what little swelling there was fell into
her feet.

Our wanderer now left the river, and after proceeding a
good distance she came to where the valley parted into two,
each leading a different course. Here a painful suspense took
place again. How truly forlorn was now the case of this poor
woman! almost ready to sink down from exhaustion, who
had now the only prospect left that, either in the right or
wrong direction, her remaining strength could not carry her
long, nor but very little way, and she began to despair—and
who would not—of ever again beholding the face of any human
creature. But the most awful and seemingly certain dangers
are sometimes providentially averted.

While her mind was thus agitated, a beautiful bird passed
close by her, fluttering slowly along near the ground, and very
remarkably took its course onward in one of the valleys before
spoken of. This drew her attention, and, while pondering
upon what it might mean, another bird like the first, in the
same manner, passed by her, and followed the same valley.
She now took it for granted that this was her course also;
and, wonderful to relate, in two days after she had wandered
in sight of the settlement on Clinch river, called New Garden.
Thus, in the third month of her captivity, she was unexpectedly though joyfully relieved from the dreadful impending death
by famine. But had she taken the other valley, she never
could have returned. The day of her arrival at New Garden
was August 11th.

Mrs. Scott relates that the Indians told her that the party
with whom she was a captive was composed of four different
nations; two of whom, she thinks, were Delawares and Min-
goes. She further relates that, during a full month of her
wanderings, viz. from July 10th to August 11th, she had no
other food to subsist upon but what she derived from chewing
and swallowing the juice of young cane stalks, sassafras leaves,
and some other plants of which she knew not the names; that
on her journey she saw buffaloes, elks, deers, and frequently
bears and wolves, not one of which, although some passed very
near her, offered her the least harm. One day a bear came
near her with a young fawn in his mouth, and on discovering
29*

her he dropped his prey and ran off. Prompted by the keen pangs of hunger, she advanced to seize upon it, but fearing the bear might return, she turned away in despair, and pursued her course; thus sparing her feelings, naturally averse to raw flesh, at the expense of increasing hunger.

Mrs. Scott continues* in a low state of health, and remains unconsolable for the loss of her family, particularly bewailing the cruel death of her little daughter.

A NARRATIVE

OF THE DESPERATE ENCOUNTER AND ESCAPE OF CAPT. WM. HUBBELL FROM THE INDIANS WHILE DESCENDING THE OHIO RIVER IN A BOAT WITH OTHERS, IN THE YEAR 1791. Originally set forth in the Western Review, and afterwards republished by Dr. Metcalf, in his " Narratives of Indian Warfare in the West."

In the year 1791, while the Indians were yet troublesome, especially on the banks of the Ohio, Capt. William Hubbell, who had previously emigrated to Kentucky from the state of Vermont, and who, after having fixed his family in the neigh-

---

* At the time the original narrative was written. It was printed in 1786.—Ed.

borhood of Frankfort, then a frontier settlement, had been compelled to go to the eastward on business, was now a second time on his way to this country. On one of the tributary streams of the Monongahela, he procured a flat-bottomed boat, and embarked in company with Mr. Daniel Light and Mr. Wm. Plascut and his family, consisting of a wife and eight children, destined for Limestone, Kentucky.

On their passage down the river, and soon after passing Pittsburgh, they saw evident traces of Indians along the banks, and there is every reason to believe that a boat which they overtook, and which, through carelessness, was suffered to run aground on an island, became a prey to these merciless savages. Though Capt. Hubbell and his party stopped some time for it in a lower part of the river, it did not arrive, and it has never, to their knowledge, been heard of.

Before they reached the mouth of the great Kenhawa they had, by several successive additions, increased their number to twenty persons, consisting of nine men, three women, and eight children. The men, besides those mentioned above, were one John Storer, an Irishman and a Dutchman whose names are not recollected, Messrs. Ray and Tucker, and a Mr. Kilpatrick, whose two daughters also were of the party. Information received at Galliopolis confirmed the expectation, which appearances had previously raised, of a serious conflict with a large body of Indians; and as Capt. Hubbell had been regularly appointed commander of the boat, every possible preparation was made for a formidable and successful resistance of the anticipated attack. The nine men were divided into three watches for the night, which were alternately to continue awake, and be on the lookout for two hours at a time.

The arms on board, which consisted principally of old muskets much out of order, were collected, put in the best possible condition for service, and loaded. At about sunset on that day, the 23d of March, 1791, our party overtook a fleet of six boats descending the river in company, and intended to have continued with them; but as their passengers seemed to be more disposed to dancing than fighting, and as, soon after dark, notwithstanding the remonstrances of Capt. Hubbell, they commenced fiddling and drinking, instead of preparing their arms and taking the necessary rest preparatory to battle, it was wisely considered, by Capt. Hubbell and his company, far more hazardous to have such companions than to proceed alone. Hence it was determined to press rapidly forward by aid of the oars, and to leave those thoughtless fellow-travellers behind. One of the boats, however, belonging to the fleet, commanded by a Capt. Greathouse, adopted the same plan, and for a while kept up with Capt. Hubbell, but all its crew at length failing asleep, that boat also ceased to be propelled by the oars, and Capt. Hubbell and his party proceeded steadily forward alone.   Early in the night a canoe was dimly seen floating down the river, in which were probably Indians reconnoitering, and other evident indications were observed of the neighborhood and hostile intentions of a formidable party of savages.

It was now agreed that should the attack, as was probable, be deferred till morning, every man should be up before the dawn, in order to make as great a show as possible of numbers and of strength; and that, whenever the action should take place, the women and children should lie down on the cabin floor, and be protected as well as they could by the trunks and other baggage, which might be placed around them.   In this perilous situation they continued during the night, and the captain, who had not slept more than one hour since he left Pittsburgh, was too deeply impressed with the imminent danger which surrounded them to obtain any rest at that time.

Just as daylight began to appear in the east, and before the men were up and at their posts agreeably to arrangement, a voice, at some distance below them, in a plaintive tone, repeatedly solicited them to come on shore, as there were some white persons who wished to obtain a passage in their boat.   This the captain very naturally and correctly concluded to be an Indian artifice, and its only effect was to rouse the men, and place every one on his guard.   The voice of entreaty was soon changed into the language of indignation and insult, and the sound of distant paddles announced the savage foe.   At length three Indian canoes were seen through the mist of the morning, rapidly advancing.   With the utmost coolness the captain and his companions prepared to receive them.   The chairs, tables, and other incumbrances were thrown into the river, in order to clear the deck for action. . Every man took his position, and was ordered not to fire till the savages had approached so near that, (to use the words of Capt. Hubbell,) "the flash from the guns might singe their eyebrows;" and a special caution was given that the men should fire successively, so that there might be no interval.

On the arrival of the canoes, they were found to contain about twenty-five or thirty Indians each.   As soon as they had approached within the reach of musket-shot, a general fire was given from one of them, which wounded Mr. Tucker through the hip so severely that his leg hung only by the flesh, and shot Mr. Light just below his ribs.   The three canoes placed themselves at the bow, stern, and on the right side of the boat, so that they had an opportunity of raking in every direction. The fire now commenced from the boat, and had a powerful effect in checking the confidence and fury of the Indians. The captain, after firing his own gun, took up that of one of the wounded men, raised it to his shoulder, and was about to discharge it, when a ball came and took away the lock of it. He coolly turned around, seized a brand of fire from the kettle which had served for a caboose, and applying it to the pan, discharged the piece with effect. A very regular and constant fire was now kept up on both sides. The captain was just in the act of raising his gun a third time, when a ball passed through his right arm, and for a moment disabled him. Scarcely had he recovered from the shock, and re-acquired the use of his hand, which had been suddenly drawn up by the wound, when he observed the Indians in one of the canoes just about to board the boat in the bow, where the horses were placed belonging to the company. So near had they approached, that some of them had actually seized with their hands the side of the boat. Severely wounded as he was, he caught up a pair of horseman's pistols and rushed forward to repel the attempt at boarding. On his approach the Indians fell back, and he discharged one of the pistols with effect at the foremost man. After firing the second pistol, he found himself with useless arms, and was compelled to retreat; but stepping back upon a pile of small wood which had been prepared for burning in the kettle, the thought struck him that it might be made use of in repelling the foe, and he continued for some time to strike with it so forcibly and actively that they were unable to enter the boat, and at length he wounded one of them so severely that with a yell they suddenly gave way.

All the canoes instantly discontinued the contest, and directed their course to Capt. Greathouse's boat, which was then in sight. Here a striking contrast was exhibited to the firmness and intrepidity which had just been displayed. Instead of resisting the attack, the people on board of that boat retired to the cabin in dismay. The Indians entered it without opposition, and rowed it to the shore, where they instantly killed the captain and a lad of about fourteen years of age. The women they placed in the centre of their canoes, and manning them with fresh hands, again pursued Capt. Hubbell. A melancholy alternative now presented itself to these brave but almost desponding men, either to fall a prey to the savages themselves, or to run the risk of shooting the women who had been placed in the canoes in the hope of deriving protection from their presence. But "self-preservation is the first law of nature," and the captain very justly remarked "that there would not be much humanity in preserving their lives at such a sacrifice, merely that they might become victims of savage cruelty at some subsequent period."

There were now but four men left on board of Capt. Hubbell's boat capable of defending it, and the captain himself was severely wounded in two places. The second attack, nevertheless, was resisted with almost incredible firmness and vigor. Whenever the Indians would rise to fire, their opponents would commonly give them the first shot, which, in almost every instance, would prove fatal. Notwithstanding the disparity of numbers, and the exhausted condition of the defenders of the boat, the Indians at length appeared to despair of success, and the canoes successively returned to the shore. Just as the last one was departing, Capt. Hubbell called to the Indian who was standing in the stern, and, on his turning round, discharged his piece at him. When the smoke, which for a moment obscured their vision, was dissipated, he was seen lying on his back, and appeared to be severely wounded, perhaps mortally.

Unfortunately, the boat now drifted near to the shore, where the Indians had collected, and a large concourse, probably between four and five hundred, were seen running down on the bank. Ray and Plascut, the only men remaining unhurt, were placed at the oars; and as the boat was not more than twenty yards from the shore, it was deemed prudent for all to lie down in as safe a position as possible, and attempt to push forward with the utmost practicable rapidity. While they continued in this situation, nine balls were shot into one oar, and ten into another, without wounding the rowers, who were hid from view and protected by the side of the boat and blankets in the stern. During this dreadful exposure to the fire of the savages, which continued about twenty minutes, Mr. Kilpatrick observed a particular Indian, whom he thought a favorable mark for his rifle, and, notwithstanding the solemn warning of Capt. Hubbell, rose up to shoot him. He immediately received a ball in his mouth, which passed out at the back part of his head, and was also, almost at the same instant, shot through the heart. He fell down among the horses that were about the same time shot down likewise; and thus was presented to his afflicted daughters and fellow-travellers, who were witnesses of the awful occurrence, a spectacle of horror which we need not further attempt to describe.

The boat was now providentially and suddenly carried out into the middle of the stream, and taken by the current beyond the reach of the enemy's balls. Our little band, reduced as they were in numbers, wounded, afflicted, and almost exhausted by fatigue, were still unsubdued in spirit, and being assembled in all their strength, men, women, and children, with an appearance of triumph, gave three hearty cheers, calling the Indians to come on again if they were fond of sport.

Thus ended this awful conflict, in which, out of nine men, two only escaped unhurt. Tucker and Kilpatric were killed on the spot, Storer was mortally wounded, and died on his arrival at Limestone, and all the rest, excepting Ray and Plascut, were severely wounded. The women and children were all uninjured, except a little son of Mr. Plascut, who, after the battle was over, came to the captain, and with great coolness requested him to take a ball out of his head. On examination it appeared that a bullet, which had passed through the side of the boat, had penetrated the forehead of this little hero, and remained under the skin. The captain took it out, and supposing this was all, as in good reason he might, was about to bestow his attention on some other momentous affair, when the little boy observed, "That is not *all*, captain," and raising his arm, exhibited a piece of bone at the point of his elbow, which had been shot off, and hung only by the skin. His mother, to whom the whole affair seems before to have been unknown, but being now present, exclaimed, "Why did you not tell me of this?" "Because," replied the son, "the captain ordered us to be silent during the fight, and I thought you would make a noise if I told you of it."

The boat made the best of its way down the river, and the object was to reach Limestone that night. The captain's arm had bled profusely, and he was compelled to close the sleeve of his coat in order to retain the blood and stop its effusion.

In this situation, tormented by excruciating pain, and faint through loss of blood, he was under the necessity of steering the boat with his left arm till about ten o'clock that night, when he was relieved by Mr. Wm. Brooks, who resided on the bank of the river, and who was induced by the calls of the suffering party to come out to their assistance. By his aid, and that of some other persons who were in the same manner brought to their relief, they were enabled to reach Limestone about twelve o'clock that night.

Immediately on the arrival of Mr. Brooks, Capt. Hubbell, relieved from labor and responsibility, sunk under the weight of pain and fatigue, and become for a while totally insensible. When the boat reached Limestone, he found himself unable to walk, and was obliged to be carried up to the tavern. Here he had his wound dressed, and continued several days, until he acquired sufficient strength to proceed homewards.

On the arrival of our party at Limestone, they found a considerable force of armed men about to march against the same Indians, from whose attacks they had so severely suffered. They now learned that, the Sunday preceding, the same party of savages had cut off a detachment of men ascending the Ohio from fort Washington, at the mouth of Licking river, and had killed with their tomahawks, without firing a gun, twenty-one out of twenty-two men, of which the detachment consisted.

Crowds of people, as might be expected, came to witness the boat which had been the scene of so much heroism, suffering, and horrid carnage, and to visit the resolute little band by whom it had been so gallantly and successfully defended. On examination it was found that the sides of the boat were literally filled with bullets and with bullet-holes. There was scarcely a space of two feet square, in the part above water, which had not either a ball remaining in it or a hole through which a ball had passed. Some persons, who had the curiosity to count the number of holes in the blankets which were hung up as curtains in the stern of the boat, affirmed that in the space of five feet square there were one hundred and twenty-two. Four horses out of five were killed, and the escape of the fifth amidst such a shower of balls appears almost miraculous.

The day after the arrival of Capt. Hubbell and his companions, the five remaining boats, which they had passed on the night preceding the battle, reached Limestone. Those on board remarked that during the action they distinctly saw the flashes, but could not hear the reports of the guns. The Indians, it appears, had met with too formidable a resistance from a single boat to attack a fleet, and suffered them to pass unmolested: and since that time it is believed that no boat has been assailed by Indians on the Ohio.

The force which marched out to disperse this formidable body of savages discovered several Indians dead on the shore near the scene of action. They also found the bodies of Capt. Greathouse and several others, men, women, and children, who had been on board of his boat. Most of them appeared to have been whipped to death, as they were found stripped, tied to trees, and marked with the appearance of lashes, and large rods which seemed to have been worn with use were observed lying near them.

Such is the plain narrative of a transaction that may serve as a specimen of the difficulties and dangers to which, but a few years since, the inhabitants of this now flourishing and beautiful country were constantly exposed.

AN ACCOUNT

OF THE SUFFERINGS OF MASSY HERBESON, AND HER FAMILY,
WHO WERE TAKEN PRISONERS BY A PARTY OF INDIANS.
GIVEN ON OATH BEFORE JOHN WILKINS, ESQ., ONE OF
THE JUSTICES OF THE PEACE FOR THE COMMONWEALTH
OF PENNSYLVANIA.

Pittsburgh, May 28, 1792

MASSY HERBESON, on her oath, according to law, being
taken before John Wilkins, Esq., one of the commonwealth's
justices of the peace in and for the county of Alleghany, de-
poseth and saith, that on the 22d day of this instant she was
taken from her own house, within two hundred yards of Reed's
block-house, which is called twenty-five miles from Pittsburgh;
her husband, being one of the spies, was from home; two of
the scouts had lodged with her that night, but had left her
house about sunrise, in order to go to the block-house, and had
left the door standing wide open.   Shortly after the two scouts
went away, a number of Indians came into the house and drew
her out of bed by the feet; the two eldest children, who also
lay in another bed, were drawn out in the same manner; a
younger child, about one year old, slept with the deponent.

The Indians then scrambled about the articles in the house; when they were at this work, the deponent went out of the house, and hollowed to the people in the block-house; one of the Indians then ran up and stopped her mouth, another ran up with his tomahawk drawn, and a third ran and seized the tomahawk and called her his squaw; this last Indian claimed her as his, and continued by her. About fifteen of the Indians then ran down towards the block-house, and fired their guns at the block and store house, in consequence of which one soldier was killed, and another wounded, one having been at the spring, and the other in coming or looking out of the store-house. This deponent then told the Indians there were about forty men in the block-house, and each man had two guns; the Indians then went to them that were firing at the block-house, and brought them back. They then began to drive the deponent and her children away; but a boy about three years old, being unwilling to leave the house, they took by the heels, and dashed it against the house, then stabbed and scalped it. They then took the deponent and the two other children to the top of the hill, where they stopped until they tied up the plunder they had got. While they were busy about this, the deponent counted them, and the number amounted to thirty-two, including two white men that were with them, painted like the Indians.

That several of the Indians could speak English, and that she knew three or four of them very well, having often seen them go up and down the Alleghany river; two of them she knew to be Senecas, and two Munsees, who had got their guns mended by her husband about two years ago. That they sent two Indians with her, and the others took their course towards Puckty. That she, the children, and the two Indians had not gone above two hundred yards, when the Indians caught two of her uncle's horses, put her and the youngest child on one, and one of the Indians and the other child on the other. That the two Indians then took her and the children to the Alleghany river, and took them over in bark canoes, as they could not get the horses to swim the river. After they had crossed the river, the oldest child, a boy of about five years of age, began to mourn for his brother; one of the Indians then tomahawked and scalped him. That they travelled all day very hard, and that night arrived at a large camp covered with bark, which, by appearance, might hold fifty men; that the camp appeared to have been occupied some time, it was very much beaten, and large beaten paths went out in different directions from it; that night they took her about three hundred yards from the camp, into a large dark bottom, bound her arms, gave her some bed clothes, and lay down one on each side of her. That the next morning they took her into a thicket on the hill-side, and one remained with her till the middle of the day, while the other went to watch the path, lest some white people should follow them. They then exchanged places during the remainder of the day. She got a piece of dry venison, about the bulk of an egg, that day, and a piece about the same size the day they were marching. That evening, (Wednesday, the 23d,) they moved her to a new place, and secured her as the night before. During the day of the 23d, she made several attempts to get the Indian's gun or tomahawk, that was guarding her, and, could she have got either, she would have put him to death. She was nearly detected in trying to get the tomahawk from his belt.

The next morning (Thursday) one of the Indians went out as on the day before to watch the path. The other lay down and fell asleep. When she found he was sleeping, she stole her short gown, handkerchief and a child's frock, and then made her escape. The sun was then about half an hour high. That she took her course from the Alleghany, in order to deceive the Indians, as they would naturally pursue her that way; that day she travelled along Conequenessing creek. The next day she altered her course, and, as she believes, fell upon the waters of Pine creek, which empties into the Alleghany. Thinking this not her best course, took over some dividing ridges, fell in on the heads of Squaw run, she lay on a dividing ridge on Friday night, and on Saturday came to Squaw run, continued down the run until an Indian, or some other person, shot at a deer; she saw the person about one hundred and fifty yards from her, the deer running and the dog pursuing it, which, from the appearance, she supposed to be an Indian dog.

She then altered her course, but again came to the same run, and continued down it until she got so tired that she was obliged to lie down, it having rained on her all that day and the night before. She lay there that night; it rained constantly. On Sunday morning she proceeded down the run until she came to the Alleghany river, and continued down the river till she came opposite to Carter's house, on the inhabited side, where she made a noise, and James Closier brought her over the river to Carter's house.

This deponent further says that, in conversing with one of the Indians, that could talk English very well, which she suspects to be George Jelloway, he asked her if she knew the prisoner that was taken by Jeffers and his Senecas, and in jail in Pittsburgh. She answered no; he said, you lie. She again said she knew nothing about him; he said she did, that he was a spy, and a great captain; that he took Butler's scalp, and that they would have him or twenty scalps; he again said that they would exchange for him; that he and two more were sent out to see what the Americans were doing; that they came round from Detroit to Venango. The Indian took paper, and showed her that he, at fort Pitt, could write and draw on it; he also asked her if a campaign was going out against the Indians this summer; she said no. He called her a liar, and said they were going out, and that the Indians would serve them as they did last year; he also said the English had guns, ammunition, &c. to give them to go to war, and that they had given them plenty last year; this deponent also says that she saw one of the Indians have Capt. Crib's sword, which she well knew. That one of the Indians asked her if she knew Thomas Girty; she said she did; he then said that Girty lived near fort Pitt; that he was a good man, but not as good as his brother at Detroit; but that his wife was a bad woman; she tells lies on the Indians, and is a friend to America. Sworn before me the day and year first above written.

JOHN WILKINS.

NARRATIVE

OF THE CAPTIVITY AND ESCAPE OF SERGEANT LENT MUN-
SON, WHO FELL INTO THE HANDS OF THE WESTERN IN-
DIANS AT THE TIME OF LIEUT. LOWRY'S DEFEAT.

As Lieut. Lowry and ensign Boyd, with about one hundred men, were escorting two hundred and fifty pack horses with provisions from fort St. Clair to General Wayne's camp, (six miles in advance of fort Jefferson,) they were furiously assailed by about half their number of concealed Indians, and totally defeated. They had encamped four miles on their journey on the night of the 16th of October, 1793, and were sufficiently warned during the whole night of what they had to undergo at early dawn. However, no attack was made until the detachment was about ready to march on the morning of the 17th. At this juncture the Indians rushed upon them with great fury, and after a short but bloody engagement the whites were dispersed in every direction. In this onset Lieut. Lowry and ensign Boyd both fell mortally wounded, and about twenty of their men were among the slain. The rest of this unfortunate escort, excepting eleven, who were taken prisoners, got back to fort St. Clair. To the smallness of the number of the Indians is to be attributed the escape of any.

Sergeant Munson was one of the eleven prisoners, and was hurried off with his companions towards the country of the Ottawas, to which nation of Indians this party belonged. They had not proceeded far when one of the prisoners, being but a boy, and weakly, was murdered and left on the way. The remaining ten were then distributed among their captors. These all had their heads shaved, which among the Ottawas denoted they were to serve as slaves.

The residence of these Indians was upon the river then called the Maumee, since, the Miami of the lakes, about thirty miles from its mouth at lake Erie. Here Mr. Munson was kept until the next June, performing the drudgery of the Indians, without anything very remarkable, for eight months, at the end of which time he made his escape in the following manner:—
He had learned so much of their language that he could understand much of their conversation, and he now learned that they were highly elated at the prospect of meeting and cutting off the army of Gen. Wayne, as they had that of Harmer and St. Clair before. They boasted that "they were fifteen hundred strong, and that they would soon cut Wayne's army to pieces." They talked with the utmost contempt of the whites; said they lied about their numbers, and that "their armies were made up of cowards and boys."

The warriors were now preparing to march to the Au Glaize, to make a stand against Gen. Wayne, and Mr. Munson anxiously awaited their departure, hoping by their absence he might take advantage and escape. His wishes were soon gratified; for on the 12th of June, 1794, the warriors left the village, and he took every precaution for flight. Accordingly, five days after, having prepared a canoe several miles below the village, on the river, under pretence of a hunting expedition he escaped to it, and in the night made all the exertions he was master of to reach the lake, which he did in two nights; not daring to sail during the day, for fear of discovery, but slyly drawing up his canoe at the approach of morning, patiently waited until the next night. And thus he found his way to Niagara, and thence to his friends in Connecticut, without material accident, where he arrived towards the end of July, 1794, after eight months' captivity.

OSEOLA.

NARRATIVE

OF THE ESCAPE OF RANSOM CLARK, (OF LIVINGSTON COUN
TY, NEW YORK,) FROM THE MASSACRE IN WHICH MAJOR
DADE AND HIS COMMAND WERE CUT OFF BY THE SEMI-
NOLE INDIANS, IN FLORIDA, on the 28th Dec. 1835; as communi-
cated by himself, while on a visit to Boston in the summer of 1837, to the
editor of the Morning Post.

[A full and particular history of the Florida War will be found in my
Book of the Indians, together with other Indian affairs.—Ed.]

Our detachment, consisting of one hundred and seventeen
men, under command of Major Dade, started from fort Brooke,
Tampa Bay, on the 23d of December, and arrived at the scene
of action about eight o'clock on the morning of the 28th. It
was on the edge of a pond, three miles from the spot where we
had bivouacked on the night previous. The pond was surrounded by tall grass, brush and small trees. A moment before we were surprised, Major Dade said to us, "We have now
got through all danger; keep up good heart, and when we get
to fort King, I 'll give you three days for Christmas."

At this time we were in a path or trail on the border of the
pond, and the first notice that we received of the presence of
the enemy was the discharge of a rifle by their chief, as a signal to commence the attack. The pond was on our right, and
the Indians were scattered round, in a semicircle, on our left,
in the rear and in advance, reaching at the two latter points
to the edge of the pond; but leaving an opening for our entrance on the path, and a similar opening on the other extremity for the egress of our advance guard, which was permitted
to pass through without being fired on, and of course uncon-
scious of the ambuscade through which they had marched.
At the time of the attack this guard was a quarter of a mile in
advance, the main body following in column two deep. The
chief's rifle was followed by a general discharge from his men,
and Major Dade, Captain Frazier and Lieut. Mudge, together
with several non-commissioned officers and privates, were
brought down by the first volley. Our rear guard had a six-
pounder, which, as soon as possible, was hauled up, and brought
to bear upon the ground occupied by the unseen enemy, secreted among the grass, brush, and trees. The discharge of
the cannon checked and made them fall back for about half an
hour. About twelve of us advanced and brought in our dead.
Among the wounded was Lieut. Mudge, who was speechless.

We set him up against a tree, and he was found there two
months after, when Gen. Gaines sent a detachment to bury the
bodies of our soldiers. All hands then commenced throwing
up a small triangular breastwork of logs ; but, just as we had
raised it about two feet, the Indians returned and renewed the
engagement. A part of our troops fought within the breastwork, and a part outside. I remained outside till I received a
ball in my right arm, and another near my right temple, which
came out at the top of my head. I next received a shot in my
thigh, which brought me down on my side, and I then got into
the breastwork. We gave them forty-nine discharges from the
cannon ; and while loading for the fiftieth, and the last shot we
had, our match went out. The Indians chiefly levelled at the
men who worked the cannon. In the mean time the main body
of our troops kept up a general fire with musketry.

The loss of the enemy must have been very great, because
we never fired until we fixed on our men ; but the cannon was
necessarily fired at random, as only two or three Indians appeared together. When the firing commenced, the van-guard
wheeled, and, in returning to the main body, were entirely cut
up. The battle lasted till about four in the afternoon, and I
was about the last man who handled a gun, while lying on my
side. At the close I received a shot in my right shoulder,
which passed into my lungs ; the blood gushed out of my
mouth in a stream, and, dropping my musket, I rolled over on
my face. The Indians then entered the breastwork, but found
not one man standing to defend it. They secured the arms,
ammunition, and the cannon, and despatched such of our fallen
soldiers as they supposed still to be alive. Their negroes then
came in to strip the dead. I had by this time somewhat revived, and a negro, observing that I was not dead, took up a musket, and shot me in the top of the shoulder, and the ball came
out at my back. After firing, he said, "Dere, d—n you, take
dat." He then stripped me of every thing but my shirt.

The enemy then disappeared to the left of the pond, and,
through weakness and apprehension, I remained still, till about
nine o'clock at night. I then commenced crawling on my
knees and left hand. As I was crawling over the dead, I put
my hand on one man who felt different from the rest ; he was
warm and limber. I roused him up, and found it was De
Courcy, an Englishman, and the son of a British officer, resi-
dent in Canada. I told him that it was best for us to attempt
to travel, as the danger appeared to be over, and we might fall
in with assistance.

As he was only wounded in the side and arm, he could walk
a little. We got along as well as we could that night, contin-

ued on till next noon, when, on a rising ground, we observed
an Indian ahead, on horseback, loading his rifle. We agreed
that he should go on one side of the road and I on the other.
The Indian took after De Courcy, and I heard the discharge
of his rifle. This gave me time to crawl into a hammock and
hide away. The Indian soon returned with his arms and legs
covered with blood, having, no doubt, according to custom, cut
De Courcy to pieces after bringing him down with his rifle.
The Indian came riding through the brush in pursuit of me,
and approached within ten feet, but gave up the search. I
then resumed my route back to fort Brooke, crawled and limped
through the nights and forenoons, and slept in the brush during the middle of the day, with no other nourishment than cold
water. I got to fort Brooke on the evening of the fifth day;
and in five months afterwards was discharged as a pensioner,
at eight dollars per month. The doctor attributes my not dying of my wounds to the circumstance that I bled a good deal,
and did not partake of any solid food during the five first days.

Two other soldiers, by the names of Thomas and Sprague,
also came in afterwards. Although badly wounded, they ascended a tree, and thus escaped the enemy, on the evening of
the battle. They joined another expedition, two months after,
but before their wounds were healed, and they soon died of
them.

THE FOLLOWING

NARRATIVE OF ONE OF THE MOST EXTRAORDINARY ES-
CAPES FROM A DREADFUL DEATH, ANYWHERE RECORDED,
IS CONTAINED IN A LETTER WRITTEN BY THE SUFFERER
TO THE EDITOR OF THE CHARLESTON (S. C.) COURIER,
IMMEDIATELY AFTER IT HAPPENED. IT TOOK PLACE AT
CAPE FLORIDA LIGHTHOUSE, IN 1836.

On the 23d of July last, about four P. M., as I was going
from the kitchen to the dwelling-house, I discovered a large
body of Indians within twenty yards of me, back of the kitch-
en. I ran for the lighthouse, and called out to the old negro
man that was with me to run, for the Indians were near; at
that moment they discharged a volley of rifle balls, which cut
my clothes and hat, and perforated the door in many places.
We got in, and as I was turning the key the savages had hold
of the door. I stationed the negro at the door, with orders to
let me know if they attempted to break in; I then took my
three muskets, which were loaded with ball and buck-shot, and
went to the second window. Seeing a large body of them op-

posite the dwelling-house, I discharged my muskets in succession among them, which put them in some confusion; they then, for the second time, began their horrid yells, and in a minute no sash or glass was left at the window, for they vented their rage at that spot. I fired at them from some of the other windows, and from the top of the house; in fact, I fired whenever I could get an Indian for a mark. I kept them from the house until dark.

They then poured in a heavy fire at all the windows and lantern; that was the time they set fire to the door and window even with the ground. The window was boarded up with plank and filled up with stone inside; but the flames spread fast, being fed with yellow pine wood. Their balls had perforated the tin tanks of oil, consisting of two hundred and twenty-five gallons; my bedding, clothing, and in fact every thing I had, was soaked in oil. I stopped at the door until driven away by the flames. I then took a keg of gunpowder, my balls, and one musket to the top of the house, then went below, and began to cut away the stairs about half way up from the bottom. I had difficulty in getting the old negro up the space I had already cut; but the flames now drove me from my labor, and I retreated to the top of the house. I covered over the scuttle that leads to the lantern, which kept the fire from me for some time; at last the awful moment arrived, the crackling flames burnt around me, the savages at the same time began their hellish yells. My poor old negro looked to me with tears in his eyes, but could not speak; we went out of the lantern, and lay down on the edge of the platform, two feet wide; the lantern now was full of flame, the lamps and glasses bursting and flying in all directions, my clothes on fire, and to move from the place where I was would be instant death from their rifles. My flesh was roasting, and to put an end to my horrible suffering, I got up, threw the keg of gunpowder down the scuttle —instantly it exploded, and shook the tower from the top to the bottom. It had not the desired effect of blowing me into eternity, but it threw down the stairs and all the wooden work near the top of the house; it damped the fire for a moment, but it soon blazed as fierce as ever; the negro man said he was wounded, which was the last word he spoke.

By this time I had received some wounds myself; and finding no chance for my life, for I was roasting alive, I took the determination to jump off. I got up, went outside the iron railing, recommending my soul to God, and was on the point of going head foremost on the rocks below, when something dictated to me to return and lie down again. I did so, and in two minutes the fire fell to the bottom of the house. It is a remarkable circumstance, that not one ball struck me when I stood up outside the railing, although they were flying all around me like hail-stones. I found the old negro man dead, being shot in several places, and literally roasted. A few minutes after the fire fell, a stiff breeze sprung up from the southward, which was a great blessing to me. I had to lie where I was, for I could not walk, having received six rifle balls, three in each foot. The Indians, thinking me dead, left the lighthouse, and set fire to the dwelling-house, kitchen and other out-houses, and began to carry their plunder to the beach; they took all the empty barrels, the drawers of the bureaus, and in fact every thing that would act as a vessel to hold any thing; my provisions were in the lighthouse, except a barrel of flour, which they took off. The next morning they hauled out of the lighthouse, by means of a pole, the tin that composed the oil tanks, no doubt to make grates to manufacture the coonty root into what we call arrow root. After loading my little sloop, about ten or twelve went into her; the rest took to the beach to meet at the other end of the island. This happened, as I judge, about ten, A. M. My eyes being much affected, prevented me from knowing their actual force, but I judge there were from forty to fifty, perhaps more. I was now almost as bad off as before; a burning fever on me, my feet shot to pieces, no clothes to cover me, nothing to eat or drink, a hot sun overhead, a dead man by my side, no friend near or any to expect, and placed between seventy and eighty feet from the earth, and no chance of getting down, my situation was truly horrible. About twelve o'clock, I thought I could perceive a vessel not far off; I took a piece of the old negro's trowsers that had escaped the flames by being wet with blood, and made a signal.

Some time in the afternoon, I saw two boats with my sloop in tow coming to the landing. I had no doubt but they were Indians, having seen my signal, and had returned to finish their murderous design: but it proved to be boats of the United States schooner Motto, Capt. Armstrong, with a detachment of seamen and marines, under the command of Lieut. Lloyd, of the sloop-of-war Concord. They had retaken my sloop, after the Indians had stripped her of her sails and rigging, and every thing of consequence belonging to her; they informed me they heard my explosion twelve miles off, and ran down to my assistance, but did not expect to find me alive. Those gentlemen did all in their power to relieve me, but, night coming on, they returned on board the Motto, after assuring me of their assistance in the morning.

Next morning, Monday, July 5, three boats landed, among them Capt. Cole, of the schooner Pee Dee, from New York.

They had made a kite during the night, to get a line to me, but without effect; they then fired twine from their muskets, made fast to a ramrod, which I received, and hauled up a tail-block and made fast round an iron stanchion, rove the twine through the block, and they below, by that means, rove a two-inch rope, and hoisted up two men, who soon landed me on terra firma. I must state here, that the Indians had made a ladder, by lashing pieces of wood across the lightning rod, near forty feet from the ground, as if to have my scalp, nolens volens. This happened on the fourth. After I got on board the Motto, every man, from the captain to the cook, tried to alleviate my sufferings. On the seventh, I was received in the military hospital, through the politeness of Lieut. Alvord, of the fourth regiment of United States Infantry. He has done every thing to make my situation as comfortable as possible.

I must not omit here to return my thanks to the citizens of Key West, generally, for their sympathy and kind offers of any thing I would wish, that it was in their power to bestow. Before I left Key West, two balls were extracted, and one remains in my right leg; but, since I am under the care of Dr. Ramsey, who has paid every attention to me, he will know best whether to extract it or not.

These lines are written to let my friends know that I am still in the land of the living, and am now in Charleston, S. C., where every attention is paid me. Although a cripple, I can eat my allowance, and walk about without the use of a cane.

Respectfully yours,
JOHN W. B. THOMPSON.

NEWS FROM NEW-ENGLAND.

BEING A TRUE AND LAST ACCOUNT OF THE PRESENT BLOODY WARS CARRIED ON BETWIXT THE INFIDELS, NATIVES, AND THE ENGLISH CHRISTIANS, AND CON-VERTED INDIANS OF *NEW-ENGLAND*, DECLARING THE MANY DREADFUL BATTLES FOUGHT BETWIXT THEM: AS ALSO THE MANY TOWNS AND VILLAGES BURNT BY THE MERCILESS HEATHENS. AND ALSO THE TRUE NUMBER OF ALL THE CHRISTIANS SLAIN SINCE THE BEGINNING OF THAT WAR, AS IT WAS SENT OVER BY A FACTOR OF *NEW-ENGLAND* TO A MERCHANT IN *LONDON*. Licensed *Aug.* 1. — Roger L'Estrange. LONDON. Printed for J. Coniers, at the Sign of the *Black Raven* in *Duck-Lane*, 1676.

[The following tract is of exceeding rarity; so much so that, not long since, but one was known to be in this country. This is reprinted from a copy of one in the library of JOHN CARTER BROWN, Esq., of Providence. To the politeness of this gentleman we are indebted for permission to make a transcript. The original is, without exception, one of the worst printed tracts of the day in which it appeared. The type on which it was printed was wretched, especially the Italic; some of the letters in many of the words not being distinguishable, and others entirely wanting. I have adhered, in this reprint, as closely to the original, in respect to orthography, capitals, and italics, as possible. Of its comparative value, in an historical point of view, it is unnecessary to remark. It is republished as a curious record of one of the most important periods in the History of New England. The Antiquary, and Student in our history, will readily perceive its value, while to the general reader it will be almost as unintelligible as though in an unknown language.

To whom belongs the authorship, we have no data on which to found even a conjecture. A few notes seemed necessary. These, and the words in the text included in brackets, are added to this edition.]

THOSE Coals of Discention which had a long time lain hid under the ashes of a secret envy; contracted by the Heathen *Indians* of New-*England*, against the English; and Christian Natives of that Country brake out in *June* 1675. both Armies being at a distance without doing any thing remarkable till the 13 of *December* following; at which time the *Mathusets* and *Plymouth* Company marching from *Seconk*, sent out a considerable number of Scouts, who kill'd & took 55. of the Enemy, returning with no other loss but two of our Men disabled, about three days after came a perfidious *Indian* to our Army pretending he was sent by the *Sachems* to treat of Peace, who was indeed no other but a Spy and was no sooner conducted out of our Camp but we had news brought us that 22 of our Stragling

Souldiers were Slain and divers barns and out houses, with Mr. *Jer. Bulls* dwelling house burnt by him and his Trecherous confederates which waited for him. The next day, as the *Connectick* Army under the Conduct of Major *Treat* was Marching to Joyn with the *Mathusets*, and *Plymouth* Company ; they were assaulted by the *Indians*, but without any loss, they taking eleaven of the Assailants Prisoners.

The 8*th* [18] of *December*, our whole Army being united under the Conduct of Major *Genr : Winslow*, went to seek out the Enemy, whom we found (there then hapening a great fall of Snow) securing themsueles in a dismal Swamp, so hard of access that there was but one was [way] for entrance, which was well lin'd with Heathen *Indians*, who presently went out to assault us ; but we falling in Pel-mell with them ; with much difficulty gained the Swamp where we found above 1500 Wiggwams, and by night, had possession [2] of the fort of which we were dispossest soon after by an unexpected recruit of fresh *Indians* out of an adjoyning Swamp, but our Noble Generals insatiable desire of victory prompted him to such brave actions, that we following his example to the enemies cost, made ourselves absolute Masters of the fort again.* Although we purchased our success at so dear a rate that we have small cause to rejoyce at the victory ; yet when we consider the vast disadvantage† they had of us in number, whom we collected ‡ have 4000 fighting men, & we not much more than half so many, we have great reason to bless God we came of so well, our dead and wounded not a Mounting to above 220, and the enemies by their own Confession to no less than 600. the chief officers kild on our side were Capt. *Davenport*, Capt. *Johnson*, Capt. *Marshal*, Capt. *Gardner*. Capt. *Gollop*. Captains wounded were 4. *vizt, Sealey*, Major *Wats*, and *Bradford*, Lieutenants wounded were 4. viz. *Savage*, *Ting*, *Upham* and *Wam*.§

In this bloody Battle we gaue so bitter a Relish of our English valour & our converted *Indians* resolutions, that they dreaded our neighborhood & thought themselves unsafe till secur'd by six or seaven miles distance from our remaining Army, where they remain'd near a month

---

* There is a little embellishment here. The English were at no time driven out of the fort. † The exact reverse is probably meant. ‡ Calculated?

§ *Swain*, very probably. There was a " Lieut. Swayne," belonging to Capt. Appleton's company. A " Lieut. *Swan* " is mentioned in one of the London tracts in our OLD INDIAN CHRONICLE, p 50, no doubt the same *Lieut Swain*

not attempting anything considerable till the first of *Feb.* at which time a certain Number of them made desperate through hunger came to *Patickset,* a Little Town near Providence & attempted the house of one Mr. Carpenter, from whom they took 20 horses 50 head of Cattle and 180 sheep. And set fire on a house at Southbury * wherein were two men. one woman and seaven Children; on the 4*th* of February the Christians received private intelligence from the *Indians* who had Sculked ever since the last Battle in certain woods scituate about 30 miles from Malbury, that they were drawn up into a body, and encamped in a well fortified Swamp, where notwithstanding the Indians [3] assaulted the Rear. wounded four of our men, and we killing so many of theirs that they thought fit to forsake their refuge, and leave both it and their wigwams to our disposal, who lodging in their Rooms that night, set fire to a 150 of their wigwams next morning, & by this light pursued them so close that we kill'd divers of them, whom age or wounds rendered incapable [3] of keeping up with their Companions. & resolving to continue the quest with all the celerity imaginable, they led us to another Swamp whose Rocky ascent propounded so great a difficulty to attain it, as would have Staggar'd the resolution of any but a resolved Mind; but we attempted it with the like resolution and success as we did the Last; the enemy by a speedy flight leaving us in full possession of all they left behind them.

We Persued them two dayes after this encounter, but then (which was on the 18*th Febr.*) finding our men wearied with Speedy marches, our provision scarce through continual expence and no recruit, our horses tir'd, and our selves hopeless of overtaking them, who had great advantage of us in passing over Rocks and through Thickets, which our Foot, not without much difficulty, could, & our horse were altogether incapable to do; our Commanders, after a Councel of warr, resolved to send the *Massathusets* & *Plymouth* Company to *Malbury,* and the *Connecticks* Army to their own homes which was accordingly done. And Major Genr. *Winslow,* only with his Troops to *Boston,* leaving the foot at *Malbury* and *South-bury,* who came home on Munday following, and were all dismist to their several habitations, except Capt. *Wadworth,* who was left

---

* Sudbury, probably.

at *Mulbury* in persuit of the Enemy, of whom he destroyed about 70, Old Men, Women and Children, who wanted strength to follow the fugitive Army.*

The Desperate heathens takeing advantage of the dismission of three Disbanded Companies, studied nothing but Massacres, outrages, and treacherous hostillitie, which within two days after those said Companies were dispers't, they found opportunity to commit, in a Town called *Nashaway*, which they set fire to, and burnt to the Ground, taking no less than 55 Persons into their Merciless captivity, and because the reader shall understand the Damnable antipathy they have to Religion and Piety, I would have him take notice how they endeavour to Signallize their Cruelty, and gratifie their enraged Spleen, chiefly on the promoters of it; for of these 55 Captives, the Minister of the Town's relations made no less than 19 of them; viz. Mrs. *Rowlonson*, the Ministers wife, and three of his Children, her sister and seaven Children, and her sister *Drew* and four Children. The Minister himself with his sisters husbands returning from *Boston* a little after the engagement, [4] to their infinite grief, found their houses burnt to the ground, and their Wives and Children t ken Captive, nor was this crueltie committed, as the extent or *Nepolus Vltria* of their vengance, but rather as an earnest of their *Bearbarity*. For no longer than the next day after, three men Going out, with the Cart, were seiz'd on by these *Indians*, one of them killed, and the other two not to be found; the day following at *Cox[c]ord*, [Concord?] they burnt one house and murder'd three persons.

In short, their outrages are so many and different, that I must intreat the reader, since they will not be brought into afluent Narration, to accept them plainly and dyurnally, according to the time, place, and manner, as they were committed, which is the only way to avoid omissions, and consequently to Satisfie the inquisitive, who, I suppose, would willingly hear of all the extremities [that] have happened to the suffering Christians in this New *England* War.

On the 17 of *Febr*. therefore, you must know, that the Town of Medfeild was begirt with a regiment of resolent *Indian[s]*, who assailed it so briskly, that maugred all the resistance made by Capt. *Jacobbs*, who was then Ingarrisoned there with a hundred Souldiers for its security, the en-

---

* If this be so, who will wonder at the fate of Capt. Wadsworth and his men?

raged Heathens never desisted their desperate attemps, Battering the Walls, and powering showers of Arrows into the bosome of the Town, they had distroyed above 50 of her inhabitants, & burnt 30 of her houses.

The 7th. of *March* following these bloody *Indians* march't to a considerable Town called *Croaton*,* where first they set fire to Major *Willard's* house, & afterwards burnt 65 more, there being Seaventy two houses at first, so that there was left standing but six houses of the whole Town ; the next day after, two men coming from *Malbury* to *Southbury* were slain : and the Sabboth day ensuing, these destroying *Indians* came to *Plymouth*, where fixing only on a house of one Mr. *Clarks*, they burnt, and murthered his wife and all his Children, himself Narrowly escaping their crueltie by happily at that juncture being at a meeting.

On the second of *April*, 1676, Major *Savage*, Capt. *Moseley*, Capt. *William Turnor*, and Captain *Whipal*,† with 300. men marching from *Malborow* to *Quabury*,‡ where they had ordered the *Connectick* Army to remain in readiness against their coming, which being effected, accordingly they joined forces, and began [5] their march towards *Northampton*, but by the way were assaulted by the *Indians*, whom they repelled without any other damage, then only Mr. *Buckly* wounded, killing about 20 of the Enemies in a hot persuit after them.

The tenth Ditto, about 700 Indians encompast *Northampton* on all sides where they fought very resolutely for the space of an hour, and then fled, leaving about 25 persons dead upon the place, the Christians loosing only 4. men and 1. woman, and had some barnes burnt ; on the 12th instant they assaulted *Warwick* with so unhappy a success that they burnt all the Town, except four Garrison houses which were left standing, six days after Captain *Peirce*, Brother to Captain *Peirce* of *London*, with 55 men and 20 Christian Indians went to seek out their Enemies, the Indians whom according to their intelligence they found rambling in an obscure Wood ; upon his approach they drew into order, and received his onset with much difficulty, being in the end forced to retreat, but it was so slowly that it scarcely deserved that name, when a fresh company of

---

* Groton, probably.   The C. may be an imperfect G. in copy.
† Probably Whipple, but hardly decidable.
‡ Quabaog ?   Brockfield.

Indians came into their assistance, beset the Christians round, Killed Captain *Pierce* and 48. of his men, besides 8. of the Christian Indians. The Fight continued about 5 hours, the Enemy bying the Victory very dearly, but at last obtained it so absolutely, that they deprived us of all means of hearing of their loss.

At *Malbrow* on the 12*th* Ditto, were several houses burnt whilst the miserable inhabitants were at a meeting, and at *Springfield* the same Lords day, these devillish Enemies of Religion seeing a man, woman, and their Children, going but towards a meeting-house, Slew them (as they said) because they thought they intended to go thither.

The 28*th*, of the same instant, *April* last, Captain *Denison* collecting a Regiment of 500, and 200 *English* Paquet Nimerass *Indians*, marcht out of New *London* in search of that Grand fomenter of this Rebellion. *Anthony** the *Secham*, whom at last near the Town call'd *Providence* he recovered, and after a hot dispute, wherein he kill'd 45 of the Sechems men, Took him their commander Prisoner, with several of his Captaines, whom they immediately put to death ; but were at strong debate whether they should send him to *Boston*, but at length they carried him to [6] New *London*, and began to examine him, why he did foment that war which would certainly be the distruction of him and all the Heathen *Indians* in the Country, to which, and many other interogatories he made no other reply but that †[he was born a Prince, & if Princes came to speak with him, he would answer them, But none of those present being Princes, he thought himself oblig'd in honour to hold his Tongue.]† This Answer, though it might Challenge their admiration, was not so prevalent as to obtain their pitty.

Notwithstanding, the Surviveing Sechems were not long in revenging his death, for, on the Sixth of *May*, they burnt all *Malborow*, except three Garrison houses, kill'd Capt. *Jacobson* and Lieutenant *Prat*, and two dayes after burnt 24 houses in *Southbury*, kill'd several of the inhabitants who vainly expected Capt. *Wedworth* and Capt. *Brookwe*‡ to their Relief ; for these unfortunate Gentlemen were inter-

---

* *Nanunteno*, unquestionably is intended ; but what is meant by *Nimerass* is beyond our comprehension.

† The printer's quotation mark.

‡ The printer was probably puzzled to make any thing of his copy *Brocklebank* is the name.

cepted by 700 *Moors*, with whom they fought for the space of 4 hours, till not only they two, but Capt. *Sharp* and 51 Christians more lay dead upon the place.

At *Woodcock*[s] 10 miles from Seconch, on the 16*th May* was a little Skirmage betwixt the *Moors* and Christians, wherein there was of the later three slain and two wounded, and only two *Indians* Kild.

May 28. 1676. Capt. *Denison* and Capt. *Evry* [Avery] with 50 English and about 150 Paquet *Indians*, Scouting among the Woods. in 8 days space kill'd 25 *Indians* and took 51 prisoners ; one whereof was Grand-child to *Dunham* * who was kill'd by Capt. *Peirce* in the engagement on the 26 *May*.

The number of Christians slain since the beginning of the late Wars in New England, are 444. Taken Prisoners, 55.

The number of *Indians* Slain in this war is uncertain, because they burn † their Dead, keeping their Death as a Secret from the Christians knowledge, but the number mentioned herein is 910.

We have Received very late news that the Christians in New *England* have had very great Victory over the Infidel Natives.

There has been a Treaty between them; the *Indians* proffer to lay down their Armes, but the *English* are not willing to agree to it, except they will give up their Armes, and go as far up into the Country, as the Court of *Boston* shall think fit.‡

---

* Perhaps *Pumham*.   † This is new and untrue.
‡ Some copies of the original tract have not this last paragraph. Mr. Brown's copy has it, but that in Harvard College library is without it. By comparing the proofs of this edition with that belonging to the College, several corrections have been made, and uncertain words made out. which could not have been done by the other copy. And here we would return our thanks to the obliging Librarian, for his kindness in affording us an opportunity to make our copy more perfect than either of the others.

FINIS.

INDEX.

INDEX.